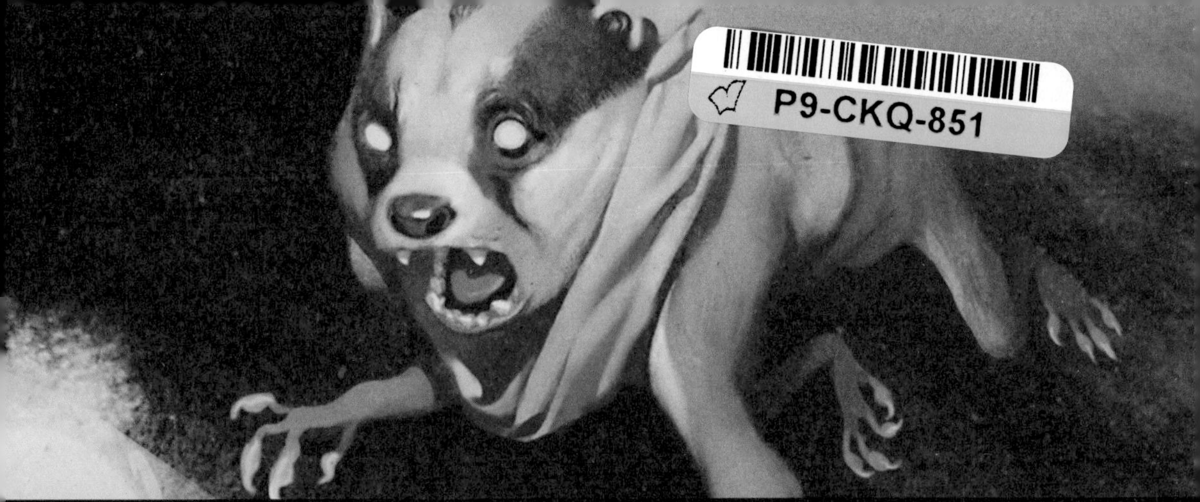

FABLES: SNOW WHITE

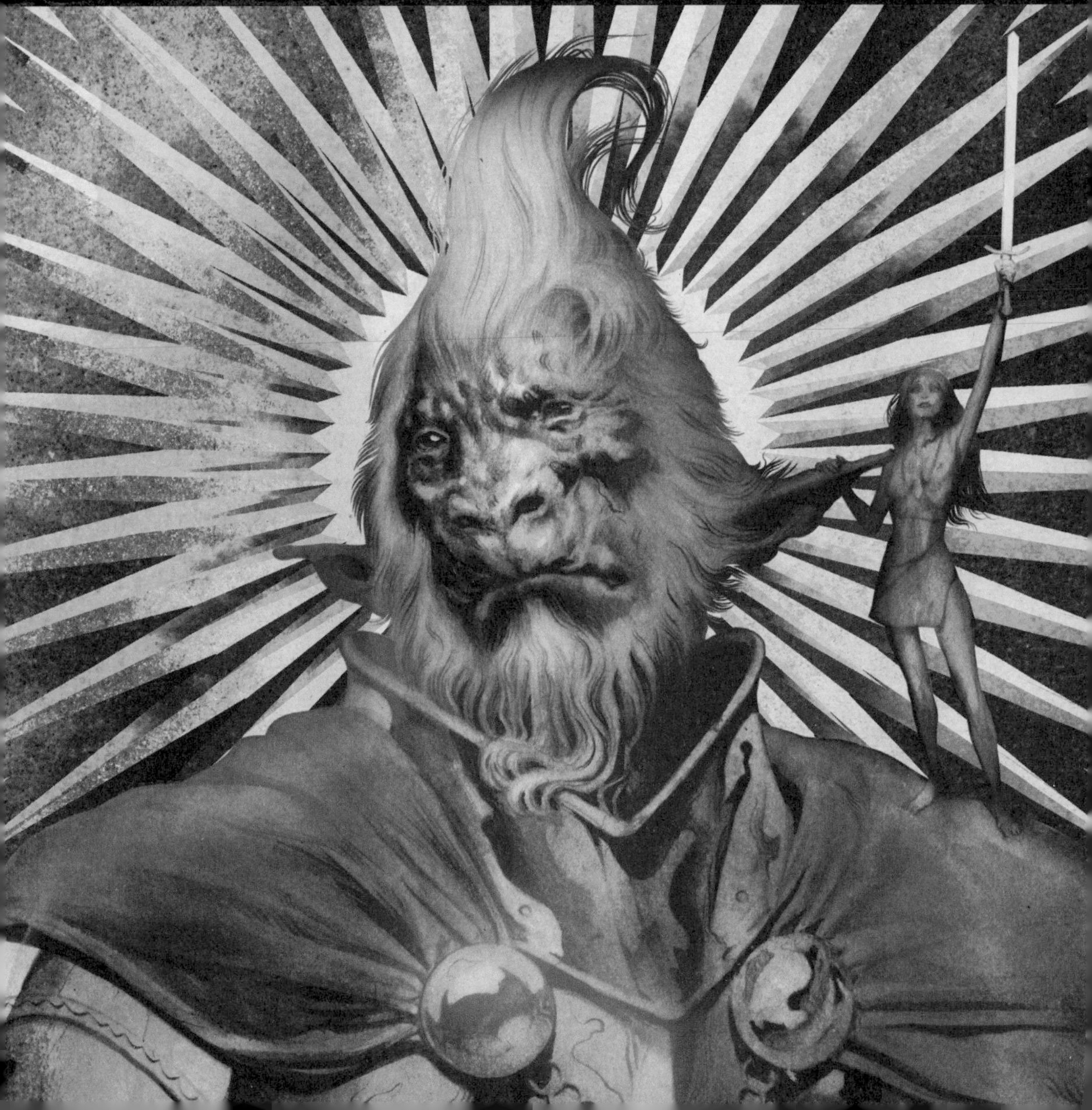

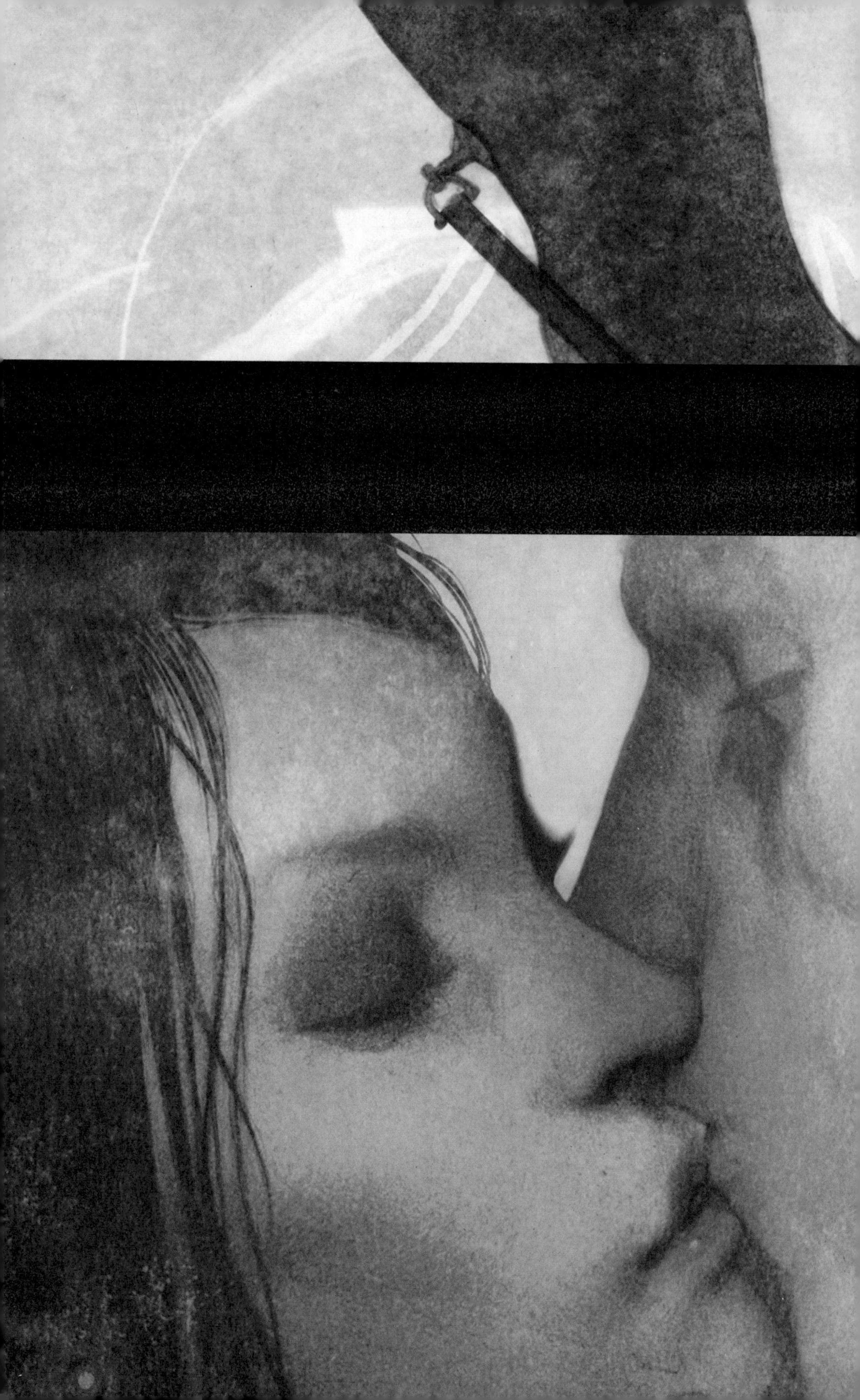

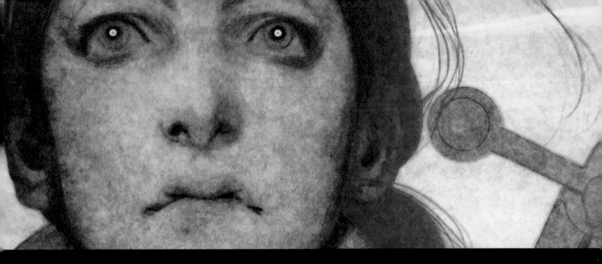

FABLES: SNOW WHITE

FABLES CREATED BY BILL WILLINGHAM

Bill Willingham
Writer

Mark Buckingham
Steve Leialoha
Shawn McManus
Andrew Pepoy
Artists

Lee Loughridge
Colorist

Todd Klein
Letterer

Mark Buckingham
Cover Art

Joao Ruas
Mark Buckingham
Original Series Covers

SHELLY BOND
Executive Editor – Vertigo and Editor – Original Series

GREGORY LOCKARD
Associate Editor – Original Series

SCOTT NYBAKKEN
Editor

ROBBIN BROSTERMAN
Design Director – Books

HANK KANALZ
Senior VP – Vertigo and Integrated Publishing

DIANE NELSON
President

DAN DIDIO and **JIM LEE**
Co-Publishers

GEOFF JOHNS
Chief Creative Officer

JOHN ROOD
Executive VP – Sales, Marketing and Business Development

AMY GENKINS
Senior VP – Business and Legal Affairs

NAIRI GARDINER
Senior VP – Finance

JEFF BOISON
VP – Publishing Planning

MARK CHIARELLO
VP – Art Direction and Design

JOHN CUNNINGHAM
VP – Marketing

TERRI CUNNINGHAM
VP – Editorial Administration

ALISON GILL
Senior VP – Manufacturing and Operations

JAY KOGAN
VP – Business and Legal Affairs, Publishing

JACK MAHAN
VP – Business Affairs, Talent

NICK NAPOLITANO
VP – Manufacturing Administration

SUE POHJA
VP – Book Sales

COURTNEY SIMMONS
Senior VP – Publicity

BOB WAYNE
Senior VP – Sales

This collection is respectfully dedicated, with gratitude, to Stacy's Rangers, those who volunteered to help us out at Fabletown and Beyond, making it the remarkable success it was.
— Bill Willingham

For Mum and Dad. Eternally supportive of me in both life and career.
— Mark Buckingham

Logo design by Nancy Ogami

FABLES: SNOW WHITE

Published by DC Comics. Copyright © 2013 Bill Willingham and DC Comics. All Rights Reserved.

Originally published in single magazine form as FABLES 114-129. Copyright © 2012, 2013 Bill Willingham and DC Comics. All Rights Reserved. All characters, their distinctive likenesses and related elements featured in this publication are trademarks of Bill Willingham. VERTIGO is a trademark of DC Comics. The stories, characters and incidents featured in this publication are entirely fictional. DC Comics does not read or accept unsolicited submissions of ideas, stories or artwork.

DC Comics, 1700 Broadway, New York, NY 10019
A Warner Bros. Entertainment Company.
Printed in the USA. First Printing.
ISBN: 978-1-4012-4248-0

Library of Congress Cataloging-in-Publication Data

Willingham, Bill.
  Fables. Volume 19, Snow White / Bill Willingham, Mark Buckingham.
    pages cm
  ISBN 978-1-4012-4248-0 (pbk.)
1. Fairy tales—Adaptations—Comic books, strips, etc.
2. Legends—Adaptations—Comic books, strips, etc. 3. Graphic novels. I. Buckingham, Mark. II. Title. III. Title: Snow White.
  PN6727.W52F433 2013
  741.5'973—dc23
                                2013030635

SUSTAINABLE FORESTRY INITIATIVE
Certified Chain of Custody
Promoting Sustainable Forestry
www.sfiprogram.org
SFI-01042
APPLIES TO TEXT STOCK ONLY

Table of Contents

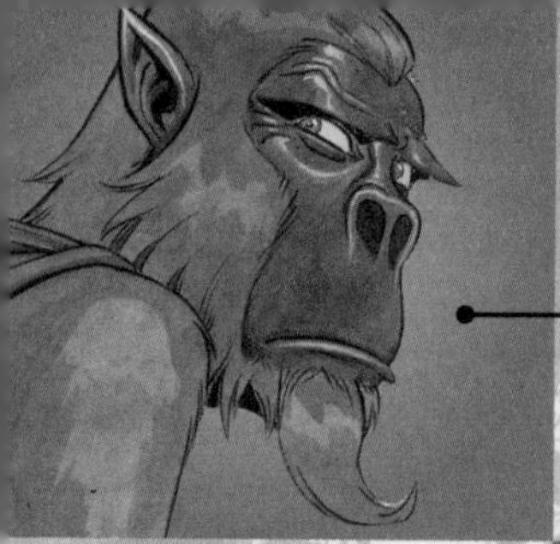

WHO'S WHO IN FABLETOWN

BUFKIN

A former member of Oz's Flying Monkey Air Corps, he now leads a rebellion against his homeland's despotic emperor, Roquat the Red.

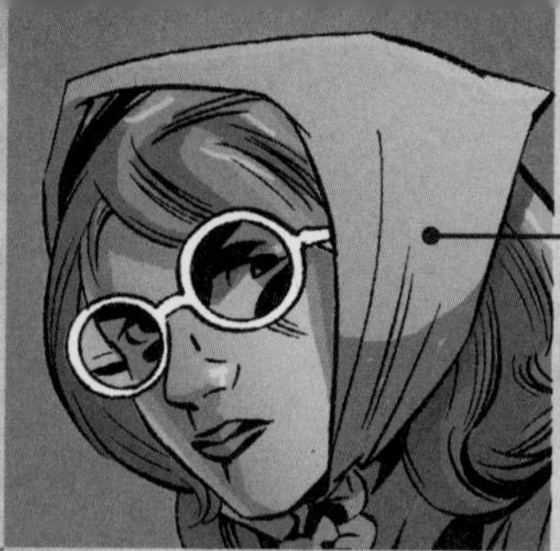

BRIAR ROSE

The Sleeping Beauty of legend, recently awoken fro her victorious slumber in the defeated Adversary's capitol

SNOW WHITE

Fabletown's former deputy mayor, wife of Bigby, and mother to their seven cubs.

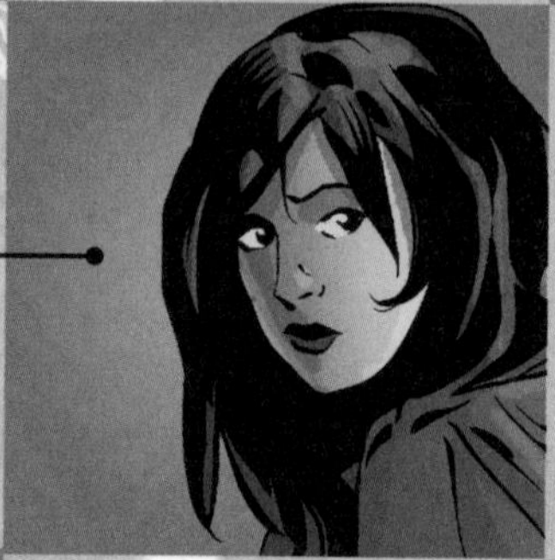

BUNGLE, SAWHORSE AND JACK PUMPKINHEAD

Three of Bufkin's top lieutenants in the ongoing Ozian insurgency.

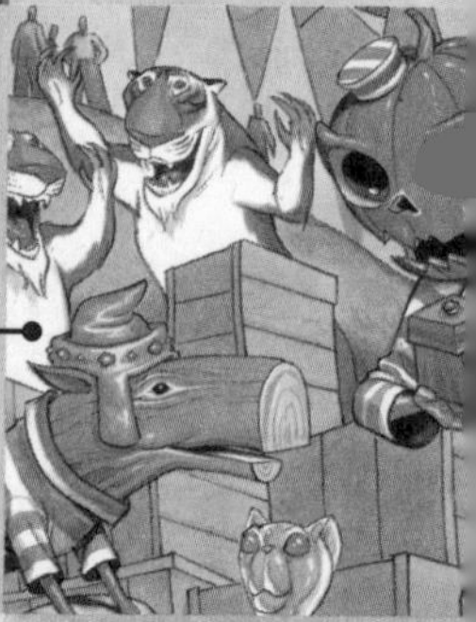

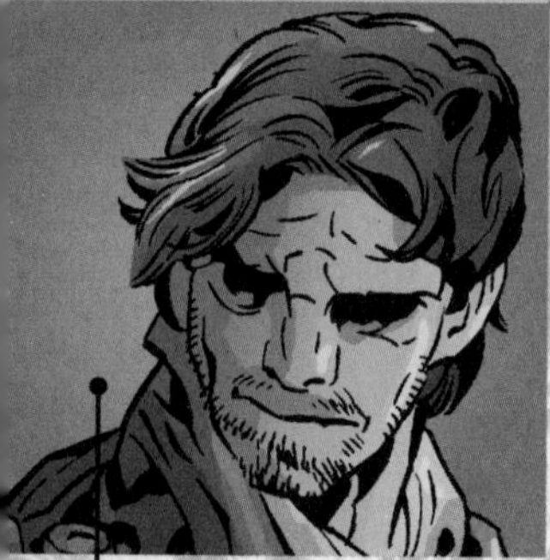

LILY MARTANION

A Barleycorn Bride with a taste for adventure and a soft spot for Bufkin.

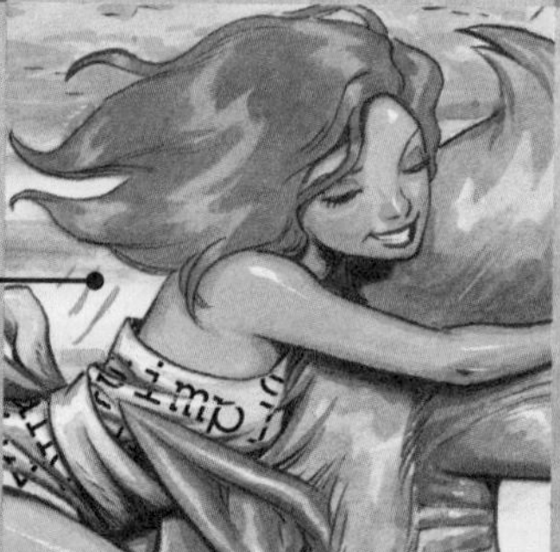

BROCK BLUEHEART

A somewhat curmudgeonly pillar of the non-human Fables community, he is more commonly known as Stinky.

BIGBY

The celebrated Big Bad Wolf and former sheriff of Fabletown.

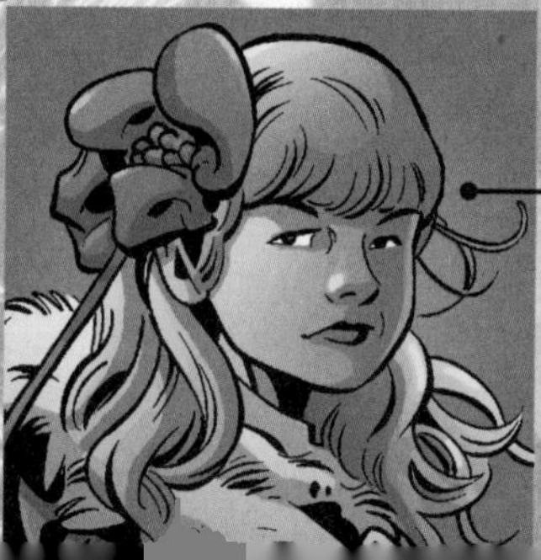

OZMA

The misleadingly youthful-looking leader of Fabletown's wizards and witches.

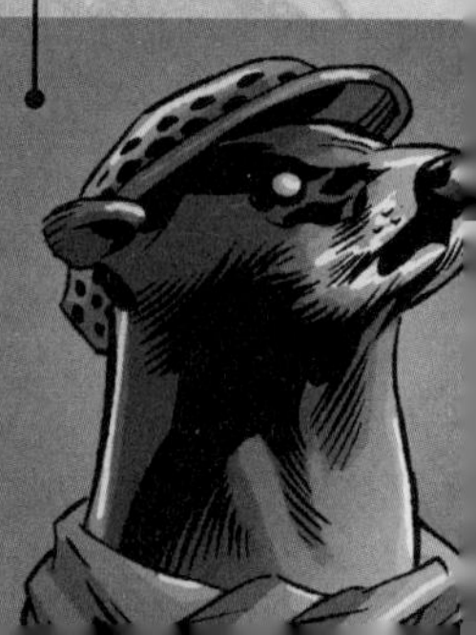

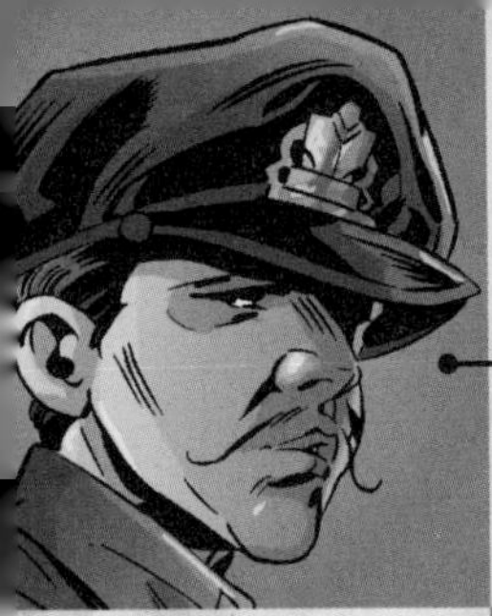

GRIMBLE

A fearsome bridge troll disguised as a dozy security guard.

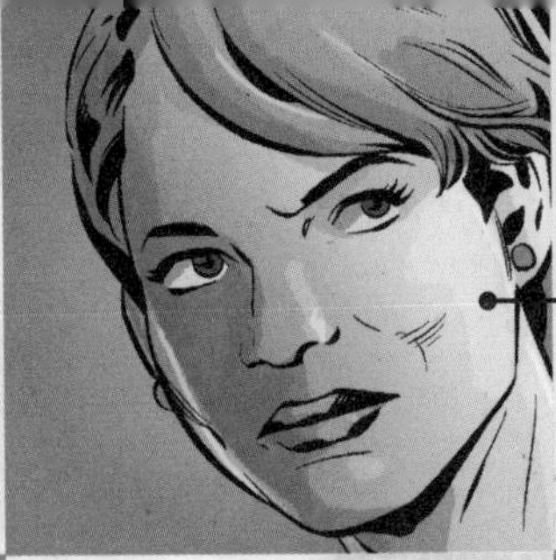

LEIGH DUGLAS

Jack Sprat's newly lean widow, groomed for revenge by her recently deceased patron, Mister Dark.

FLYCATCHER

The former Frog Prince and Fabletown janitor, now the ruler of the Kingdom of Haven in the liberated Homelands.

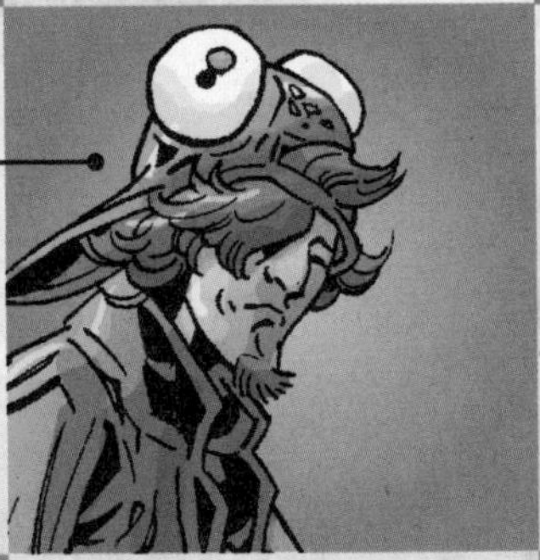

GEPPETTO

Fabletown's former Adversary, now a much-reviled fellow citizen.

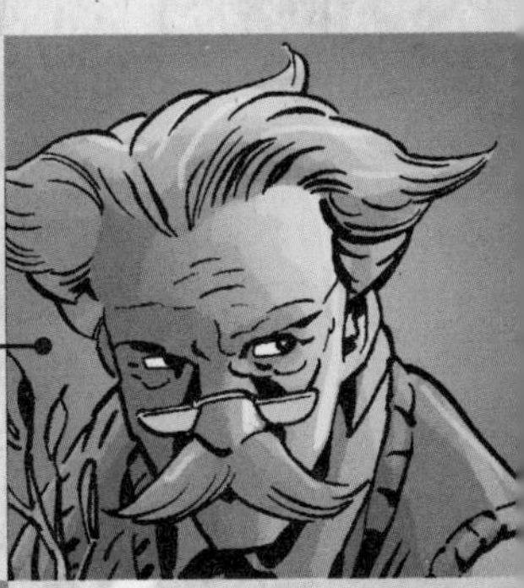

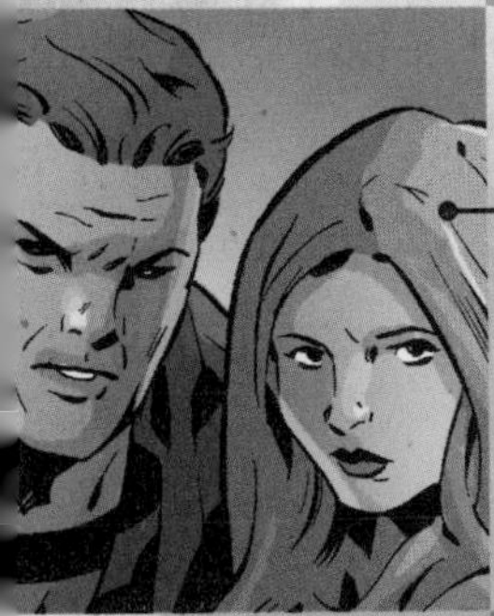

BEAUTY AND BEAST

Fabletown's husband-and-wife deputy mayor and sheriff.

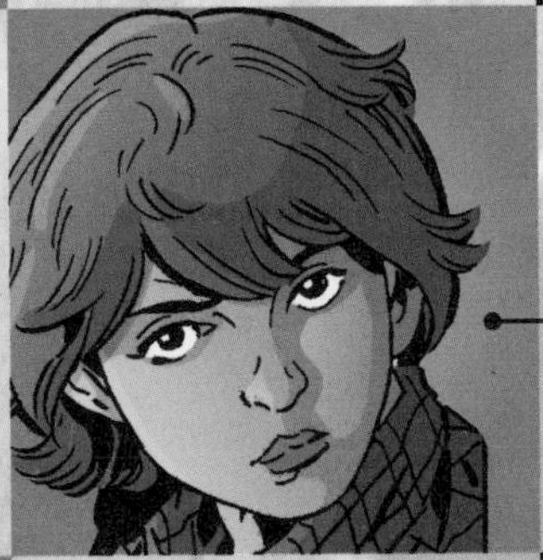

ROSE RED

Snow White's sister and the leader of the non-human Fable community.

KING COLE

The once and future mayor of Fabletown.

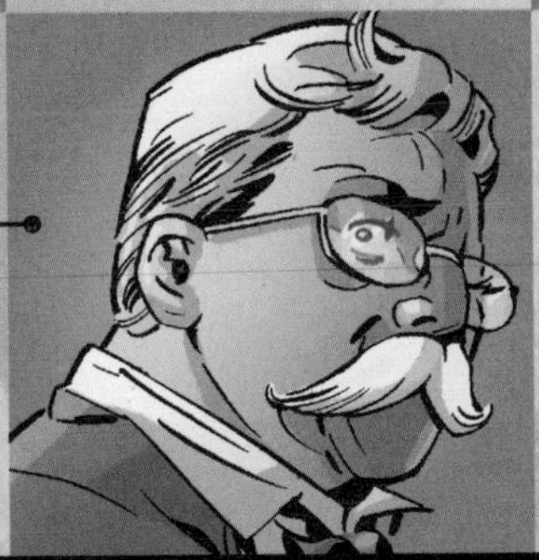

THE BLUE FAIRY

A being of powerful magic with an equally powerful grudge against a certain ambitious woodcarver.

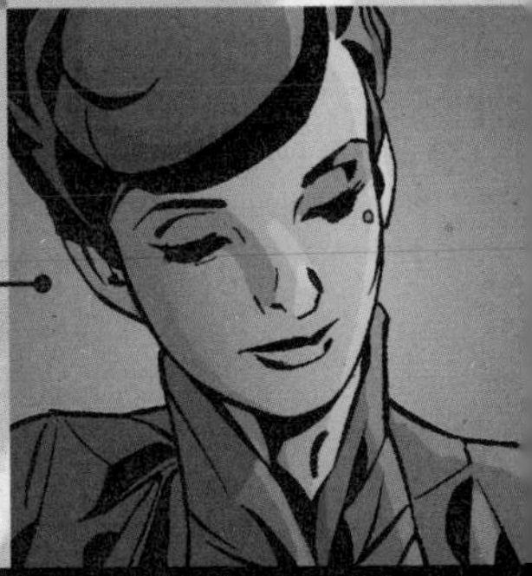

THE STORY SO FAR

After successfully defending Fabletown's lost business office from the depredations of Baba Yaga, native Ozian Bufkin returned to his homeland only to find it in the cruel grip of a new dictator. Quickly joining the grassroots insurrection against the tyrannical Nome King, Bufkin was just as quickly captured and sent to the gallows for execution.

Meanwhile, back in the Mundane World, the inhabitants of Fabletown continue to reoccupy the labyrinthine halls of Castle Dark, their transformed stronghold in New York City. But for Bigby and Snow, only one mission matters now: tracking down their two lost cubs, Darien and Therese, every trace of whom has vanished from the Earth.

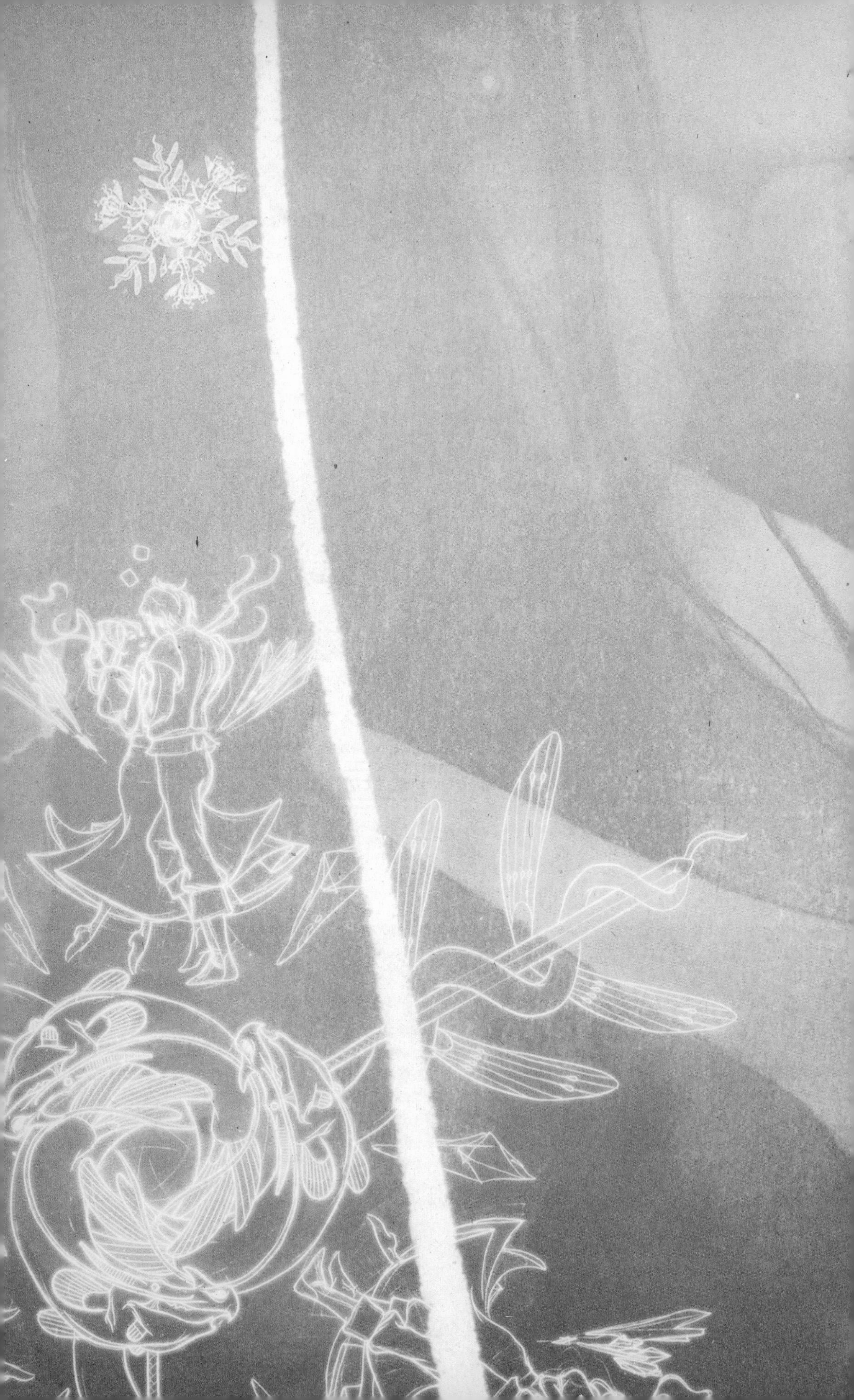

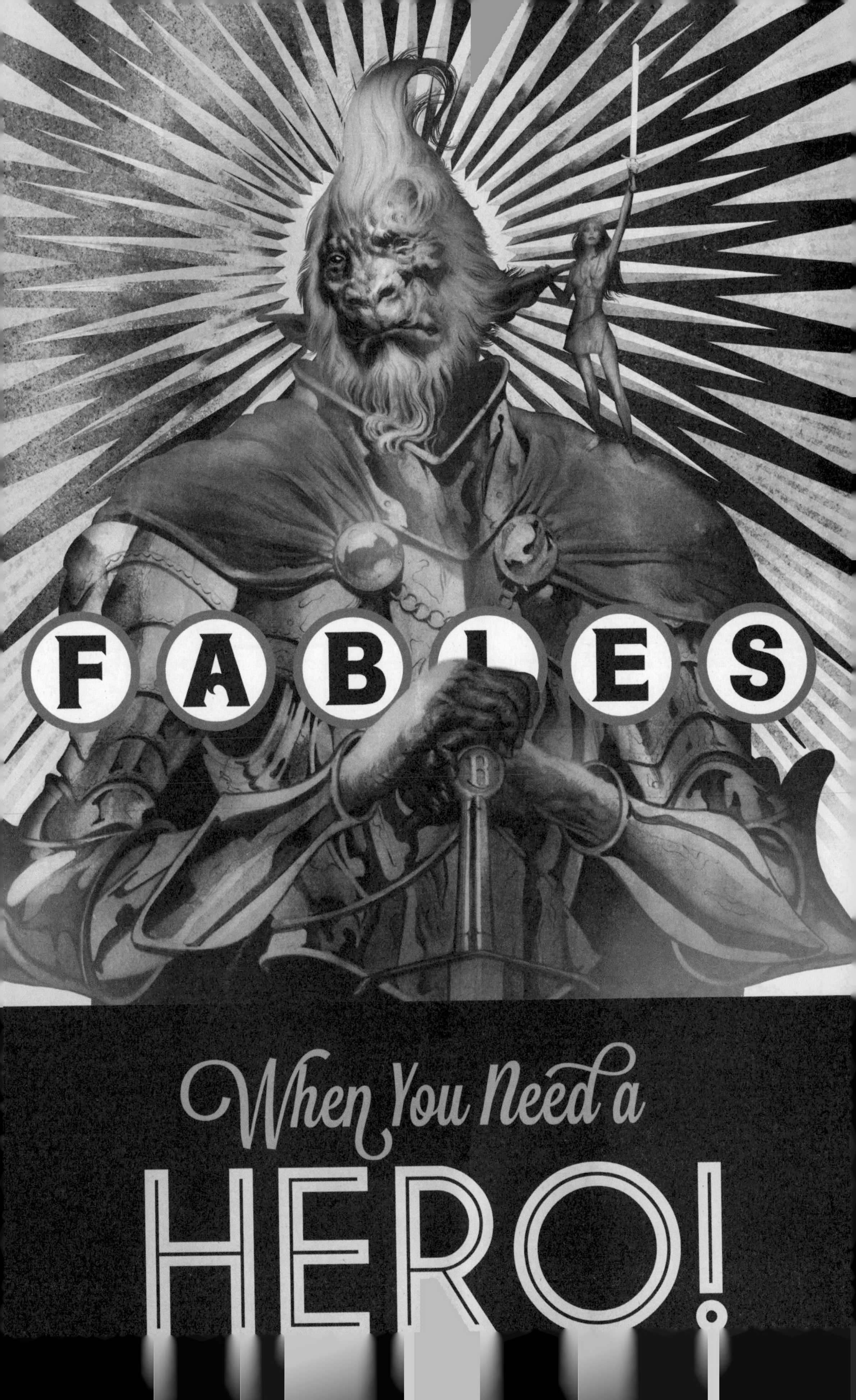
FABLES
When You Need a
HERO!

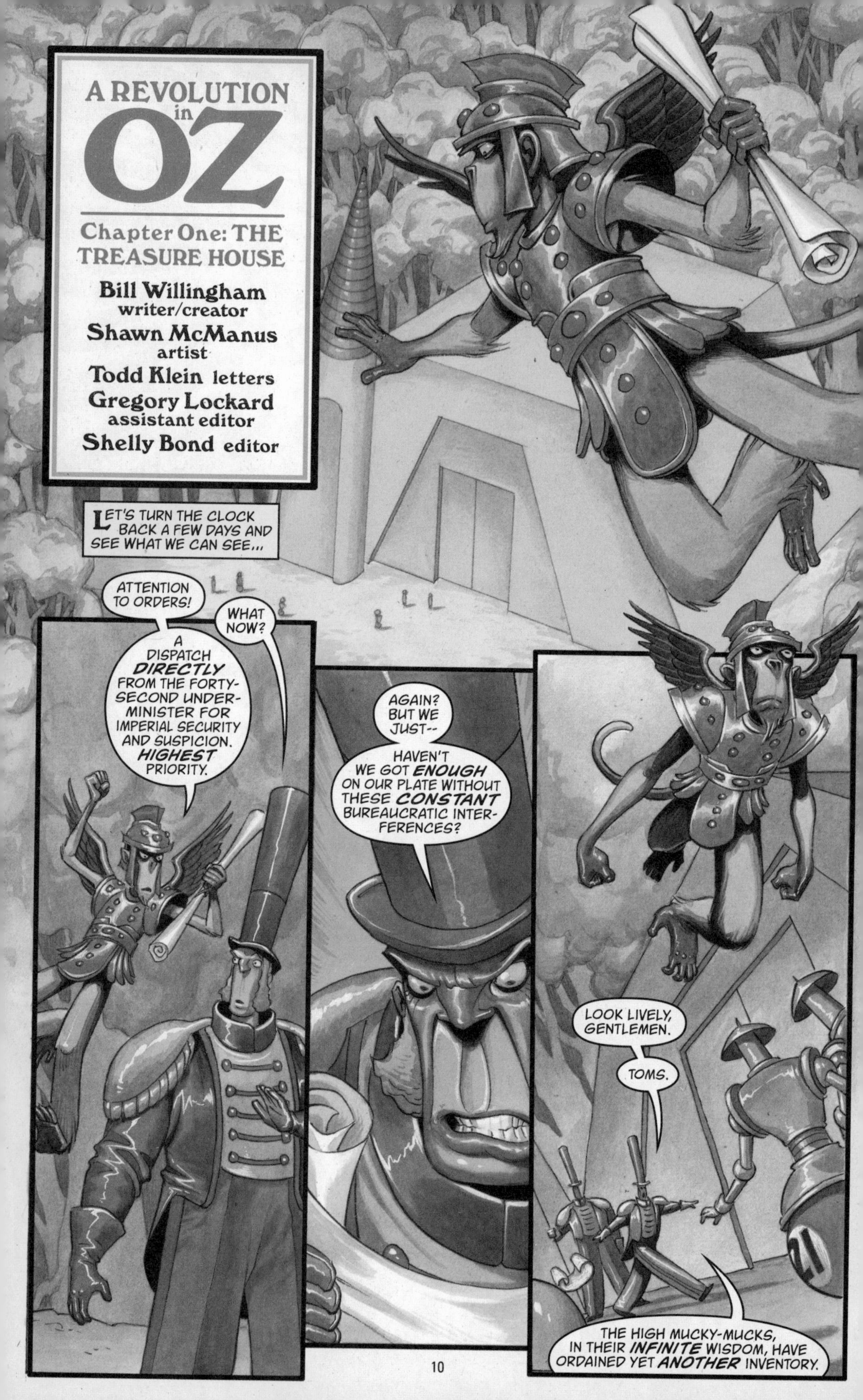
A REVOLUTION in OZ
Chapter One: THE TREASURE HOUSE
Bill Willingham writer/creator
Shawn McManus artist
Todd Klein letters
Gregory Lockard assistant editor
Shelly Bond editor
LET'S TURN THE CLOCK BACK A FEW DAYS AND SEE WHAT WE CAN SEE...
ATTENTION TO ORDERS!
WHAT NOW?
A DISPATCH DIRECTLY FROM THE FORTY-SECOND UNDER-MINISTER FOR IMPERIAL SECURITY AND SUSPICION. HIGHEST PRIORITY.
AGAIN? BUT WE JUST--
HAVEN'T WE GOT ENOUGH ON OUR PLATE WITHOUT THESE CONSTANT BUREAUCRATIC INTERFERENCES?
LOOK LIVELY, GENTLEMEN.
TOMS.
THE HIGH MUCKY-MUCKS, IN THEIR INFINITE WISDOM, HAVE ORDAINED YET ANOTHER INVENTORY.

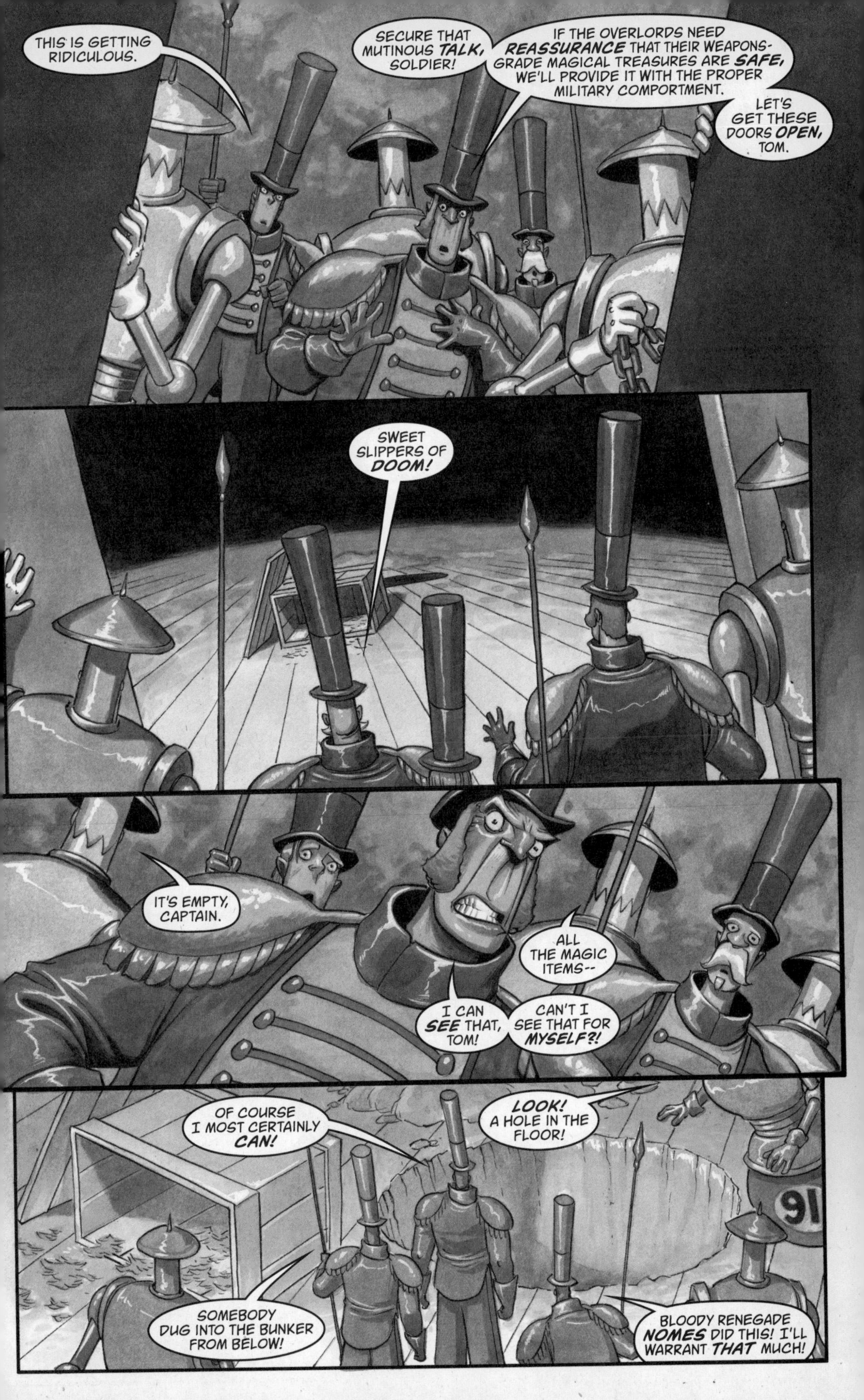

THIS IS GETTING RIDICULOUS.
SECURE THAT MUTINOUS TALK, SOLDIER!
IF THE OVERLORDS NEED REASSURANCE THAT THEIR WEAPONS-GRADE MAGICAL TREASURES ARE SAFE, WE'LL PROVIDE IT WITH THE PROPER MILITARY COMPORTMENT.
LET'S GET THESE DOORS OPEN, TOM.
SWEET SLIPPERS OF DOOM!
IT'S EMPTY, CAPTAIN.
ALL THE MAGIC ITEMS--
I CAN SEE THAT, TOM!
CAN'T I SEE THAT FOR MYSELF?!
OF COURSE I MOST CERTAINLY CAN!
LOOK! A HOLE IN THE FLOOR!
91
SOMEBODY DUG INTO THE BUNKER FROM BELOW!
BLOODY RENEGADE NOMES DID THIS! I'LL WARRANT THAT MUCH!

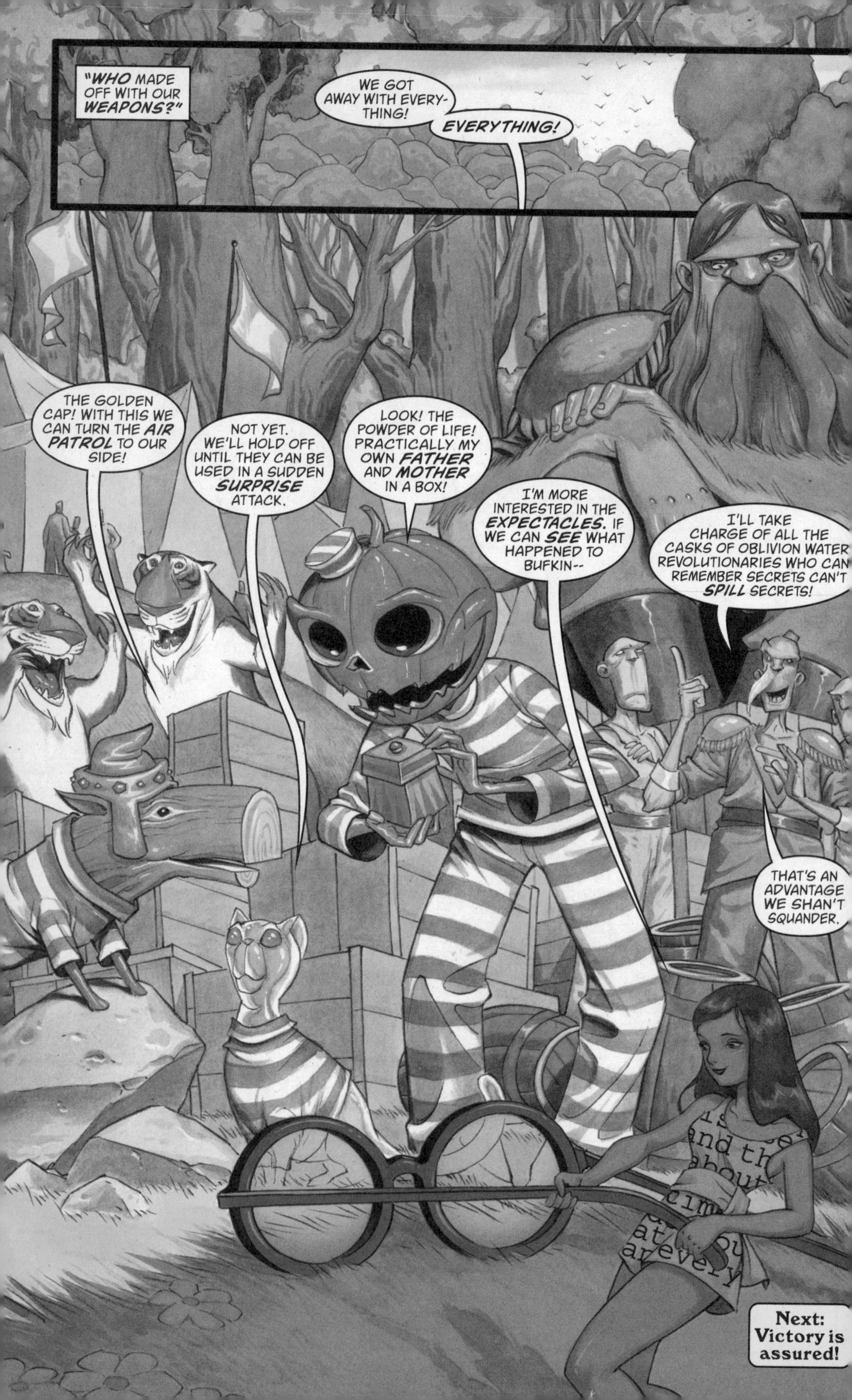
"WHO MADE OFF WITH OUR WEAPONS?"
WE GOT AWAY WITH EVERY-THING!
EVERYTHING!
THE GOLDEN CAP! WITH THIS WE CAN TURN THE AIR PATROL TO OUR SIDE!
NOT YET. WE'LL HOLD OFF UNTIL THEY CAN BE USED IN A SUDDEN SURPRISE ATTACK.
LOOK! THE POWDER OF LIFE! PRACTICALLY MY OWN FATHER AND MOTHER IN A BOX!
I'M MORE INTERESTED IN THE EXPECTACLES. IF WE CAN SEE WHAT HAPPENED TO BUFKIN--
I'LL TAKE CHARGE OF ALL THE CASKS OF OBLIVION WATER. REVOLUTIONARIES WHO CAN REMEMBER SECRETS CAN'T SPILL SECRETS!
THAT'S AN ADVANTAGE WE SHAN'T SQUANDER.
Next: Victory is assured!

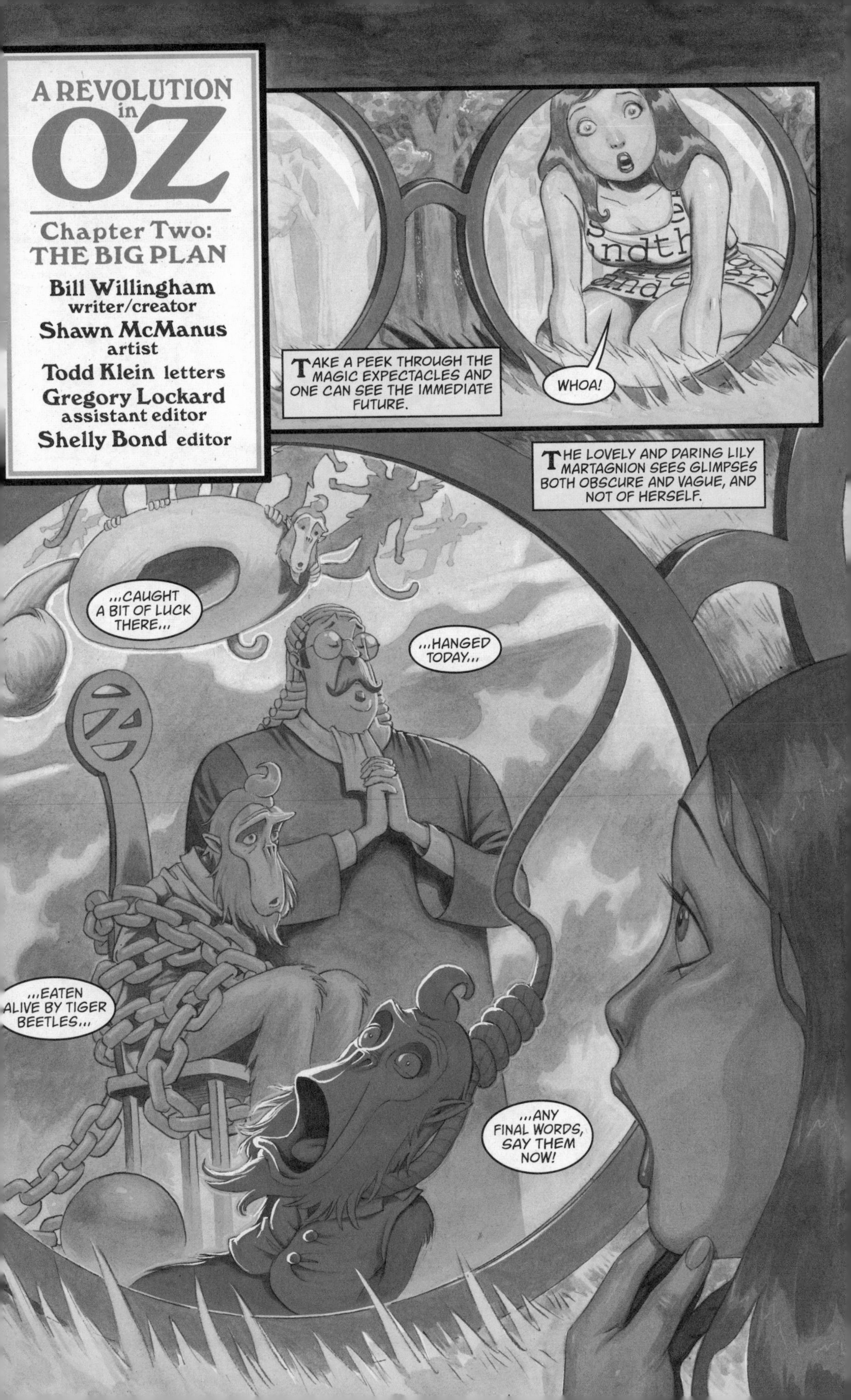
A REVOLUTION in OZ
Chapter Two: THE BIG PLAN
Bill Willingham writer/creator
Shawn McManus artist
Todd Klein letters
Gregory Lockard assistant editor
Shelly Bond editor
TAKE A PEEK THROUGH THE MAGIC EXPECTACLES AND ONE CAN SEE THE IMMEDIATE FUTURE.
WHOA!
THE LOVELY AND DARING LILY MARTAGNION SEES GLIMPSES BOTH OBSCURE AND VAGUE, AND NOT OF HERSELF.
...CAUGHT A BIT OF LUCK THERE...
...HANGED TODAY...
...EATEN ALIVE BY TIGER BEETLES...
...ANY FINAL WORDS, SAY THEM NOW!

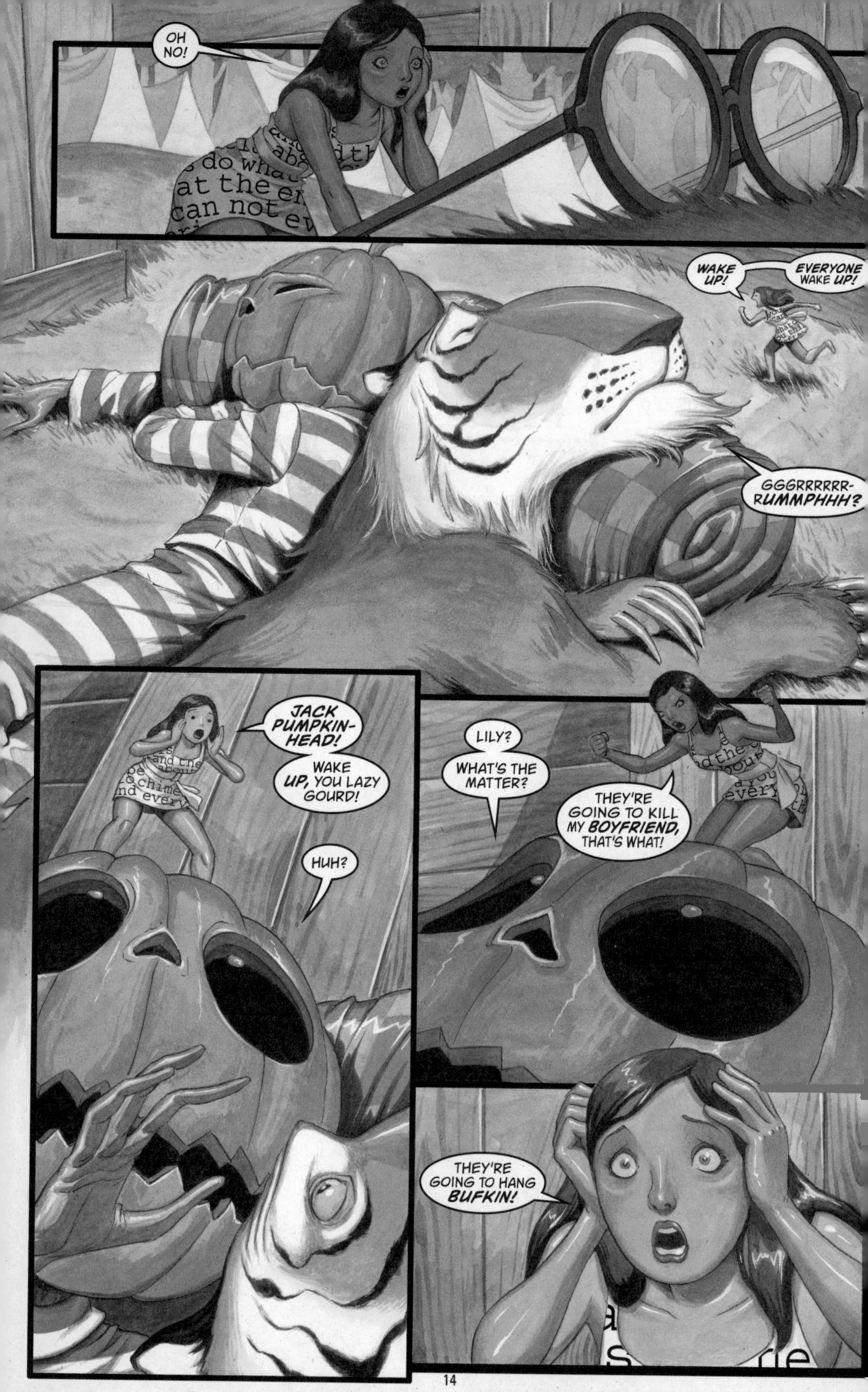
OH NO!
WAKE UP!
EVERYONE WAKE UP!
GGGRRRRRR-RUMMPHHH?
JACK PUMPKIN-HEAD!
WAKE UP, YOU LAZY GOURD!
HUH?
LILY?
WHAT'S THE MATTER?
THEY'RE GOING TO KILL MY BOYFRIEND, THAT'S WHAT!
THEY'RE GOING TO HANG BUFKIN!

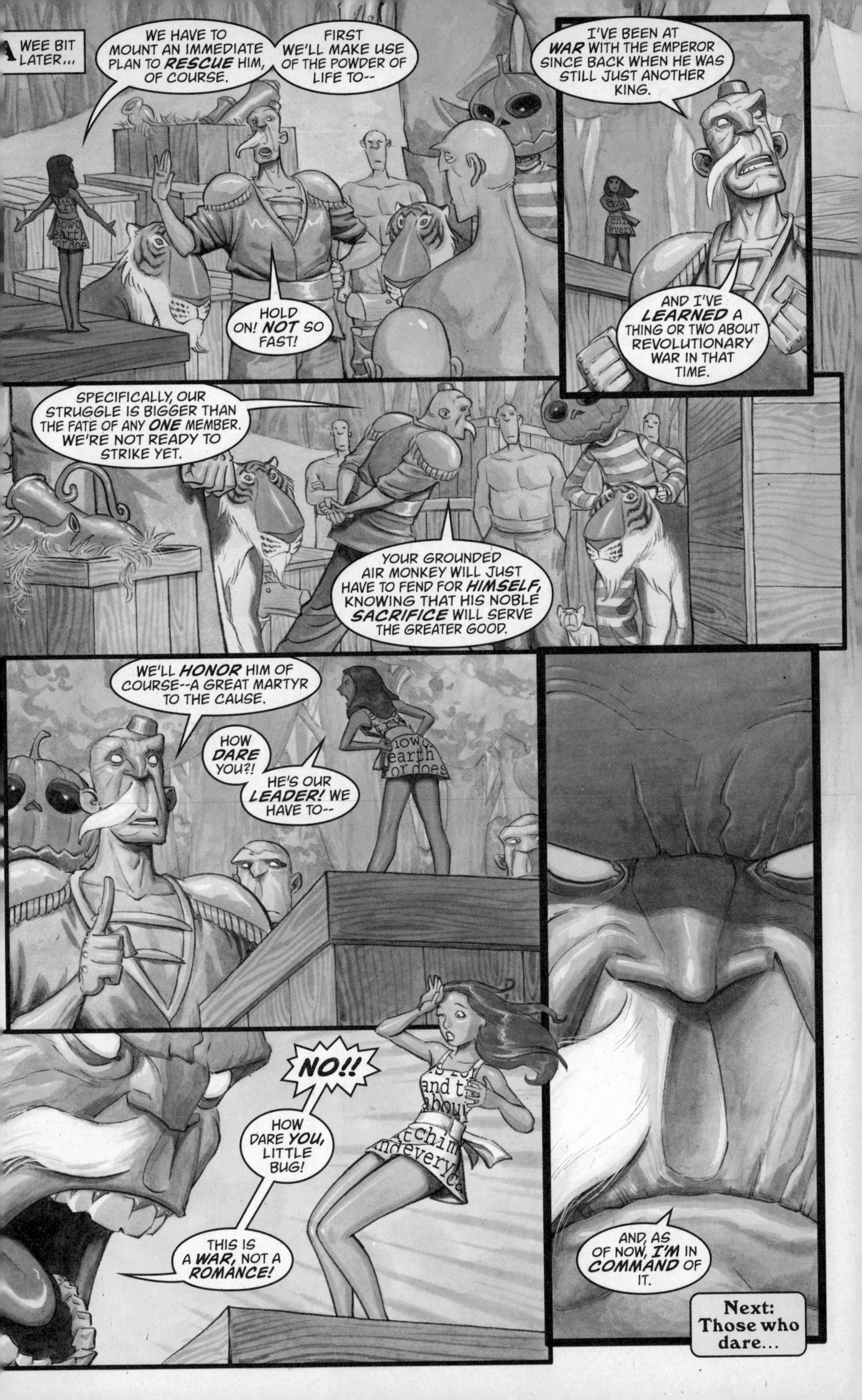
A WEE BIT LATER...
WE HAVE TO MOUNT AN IMMEDIATE PLAN TO RESCUE HIM, OF COURSE.
FIRST WE'LL MAKE USE OF THE POWDER OF LIFE TO--
HOLD ON! NOT SO FAST!
I'VE BEEN AT WAR WITH THE EMPEROR SINCE BACK WHEN HE WAS STILL JUST ANOTHER KING.
AND I'VE LEARNED A THING OR TWO ABOUT REVOLUTIONARY WAR IN THAT TIME.
SPECIFICALLY, OUR STRUGGLE IS BIGGER THAN THE FATE OF ANY ONE MEMBER. WE'RE NOT READY TO STRIKE YET.
YOUR GROUNDED AIR MONKEY WILL JUST HAVE TO FEND FOR HIMSELF, KNOWING THAT HIS NOBLE SACRIFICE WILL SERVE THE GREATER GOOD.
WE'LL HONOR HIM OF COURSE--A GREAT MARTYR TO THE CAUSE.
HOW DARE YOU?!
HE'S OUR LEADER! WE HAVE TO--
NO!!
HOW DARE YOU, LITTLE BUG!
THIS IS A WAR, NOT A ROMANCE!
AND, AS OF NOW, I'M IN COMMAND OF IT.
Next: Those who dare...

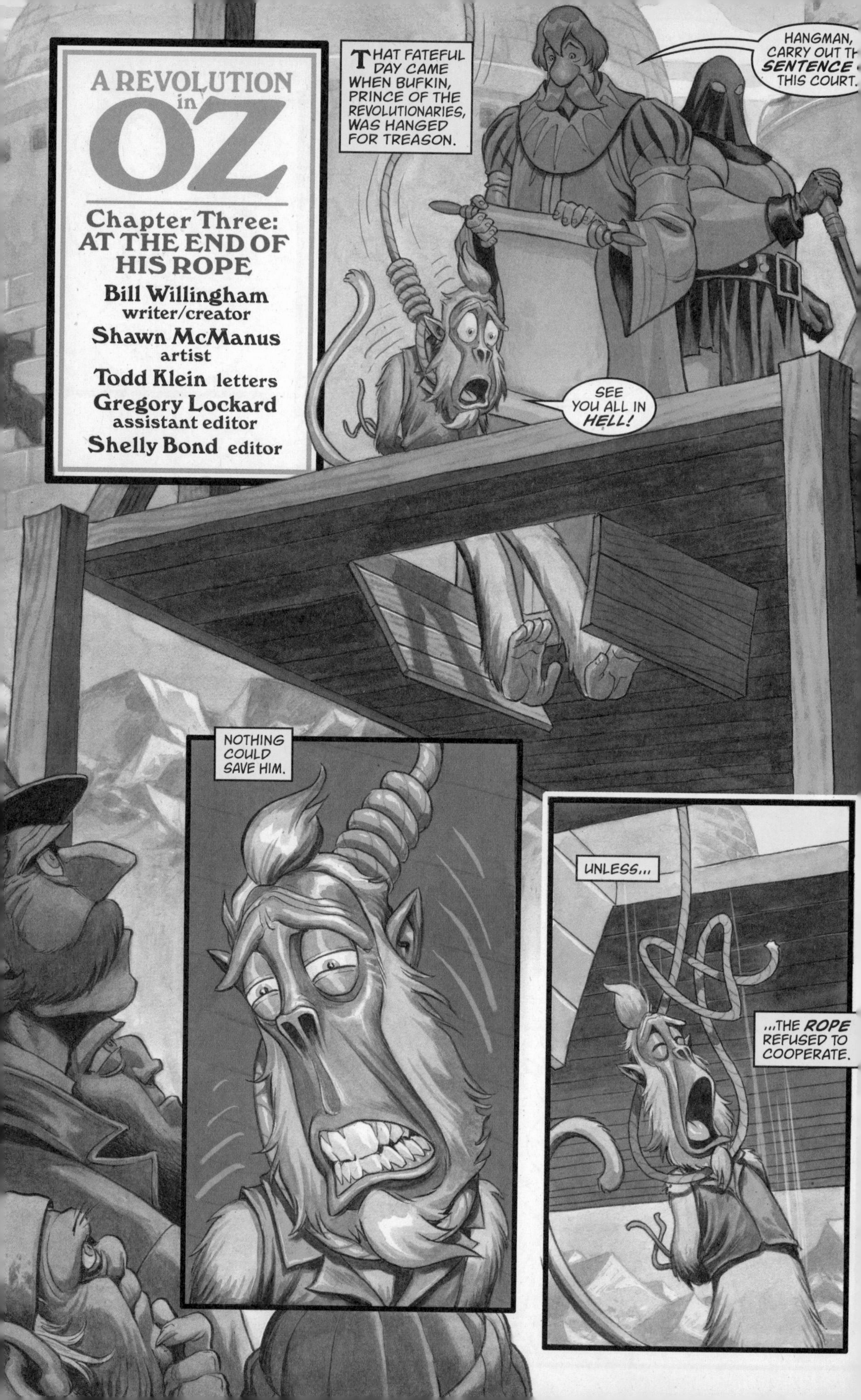
A REVOLUTION in OZ
Chapter Three: AT THE END OF HIS ROPE
Bill Willingham writer/creator
Shawn McManus artist
Todd Klein letters
Gregory Lockard assistant editor
Shelly Bond editor
THAT FATEFUL DAY CAME WHEN BUFKIN, PRINCE OF THE REVOLUTIONARIES, WAS HANGED FOR TREASON.
HANGMAN, CARRY OUT TH SENTENCE THIS COURT.
SEE YOU ALL IN HELL!
NOTHING COULD SAVE HIM.
UNLESS...
...THE ROPE REFUSED TO COOPERATE.

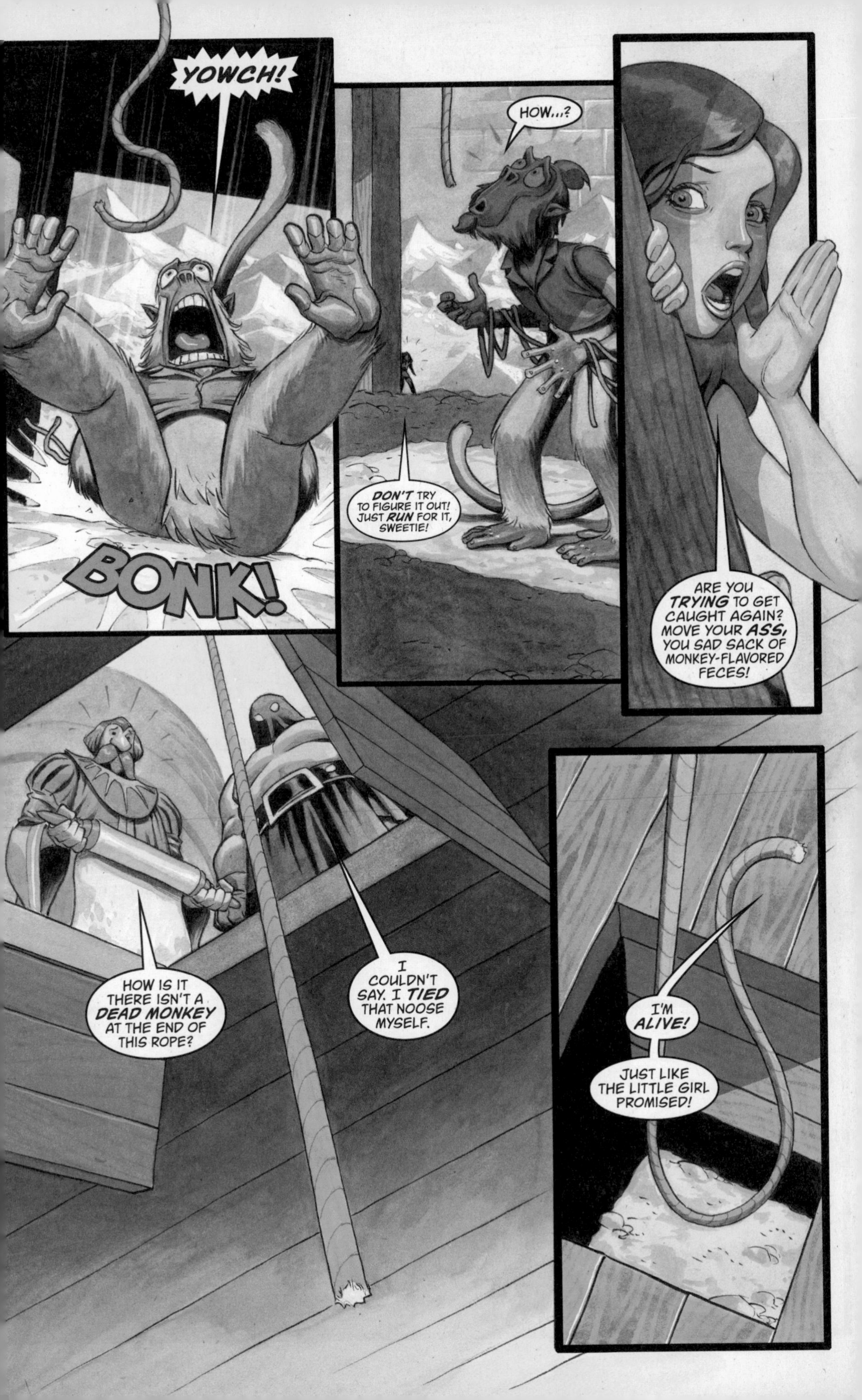
YOWCH!
BONK!
HOW...?
DON'T TRY TO FIGURE IT OUT! JUST RUN FOR IT, SWEETIE!
ARE YOU TRYING TO GET CAUGHT AGAIN? MOVE YOUR ASS, YOU SAD SACK OF MONKEY-FLAVORED FECES!
HOW IS IT THERE ISN'T A DEAD MONKEY AT THE END OF THIS ROPE?
I COULDN'T SAY. I TIED THAT NOOSE MYSELF.
I'M ALIVE!
JUST LIKE THE LITTLE GIRL PROMISED!

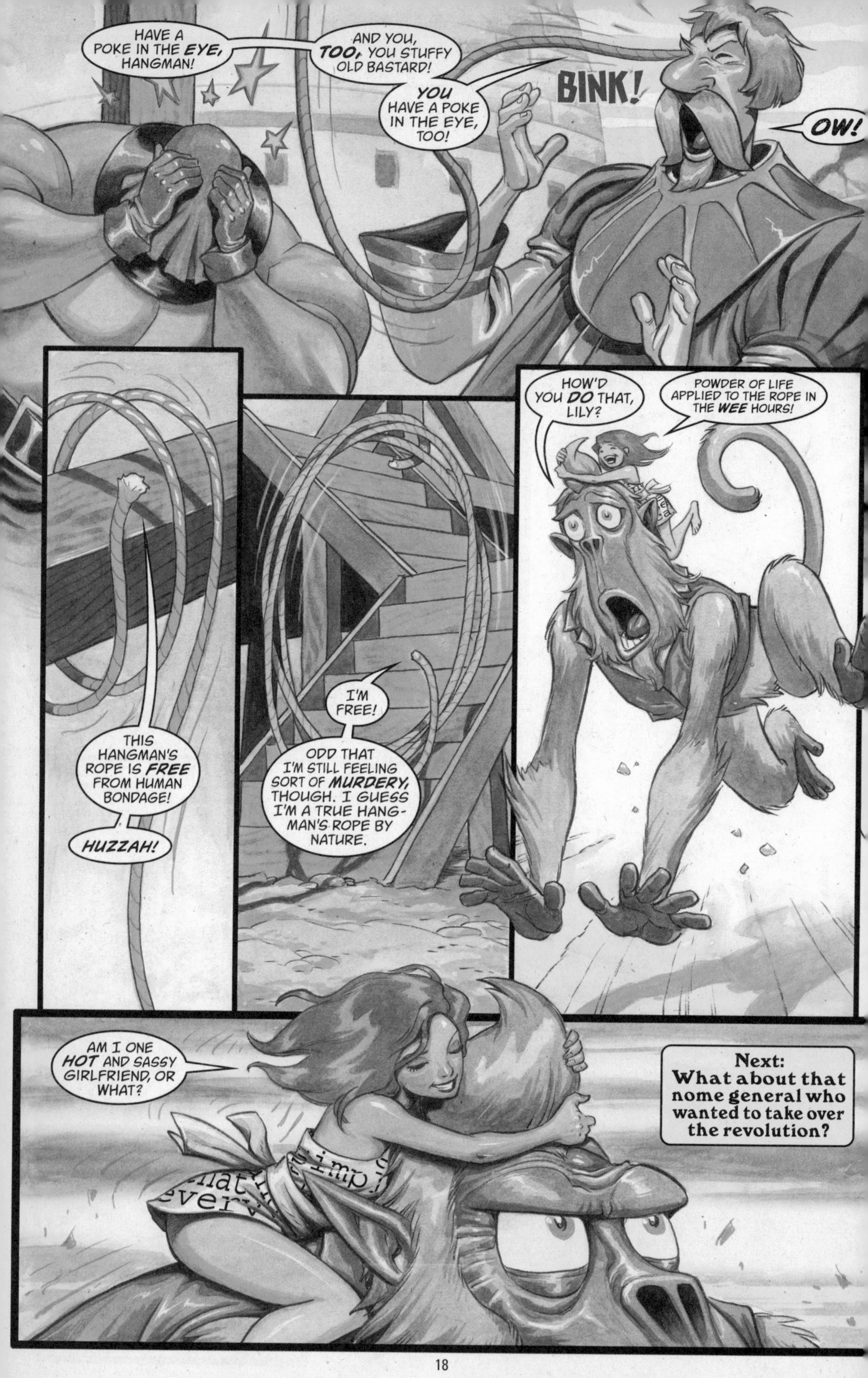
HAVE A POKE IN THE EYE, HANGMAN!
AND YOU, TOO, YOU STUFFY OLD BASTARD!
YOU HAVE A POKE IN THE EYE, TOO!
BINK!
OW!
THIS HANGMAN'S ROPE IS FREE FROM HUMAN BONDAGE!
HUZZAH!
I'M FREE!
ODD THAT I'M STILL FEELING SORT OF MURDERY, THOUGH. I GUESS I'M A TRUE HANG-MAN'S ROPE BY NATURE.
HOW'D YOU DO THAT, LILY?
POWDER OF LIFE APPLIED TO THE ROPE IN THE WEE HOURS!
AM I ONE HOT AND SASSY GIRLFRIEND, OR WHAT?
Next: What about that nome general who wanted to take over the revolution?

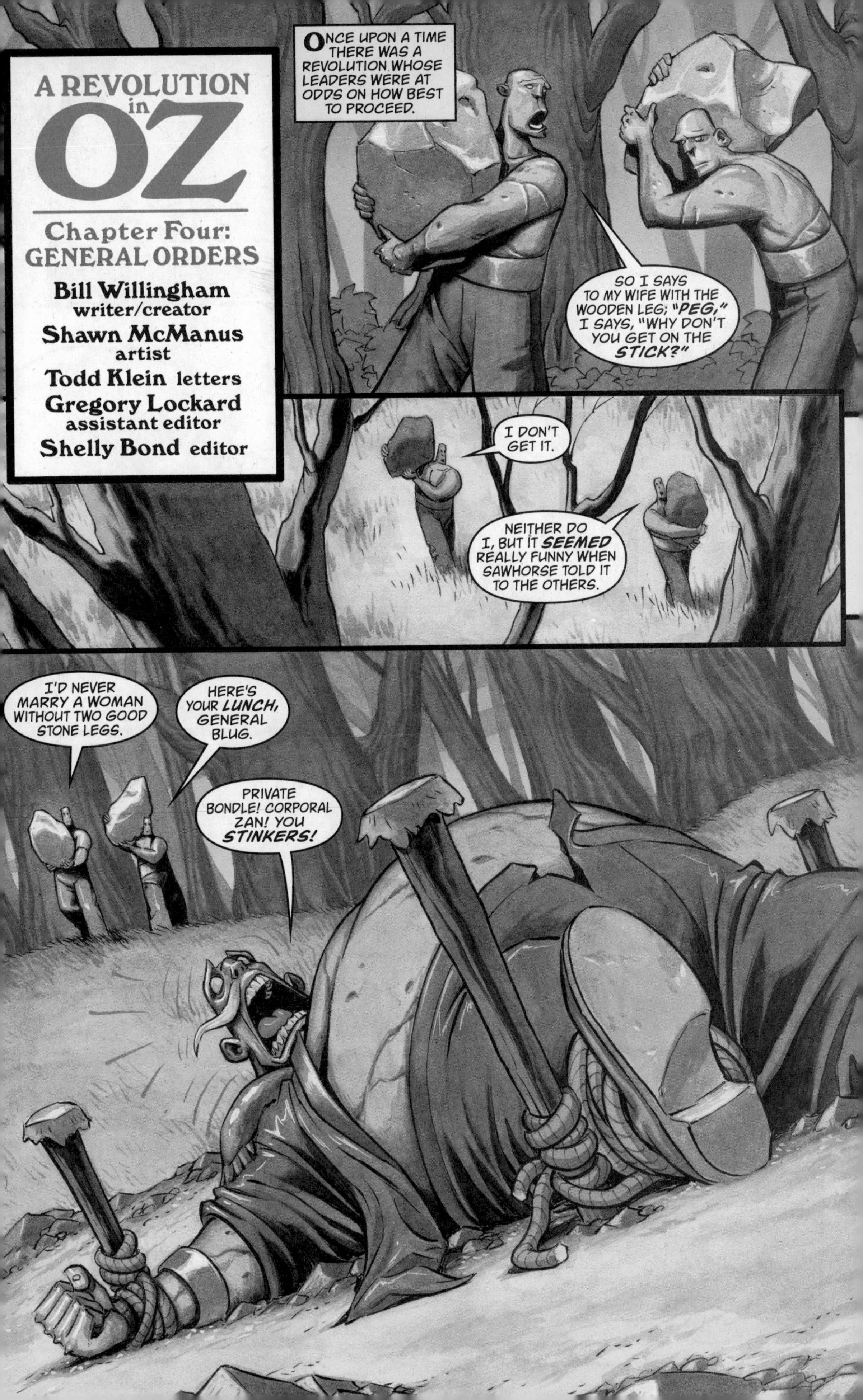
A REVOLUTION in OZ
Chapter Four: GENERAL ORDERS
Bill Willingham writer/creator
Shawn McManus artist
Todd Klein letters
Gregory Lockard assistant editor
Shelly Bond editor
ONCE UPON A TIME THERE WAS A REVOLUTION WHOSE LEADERS WERE AT ODDS ON HOW BEST TO PROCEED.
SO I SAYS TO MY WIFE WITH THE WOODEN LEG; "PEG," I SAYS, "WHY DON'T YOU GET ON THE STICK?"
I DON'T GET IT.
NEITHER DO I, BUT IT SEEMED REALLY FUNNY WHEN SAWHORSE TOLD IT TO THE OTHERS.
I'D NEVER MARRY A WOMAN WITHOUT TWO GOOD STONE LEGS.
HERE'S YOUR LUNCH, GENERAL BLUG.
PRIVATE BONDLE! CORPORAL ZAN! YOU STINKERS!

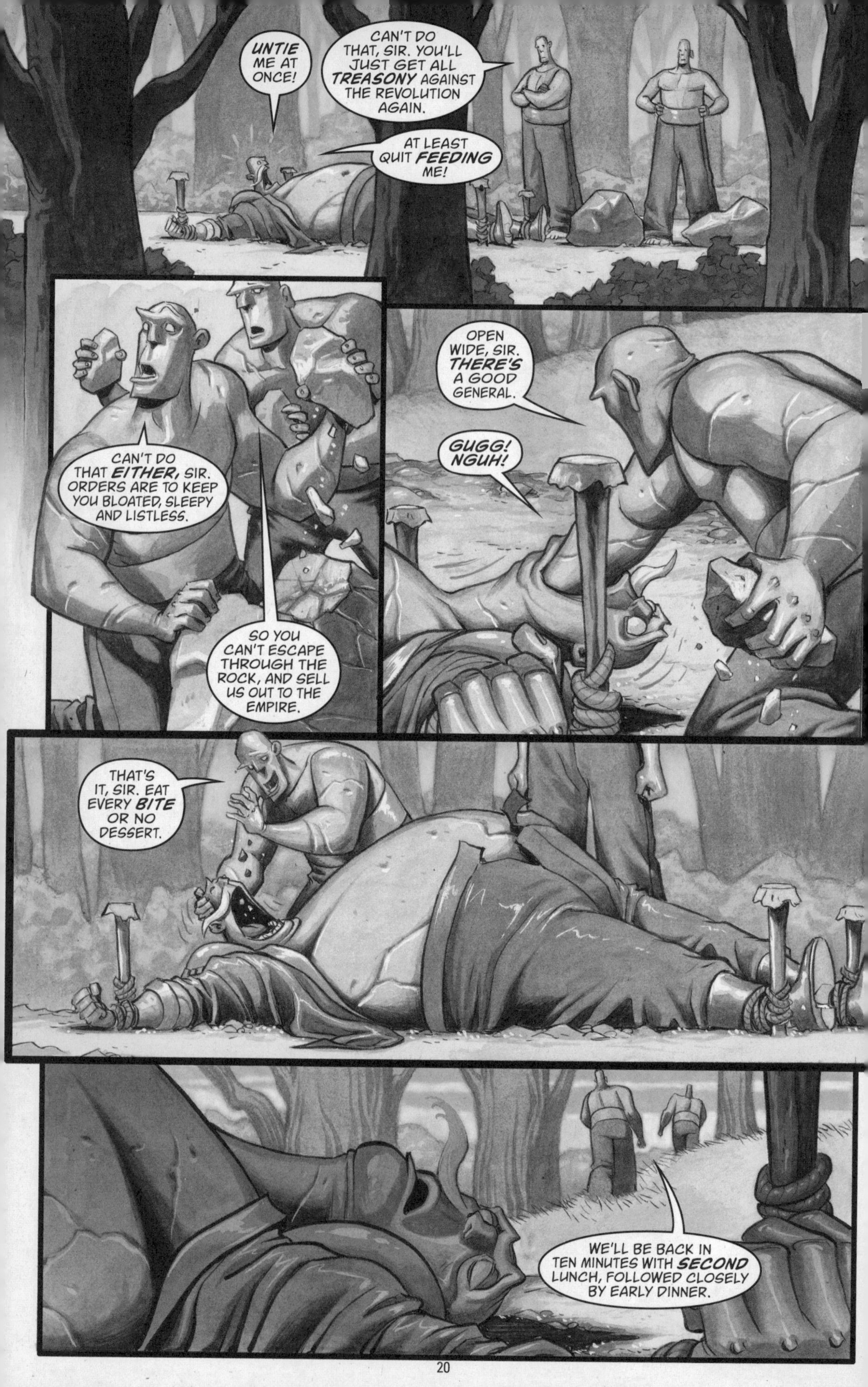
UNTIE ME AT ONCE!
CAN'T DO THAT, SIR. YOU'LL JUST GET ALL TREASONY AGAINST THE REVOLUTION AGAIN.
AT LEAST QUIT FEEDING ME!
CAN'T DO THAT EITHER, SIR. ORDERS ARE TO KEEP YOU BLOATED, SLEEPY AND LISTLESS.
SO YOU CAN'T ESCAPE THROUGH THE ROCK, AND SELL US OUT TO THE EMPIRE.
OPEN WIDE, SIR. THERE'S A GOOD GENERAL.
GUGG! NGUH!
THAT'S IT, SIR. EAT EVERY BITE OR NO DESSERT.
WE'LL BE BACK IN TEN MINUTES WITH SECOND LUNCH, FOLLOWED CLOSELY BY EARLY DINNER.

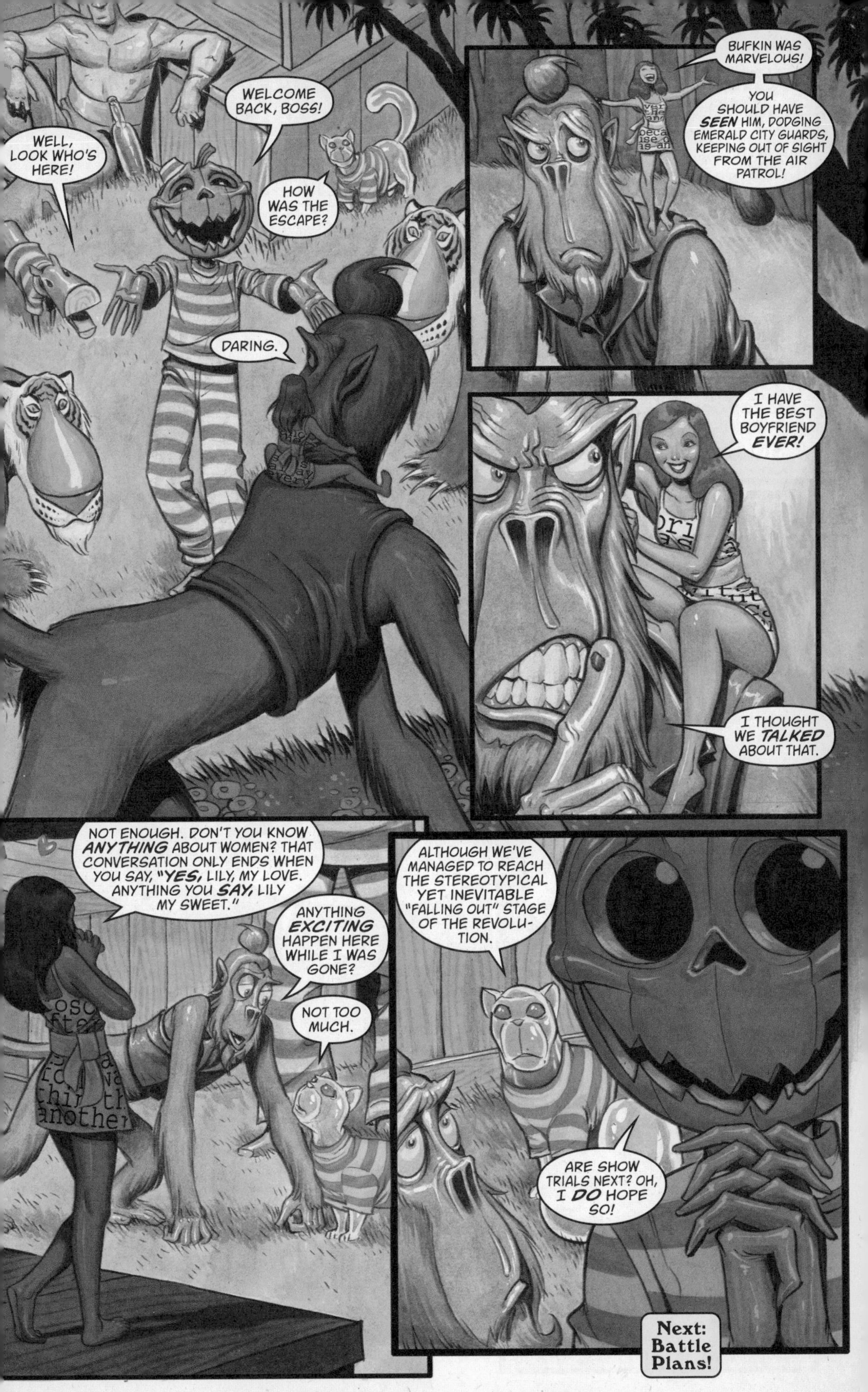
WELL, LOOK WHO'S HERE!
WELCOME BACK, BOSS!
HOW WAS THE ESCAPE?
DARING.
BUFKIN WAS MARVELOUS!
YOU SHOULD HAVE SEEN HIM, DODGING EMERALD CITY GUARDS, KEEPING OUT OF SIGHT FROM THE AIR PATROL!
I HAVE THE BEST BOYFRIEND EVER!
I THOUGHT WE TALKED ABOUT THAT.
NOT ENOUGH. DON'T YOU KNOW ANYTHING ABOUT WOMEN? THAT CONVERSATION ONLY ENDS WHEN YOU SAY, "YES, LILY, MY LOVE. ANYTHING YOU SAY, LILY MY SWEET."
ANYTHING EXCITING HAPPEN HERE WHILE I WAS GONE?
NOT TOO MUCH.
ALTHOUGH WE'VE MANAGED TO REACH THE STEREOTYPICAL YET INEVITABLE "FALLING OUT" STAGE OF THE REVOLUTION.
ARE SHOW TRIALS NEXT? OH, I DO HOPE SO!
Next: Battle Plans!

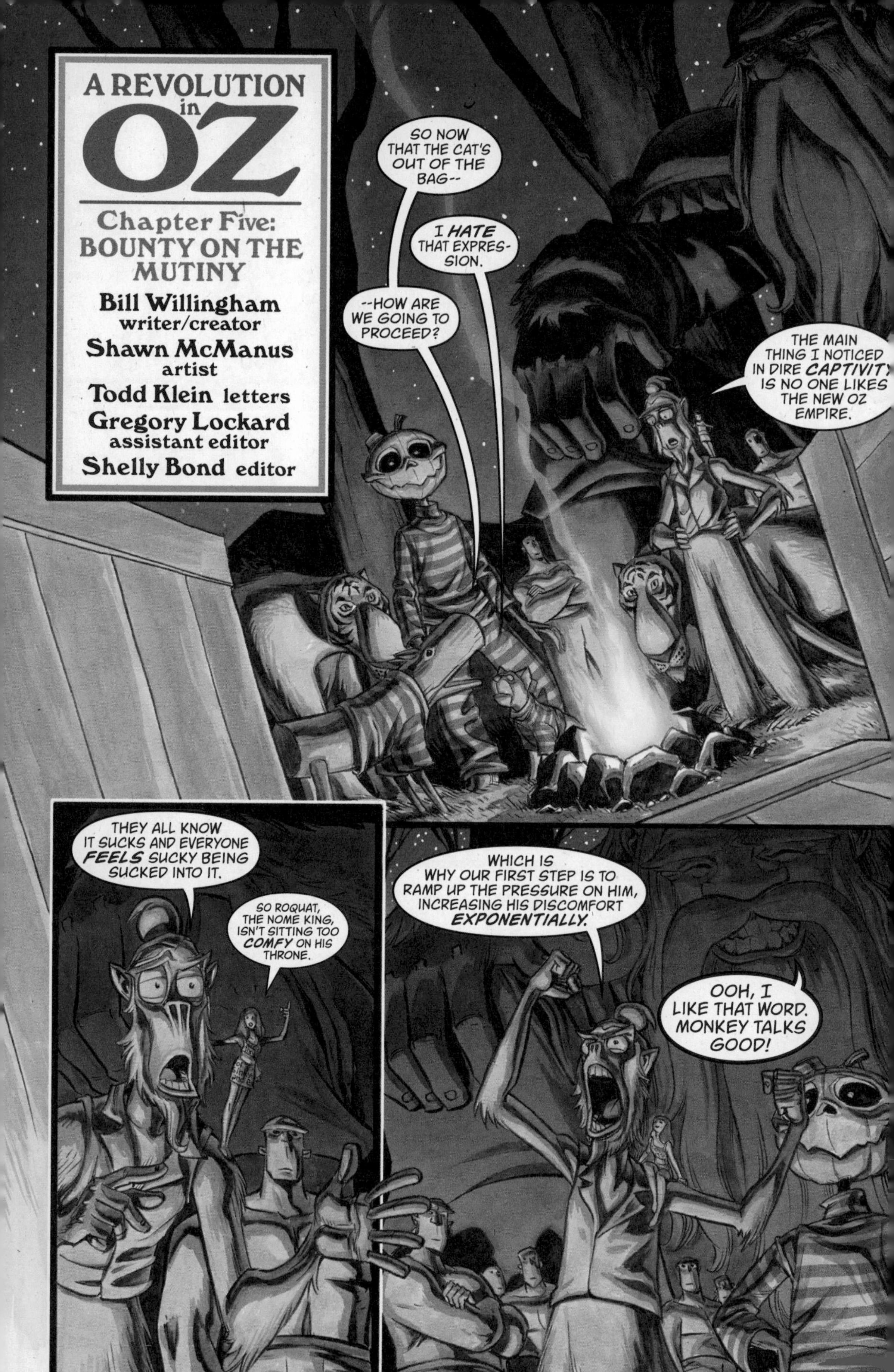
A REVOLUTION in OZ
Chapter Five: BOUNTY ON THE MUTINY
Bill Willingham writer/creator
Shawn McManus artist
Todd Klein letters
Gregory Lockard assistant editor
Shelly Bond editor
SO NOW THAT THE CAT'S OUT OF THE BAG--
I HATE THAT EXPRESSION.
--HOW ARE WE GOING TO PROCEED?
THE MAIN THING I NOTICED IN DIRE CAPTIVITY IS NO ONE LIKES THE NEW OZ EMPIRE.
THEY ALL KNOW IT SUCKS AND EVERYONE FEELS SUCKY BEING SUCKED INTO IT.
SO ROQUAT, THE NOME KING, ISN'T SITTING TOO COMFY ON HIS THRONE.
WHICH IS WHY OUR FIRST STEP IS TO RAMP UP THE PRESSURE ON HIM, INCREASING HIS DISCOMFORT EXPONENTIALLY.
OOH, I LIKE THAT WORD. MONKEY TALKS GOOD!

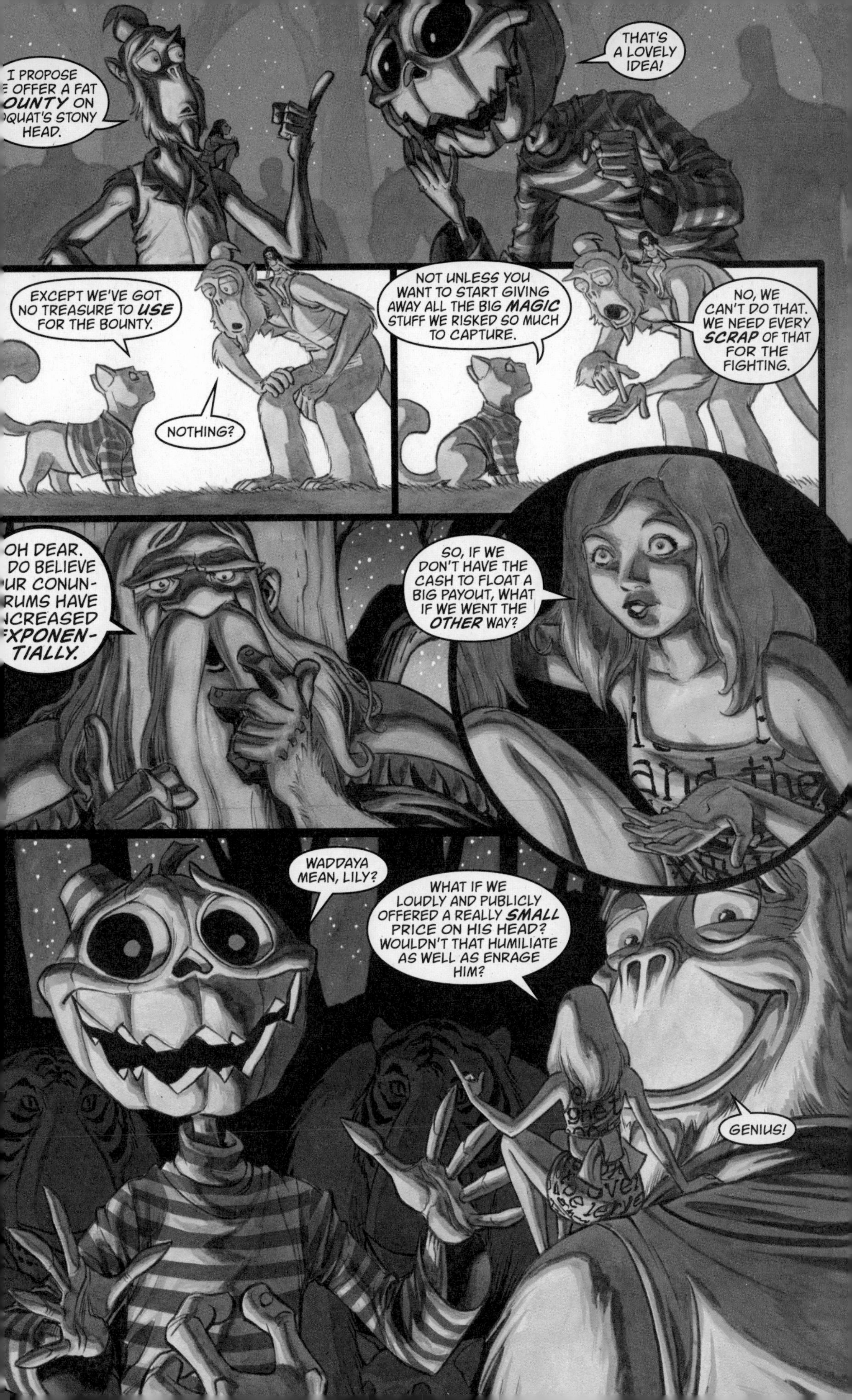

I PROPOSE E OFFER A FAT OUNTY ON OQUAT'S STONY HEAD.
THAT'S A LOVELY IDEA!
EXCEPT WE'VE GOT NO TREASURE TO USE FOR THE BOUNTY.
NOTHING?
NOT UNLESS YOU WANT TO START GIVING AWAY ALL THE BIG MAGIC STUFF WE RISKED SO MUCH TO CAPTURE.
NO, WE CAN'T DO THAT. WE NEED EVERY SCRAP OF THAT FOR THE FIGHTING.
OH DEAR. DO BELIEVE UR CONUN-RUMS HAVE NCREASED XPONEN-TIALLY.
SO, IF WE DON'T HAVE THE CASH TO FLOAT A BIG PAYOUT, WHAT IF WE WENT THE OTHER WAY?
WADDAYA MEAN, LILY?
WHAT IF WE LOUDLY AND PUBLICLY OFFERED A REALLY SMALL PRICE ON HIS HEAD? WOULDN'T THAT HUMILIATE AS WELL AS ENRAGE HIM?
GENIUS!

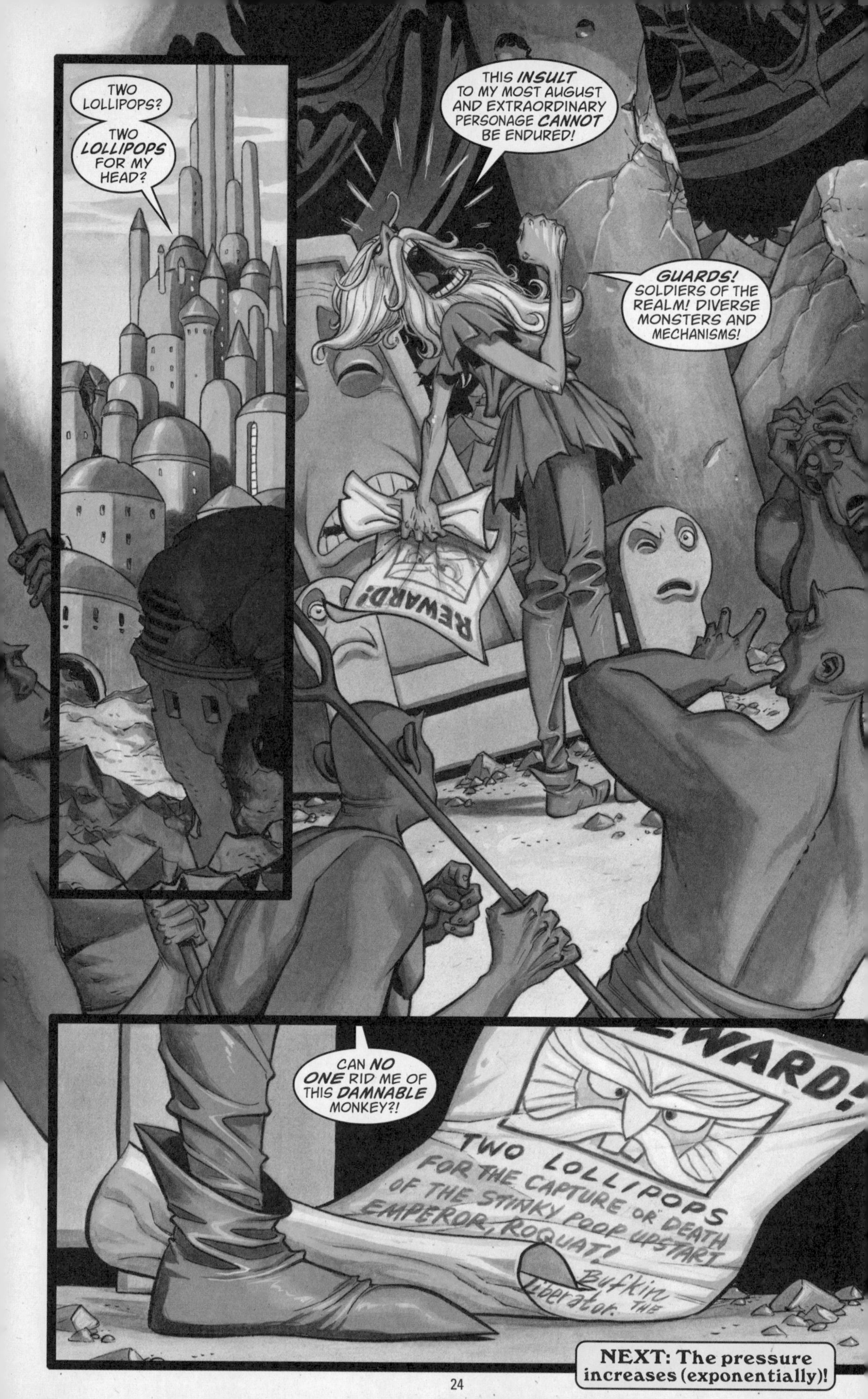
TWO LOLLIPOPS?
TWO LOLLIPOPS FOR MY HEAD?
THIS INSULT TO MY MOST AUGUST AND EXTRAORDINARY PERSONAGE CANNOT BE ENDURED!
GUARDS! SOLDIERS OF THE REALM! DIVERSE MONSTERS AND MECHANISMS!
REWARD!
CAN NO ONE RID ME OF THIS DAMNABLE MONKEY?!
REWARD!
TWO LOLLIPOPS FOR THE CAPTURE OR DEATH OF THE STINKY POOP UPSTART EMPEROR, ROQUAT!
Bufkin THE liberator.
NEXT: The pressure increases (exponentially)!

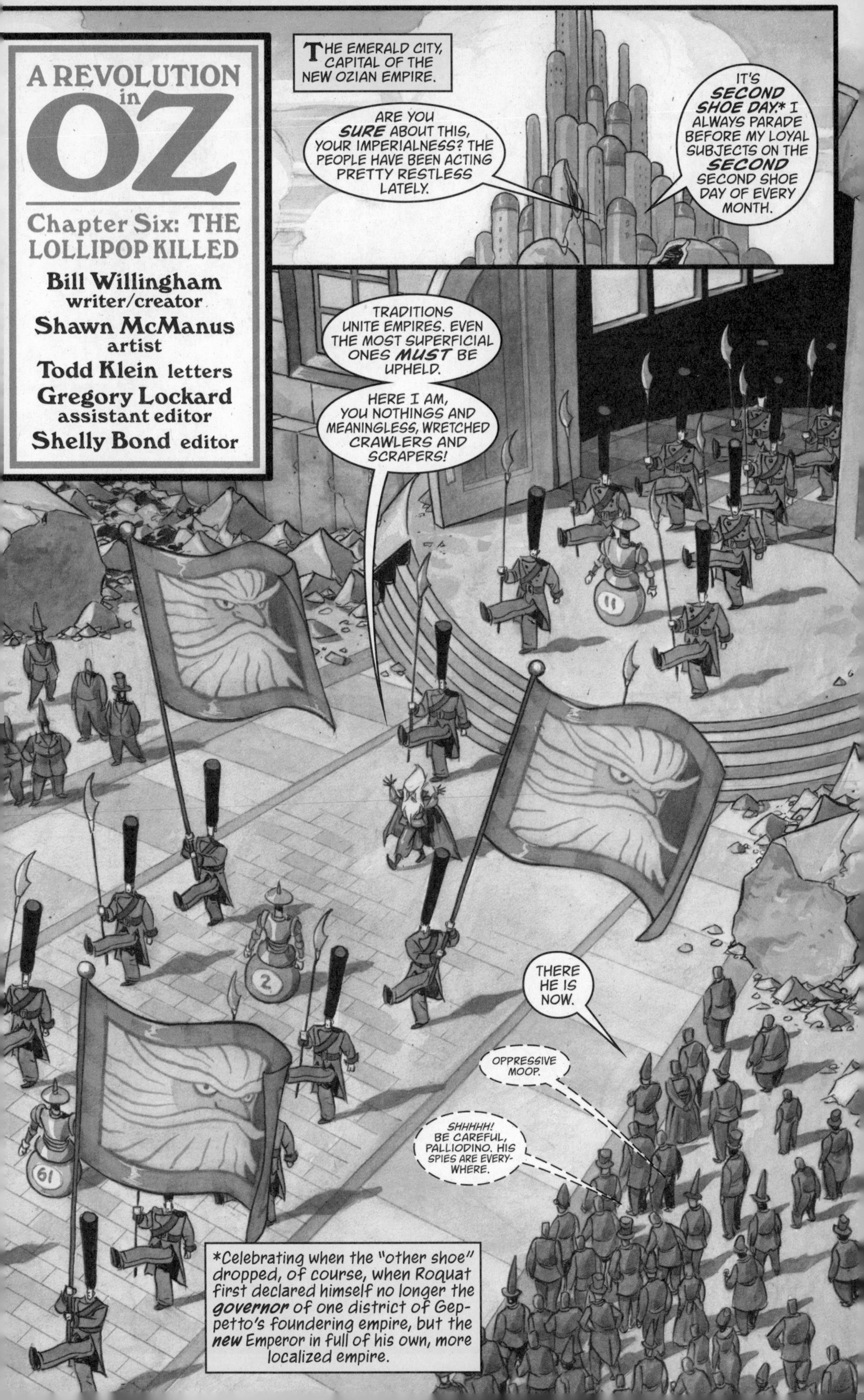
A REVOLUTION in OZ
Chapter Six: THE LOLLIPOP KILLED
Bill Willingham writer/creator
Shawn McManus artist
Todd Klein letters
Gregory Lockard assistant editor
Shelly Bond editor
THE EMERALD CITY, CAPITAL OF THE NEW OZIAN EMPIRE.
ARE YOU SURE ABOUT THIS, YOUR IMPERIALNESS? THE PEOPLE HAVE BEEN ACTING PRETTY RESTLESS LATELY.
IT'S SECOND SHOE DAY.* I ALWAYS PARADE BEFORE MY LOYAL SUBJECTS ON THE SECOND SECOND SHOE DAY OF EVERY MONTH.
TRADITIONS UNITE EMPIRES. EVEN THE MOST SUPERFICIAL ONES MUST BE UPHELD.
HERE I AM, YOU NOTHINGS AND MEANINGLESS, WRETCHED CRAWLERS AND SCRAPERS!
THERE HE IS NOW.
OPPRESSIVE MOOP.
SHHHHH! BE CAREFUL, PALLIODINO. HIS SPIES ARE EVERYWHERE.
*Celebrating when the "other shoe" dropped, of course, when Roquat first declared himself no longer the governor of one district of Geppetto's foundering empire, but the new Emperor in full of his own, more localized empire.

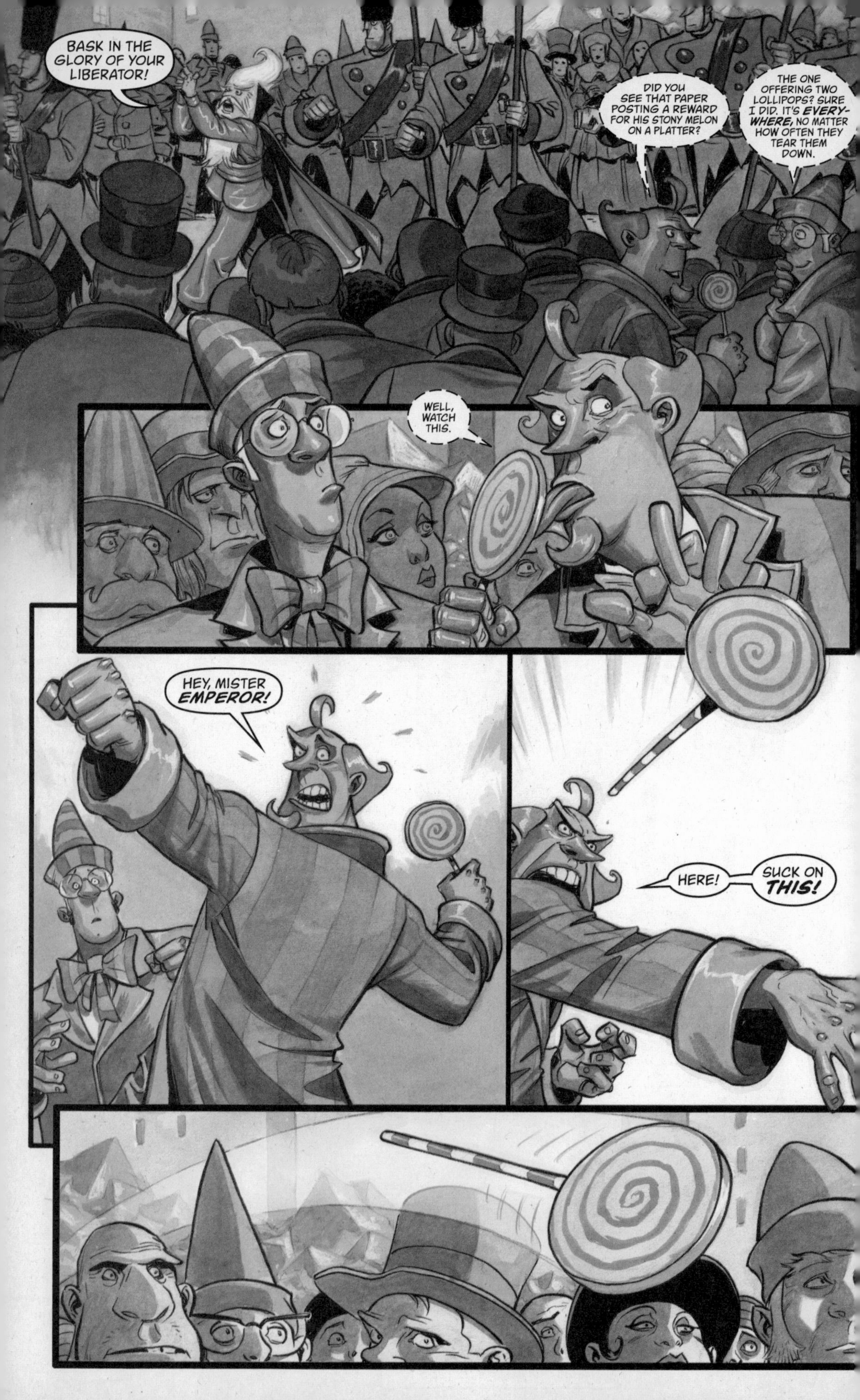
BASK IN THE GLORY OF YOUR LIBERATOR!
DID YOU SEE THAT PAPER POSTING A REWARD FOR HIS STONY MELON ON A PLATTER?
THE ONE OFFERING TWO LOLLIPOPS? SURE I DID. IT'S EVERY-WHERE, NO MATTER HOW OFTEN THEY TEAR THEM DOWN.
WELL, WATCH THIS.
HEY, MISTER EMPEROR!
HERE!
SUCK ON THIS!

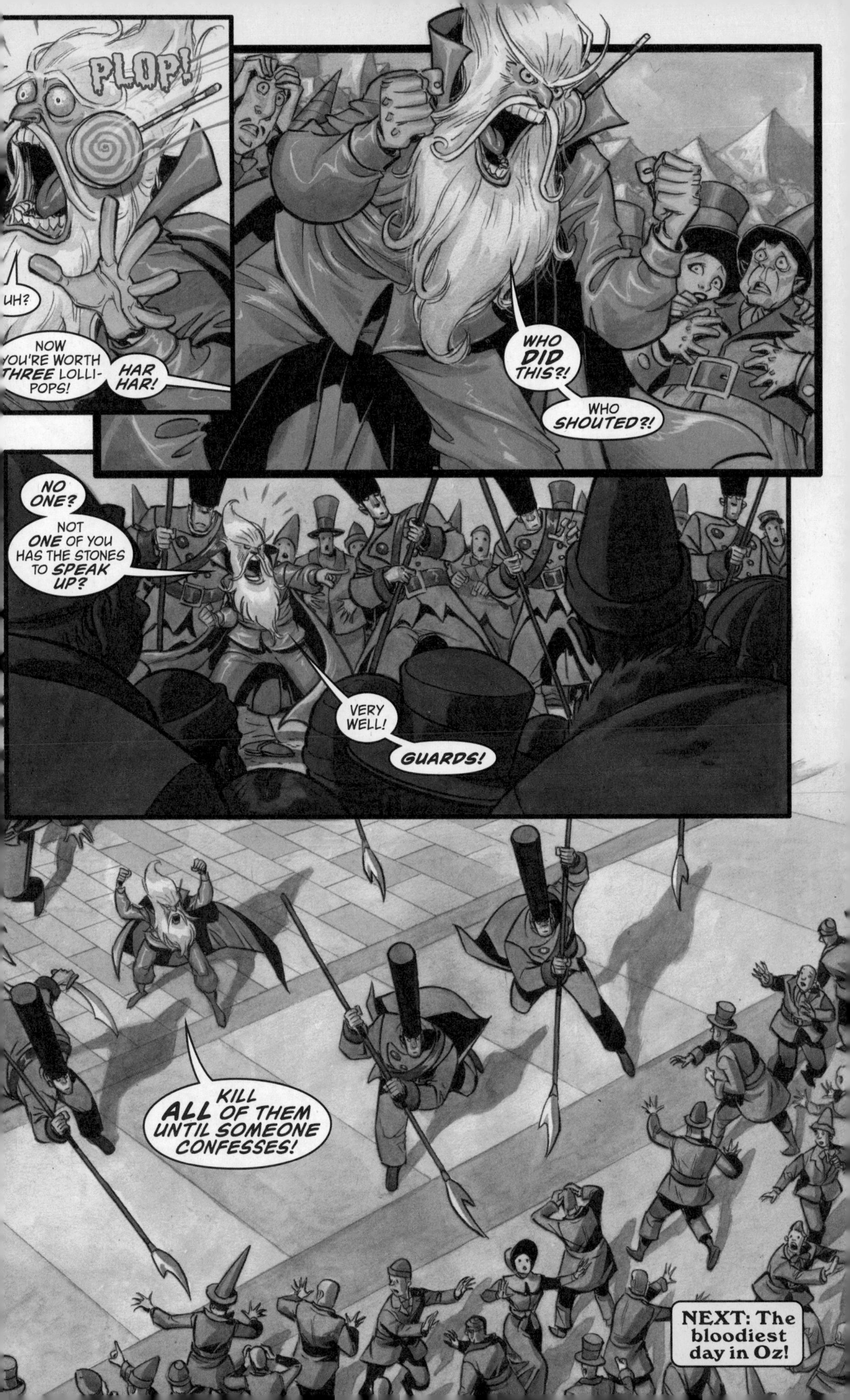
PLOP!
UH?
NOW YOU'RE WORTH THREE LOLLI-POPS!
HAR HAR!
WHO DID THIS?!
WHO SHOUTED?!
NO ONE?
NOT ONE OF YOU HAS THE STONES TO SPEAK UP?
VERY WELL!
GUARDS!
KILL ALL OF THEM UNTIL SOMEONE CONFESSES!
NEXT: The bloodiest day in Oz!

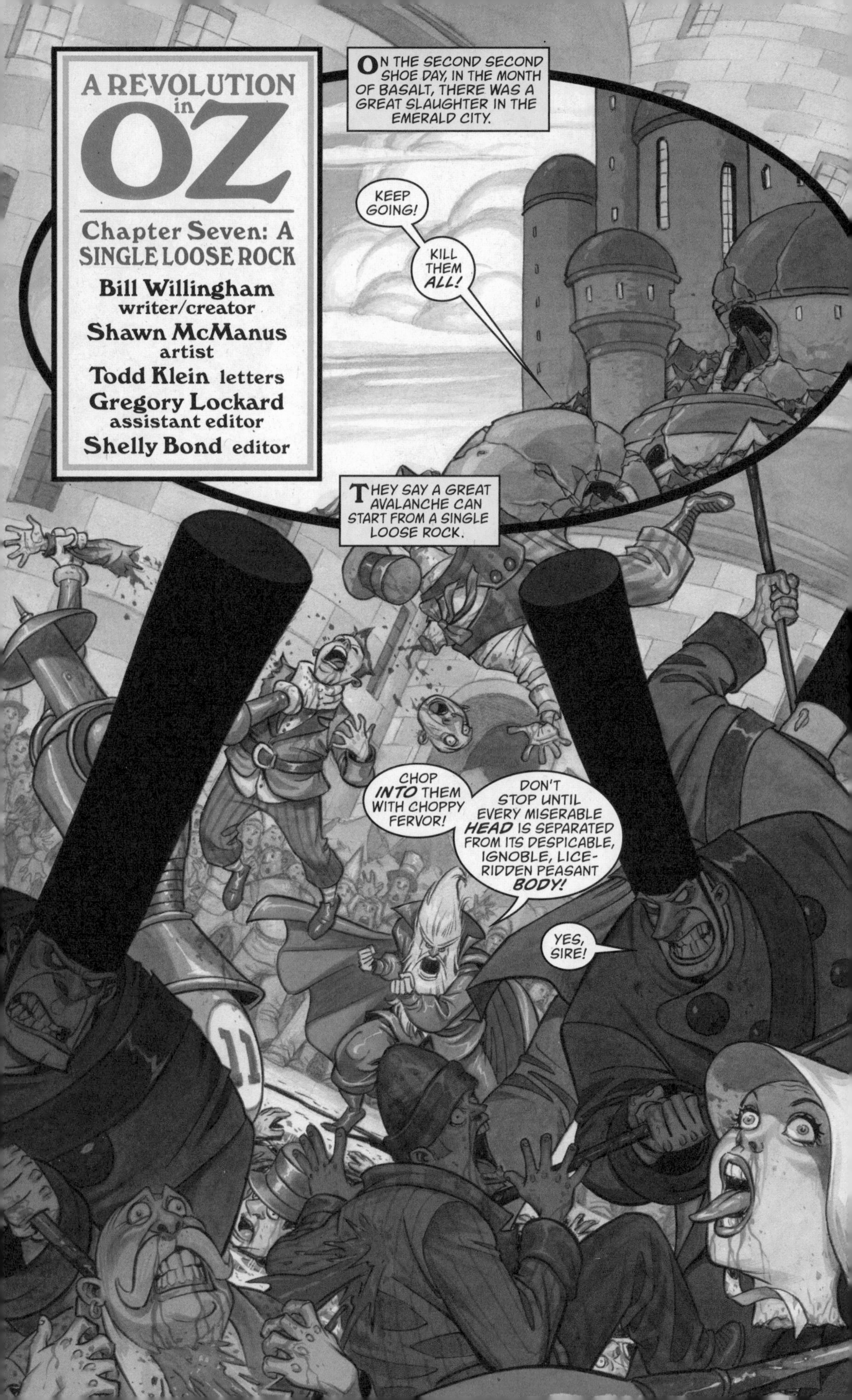
A REVOLUTION in OZ
Chapter Seven: A SINGLE LOOSE ROCK
Bill Willingham writer/creator
Shawn McManus artist
Todd Klein letters
Gregory Lockard assistant editor
Shelly Bond editor
ON THE SECOND SECOND SHOE DAY, IN THE MONTH OF BASALT, THERE WAS A GREAT SLAUGHTER IN THE EMERALD CITY.
KEEP GOING!
KILL THEM ALL!
THEY SAY A GREAT AVALANCHE CAN START FROM A SINGLE LOOSE ROCK.
CHOP INTO THEM WITH CHOPPY FERVOR!
DON'T STOP UNTIL EVERY MISERABLE HEAD IS SEPARATED FROM ITS DESPICABLE, IGNOBLE, LICE-RIDDEN PEASANT BODY!
YES, SIRE!
11

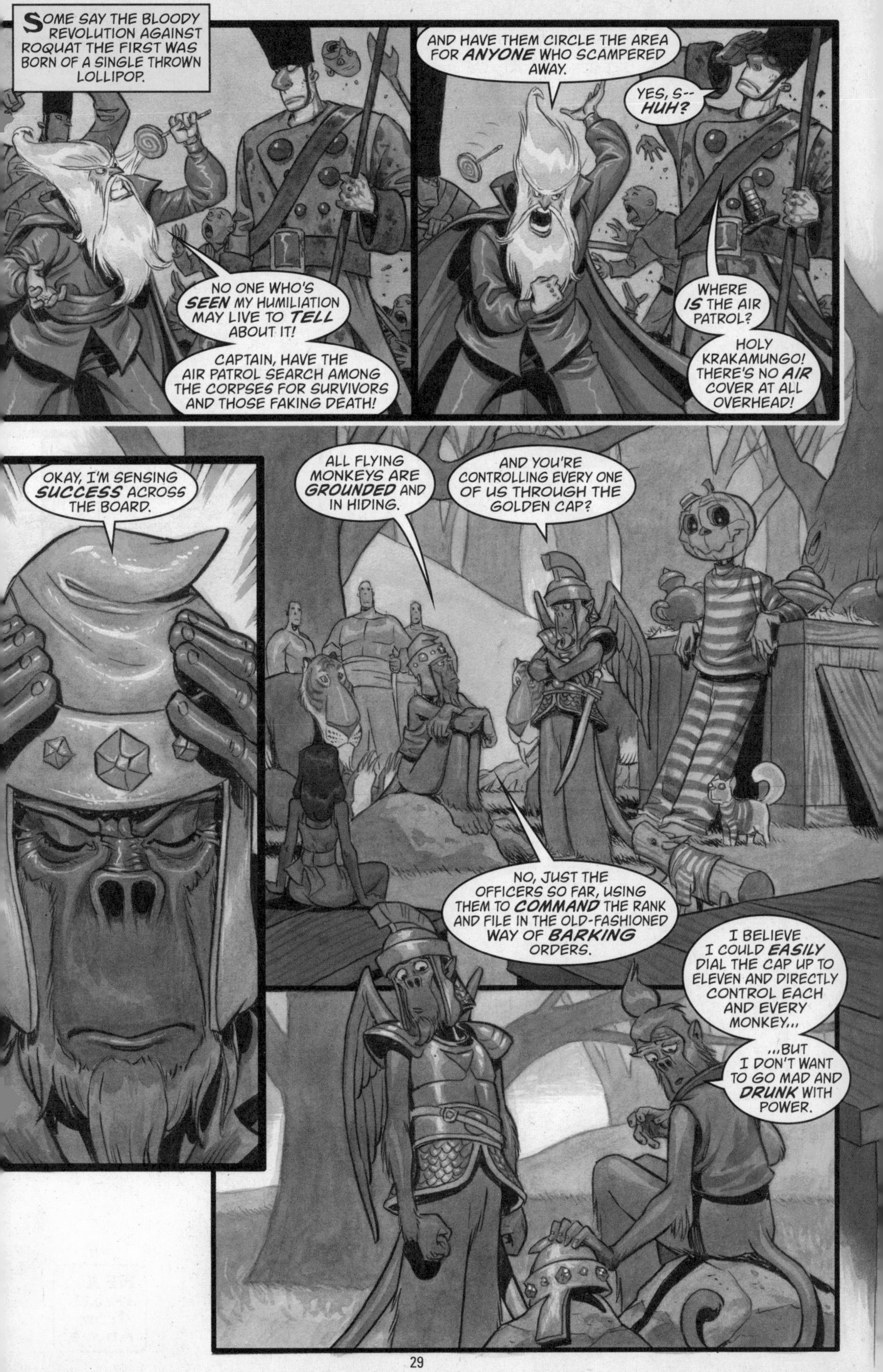
SOME SAY THE BLOODY REVOLUTION AGAINST ROQUAT THE FIRST WAS BORN OF A SINGLE THROWN LOLLIPOP.
NO ONE WHO'S SEEN MY HUMILIATION MAY LIVE TO TELL ABOUT IT!
CAPTAIN, HAVE THE AIR PATROL SEARCH AMONG THE CORPSES FOR SURVIVORS AND THOSE FAKING DEATH!
AND HAVE THEM CIRCLE THE AREA FOR ANYONE WHO SCAMPERED AWAY.
YES, S-- HUH?
WHERE IS THE AIR PATROL?
HOLY KRAKAMUNGO! THERE'S NO AIR COVER AT ALL OVERHEAD!
OKAY, I'M SENSING SUCCESS ACROSS THE BOARD.
ALL FLYING MONKEYS ARE GROUNDED AND IN HIDING.
AND YOU'RE CONTROLLING EVERY ONE OF US THROUGH THE GOLDEN CAP?
NO, JUST THE OFFICERS SO FAR, USING THEM TO COMMAND THE RANK AND FILE IN THE OLD-FASHIONED WAY OF BARKING ORDERS.
I BELIEVE I COULD EASILY DIAL THE CAP UP TO ELEVEN AND DIRECTLY CONTROL EACH AND EVERY MONKEY...
...BUT I DON'T WANT TO GO MAD AND DRUNK WITH POWER.

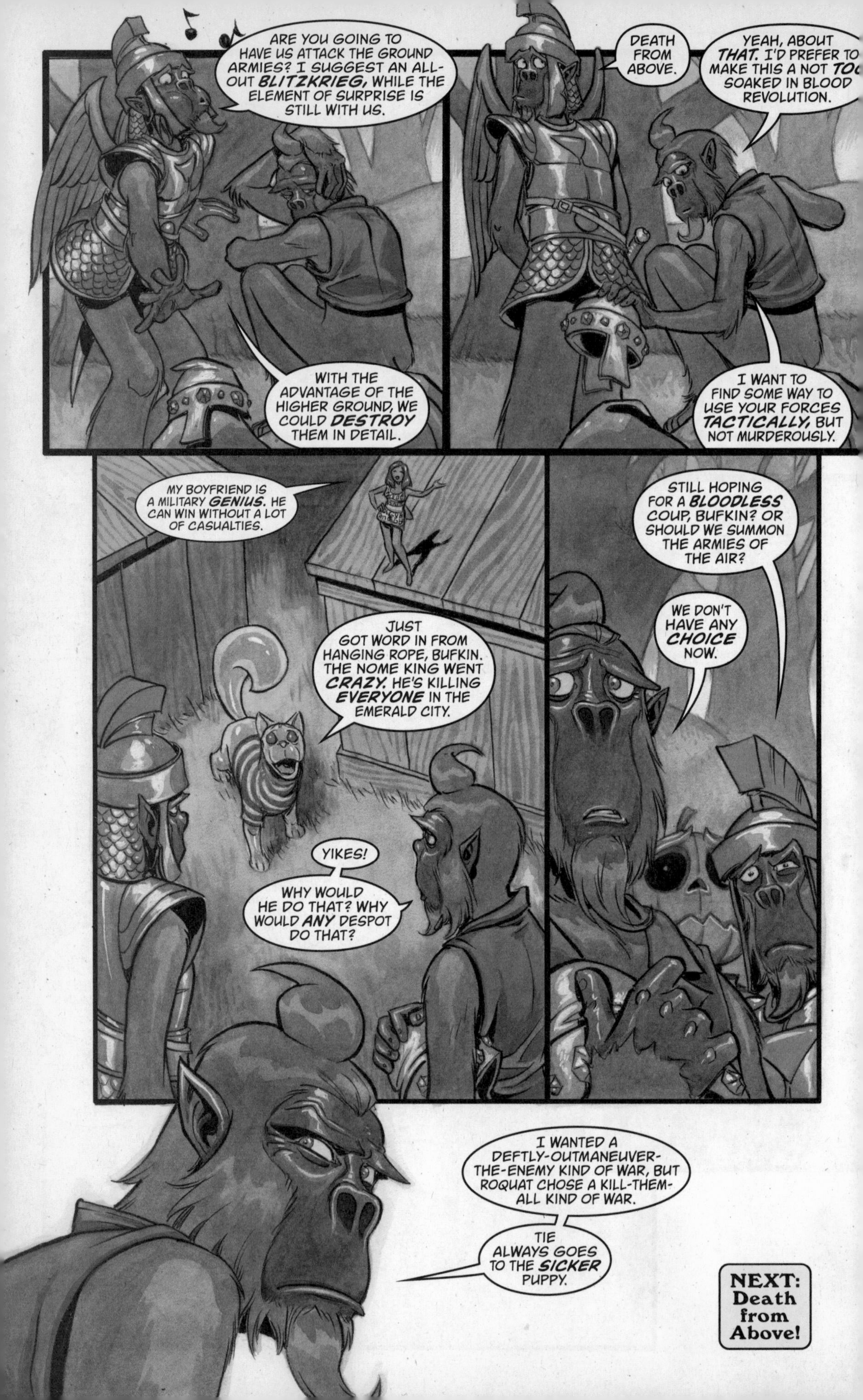
ARE YOU GOING TO HAVE US ATTACK THE GROUND ARMIES? I SUGGEST AN ALL-OUT BLITZKRIEG, WHILE THE ELEMENT OF SURPRISE IS STILL WITH US.
WITH THE ADVANTAGE OF THE HIGHER GROUND, WE COULD DESTROY THEM IN DETAIL.
DEATH FROM ABOVE.
YEAH, ABOUT THAT. I'D PREFER TO MAKE THIS A NOT TOO SOAKED IN BLOOD REVOLUTION.
I WANT TO FIND SOME WAY TO USE YOUR FORCES TACTICALLY, BUT NOT MURDEROUSLY.
MY BOYFRIEND IS A MILITARY GENIUS. HE CAN WIN WITHOUT A LOT OF CASUALTIES.
JUST GOT WORD IN FROM HANGING ROPE, BUFKIN. THE NOME KING WENT CRAZY. HE'S KILLING EVERYONE IN THE EMERALD CITY.
YIKES!
WHY WOULD HE DO THAT? WHY WOULD ANY DESPOT DO THAT?
STILL HOPING FOR A BLOODLESS COUP, BUFKIN? OR SHOULD WE SUMMON THE ARMIES OF THE AIR?
WE DON'T HAVE ANY CHOICE NOW.
I WANTED A DEFTLY-OUTMANEUVER-THE-ENEMY KIND OF WAR, BUT ROQUAT CHOSE A KILL-THEM-ALL KIND OF WAR.
TIE ALWAYS GOES TO THE SICKER PUPPY.
NEXT: Death from Above!

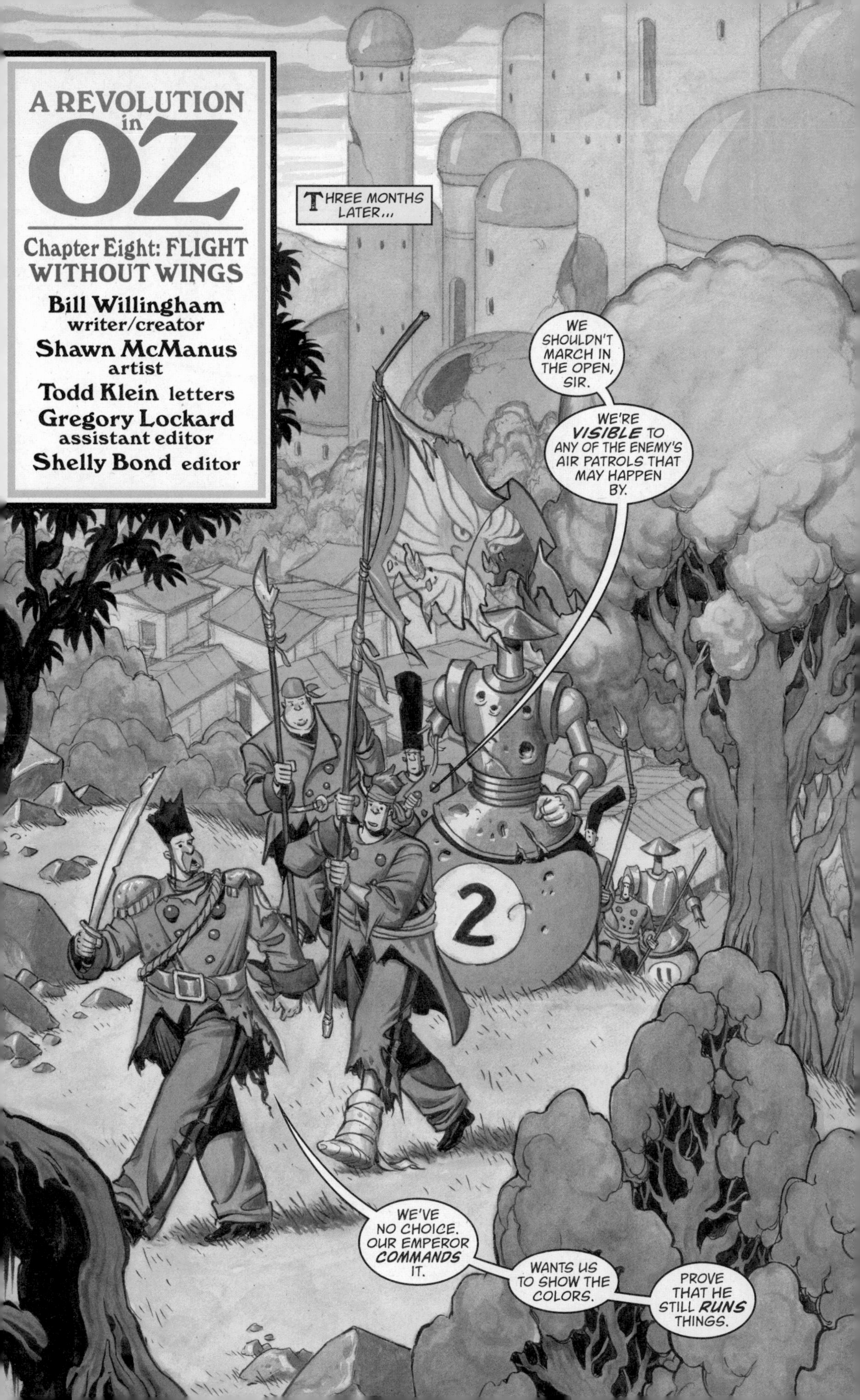
A REVOLUTION in OZ
Chapter Eight: FLIGHT WITHOUT WINGS
Bill Willingham writer/creator
Shawn McManus artist
Todd Klein letters
Gregory Lockard assistant editor
Shelly Bond editor
THREE MONTHS LATER...
WE SHOULDN'T MARCH IN THE OPEN, SIR.
WE'RE VISIBLE TO ANY OF THE ENEMY'S AIR PATROLS THAT MAY HAPPEN BY.
WE'VE NO CHOICE. OUR EMPEROR COMMANDS IT.
WANTS US TO SHOW THE COLORS.
PROVE THAT HE STILL RUNS THINGS.

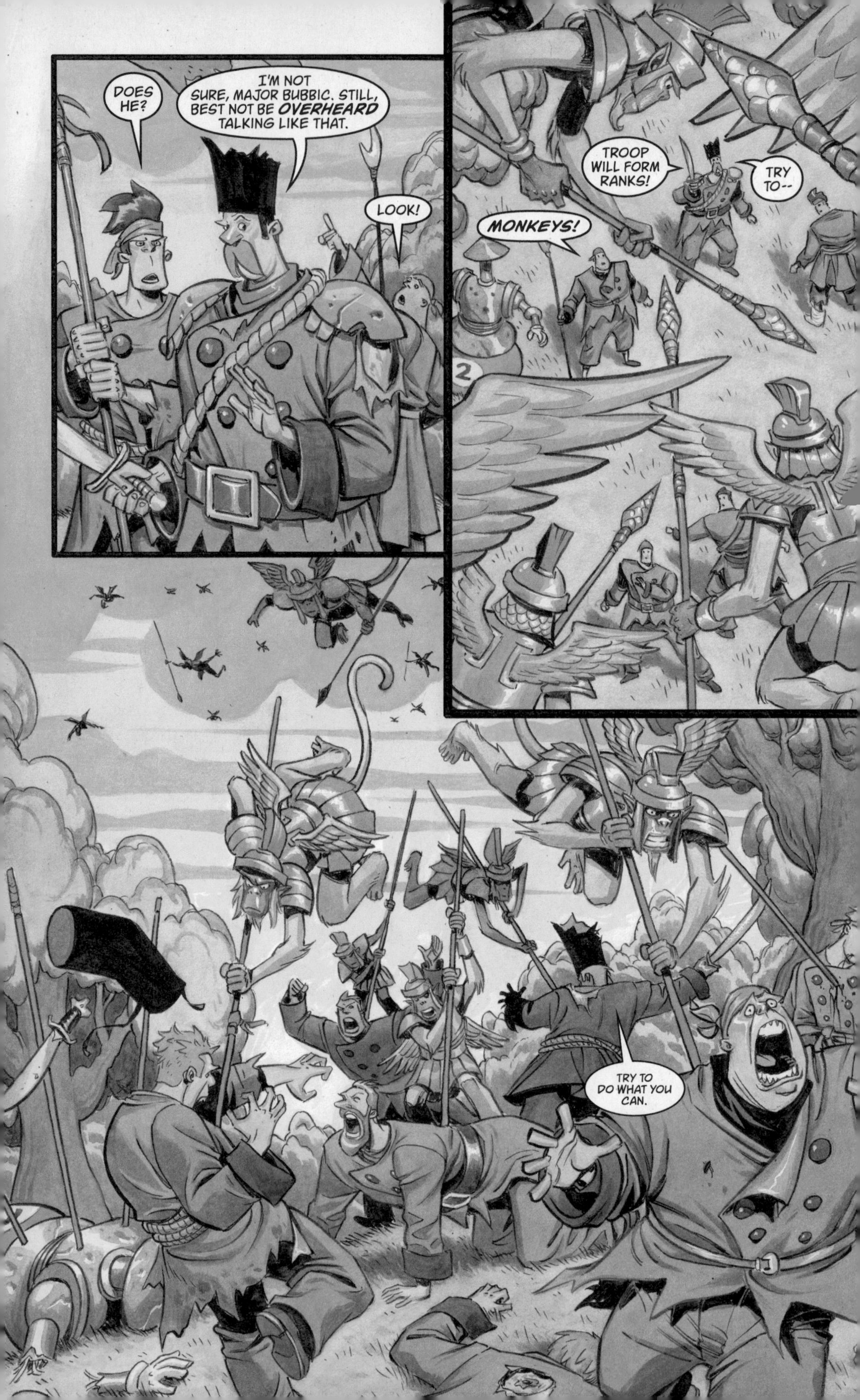
DOES HE?
I'M NOT SURE, MAJOR BUBBIC. STILL, BEST NOT BE OVERHEARD TALKING LIKE THAT.
LOOK!
MONKEYS!
TROOP WILL FORM RANKS!
TRY TO--
TRY TO DO WHAT YOU CAN.

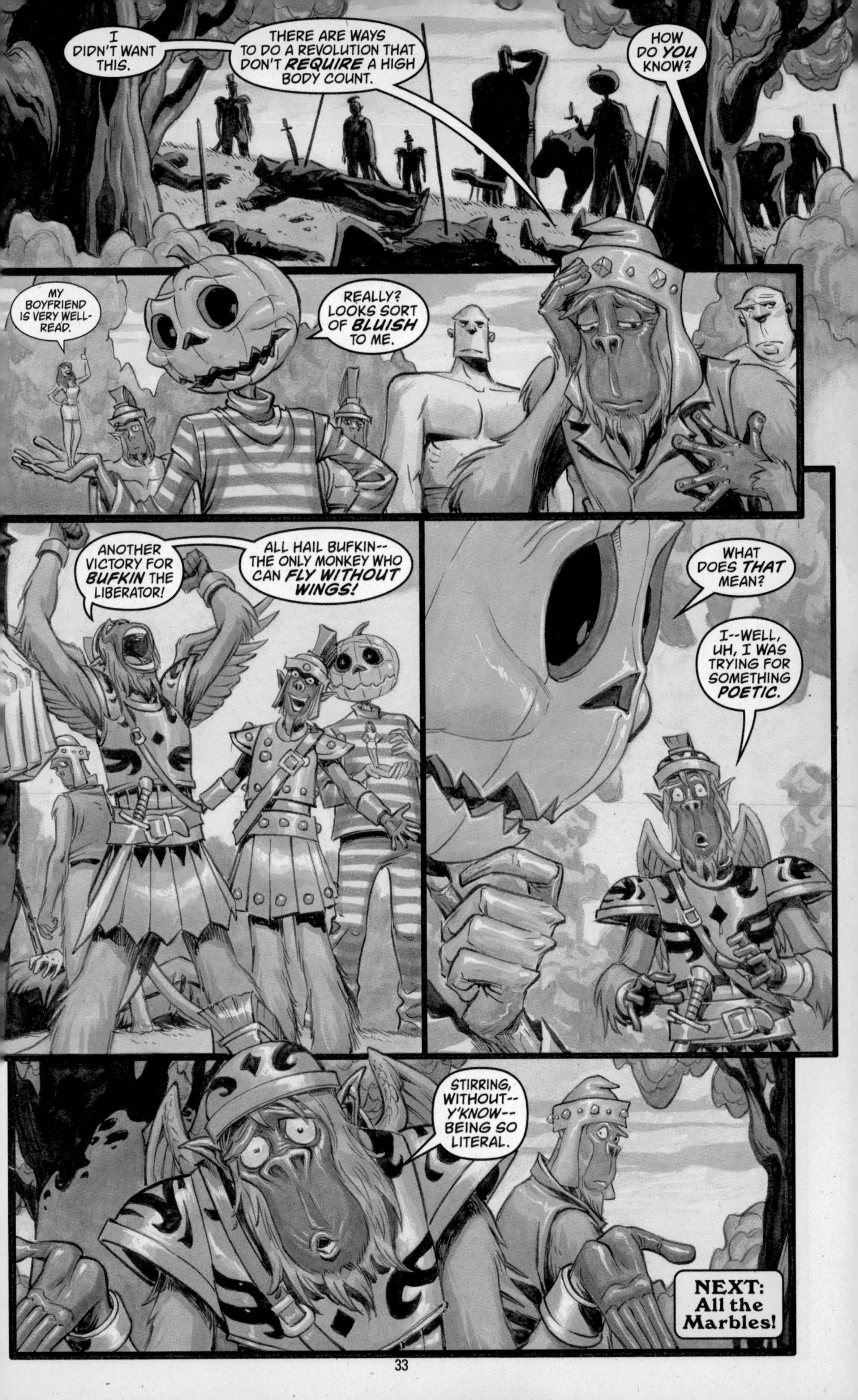
I DIDN'T WANT THIS.
THERE ARE WAYS TO DO A REVOLUTION THAT DON'T *REQUIRE* A HIGH BODY COUNT.
HOW DO *YOU* KNOW?
MY BOYFRIEND IS VERY WELL-READ.
REALLY? LOOKS SORT OF *BLUISH* TO ME.
ANOTHER VICTORY FOR *BUFKIN* THE LIBERATOR!
ALL HAIL BUFKIN-- THE ONLY MONKEY WHO CAN *FLY WITHOUT WINGS!*
WHAT DOES *THAT* MEAN?
I--WELL, UH, I WAS TRYING FOR SOMETHING *POETIC*.
STIRRING, WITHOUT-- *Y'KNOW*-- BEING SO LITERAL.
NEXT: All the Marbles!

A REVOLUTION in OZ

Chapter Nine: ALL THE MARBLES

Bill Willingham writer/creator
Shawn McManus artist
Todd Klein letters
Gregory Lockard assistant editor
Shelly Bond editor

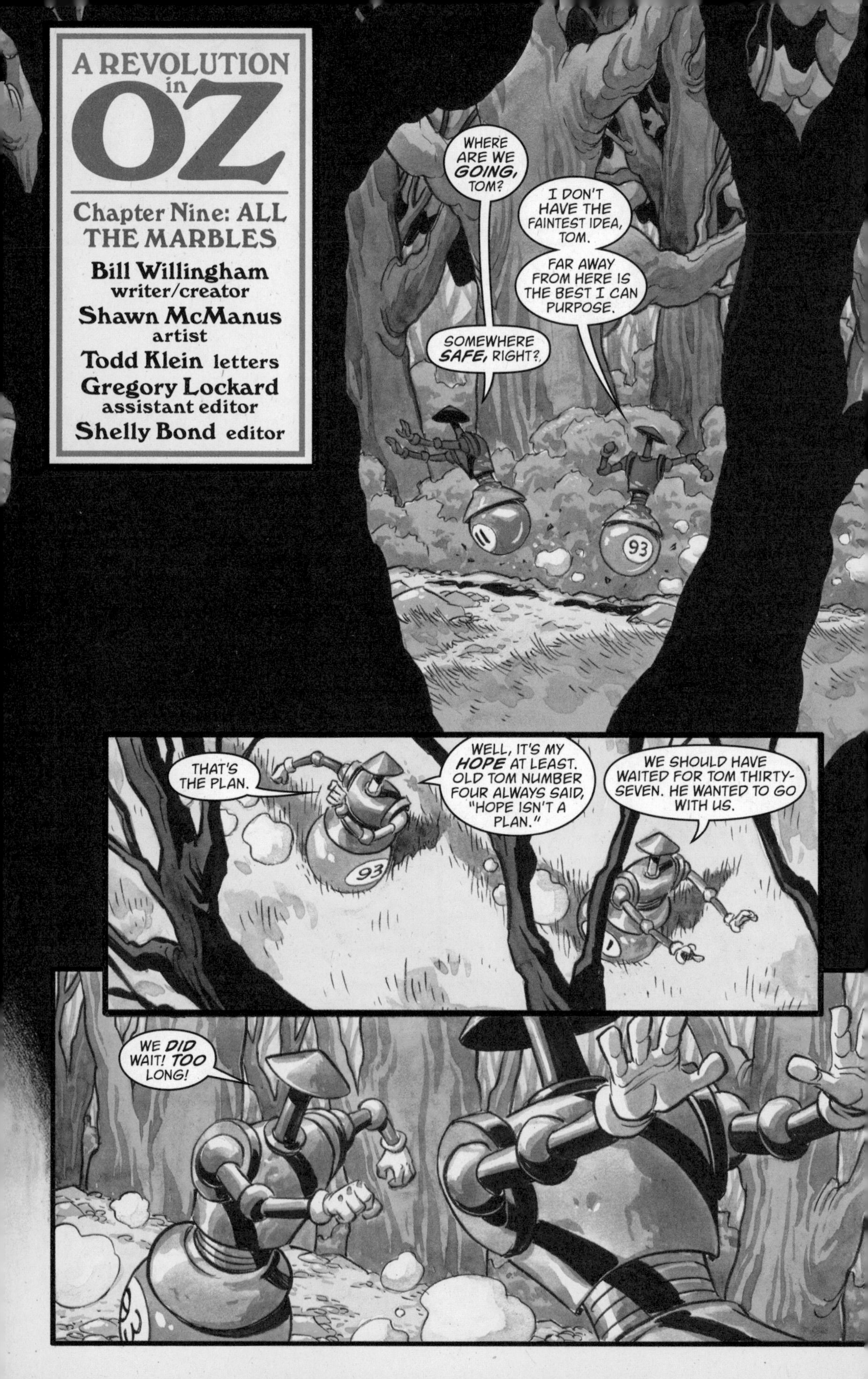
WHERE ARE WE *GOING,* TOM?
I DON'T HAVE THE FAINTEST IDEA, TOM.
FAR AWAY FROM HERE IS THE BEST I CAN PURPOSE.
SOMEWHERE *SAFE,* RIGHT?
THAT'S THE PLAN.
WELL, IT'S MY *HOPE* AT LEAST. OLD TOM NUMBER FOUR ALWAYS SAID, "HOPE ISN'T A PLAN."
WE SHOULD HAVE WAITED FOR TOM THIRTY-SEVEN. HE WANTED TO GO WITH US.
WE *DID* WAIT! *TOO* LONG!

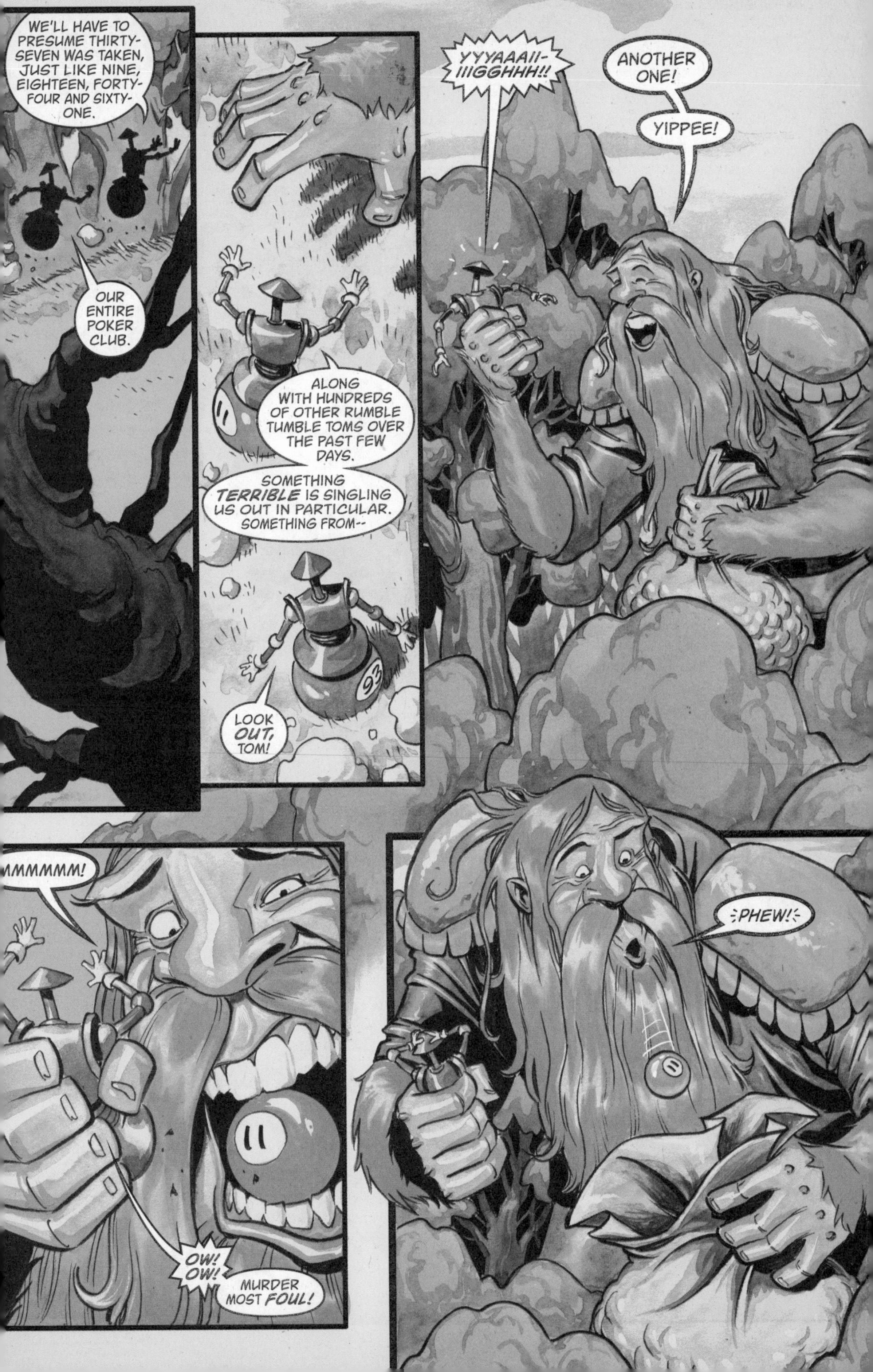

WE'LL HAVE TO PRESUME THIRTY-SEVEN WAS TAKEN, JUST LIKE NINE, EIGHTEEN, FORTY-FOUR AND SIXTY-ONE.
OUR ENTIRE POKER CLUB.
ALONG WITH HUNDREDS OF OTHER RUMBLE TUMBLE TOMS OVER THE PAST FEW DAYS.
SOMETHING TERRIBLE IS SINGLING US OUT IN PARTICULAR. SOMETHING FROM--
LOOK OUT, TOM!
YYYAAAII-IIIGGHHH!!
ANOTHER ONE!
YIPPEE!
MMMMMM!
OW! OW!
MURDER MOST FOUL!
PHEW!

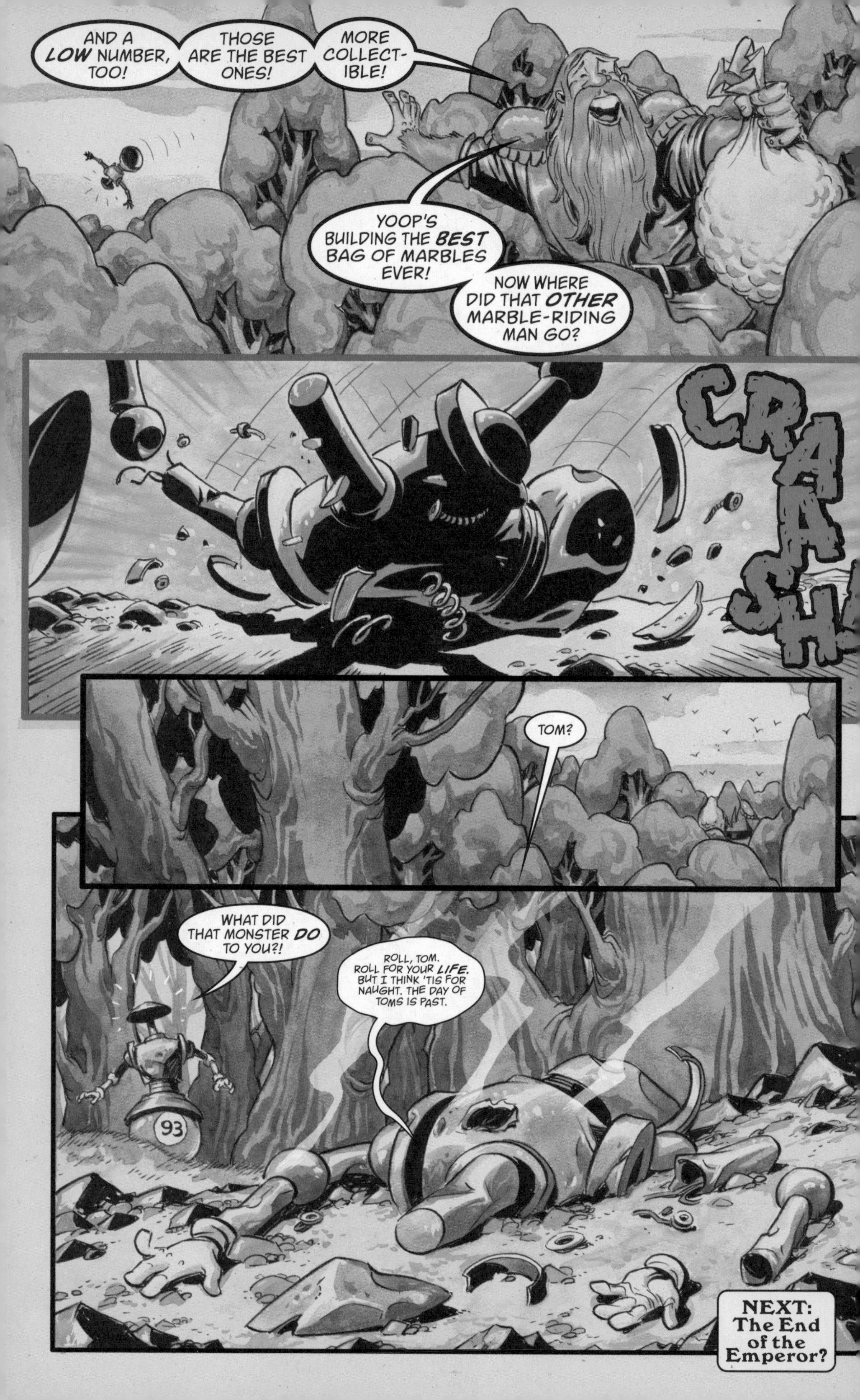
AND A LOW NUMBER, TOO!
THOSE ARE THE BEST ONES!
MORE COLLECT-IBLE!
YOOP'S BUILDING THE BEST BAG OF MARBLES EVER!
NOW WHERE DID THAT OTHER MARBLE-RIDING MAN GO?
CRASH
TOM?
WHAT DID THAT MONSTER DO TO YOU?!
ROLL, TOM. ROLL FOR YOUR LIFE. BUT I THINK 'TIS FOR NAUGHT. THE DAY OF TOMS IS PAST.
93
NEXT: The End of the Emperor?

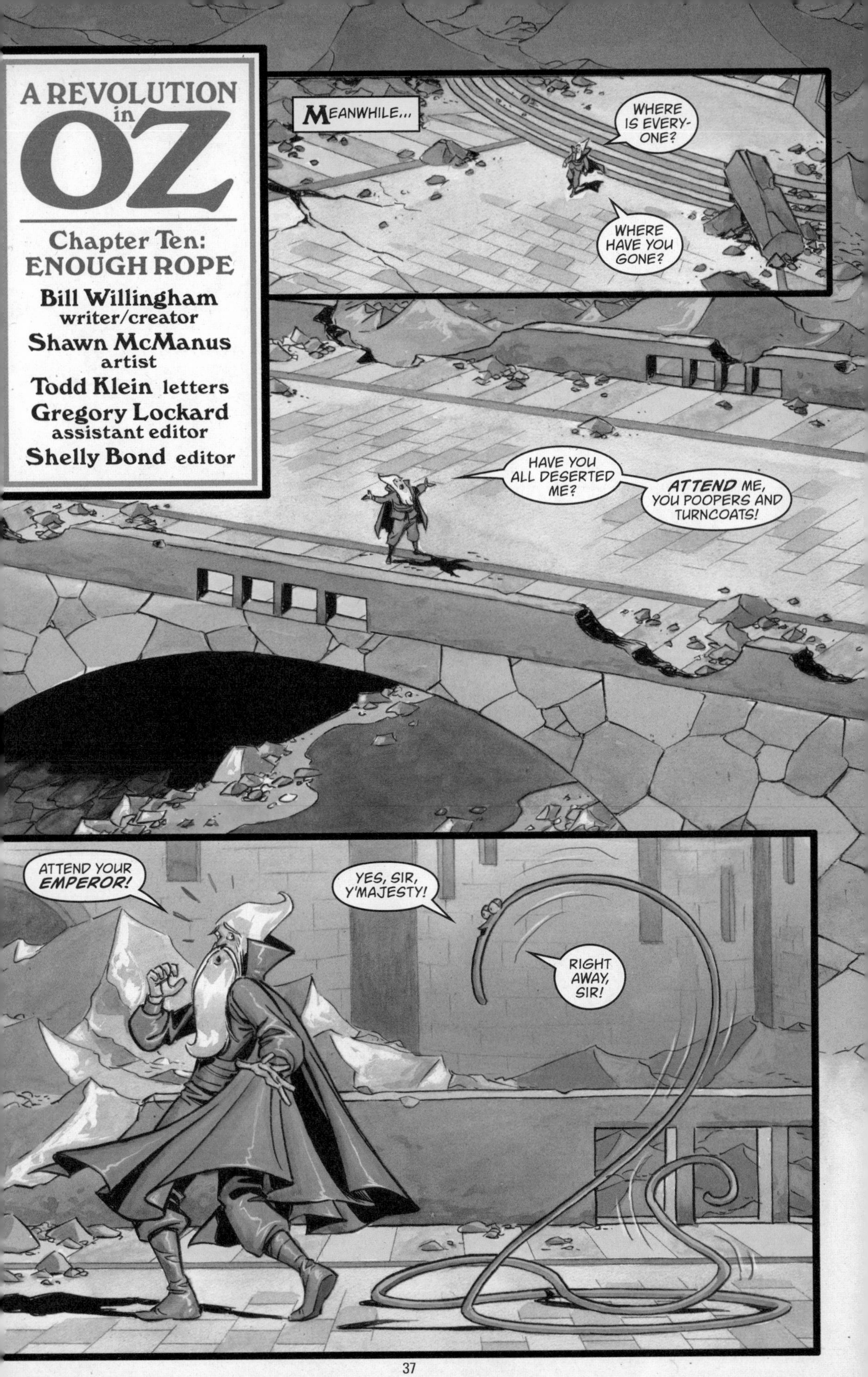
A REVOLUTION in OZ
Chapter Ten: ENOUGH ROPE
Bill Willingham writer/creator
Shawn McManus artist
Todd Klein letters
Gregory Lockard assistant editor
Shelly Bond editor
MEANWHILE...
WHERE IS EVERY-ONE?
WHERE HAVE YOU GONE?
HAVE YOU ALL DESERTED ME?
ATTEND ME, YOU POOPERS AND TURNCOATS!
ATTEND YOUR EMPEROR!
YES, SIR, Y'MAJESTY!
RIGHT AWAY, SIR!

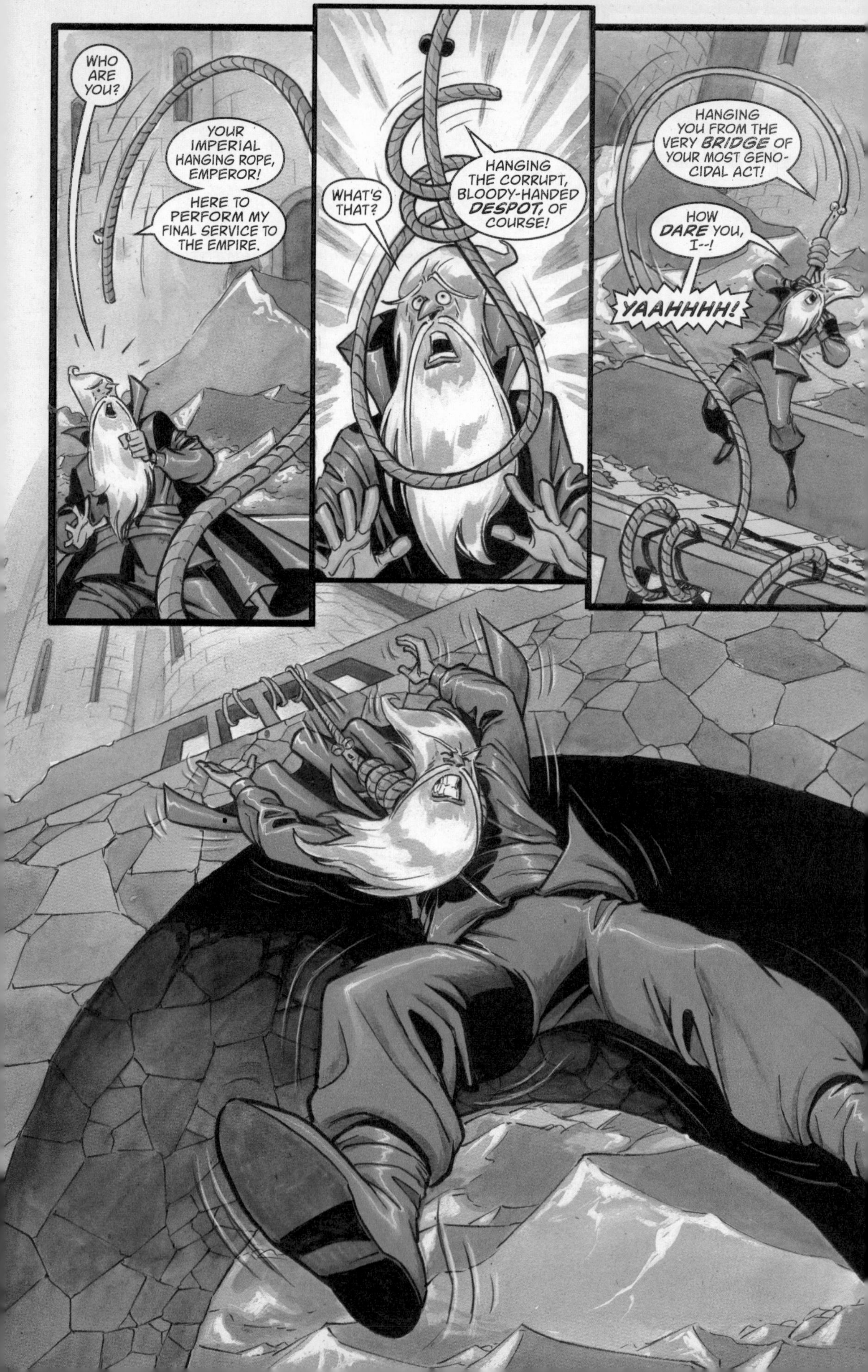
WHO ARE YOU?
YOUR IMPERIAL HANGING ROPE, EMPEROR!
HERE TO PERFORM MY FINAL SERVICE TO THE EMPIRE.
WHAT'S THAT?
HANGING THE CORRUPT, BLOODY-HANDED DESPOT, OF COURSE!
HANGING YOU FROM THE VERY BRIDGE OF YOUR MOST GENOCIDAL ACT!
HOW DARE YOU, I--!
YAAHHHH!

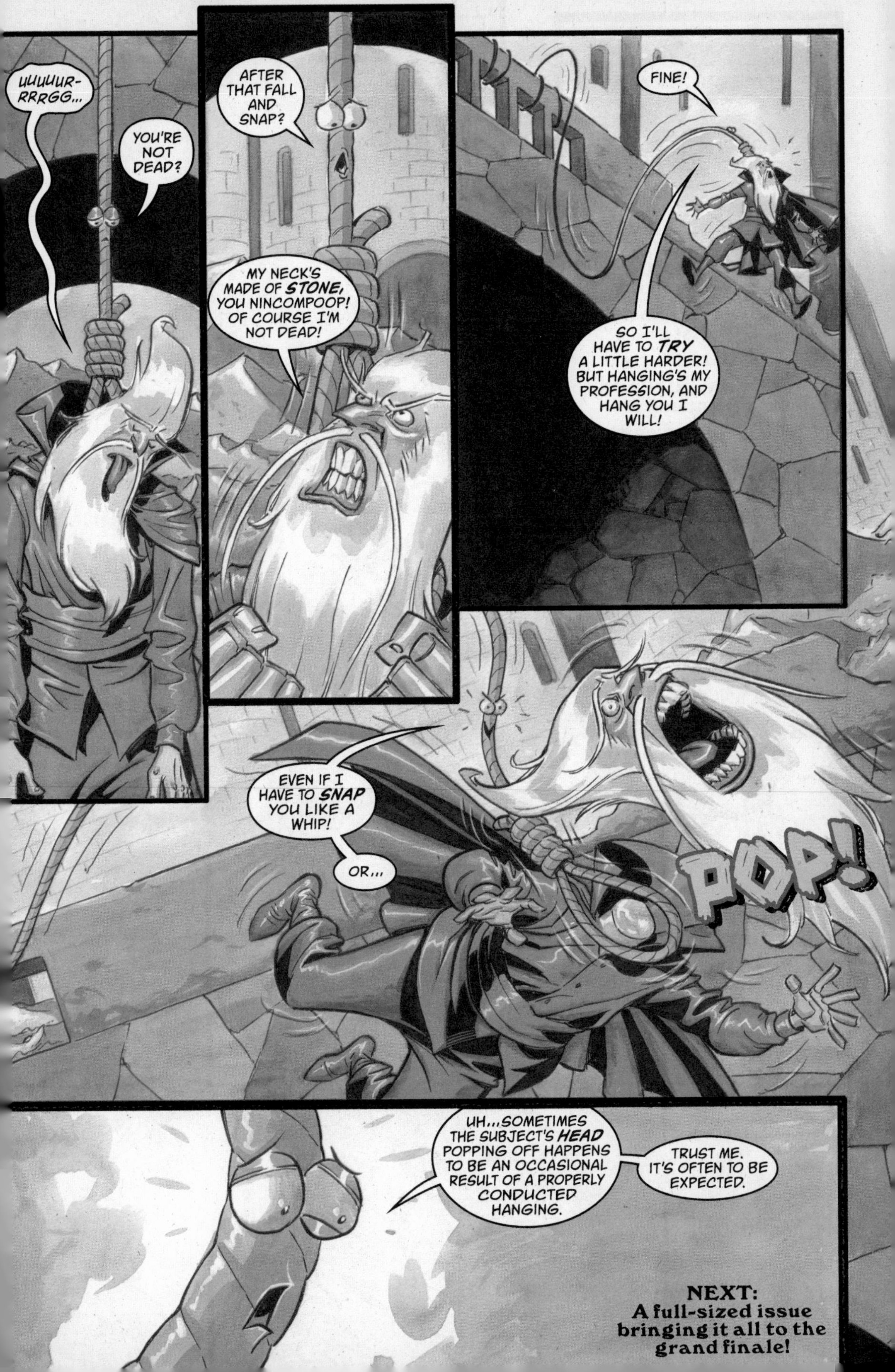
UUUUUR-RRRGG...
YOU'RE NOT DEAD?
AFTER THAT FALL AND SNAP?
MY NECK'S MADE OF STONE, YOU NINCOMPOOP! OF COURSE I'M NOT DEAD!
FINE!
SO I'LL HAVE TO TRY A LITTLE HARDER! BUT HANGING'S MY PROFESSION, AND HANG YOU I WILL!
EVEN IF I HAVE TO SNAP YOU LIKE A WHIP!
OR...
POP!
UH...SOMETIMES THE SUBJECT'S HEAD POPPING OFF HAPPENS TO BE AN OCCASIONAL RESULT OF A PROPERLY CONDUCTED HANGING.
TRUST ME. IT'S OFTEN TO BE EXPECTED.
NEXT: A full-sized issue bringing it all to the grand finale!

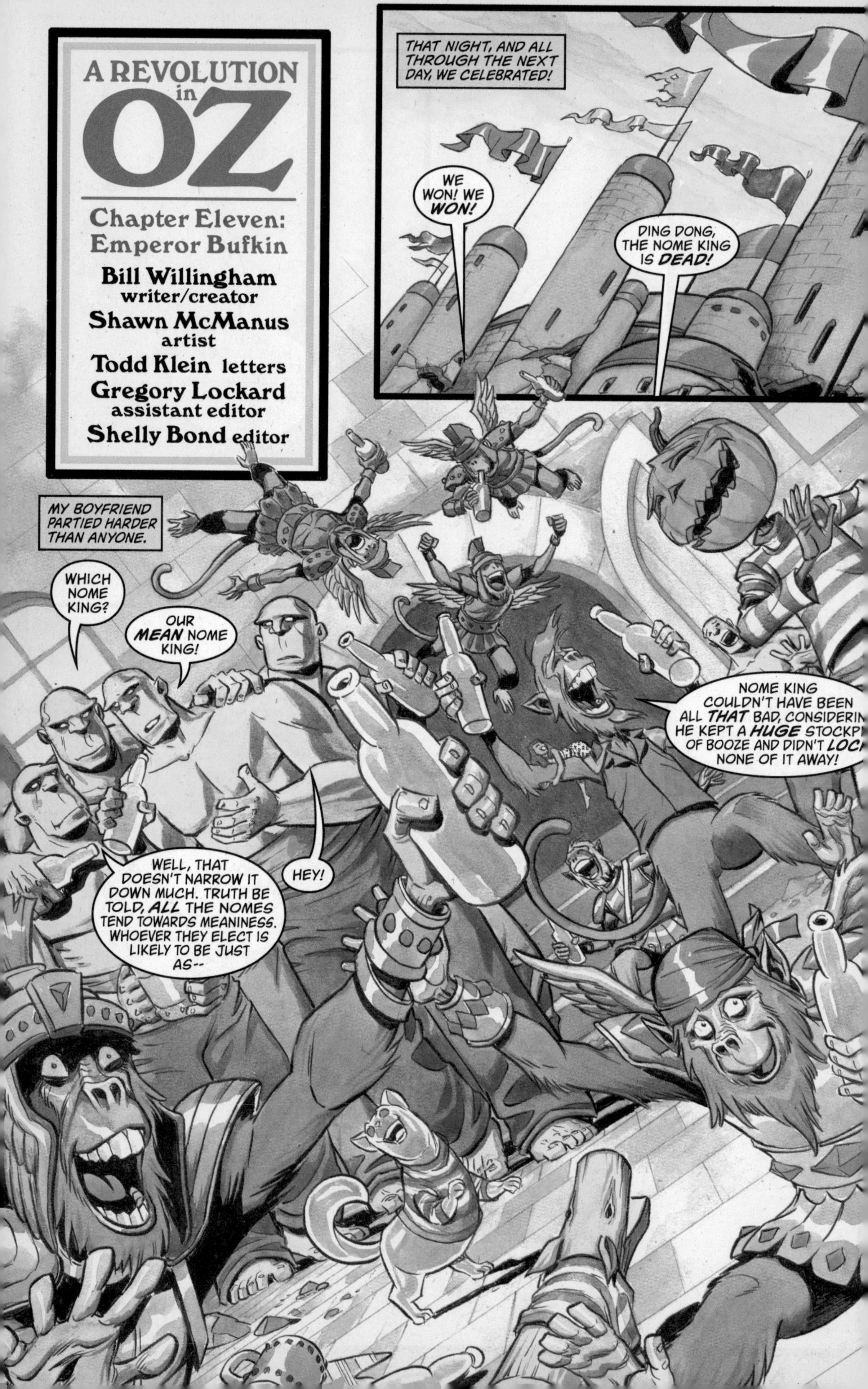
A REVOLUTION in OZ
Chapter Eleven: Emperor Bufkin
Bill Willingham writer/creator
Shawn McManus artist
Todd Klein letters
Gregory Lockard assistant editor
Shelly Bond editor
THAT NIGHT, AND ALL THROUGH THE NEXT DAY, WE CELEBRATED!
WE WON! WE WON!
DING DONG, THE NOME KING IS DEAD!
MY BOYFRIEND PARTIED HARDER THAN ANYONE.
WHICH NOME KING?
OUR MEAN NOME KING!
NOME KING COULDN'T HAVE BEEN ALL THAT BAD, CONSIDERIN HE KEPT A HUGE STOCKPI OF BOOZE AND DIDN'T LOC NONE OF IT AWAY!
WELL, THAT DOESN'T NARROW IT DOWN MUCH. TRUTH BE TOLD, ALL THE NOMES TEND TOWARDS MEANINESS. WHOEVER THEY ELECT IS LIKELY TO BE JUST AS--
HEY!

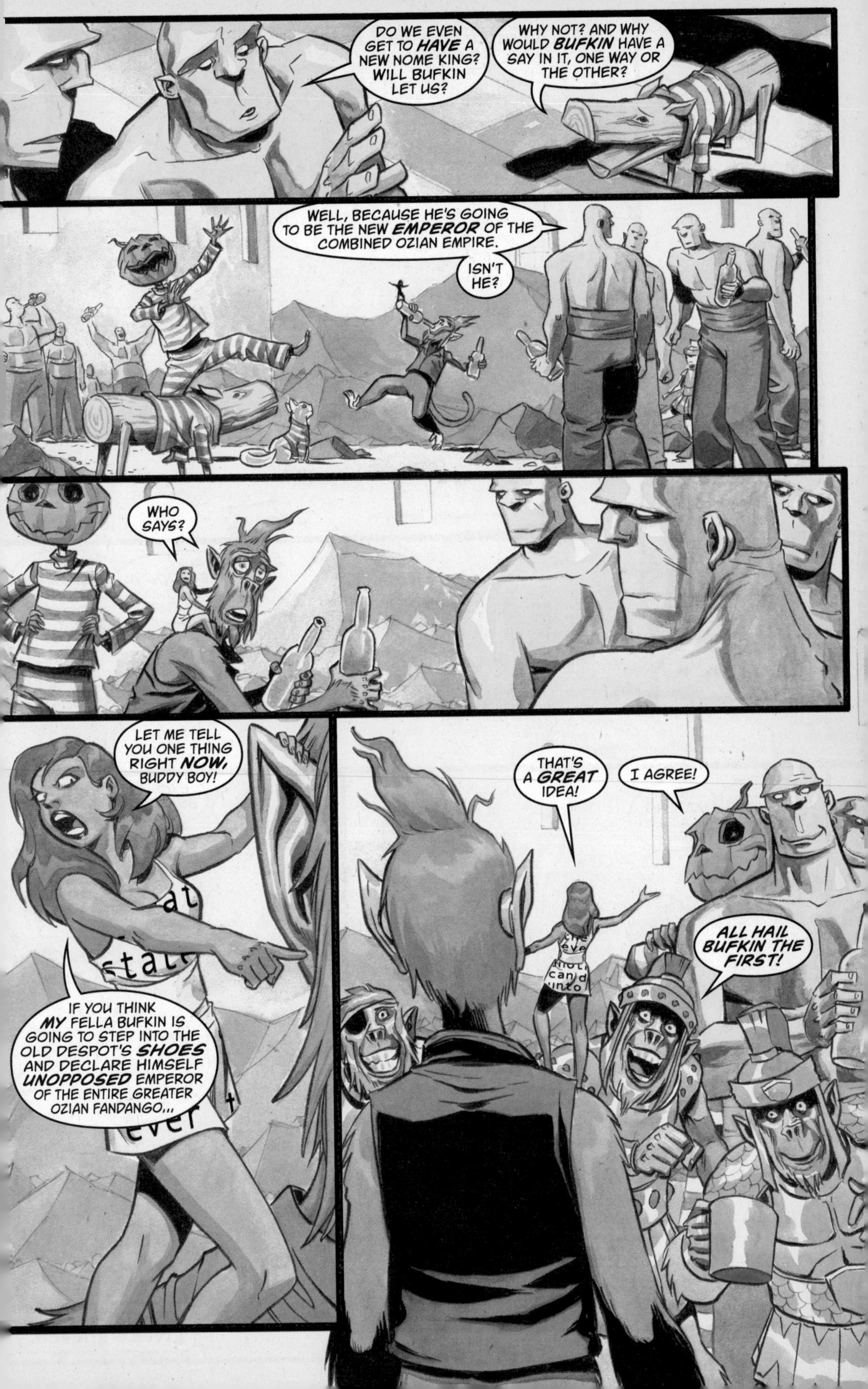
DO WE EVEN GET TO HAVE A NEW NOME KING? WILL BUFKIN LET US?
WHY NOT? AND WHY WOULD BUFKIN HAVE A SAY IN IT, ONE WAY OR THE OTHER?
WELL, BECAUSE HE'S GOING TO BE THE NEW EMPEROR OF THE COMBINED OZIAN EMPIRE.
ISN'T HE?
WHO SAYS?
LET ME TELL YOU ONE THING RIGHT NOW, BUDDY BOY!
IF YOU THINK MY FELLA BUFKIN IS GOING TO STEP INTO THE OLD DESPOT'S SHOES AND DECLARE HIMSELF UNOPPOSED EMPEROR OF THE ENTIRE GREATER OZIAN FANDANGO...
THAT'S A GREAT IDEA!
I AGREE!
ALL HAIL BUFKIN THE FIRST!

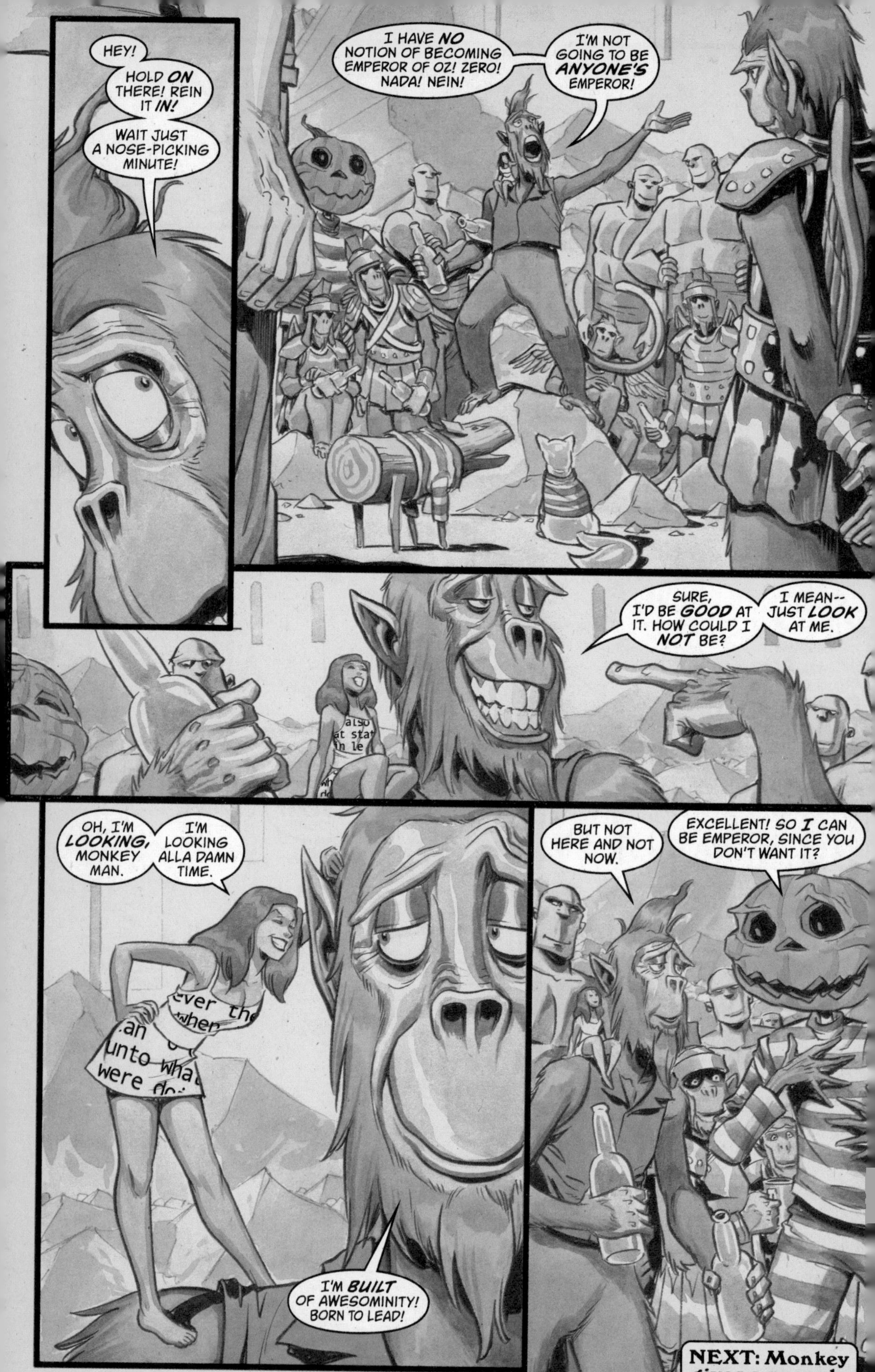
HEY!
HOLD ON THERE! REIN IT IN!
WAIT JUST A NOSE-PICKING MINUTE!
I HAVE NO NOTION OF BECOMING EMPEROR OF OZ! ZERO! NADA! NEIN!
I'M NOT GOING TO BE ANYONE'S EMPEROR!
SURE, I'D BE GOOD AT IT. HOW COULD I NOT BE?
I MEAN-- JUST LOOK AT ME.
OH, I'M LOOKING, MONKEY MAN.
I'M LOOKING ALLA DAMN TIME.
I'M BUILT OF AWESOMINITY! BORN TO LEAD!
BUT NOT HERE AND NOT NOW.
EXCELLENT! SO I CAN BE EMPEROR, SINCE YOU DON'T WANT IT?
NEXT: Monkey gives a speech.

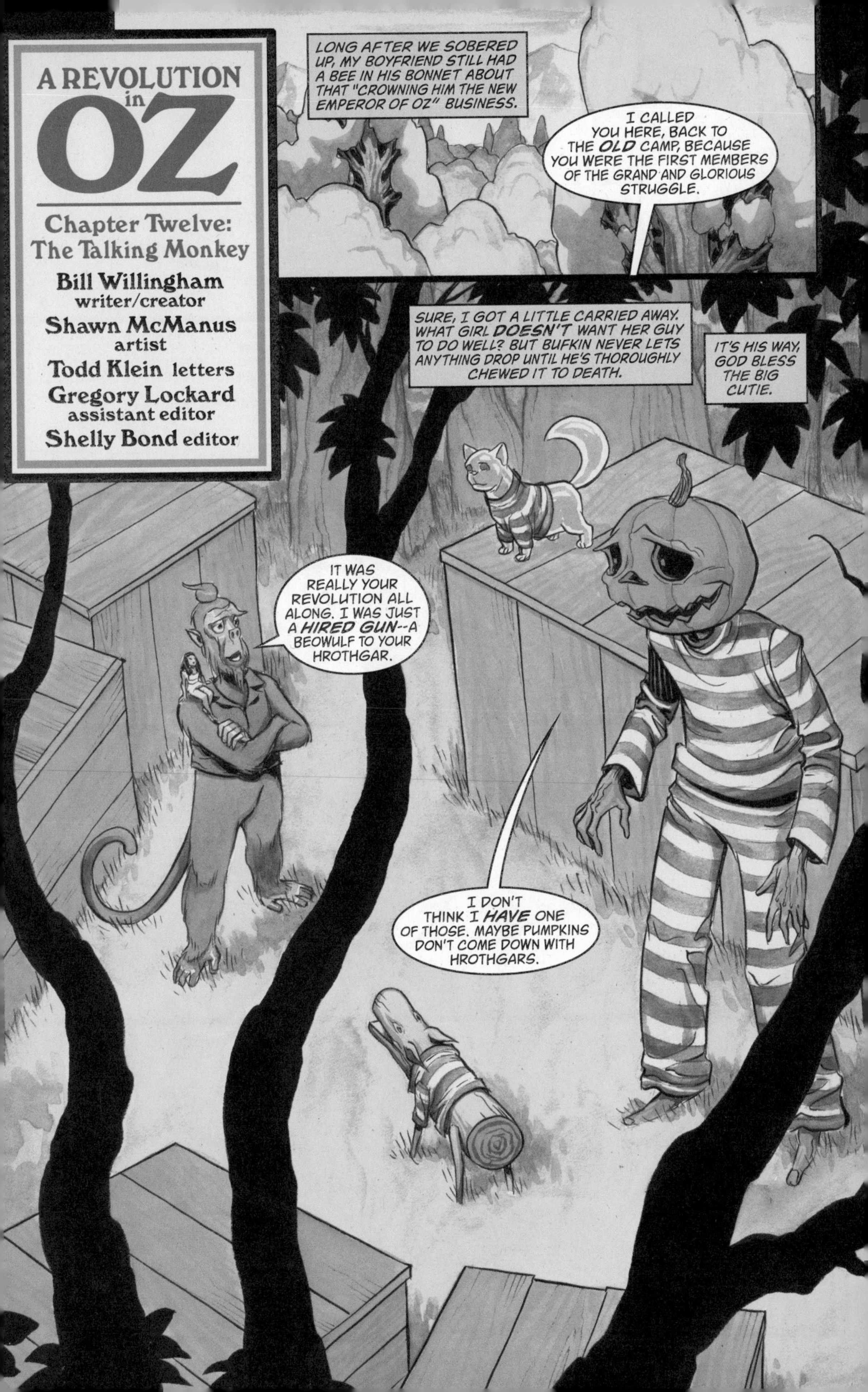
A REVOLUTION in OZ
Chapter Twelve: The Talking Monkey
Bill Willingham writer/creator
Shawn McManus artist
Todd Klein letters
Gregory Lockard assistant editor
Shelly Bond editor
LONG AFTER WE SOBERED UP, MY BOYFRIEND STILL HAD A BEE IN HIS BONNET ABOUT THAT "CROWNING HIM THE NEW EMPEROR OF OZ" BUSINESS.
I CALLED YOU HERE, BACK TO THE OLD CAMP, BECAUSE YOU WERE THE FIRST MEMBERS OF THE GRAND AND GLORIOUS STRUGGLE.
SURE, I GOT A LITTLE CARRIED AWAY. WHAT GIRL DOESN'T WANT HER GUY TO DO WELL? BUT BUFKIN NEVER LETS ANYTHING DROP UNTIL HE'S THOROUGHLY CHEWED IT TO DEATH.
IT'S HIS WAY, GOD BLESS THE BIG CUTIE.
IT WAS REALLY YOUR REVOLUTION ALL ALONG. I WAS JUST A HIRED GUN--A BEOWULF TO YOUR HROTHGAR.
I DON'T THINK I HAVE ONE OF THOSE. MAYBE PUMPKINS DON'T COME DOWN WITH HROTHGARS.

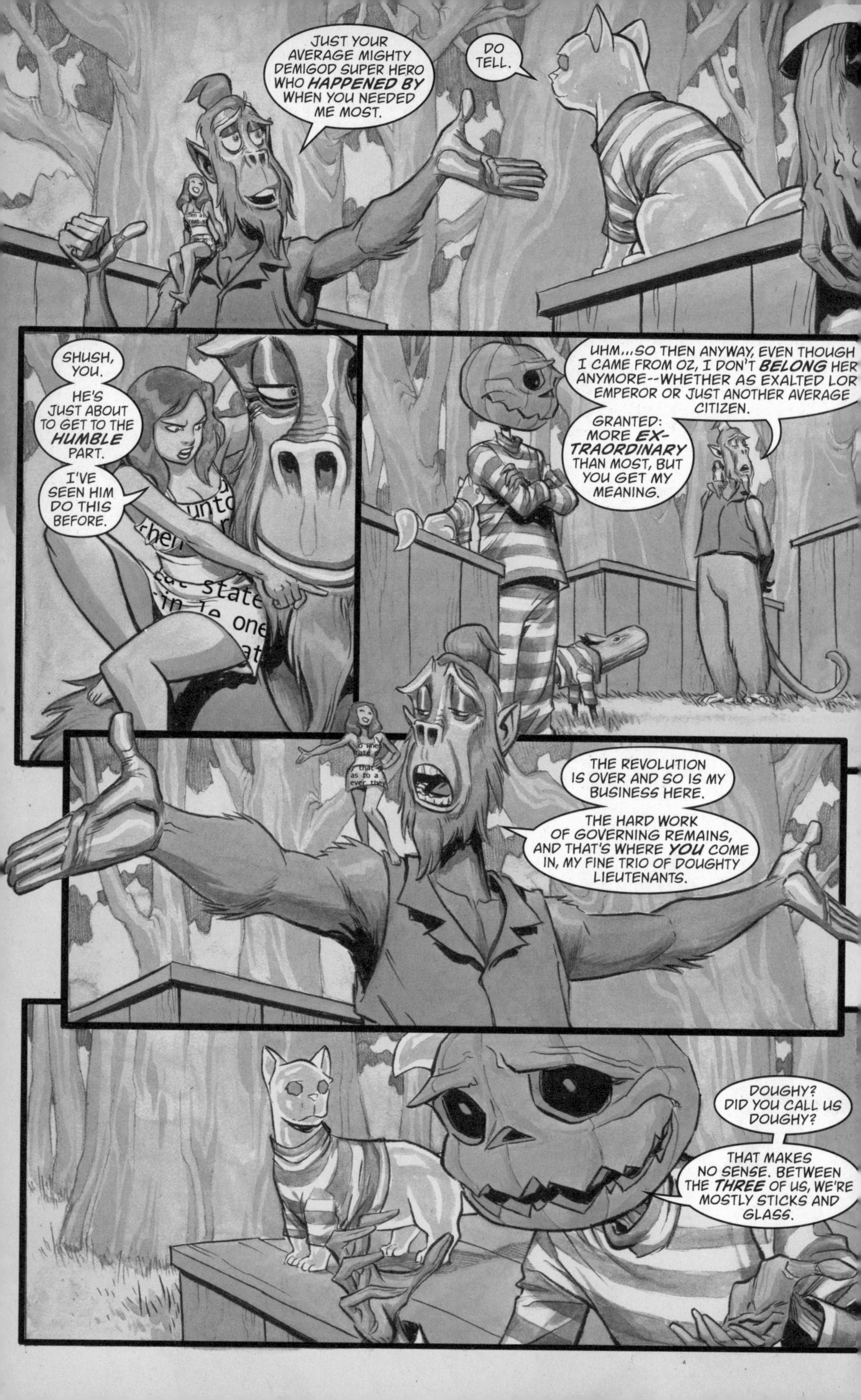

JUST YOUR AVERAGE MIGHTY DEMIGOD SUPER HERO WHO HAPPENED BY WHEN YOU NEEDED ME MOST.
DO TELL.
SHUSH, YOU.
HE'S JUST ABOUT TO GET TO THE HUMBLE PART.
I'VE SEEN HIM DO THIS BEFORE.
UHM...SO THEN ANYWAY, EVEN THOUGH I CAME FROM OZ, I DON'T BELONG HER ANYMORE--WHETHER AS EXALTED LOR EMPEROR OR JUST ANOTHER AVERAGE CITIZEN.
GRANTED: MORE EX-TRAORDINARY THAN MOST, BUT YOU GET MY MEANING.
THE REVOLUTION IS OVER AND SO IS MY BUSINESS HERE.
THE HARD WORK OF GOVERNING REMAINS, AND THAT'S WHERE YOU COME IN, MY FINE TRIO OF DOUGHTY LIEUTENANTS.
DOUGHY? DID YOU CALL US DOUGHY?
THAT MAKES NO SENSE. BETWEEN THE THREE OF US, WE'RE MOSTLY STICKS AND GLASS.

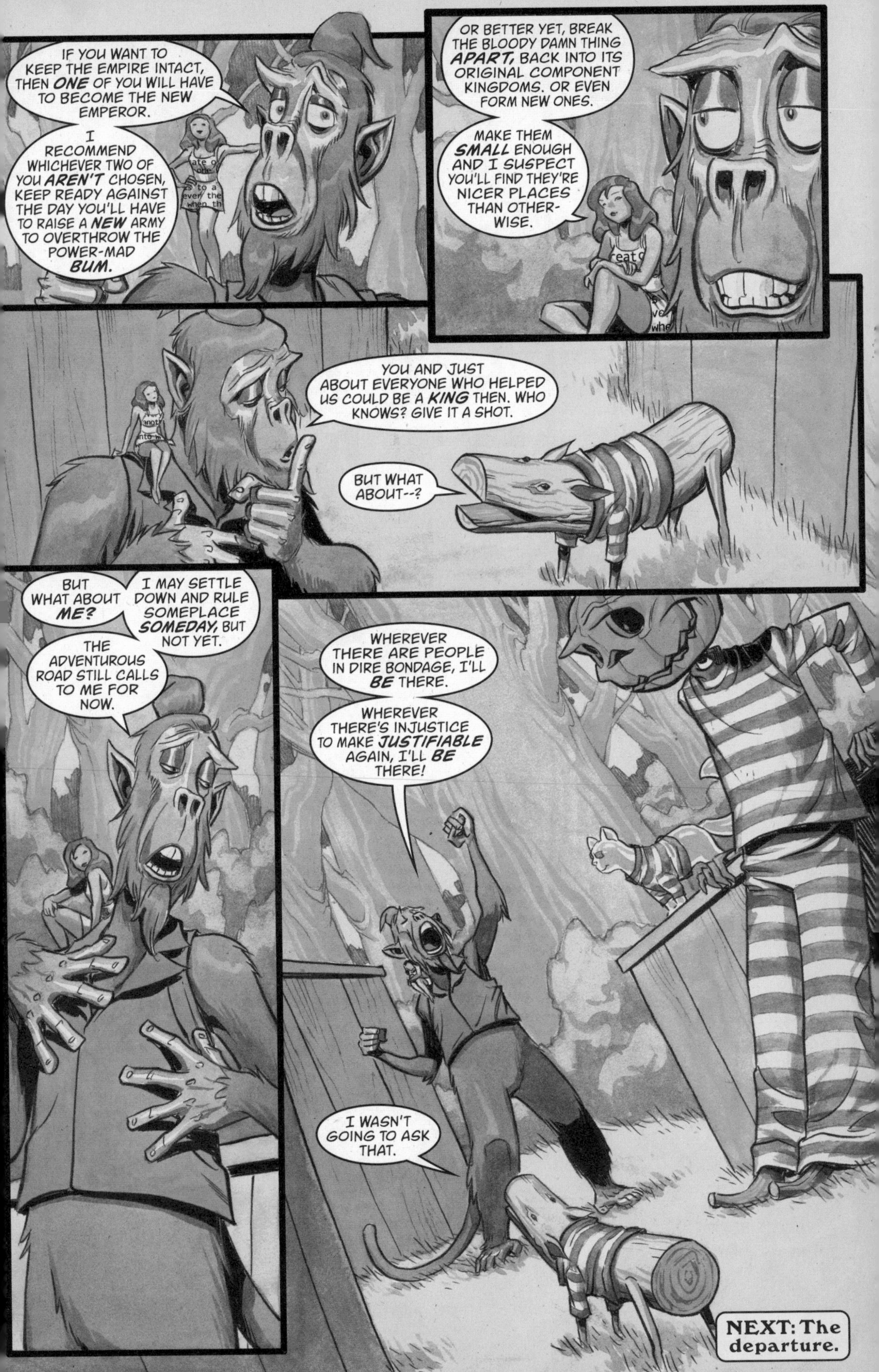
IF YOU WANT TO KEEP THE EMPIRE INTACT, THEN ONE OF YOU WILL HAVE TO BECOME THE NEW EMPEROR.
I RECOMMEND WHICHEVER TWO OF YOU AREN'T CHOSEN, KEEP READY AGAINST THE DAY YOU'LL HAVE TO RAISE A NEW ARMY TO OVERTHROW THE POWER-MAD BUM.
OR BETTER YET, BREAK THE BLOODY DAMN THING APART, BACK INTO ITS ORIGINAL COMPONENT KINGDOMS. OR EVEN FORM NEW ONES.
MAKE THEM SMALL ENOUGH AND I SUSPECT YOU'LL FIND THEY'RE NICER PLACES THAN OTHER-WISE.
YOU AND JUST ABOUT EVERYONE WHO HELPED US COULD BE A KING THEN. WHO KNOWS? GIVE IT A SHOT.
BUT WHAT ABOUT--?
BUT WHAT ABOUT ME?
I MAY SETTLE DOWN AND RULE SOMEPLACE SOMEDAY, BUT NOT YET.
THE ADVENTUROUS ROAD STILL CALLS TO ME FOR NOW.
WHEREVER THERE ARE PEOPLE IN DIRE BONDAGE, I'LL BE THERE.
WHEREVER THERE'S INJUSTICE TO MAKE JUSTIFIABLE AGAIN, I'LL BE THERE!
I WASN'T GOING TO ASK THAT.
NEXT: The departure.

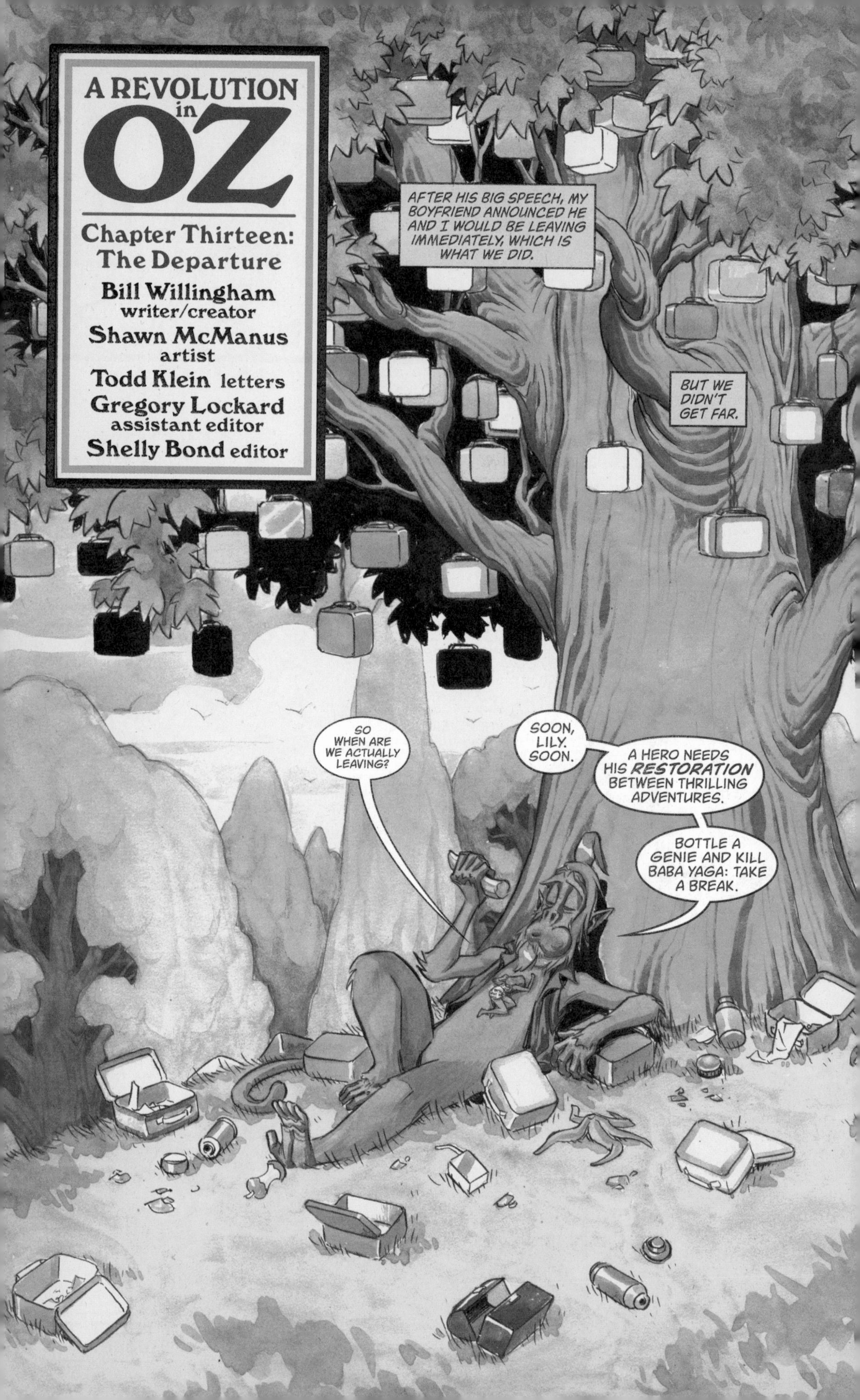
A REVOLUTION in OZ
Chapter Thirteen: The Departure
Bill Willingham writer/creator
Shawn McManus artist
Todd Klein letters
Gregory Lockard assistant editor
Shelly Bond editor
AFTER HIS BIG SPEECH, MY BOYFRIEND ANNOUNCED HE AND I WOULD BE LEAVING IMMEDIATELY, WHICH IS WHAT WE DID.
BUT WE DIDN'T GET FAR.
SO WHEN ARE WE ACTUALLY LEAVING?
SOON, LILY. SOON.
A HERO NEEDS HIS RESTORATION BETWEEN THRILLING ADVENTURES.
BOTTLE A GENIE AND KILL BABA YAGA: TAKE A BREAK.

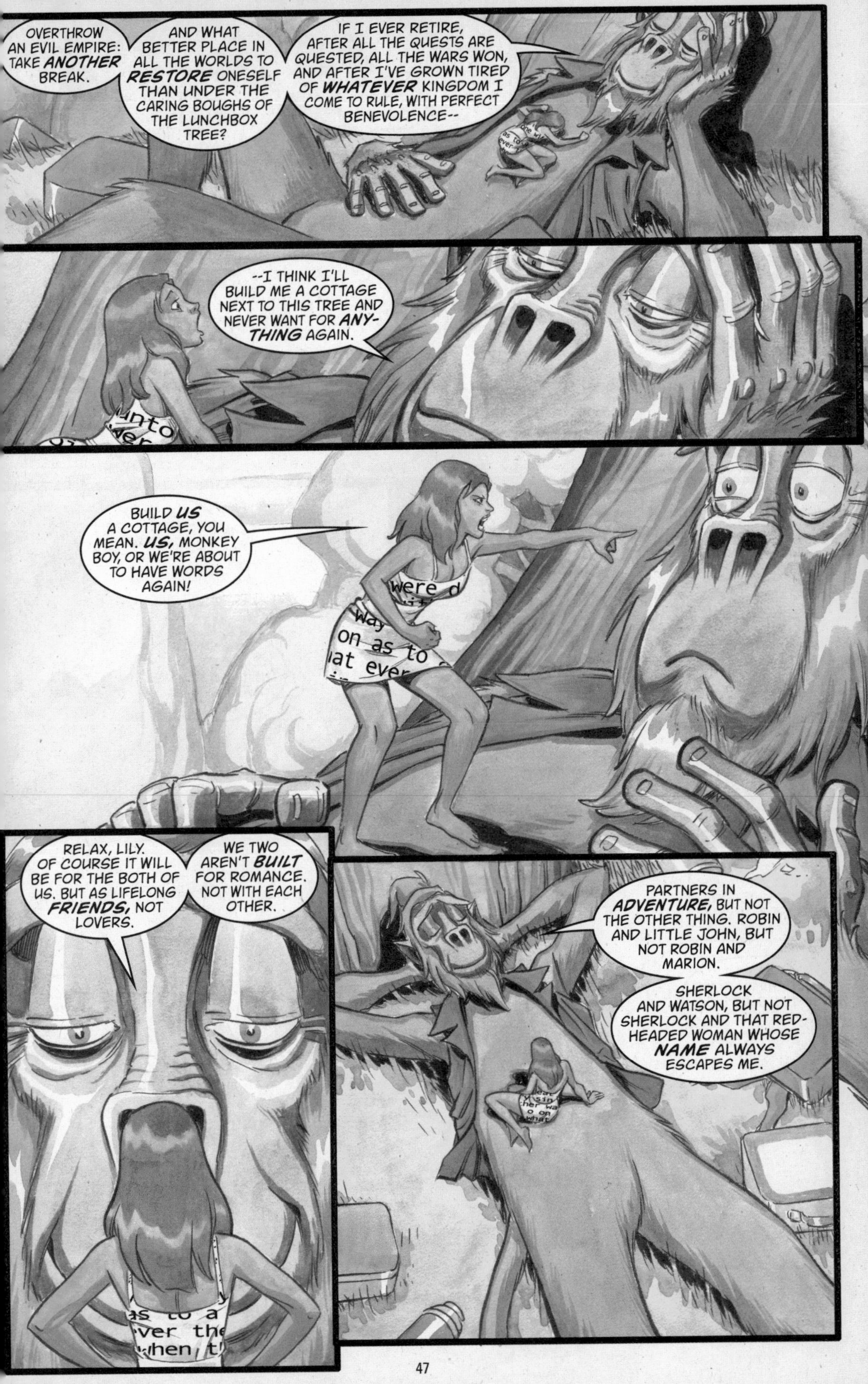
OVERTHROW AN EVIL EMPIRE: TAKE ANOTHER BREAK.
AND WHAT BETTER PLACE IN ALL THE WORLDS TO RESTORE ONESELF THAN UNDER THE CARING BOUGHS OF THE LUNCHBOX TREE?
IF I EVER RETIRE, AFTER ALL THE QUESTS ARE QUESTED, ALL THE WARS WON, AND AFTER I'VE GROWN TIRED OF WHATEVER KINGDOM I COME TO RULE, WITH PERFECT BENEVOLENCE--
--I THINK I'LL BUILD ME A COTTAGE NEXT TO THIS TREE AND NEVER WANT FOR ANYTHING AGAIN.
BUILD US A COTTAGE, YOU MEAN. US, MONKEY BOY, OR WE'RE ABOUT TO HAVE WORDS AGAIN!
were d
way
on as to
at ever
RELAX, LILY. OF COURSE IT WILL BE FOR THE BOTH OF US. BUT AS LIFELONG FRIENDS, NOT LOVERS.
WE TWO AREN'T BUILT FOR ROMANCE. NOT WITH EACH OTHER.
as to a
ver the
when
PARTNERS IN ADVENTURE, BUT NOT THE OTHER THING. ROBIN AND LITTLE JOHN, BUT NOT ROBIN AND MARION.
SHERLOCK AND WATSON, BUT NOT SHERLOCK AND THAT RED-HEADED WOMAN WHOSE NAME ALWAYS ESCAPES ME.

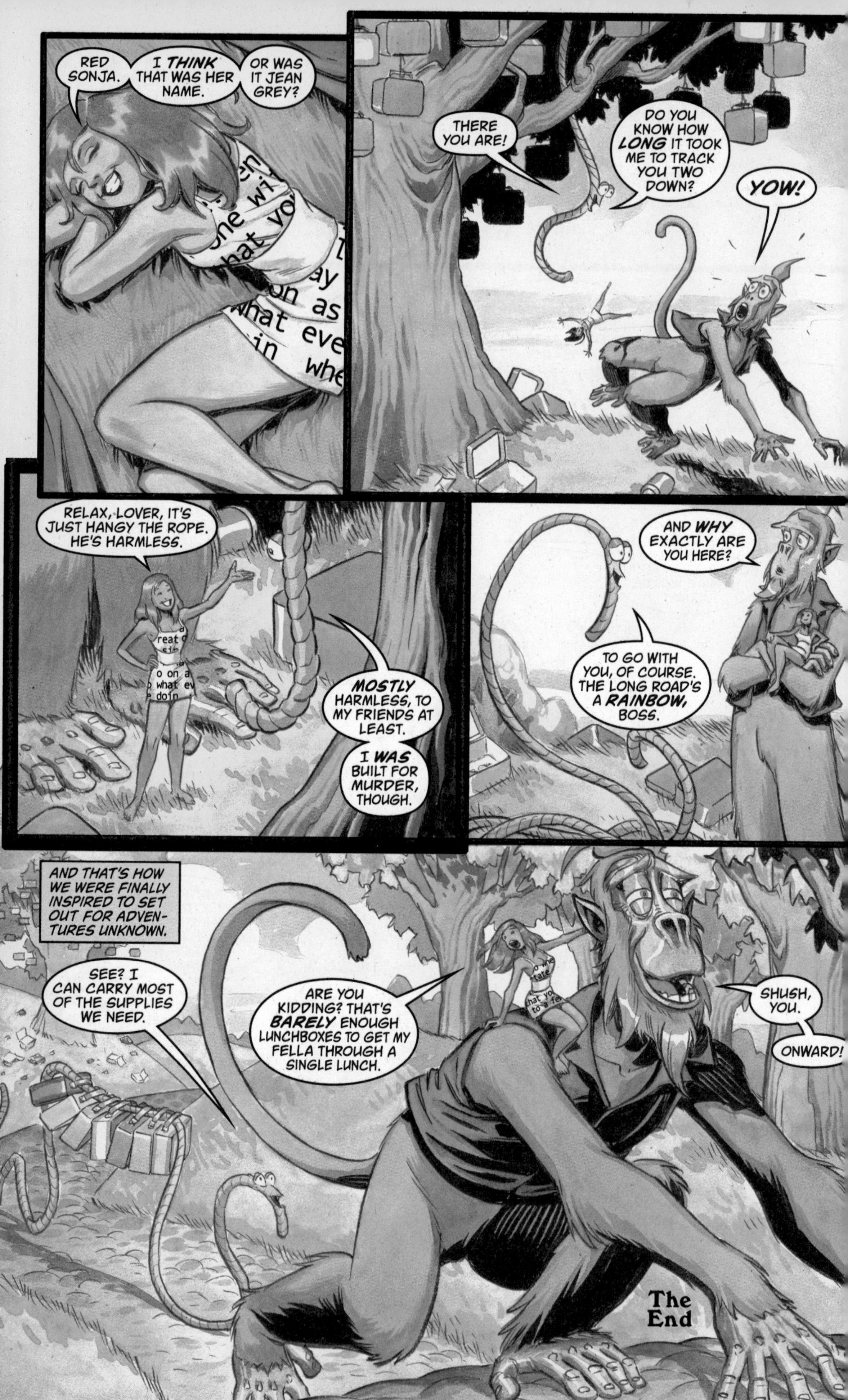
RED SONJA.
I THINK THAT WAS HER NAME.
OR WAS IT JEAN GREY?
THERE YOU ARE!
DO YOU KNOW HOW LONG IT TOOK ME TO TRACK YOU TWO DOWN?
YOW!
RELAX, LOVER, IT'S JUST HANGY THE ROPE. HE'S HARMLESS.
MOSTLY HARMLESS, TO MY FRIENDS AT LEAST.
I WAS BUILT FOR MURDER, THOUGH.
AND WHY EXACTLY ARE YOU HERE?
TO GO WITH YOU, OF COURSE. THE LONG ROAD'S A RAINBOW, BOSS.
AND THAT'S HOW WE WERE FINALLY INSPIRED TO SET OUT FOR ADVENTURES UNKNOWN.
SEE? I CAN CARRY MOST OF THE SUPPLIES WE NEED.
ARE YOU KIDDING? THAT'S BARELY ENOUGH LUNCHBOXES TO GET MY FELLA THROUGH A SINGLE LUNCH.
SHUSH, YOU.
ONWARD!
The End

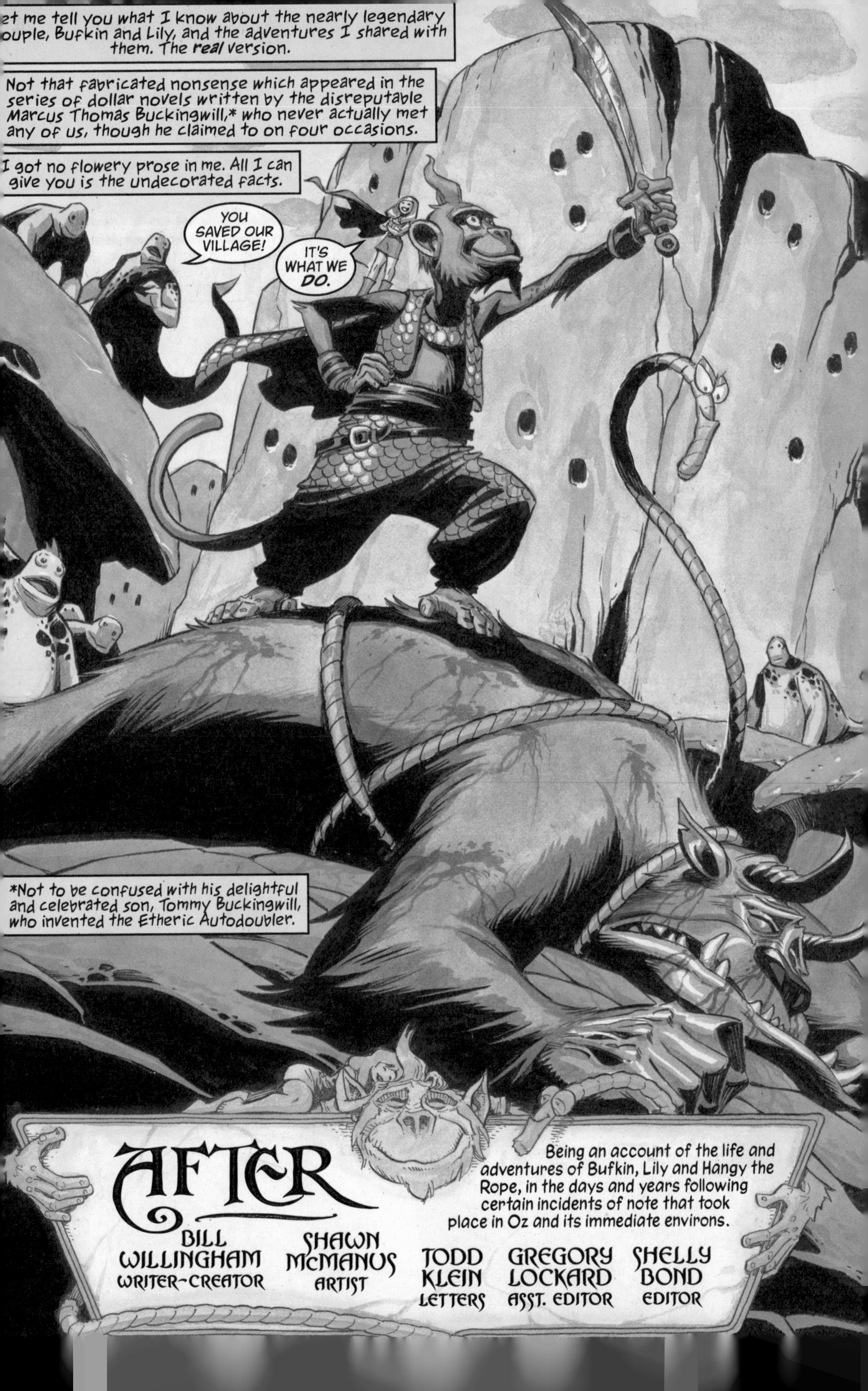
et me tell you what I know about the nearly legendary ouple, Bufkin and Lily, and the adventures I shared with them. The *real* version.
Not that fabricated nonsense which appeared in the series of dollar novels written by the disreputable Marcus Thomas Buckingwill,* who never actually met any of us, though he claimed to on four occasions.
I got no flowery prose in me. All I can give you is the undecorated facts.
YOU SAVED OUR VILLAGE!
IT'S WHAT WE *DO.*
*Not to be confused with his delightful and celebrated son, Tommy Buckingwill, who invented the Etheric Autodoubler.
AFTER
Being an account of the life and adventures of Bufkin, Lily and Hangy the Rope, in the days and years following certain incidents of note that took place in Oz and its immediate environs.
BILL WILLINGHAM WRITER-CREATOR
SHAWN McMANUS ARTIST
TODD KLEIN LETTERS
GREGORY LOCKARD ASST. EDITOR
SHELLY BOND EDITOR

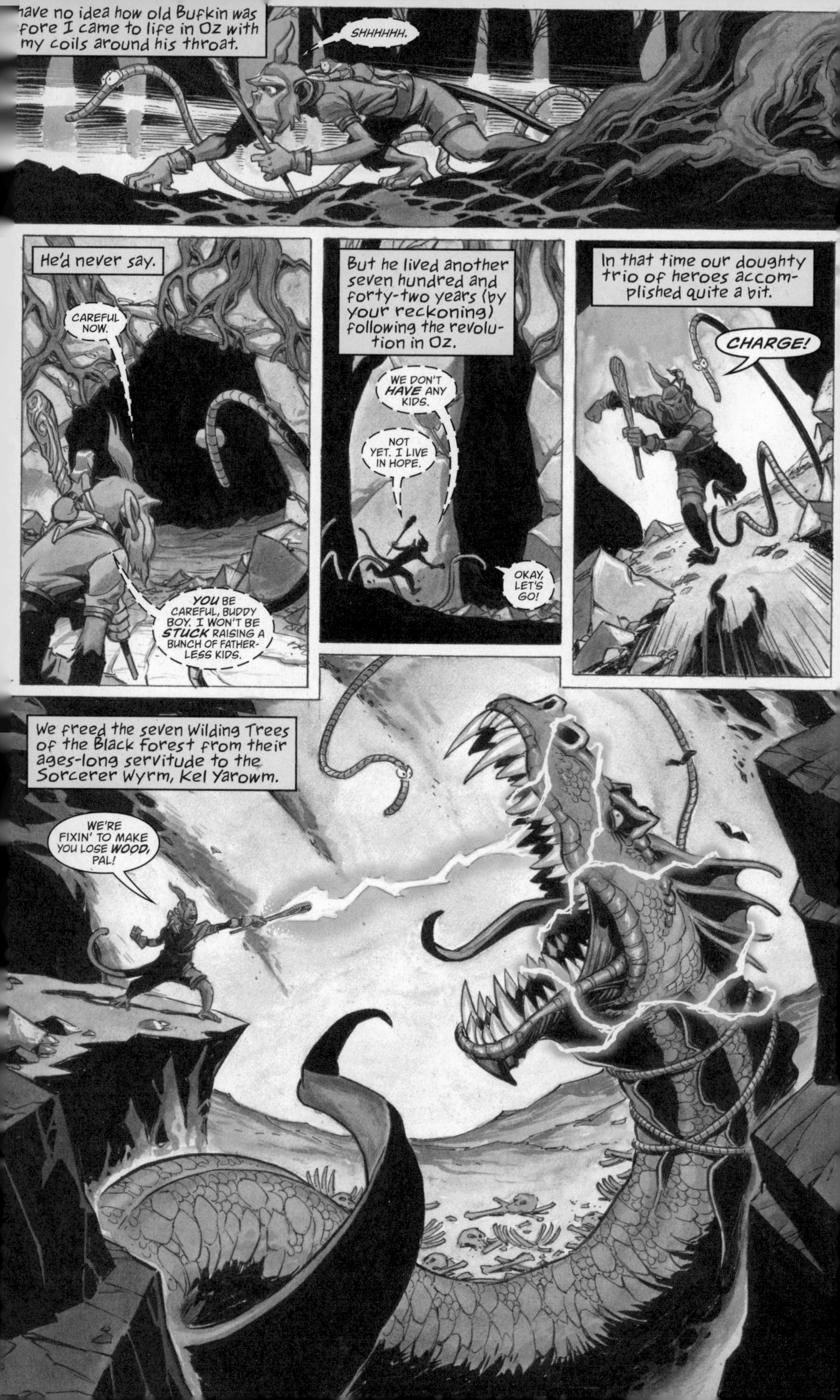

have no idea how old Bufkin was
fore I came to life in Oz with
my coils around his throat.
SHHHHHH.
He'd never say.
CAREFUL NOW.
YOU BE CAREFUL, BUDDY BOY. I WON'T BE STUCK RAISING A BUNCH OF FATHERLESS KIDS.
But he lived another seven hundred and forty-two years (by your reckoning) following the revolution in Oz.
WE DON'T HAVE ANY KIDS.
NOT YET. I LIVE IN HOPE.
OKAY, LET'S GO!
In that time our doughty trio of heroes accomplished quite a bit.
CHARGE!
We freed the seven Wilding Trees of the Black Forest from their ages-long servitude to the Sorcerer Wyrm, Kel Yarowm.
WE'RE FIXIN' TO MAKE YOU LOSE WOOD, PAL!

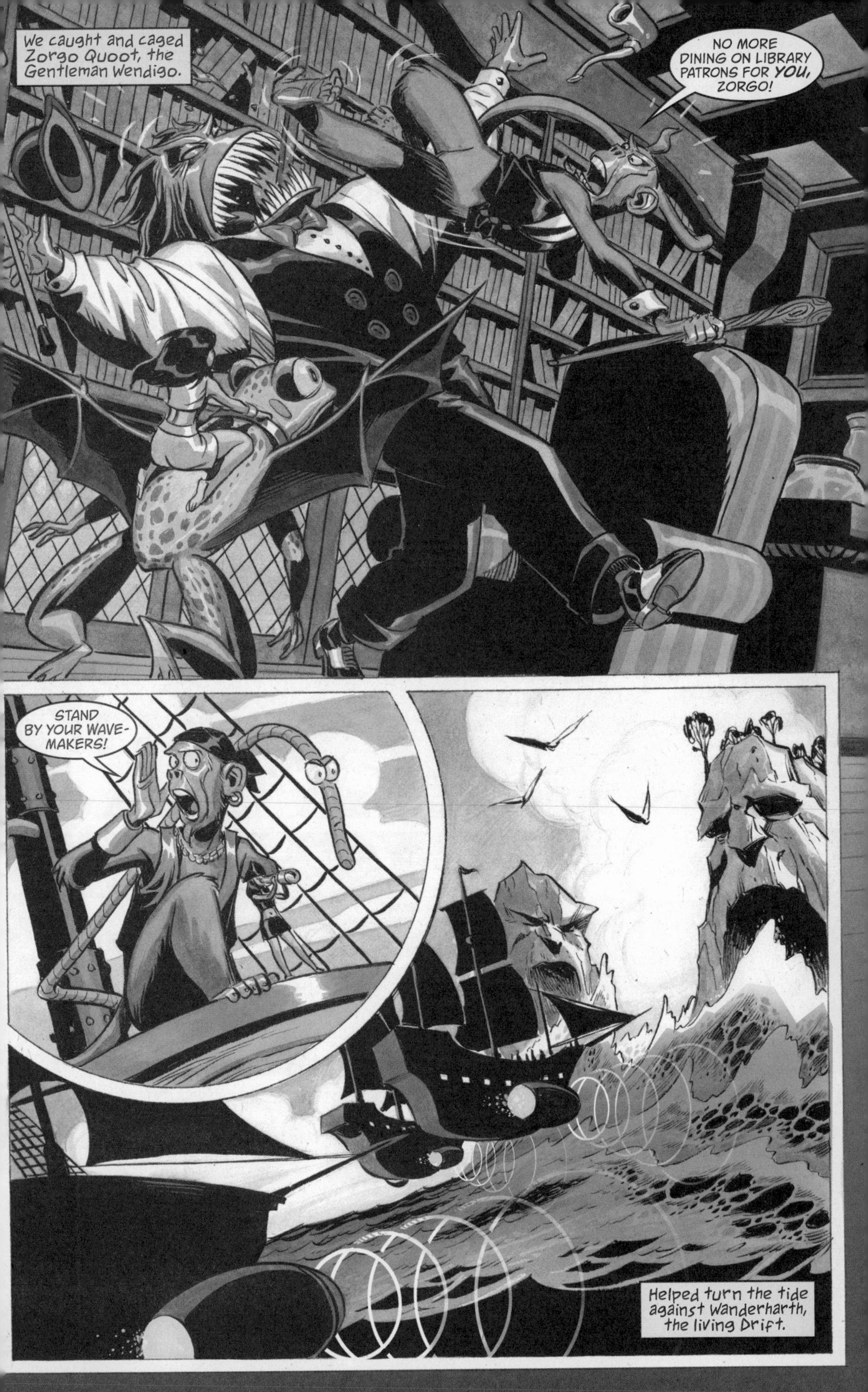

We caught and caged Zorgo Quoot, the Gentleman Wendigo.
NO MORE DINING ON LIBRARY PATRONS FOR YOU, ZORGO!
STAND BY YOUR WAVE-MAKERS!
Helped turn the tide against Wanderharth, the living Drift.

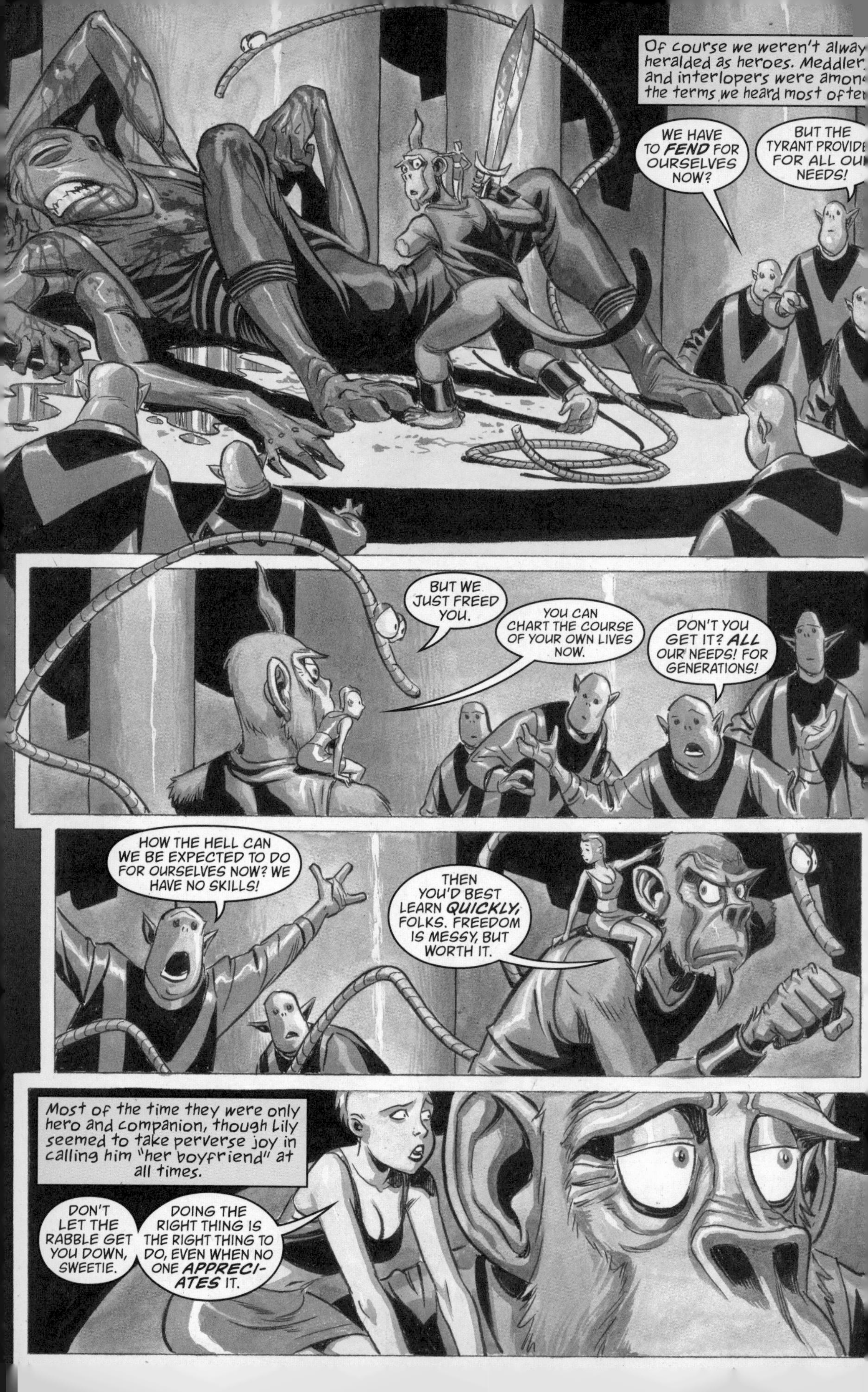
Of course we weren't alway
heralded as heroes. Meddler
and interlopers were amon
the terms we heard most ofte
WE HAVE TO FEND FOR OURSELVES NOW?
BUT THE TYRANT PROVIDE FOR ALL OU NEEDS!
BUT WE JUST FREED YOU.
YOU CAN CHART THE COURSE OF YOUR OWN LIVES NOW.
DON'T YOU GET IT? ALL OUR NEEDS! FOR GENERATIONS!
HOW THE HELL CAN WE BE EXPECTED TO DO FOR OURSELVES NOW? WE HAVE NO SKILLS!
THEN YOU'D BEST LEARN QUICKLY, FOLKS. FREEDOM IS MESSY, BUT WORTH IT.
Most of the time they were only hero and companion, though Lily seemed to take perverse joy in calling him "her boyfriend" at all times.
DON'T LET THE RABBLE GET YOU DOWN, SWEETIE.
DOING THE RIGHT THING IS THE RIGHT THING TO DO, EVEN WHEN NO ONE APPRECIATES IT.

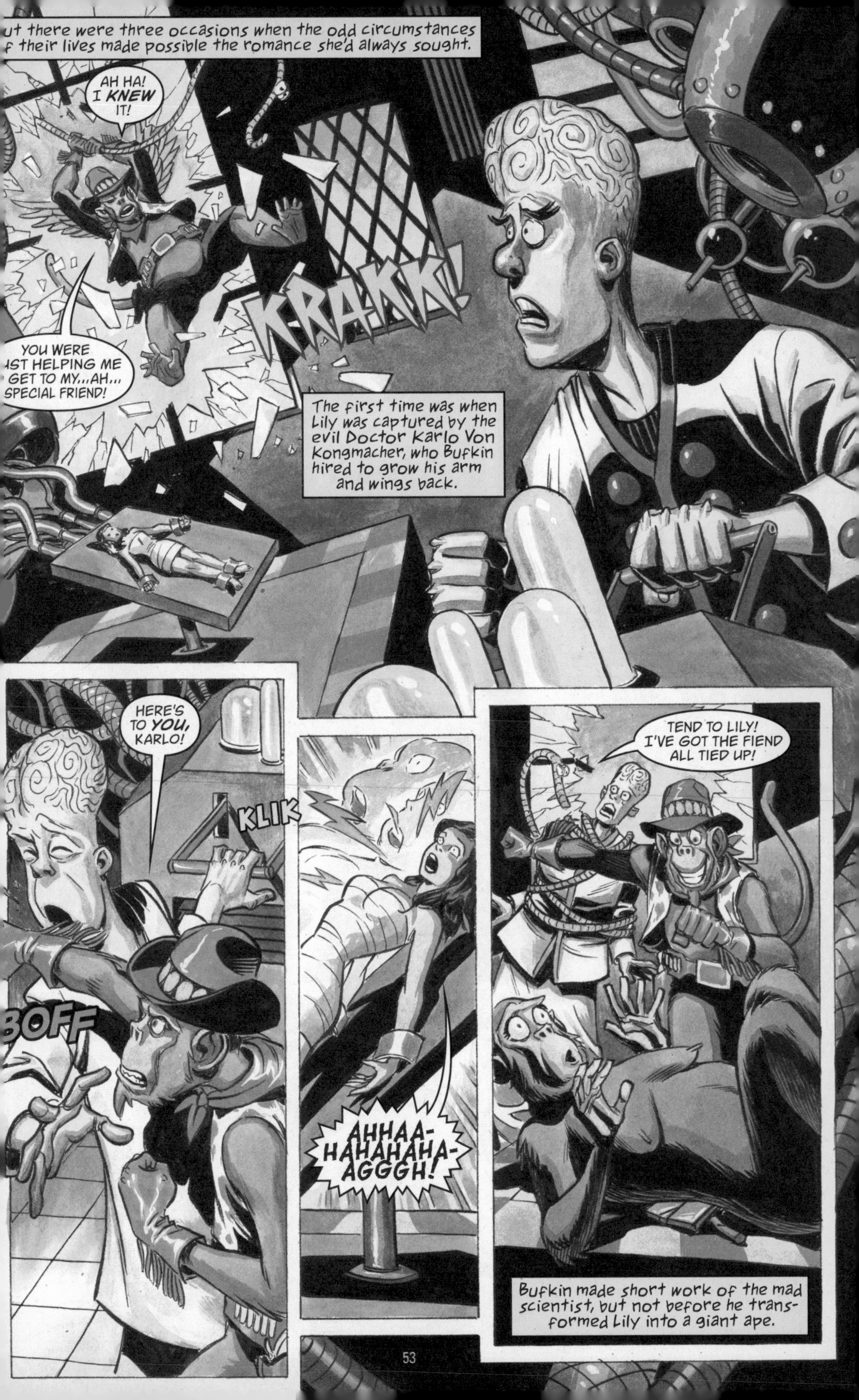
ut there were three occasions when the odd circumstances f their lives made possible the romance she'd always sought.
AH HA! I KNEW IT!
YOU WERE ST HELPING ME GET TO MY...AH... SPECIAL FRIEND!
KRAKK!
The first time was when Lily was captured by the evil Doctor Karlo Von Kongmacher, who Bufkin hired to grow his arm and wings back.
HERE'S TO YOU, KARLO!
KLIK
BOFF
AHHAA-HAHAHAHA-AGGGH!
TEND TO LILY! I'VE GOT THE FIEND ALL TIED UP!
Bufkin made short work of the mad scientist, but not before he transformed Lily into a giant ape.

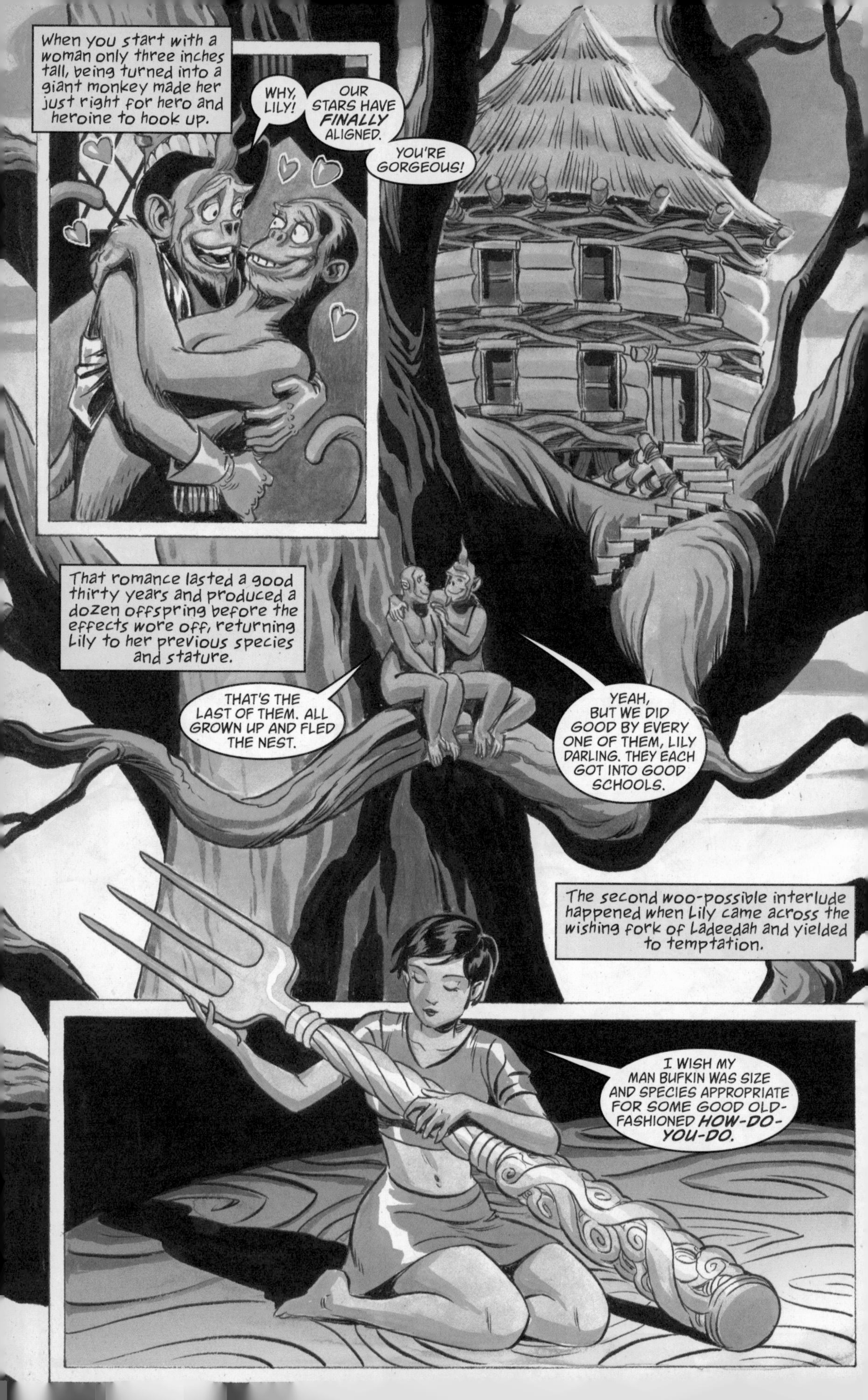

When you start with a woman only three inches tall, being turned into a giant monkey made her just right for hero and heroine to hook up.
WHY, LILY!
OUR STARS HAVE FINALLY ALIGNED.
YOU'RE GORGEOUS!
That romance lasted a good thirty years and produced a dozen offspring before the effects wore off, returning Lily to her previous species and stature.
THAT'S THE LAST OF THEM. ALL GROWN UP AND FLED THE NEST.
YEAH, BUT WE DID GOOD BY EVERY ONE OF THEM, LILY DARLING. THEY EACH GOT INTO GOOD SCHOOLS.
The second woo-possible interlude happened when Lily came across the wishing fork of Ladeedah and yielded to temptation.
I WISH MY MAN BUFKIN WAS SIZE AND SPECIES APPROPRIATE FOR SOME GOOD OLD-FASHIONED HOW-DO-YOU-DO.

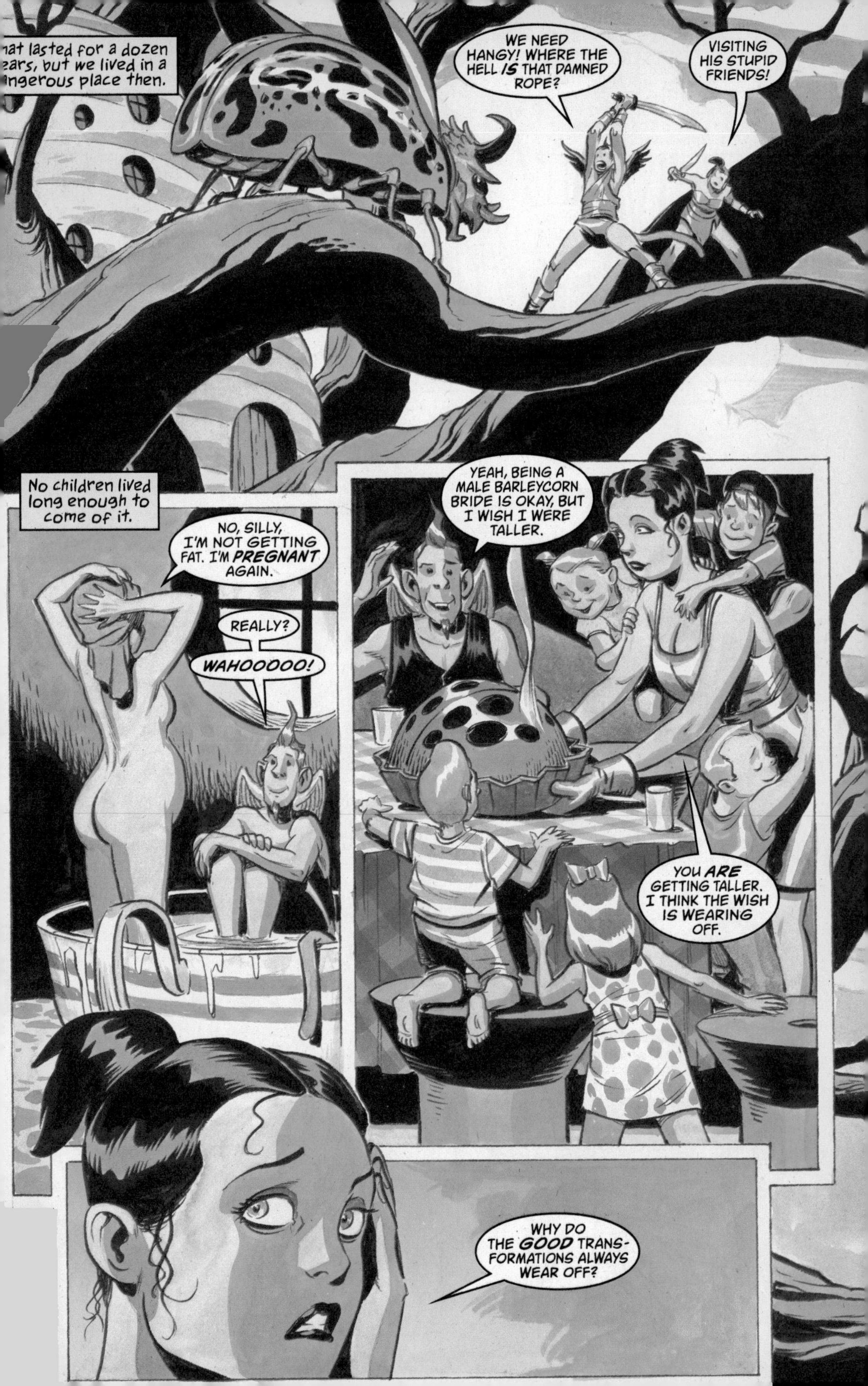
hat lasted for a dozen
ears, but we lived in a
ngerous place then.
WE NEED HANGY! WHERE THE HELL *IS* THAT DAMNED ROPE?
VISITING HIS STUPID FRIENDS!
No children lived long enough to come of it.
NO, SILLY, I'M NOT GETTING FAT. I'M *PREGNANT* AGAIN.
REALLY?
WAHOOOOO!
YEAH, BEING A MALE BARLEYCORN BRIDE IS OKAY, BUT I WISH I WERE TALLER.
YOU *ARE* GETTING TALLER. I THINK THE WISH IS WEARING OFF.
WHY DO THE *GOOD* TRANS-FORMATIONS ALWAYS WEAR OFF?

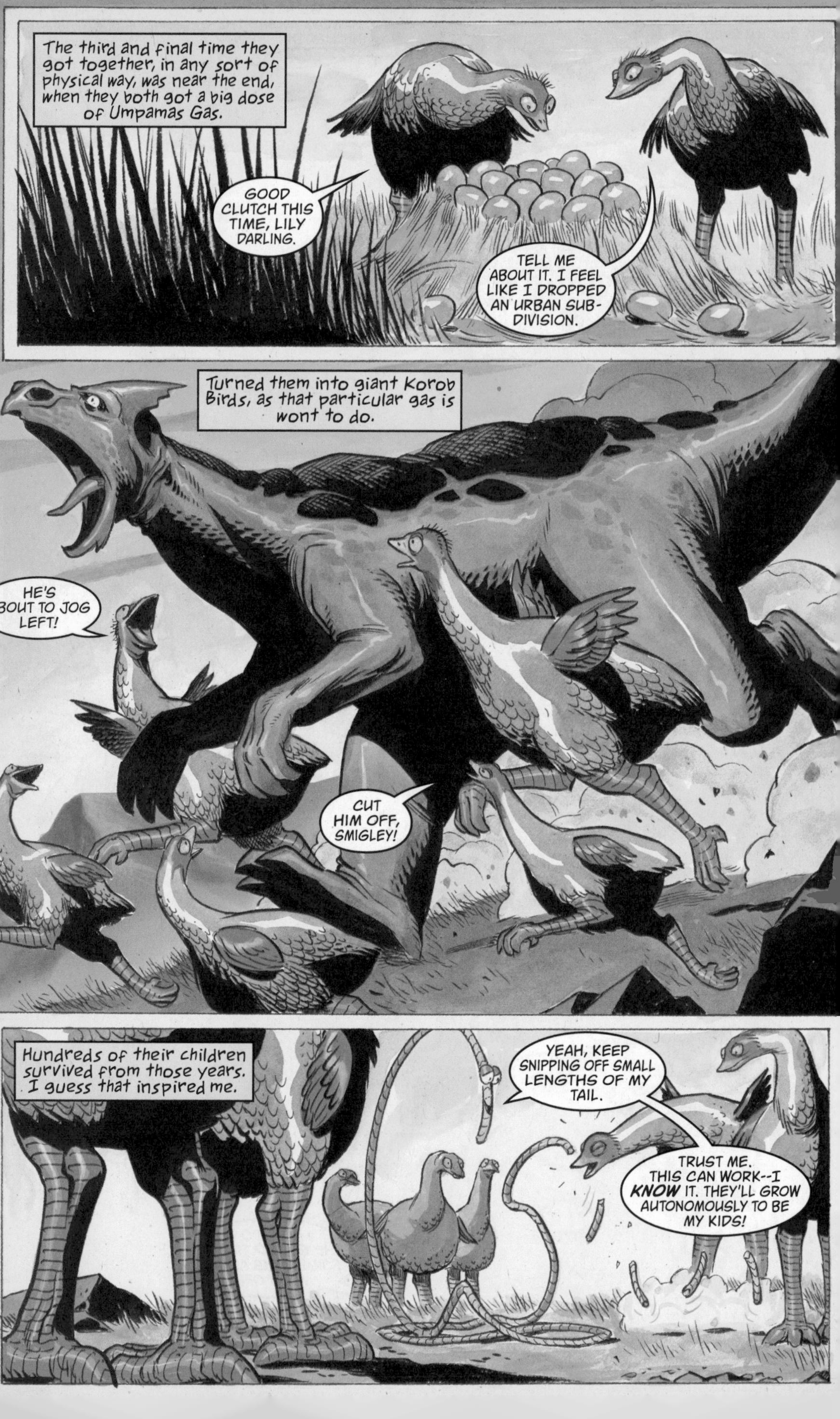
The third and final time they got together, in any sort of physical way, was near the end, when they both got a big dose of Umpamas Gas.
GOOD CLUTCH THIS TIME, LILY DARLING.
TELL ME ABOUT IT. I FEEL LIKE I DROPPED AN URBAN SUB-DIVISION.
Turned them into giant Korob Birds, as that particular gas is wont to do.
HE'S ABOUT TO JOG LEFT!
CUT HIM OFF, SMIGLEY!
Hundreds of their children survived from those years. I guess that inspired me.
YEAH, KEEP SNIPPING OFF SMALL LENGTHS OF MY TAIL.
TRUST ME. THIS CAN WORK--I KNOW IT. THEY'LL GROW AUTONOMOUSLY TO BE MY KIDS!

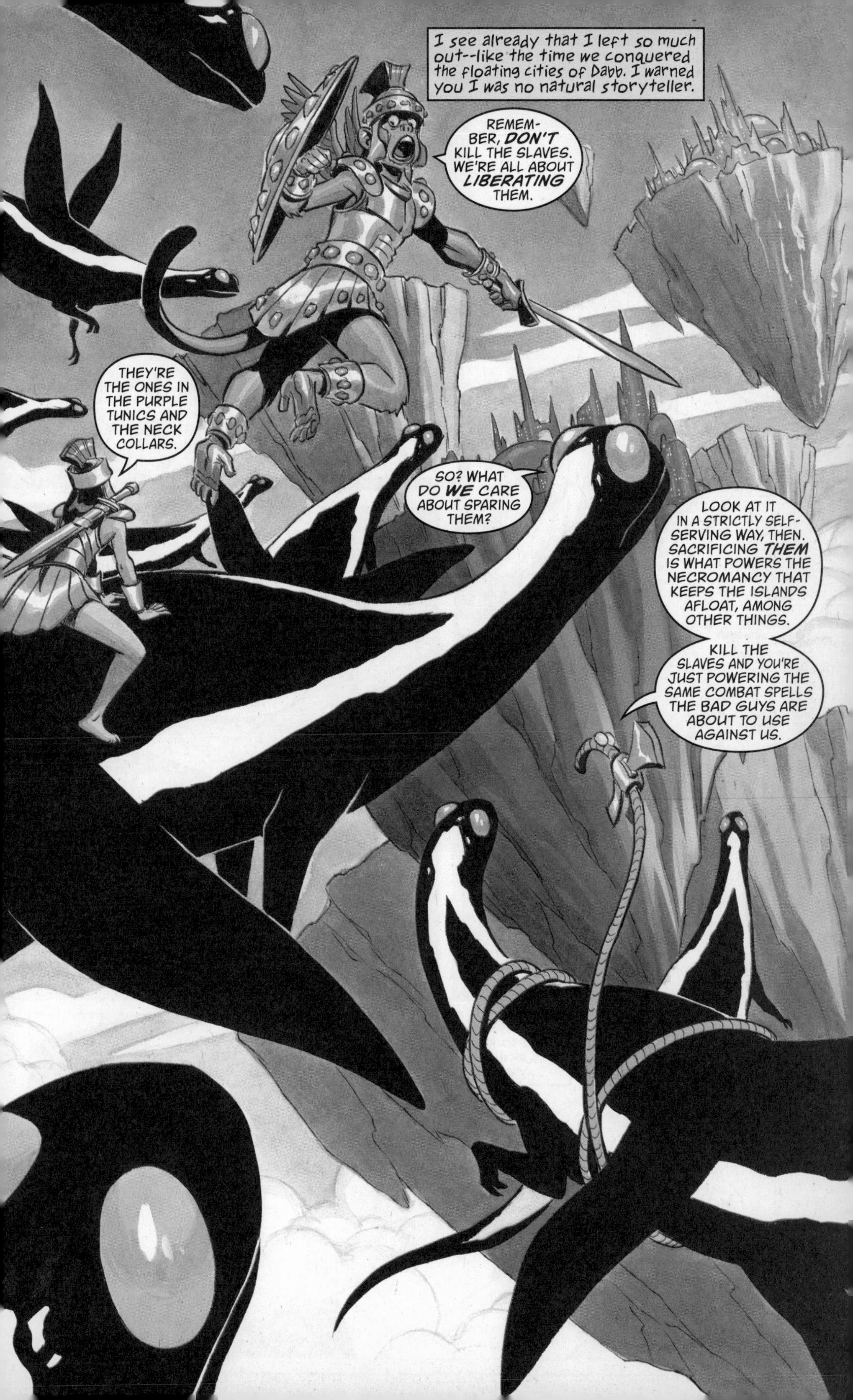
I see already that I left so much out--like the time we conquered the floating cities of Dabb. I warned you I was no natural storyteller.
REMEMBER, DON'T KILL THE SLAVES. WE'RE ALL ABOUT LIBERATING THEM.
THEY'RE THE ONES IN THE PURPLE TUNICS AND THE NECK COLLARS.
SO? WHAT DO WE CARE ABOUT SPARING THEM?
LOOK AT IT IN A STRICTLY SELF-SERVING WAY, THEN. SACRIFICING THEM IS WHAT POWERS THE NECROMANCY THAT KEEPS THE ISLANDS AFLOAT, AMONG OTHER THINGS.
KILL THE SLAVES AND YOU'RE JUST POWERING THE SAME COMBAT SPELLS THE BAD GUYS ARE ABOUT TO USE AGAINST US.

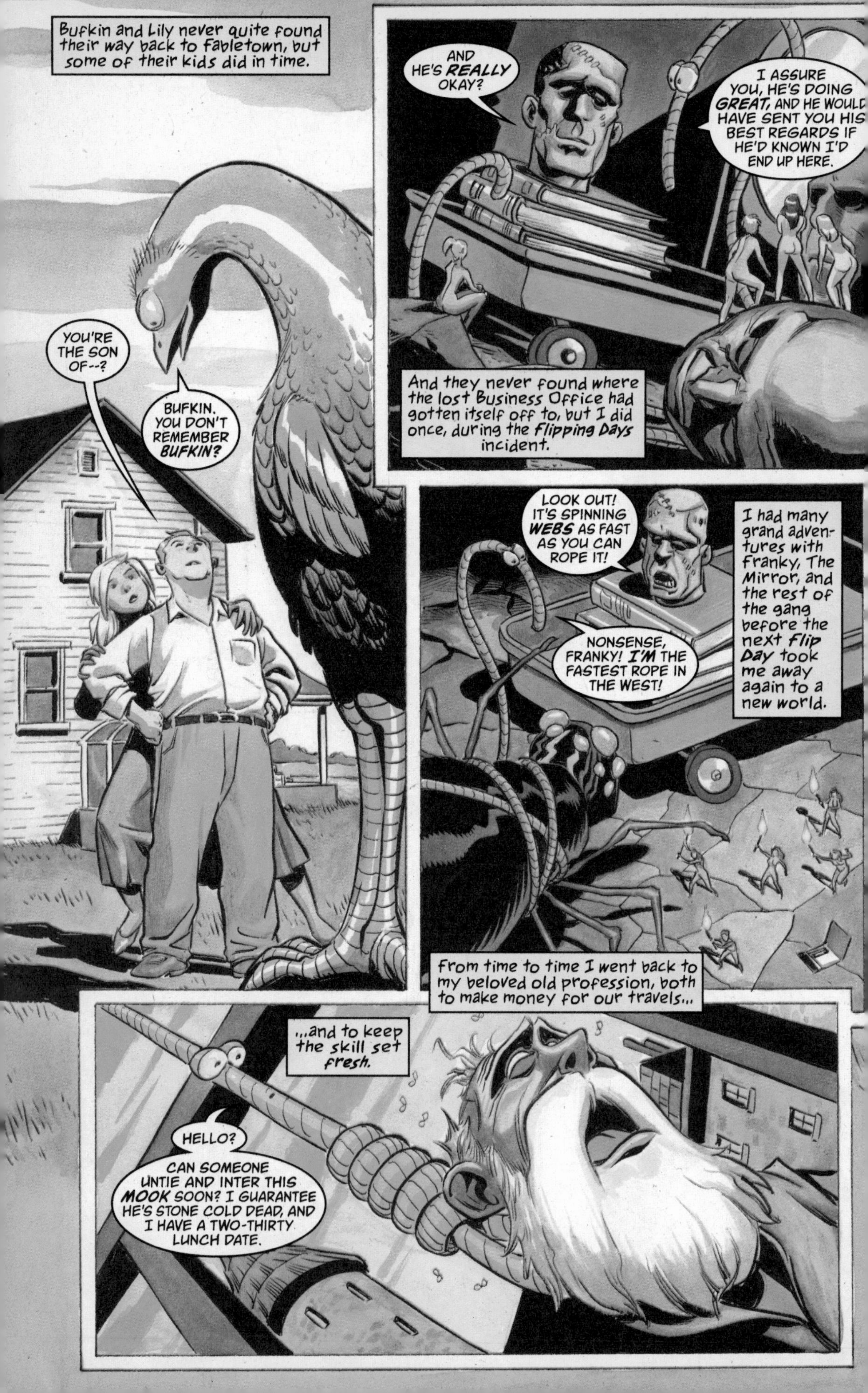
Bufkin and Lily never quite found their way back to Fabletown, but some of their kids did in time.
YOU'RE THE SON OF--?
BUFKIN. YOU DON'T REMEMBER BUFKIN?
AND HE'S REALLY OKAY?
I ASSURE YOU, HE'S DOING GREAT, AND HE WOULD HAVE SENT YOU HIS BEST REGARDS IF HE'D KNOWN I'D END UP HERE.
And they never found where the lost Business Office had gotten itself off to, but I did once, during the Flipping Days incident.
LOOK OUT! IT'S SPINNING WEBS AS FAST AS YOU CAN ROPE IT!
NONSENSE, FRANKY! I'M THE FASTEST ROPE IN THE WEST!
I had many grand adventures with Franky, The Mirror, and the rest of the gang before the next Flip Day took me away again to a new world.
From time to time I went back to my beloved old profession, both to make money for our travels...
...and to keep the skill set fresh.
HELLO?
CAN SOMEONE UNTIE AND INTER THIS MOOK SOON? I GUARANTEE HE'S STONE COLD DEAD, AND I HAVE A TWO-THIRTY LUNCH DATE.

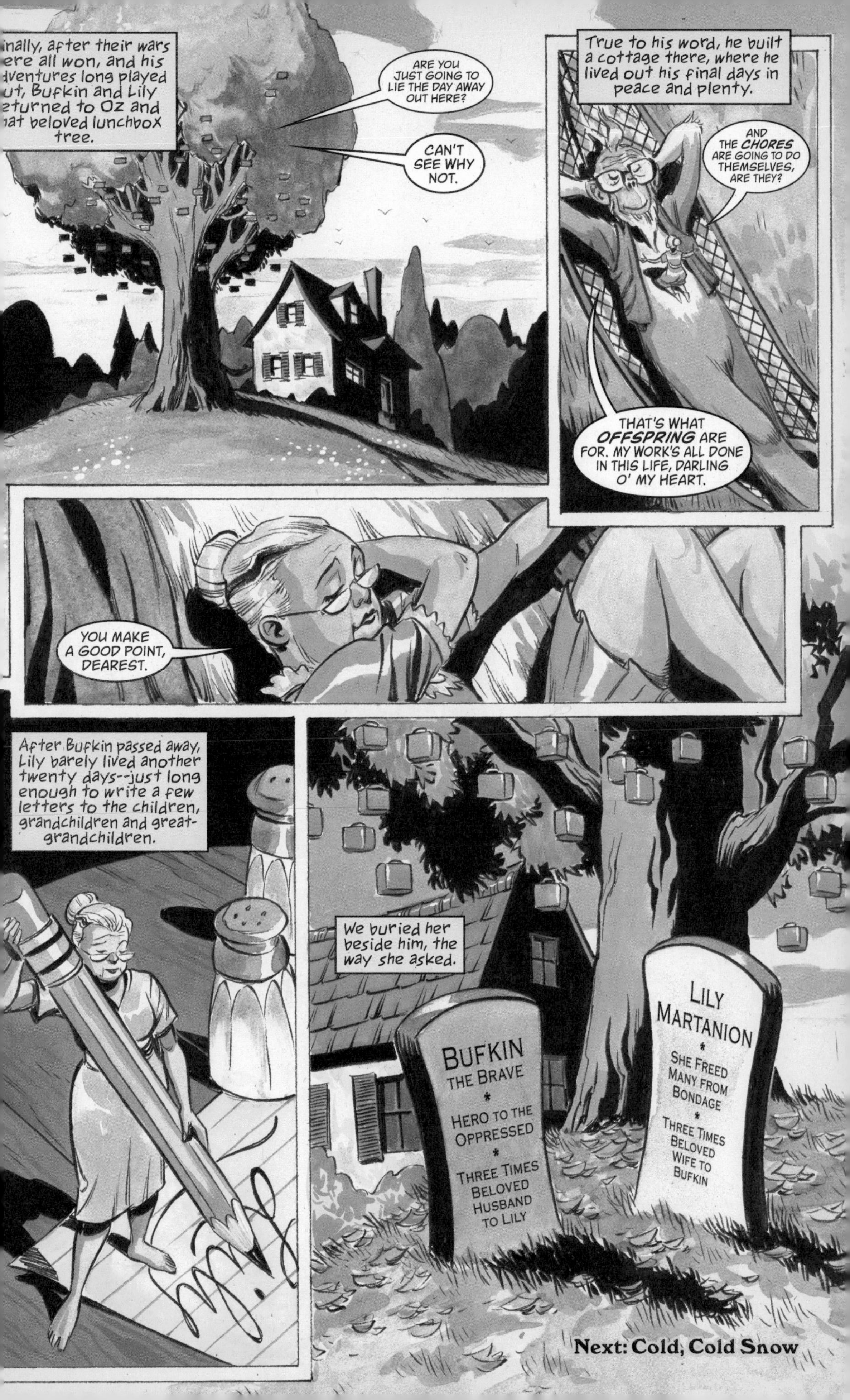
inally, after their wars
ere all won, and his
dventures long played
ut, Bufkin and Lily
eturned to Oz and
hat beloved lunchbox
tree.
ARE YOU JUST GOING TO LIE THE DAY AWAY OUT HERE?
CAN'T SEE WHY NOT.
True to his word, he built a cottage there, where he lived out his final days in peace and plenty.
AND THE CHORES ARE GOING TO DO THEMSELVES, ARE THEY?
THAT'S WHAT OFFSPRING ARE FOR. MY WORK'S ALL DONE IN THIS LIFE, DARLING O' MY HEART.
YOU MAKE A GOOD POINT, DEAREST.
After Bufkin passed away, Lily barely lived another twenty days--just long enough to write a few letters to the children, grandchildren and great-grandchildren.
We buried her beside him, the way she asked.
BUFKIN THE BRAVE * HERO TO THE OPPRESSED * THREE TIMES BELOVED HUSBAND TO LILY
LILY MARTANION * SHE FREED MANY FROM BONDAGE * THREE TIMES BELOVED WIFE TO BUFKIN
Next: Cold, Cold Snow

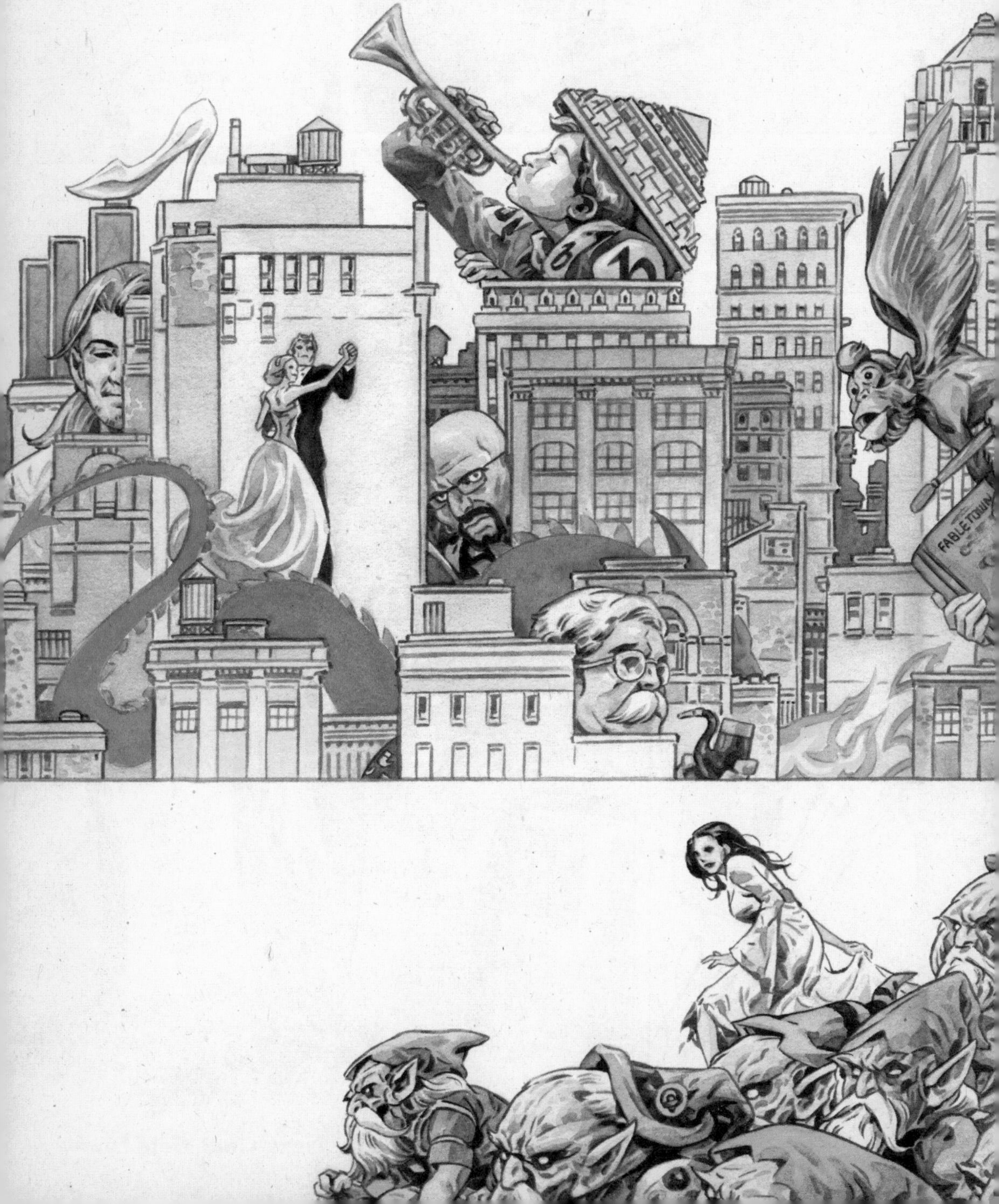
FABLETOWN

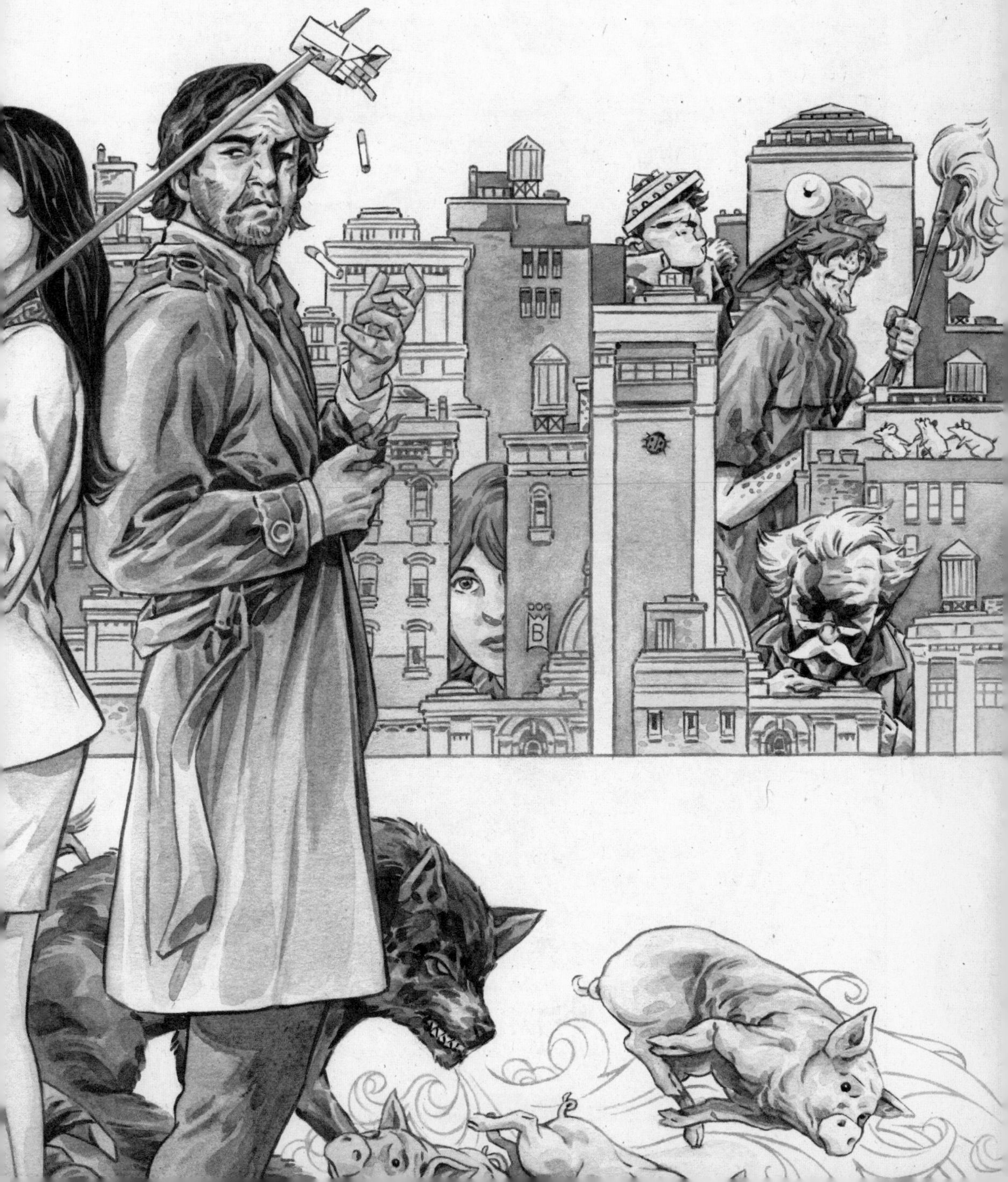

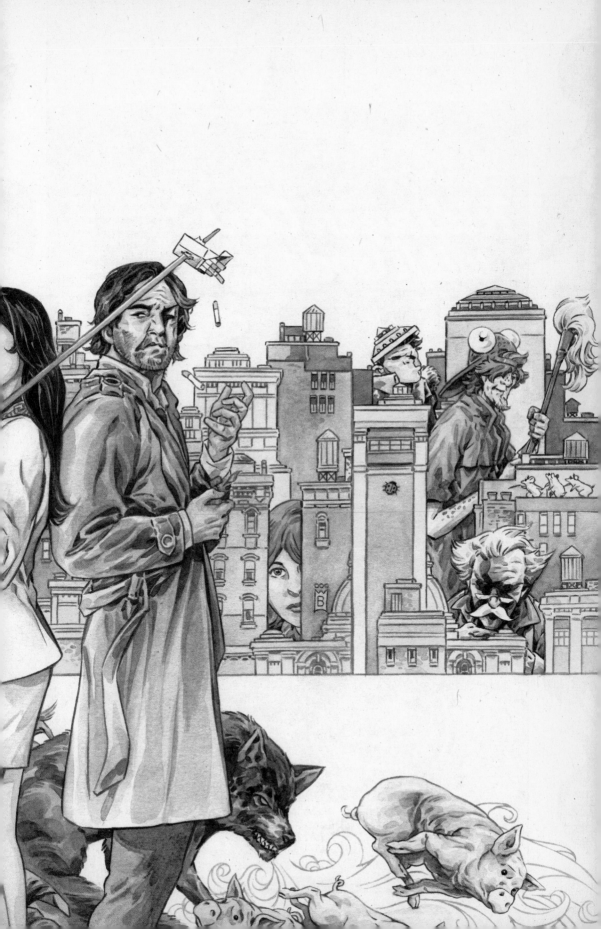

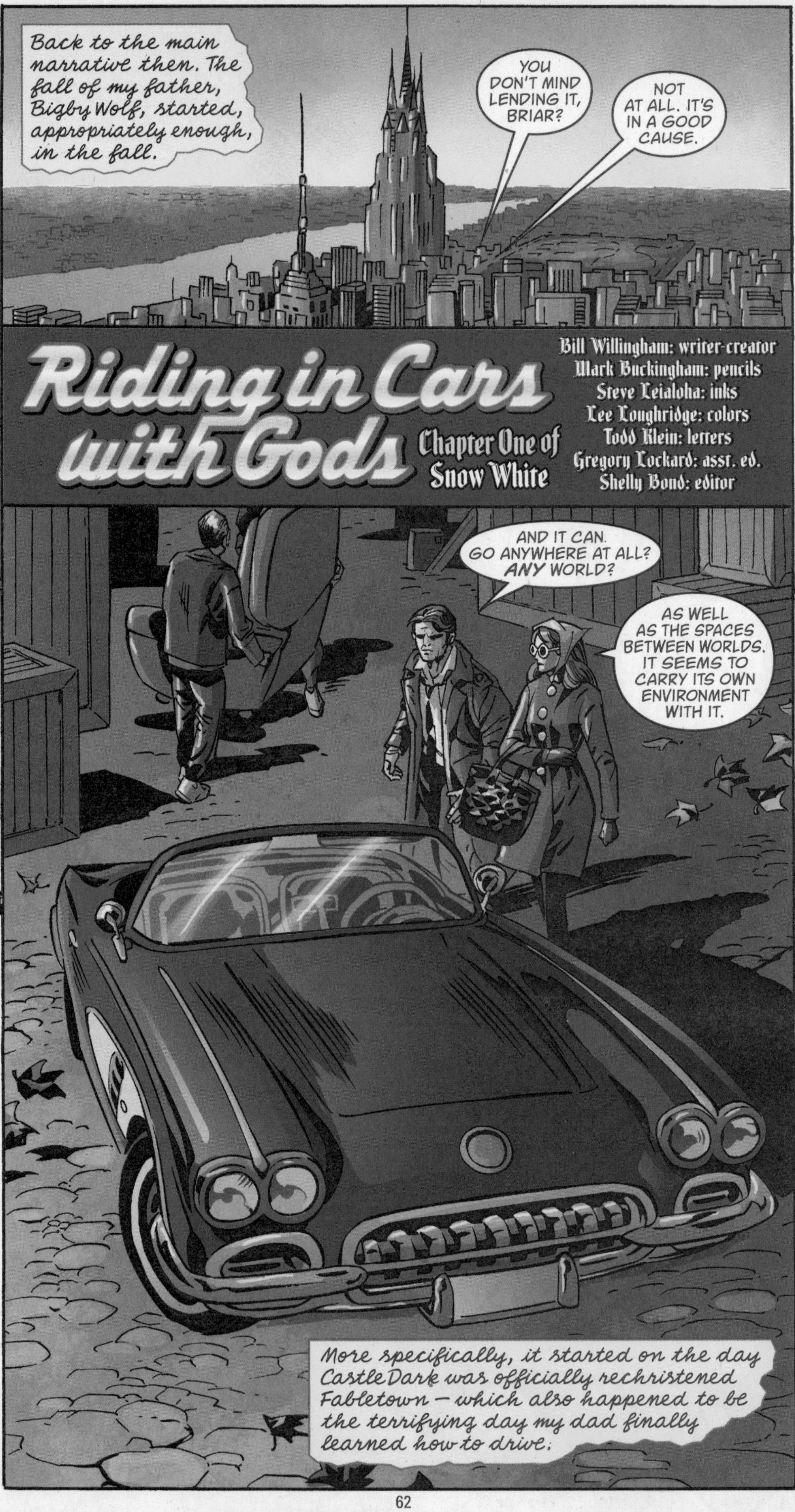

Back to the main narrative then. The fall of my father, Bigby Wolf, started, appropriately enough, in the fall.
YOU DON'T MIND LENDING IT, BRIAR?
NOT AT ALL. IT'S IN A GOOD CAUSE.
Riding in Cars with Gods
Chapter One of Snow White
Bill Willingham: writer-creator
Mark Buckingham: pencils
Steve Leialoha: inks
Lee Loughridge: colors
Todd Klein: letters
Gregory Lockard: asst. ed.
Shelly Bond: editor
AND IT CAN. GO ANYWHERE AT ALL? ANY WORLD?
AS WELL AS THE SPACES BETWEEN WORLDS. IT SEEMS TO CARRY ITS OWN ENVIRONMENT WITH IT.
More specifically, it started on the day Castle Dark was officially rechristened Fabletown — which also happened to be the terrifying day my dad finally learned how to drive.

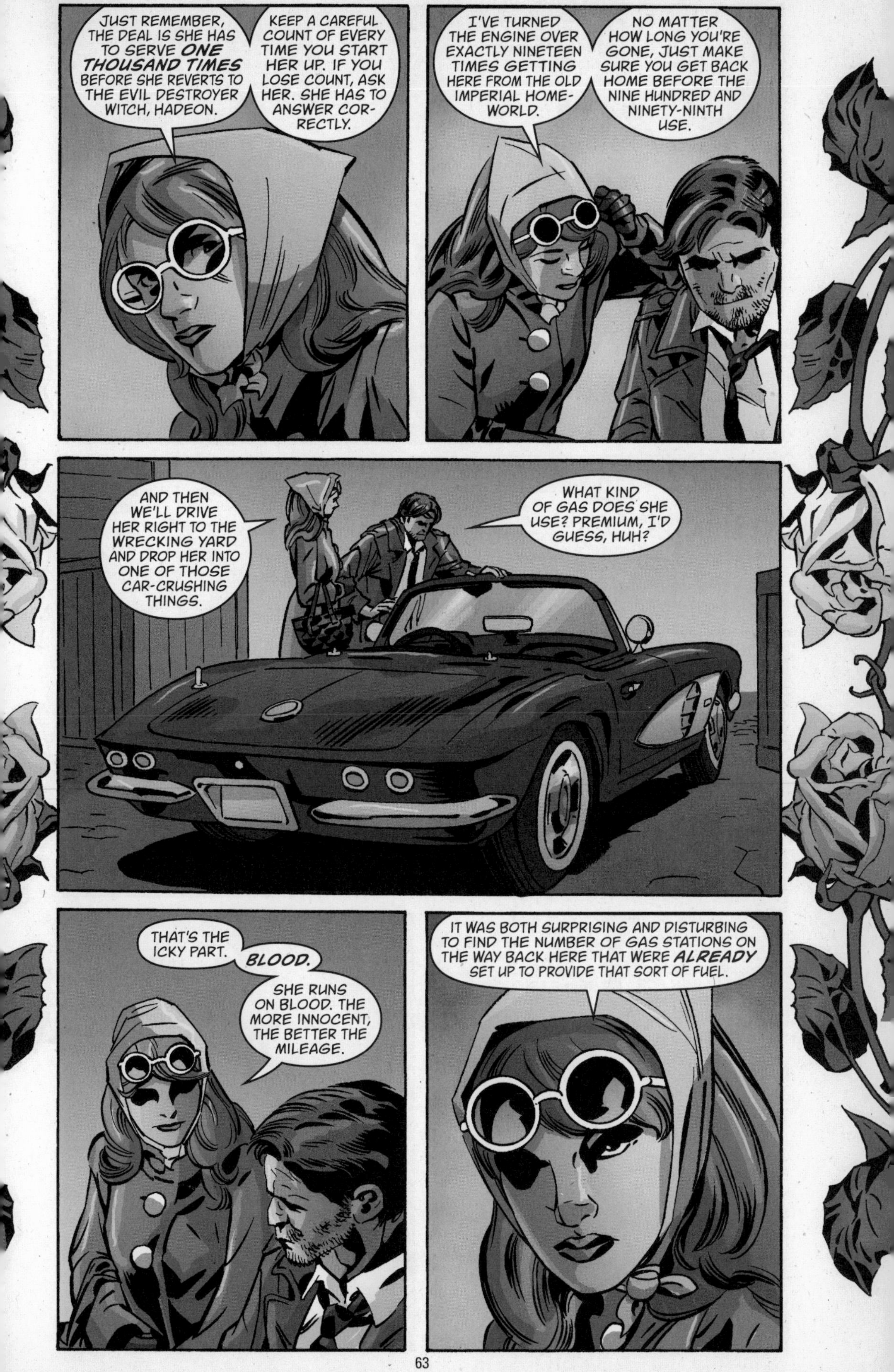
JUST REMEMBER, THE DEAL IS SHE HAS TO SERVE ONE THOUSAND TIMES BEFORE SHE REVERTS TO THE EVIL DESTROYER WITCH, HADEON.
KEEP A CAREFUL COUNT OF EVERY TIME YOU START HER UP. IF YOU LOSE COUNT, ASK HER. SHE HAS TO ANSWER CORRECTLY.
I'VE TURNED THE ENGINE OVER EXACTLY NINETEEN TIMES GETTING HERE FROM THE OLD IMPERIAL HOMEWORLD.
NO MATTER HOW LONG YOU'RE GONE, JUST MAKE SURE YOU GET BACK HOME BEFORE THE NINE HUNDRED AND NINETY-NINTH USE.
AND THEN WE'LL DRIVE HER RIGHT TO THE WRECKING YARD AND DROP HER INTO ONE OF THOSE CAR-CRUSHING THINGS.
WHAT KIND OF GAS DOES SHE USE? PREMIUM, I'D GUESS, HUH?
THAT'S THE ICKY PART.
BLOOD.
SHE RUNS ON BLOOD. THE MORE INNOCENT, THE BETTER THE MILEAGE.
IT WAS BOTH SURPRISING AND DISTURBING TO FIND THE NUMBER OF GAS STATIONS ON THE WAY BACK HERE THAT WERE ALREADY SET UP TO PROVIDE THAT SORT OF FUEL.

I REPACKED YOUR BAGS FOR THE TRIP.

TYPICALLY, YOU HADN'T PACKED NEARLY ENOUGH.

SNOW. STINKY.

I'M NOT STINKY ANYMORE-- uh--MEANING I'M NOT *NAMED* STINKY.

I KNOW YOU'VE BEEN OUT OF CIRCULATION FOR A WHILE, BUT YOU NEED TO CATCH UP ON A *LOT* OF STUFF, MISSY ROSE.

BRIAR ROSE.

IT'S SO WONDERFUL TO SEE YOU MADE IT HOME, AT LONG LAST.

WELCOME BACK.

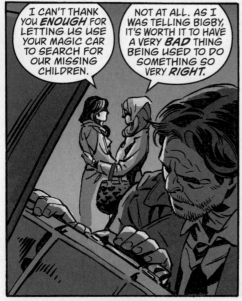

I CAN'T THANK YOU *ENOUGH* FOR LETTING US USE YOUR MAGIC CAR TO SEARCH FOR OUR MISSING CHILDREN.

NOT AT ALL. AS I WAS TELLING BIGBY, IT'S WORTH IT TO HAVE A VERY *BAD* THING BEING USED TO DO SOMETHING SO VERY *RIGHT*.

IT'S YOURS FOR AS LONG AS YOU NEED IT.

WE SHOULD BE GOING SOON. SNOW, ANY LUCK ON FINDING A CO-DRIVER TO GO WITH ME?

THAT'S ME. *I'M* GOING WITH YOU.

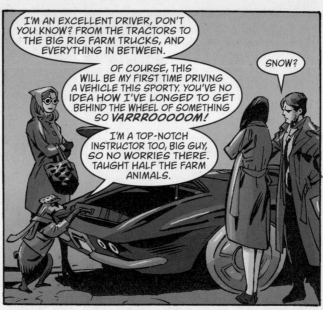

I'M AN EXCELLENT DRIVER, DON'T YOU KNOW? FROM THE TRACTORS TO THE BIG RIG FARM TRUCKS, AND EVERYTHING IN BETWEEN.

OF COURSE, THIS WILL BE MY FIRST TIME DRIVING A VEHICLE THIS SPORTY. YOU'VE NO IDEA HOW I'VE LONGED TO GET BEHIND THE WHEEL OF SOMETHING SO *VARRROOOOOM!*

SNOW?

I'M A TOP-NOTCH INSTRUCTOR TOO, BIG GUY, SO NO WORRIES THERE. TAUGHT HALF THE FARM ANIMALS.

BAG'S ALL PACKED. FAREWELLS MADE. I'M READY TO GO, AS SOON AS YOU ARE.

I'LL MAKE MYSELF A WEE BIT BIGGER HERE, TO SEE OVER THE DASH.

WHO'S GOT THE KEYS?

HE WAS THE BEST I COULD DO.

TAKE CARE, *BOTH* OF YOU.

AND BRING MY BABIES HOME.

WAHOOOOOOO! *ROAD TRIP!*

HANG ON, PAL! IMMA BOUTTA PUT THE *PEDAL* TO THE *METAL!*

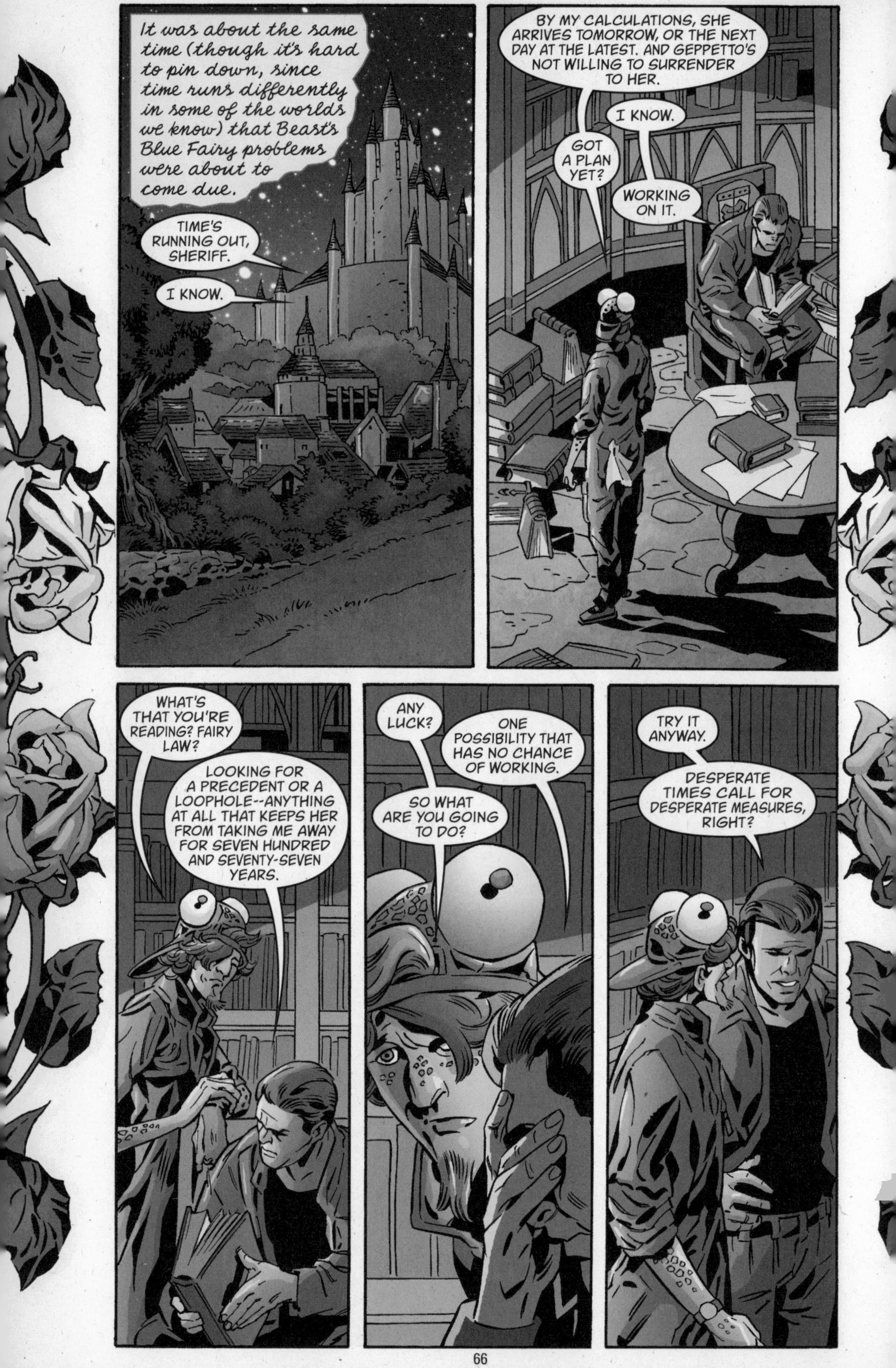
It was about the same time (though it's hard to pin down, since time runs differently in some of the worlds we know) that Beast's Blue Fairy problems were about to come due.
TIME'S RUNNING OUT, SHERIFF.
I KNOW.
BY MY CALCULATIONS, SHE ARRIVES TOMORROW, OR THE NEXT DAY AT THE LATEST. AND GEPPETTO'S NOT WILLING TO SURRENDER TO HER.
I KNOW.
GOT A PLAN YET?
WORKING ON IT.
WHAT'S THAT YOU'RE READING? FAIRY LAW?
LOOKING FOR A PRECEDENT OR A LOOPHOLE--ANYTHING AT ALL THAT KEEPS HER FROM TAKING ME AWAY FOR SEVEN HUNDRED AND SEVENTY-SEVEN YEARS.
ANY LUCK?
ONE POSSIBILITY THAT HAS NO CHANCE OF WORKING.
SO WHAT ARE YOU GOING TO DO?
TRY IT ANYWAY.
DESPERATE TIMES CALL FOR DESPERATE MEASURES, RIGHT?

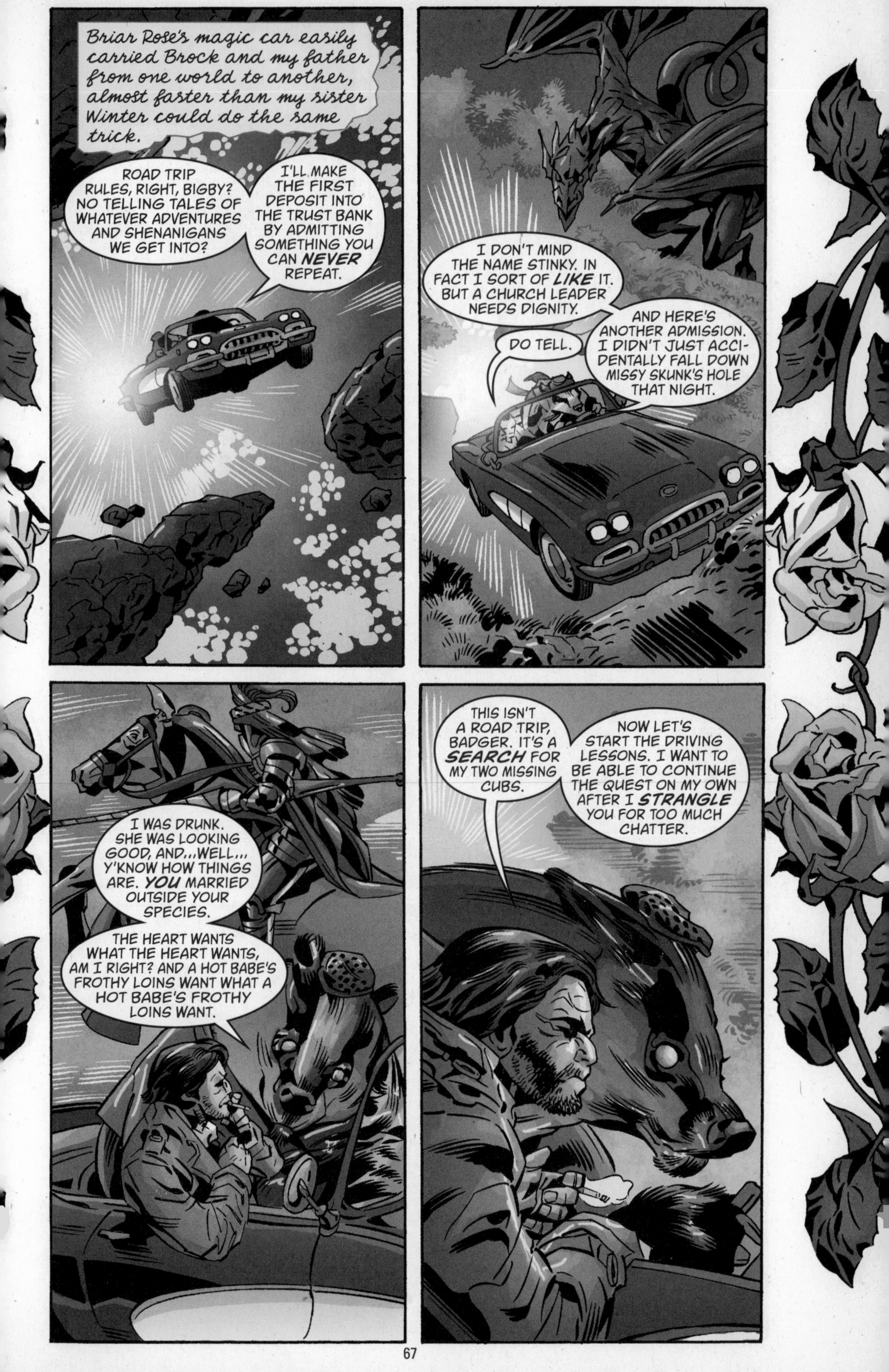

Briar Rose's magic car easily carried Brock and my father from one world to another, almost faster than my sister Winter could do the same trick.
ROAD TRIP RULES, RIGHT, BIGBY? NO TELLING TALES OF WHATEVER ADVENTURES AND SHENANIGANS WE GET INTO?
I'LL MAKE THE FIRST DEPOSIT INTO THE TRUST BANK BY ADMITTING SOMETHING YOU CAN NEVER REPEAT.
I DON'T MIND THE NAME STINKY. IN FACT I SORT OF LIKE IT. BUT A CHURCH LEADER NEEDS DIGNITY.
DO TELL.
AND HERE'S ANOTHER ADMISSION. I DIDN'T JUST ACCIDENTALLY FALL DOWN MISSY SKUNK'S HOLE THAT NIGHT.
I WAS DRUNK. SHE WAS LOOKING GOOD, AND...WELL... Y'KNOW HOW THINGS ARE. YOU MARRIED OUTSIDE YOUR SPECIES.
THE HEART WANTS WHAT THE HEART WANTS, AM I RIGHT? AND A HOT BABE'S FROTHY LOINS WANT WHAT A HOT BABE'S FROTHY LOINS WANT.
THIS ISN'T A ROAD TRIP, BADGER. IT'S A SEARCH FOR MY TWO MISSING CUBS.
NOW LET'S START THE DRIVING LESSONS. I WANT TO BE ABLE TO CONTINUE THE QUEST ON MY OWN AFTER I STRANGLE YOU FOR TOO MUCH CHATTER.

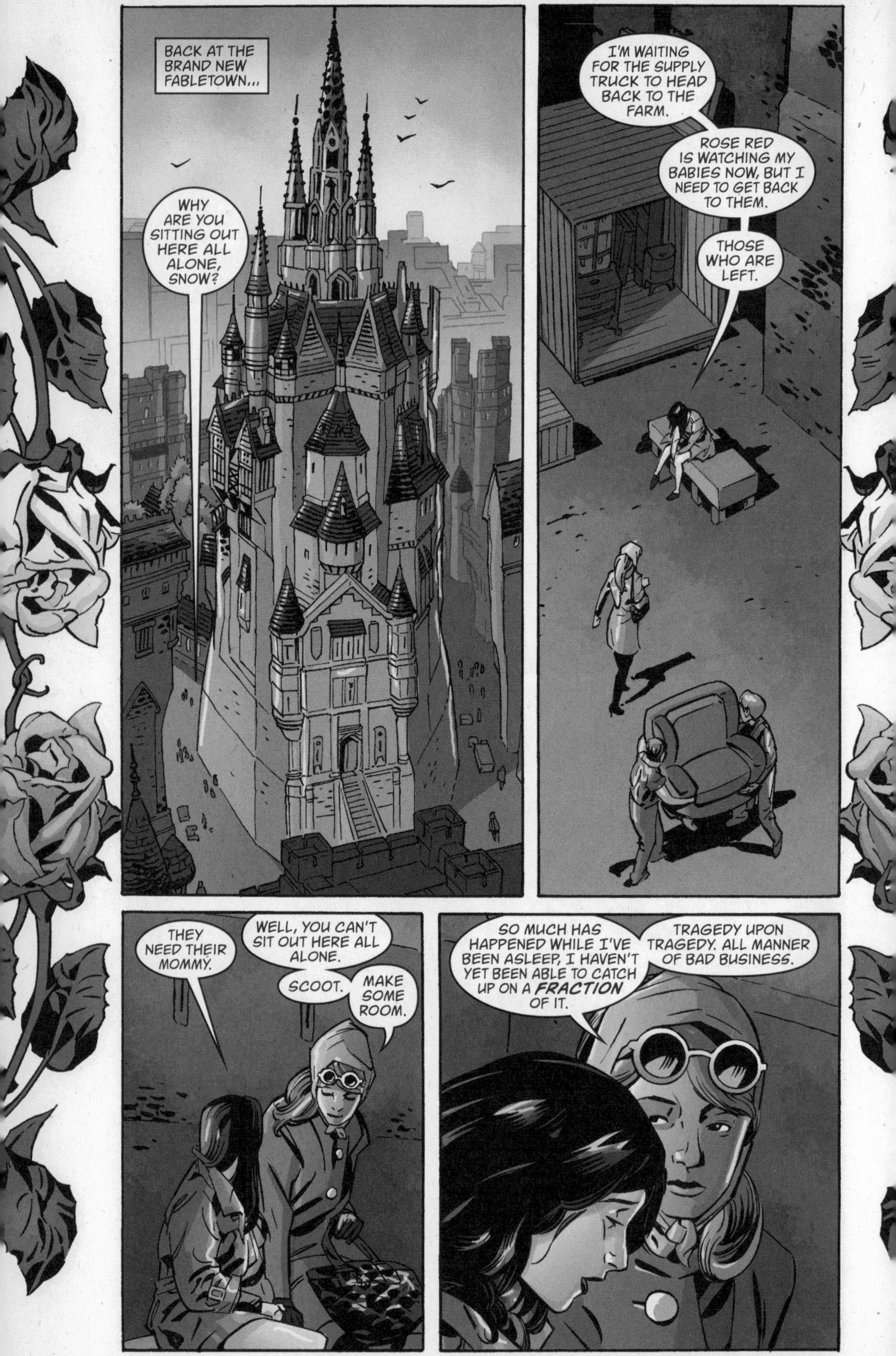
BACK AT THE BRAND NEW FABLETOWN...
WHY ARE YOU SITTING OUT HERE ALL ALONE, SNOW?
I'M WAITING FOR THE SUPPLY TRUCK TO HEAD BACK TO THE FARM.
ROSE RED IS WATCHING MY BABIES NOW, BUT I NEED TO GET BACK TO THEM.
THOSE WHO ARE LEFT.
THEY NEED THEIR MOMMY.
WELL, YOU CAN'T SIT OUT HERE ALL ALONE.
SCOOT.
MAKE SOME ROOM.
SO MUCH HAS HAPPENED WHILE I'VE BEEN ASLEEP, I HAVEN'T YET BEEN ABLE TO CATCH UP ON A *FRACTION* OF IT.
TRAGEDY UPON TRAGEDY. ALL MANNER OF BAD BUSINESS.

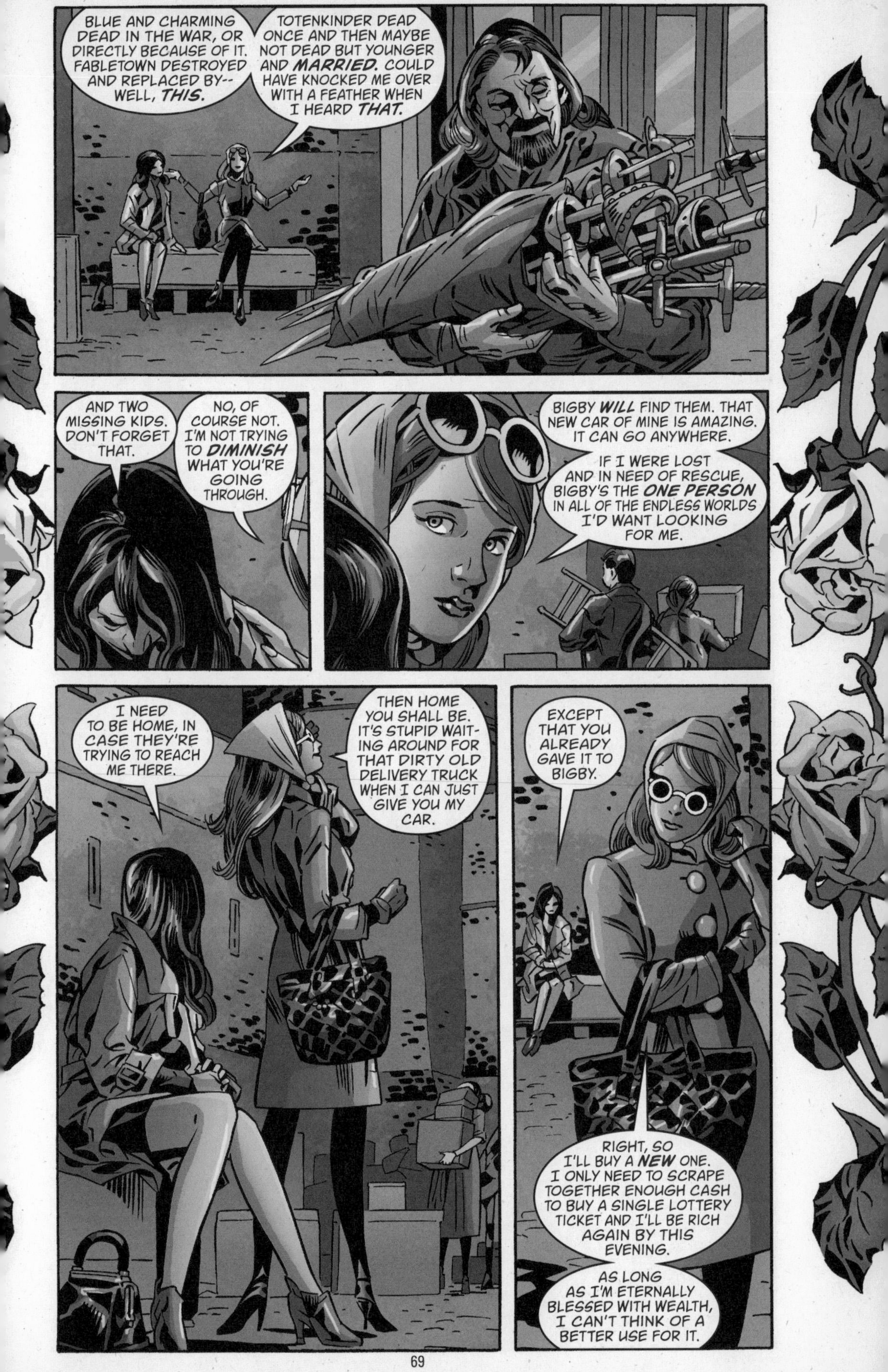
BLUE AND CHARMING DEAD IN THE WAR, OR DIRECTLY BECAUSE OF IT. FABLETOWN DESTROYED AND REPLACED BY-- WELL, THIS.
TOTENKINDER DEAD ONCE AND THEN MAYBE NOT DEAD BUT YOUNGER AND MARRIED. COULD HAVE KNOCKED ME OVER WITH A FEATHER WHEN I HEARD THAT.
AND TWO MISSING KIDS. DON'T FORGET THAT.
NO, OF COURSE NOT. I'M NOT TRYING TO DIMINISH WHAT YOU'RE GOING THROUGH.
BIGBY WILL FIND THEM. THAT NEW CAR OF MINE IS AMAZING. IT CAN GO ANYWHERE.
IF I WERE LOST AND IN NEED OF RESCUE, BIGBY'S THE ONE PERSON IN ALL OF THE ENDLESS WORLDS I'D WANT LOOKING FOR ME.
I NEED TO BE HOME, IN CASE THEY'RE TRYING TO REACH ME THERE.
THEN HOME YOU SHALL BE. IT'S STUPID WAITING AROUND FOR THAT DIRTY OLD DELIVERY TRUCK WHEN I CAN JUST GIVE YOU MY CAR.
EXCEPT THAT YOU ALREADY GAVE IT TO BIGBY.
RIGHT, SO I'LL BUY A NEW ONE. I ONLY NEED TO SCRAPE TOGETHER ENOUGH CASH TO BUY A SINGLE LOTTERY TICKET AND I'LL BE RICH AGAIN BY THIS EVENING.
AS LONG AS I'M ETERNALLY BLESSED WITH WEALTH, I CAN'T THINK OF A BETTER USE FOR IT.

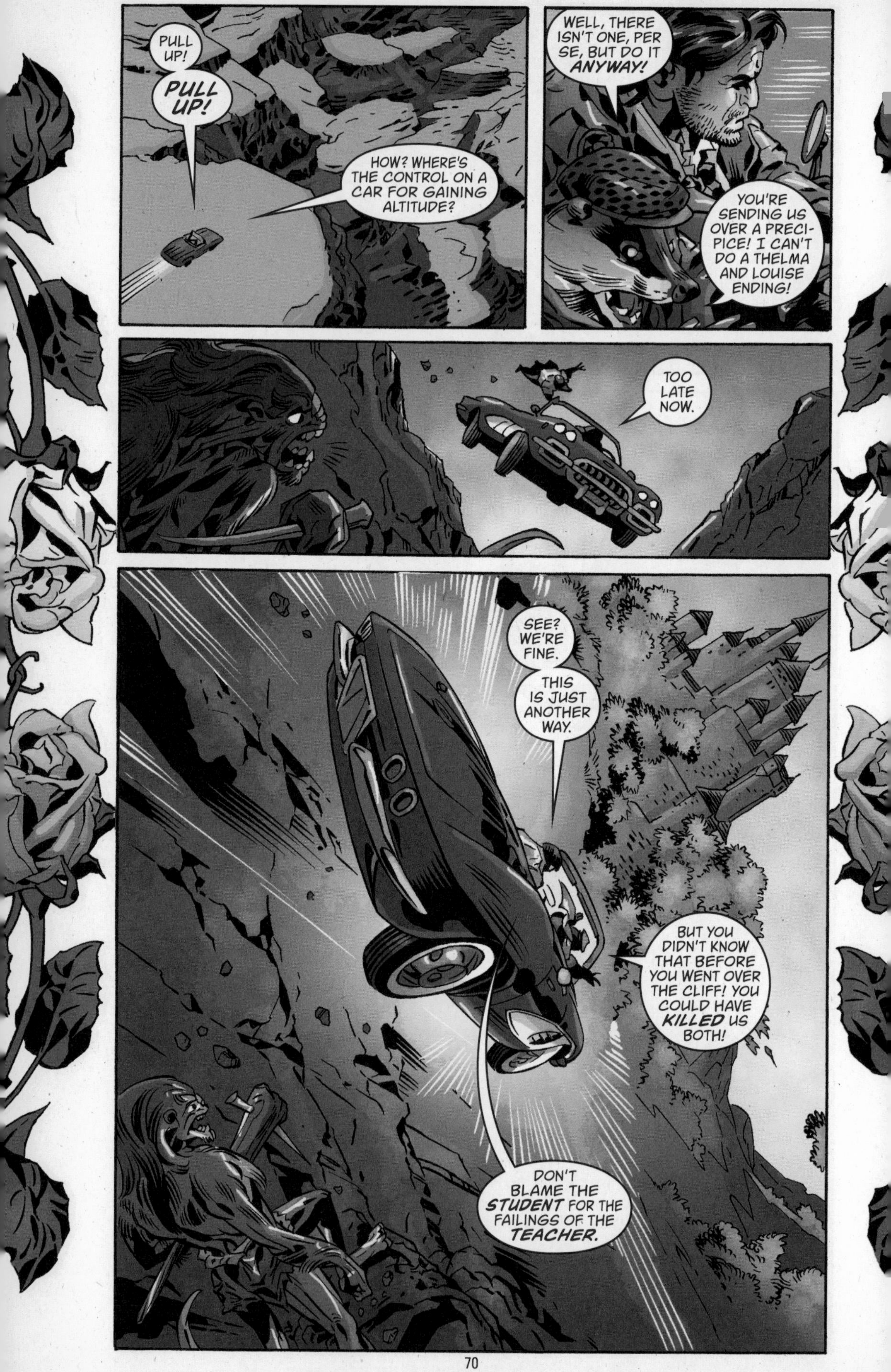
PULL UP!
PULL UP!
HOW? WHERE'S THE CONTROL ON A CAR FOR GAINING ALTITUDE?
WELL, THERE ISN'T ONE, PER SE, BUT DO IT ANYWAY!
YOU'RE SENDING US OVER A PRECI-PICE! I CAN'T DO A THELMA AND LOUISE ENDING!
TOO LATE NOW.
SEE? WE'RE FINE.
THIS IS JUST ANOTHER WAY.
BUT YOU DIDN'T KNOW THAT BEFORE YOU WENT OVER THE CLIFF! YOU COULD HAVE KILLED US BOTH!
DON'T BLAME THE STUDENT FOR THE FAILINGS OF THE TEACHER.

I'M BEGINNING TO GET IT BACK.

THE OLD SKILLS.

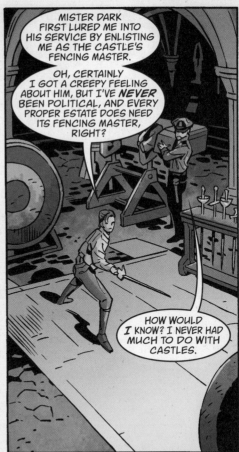

MISTER DARK FIRST LURED ME INTO HIS SERVICE BY ENLISTING ME AS THE CASTLE'S FENCING MASTER.

OH, CERTAINLY I GOT A CREEPY FEELING ABOUT HIM, BUT I'VE *NEVER* BEEN POLITICAL, AND EVERY PROPER ESTATE DOES NEED ITS FENCING MASTER, RIGHT?

HOW WOULD *I* KNOW? I NEVER HAD MUCH TO DO WITH CASTLES.

I WAS BASICALLY A BRIDGE TROLL UNTIL I CROSSED OVER TO THE MUNDY WORLD.

WELL, TRUST ME, SQUIRE GRIMBLE. IT WOULD BE A *SCANDAL* NOT TO HAVE ONE.

I NEED MORE THAN THIS, THOUGH.

A THOUSAND PRACTICE LUNGES A DAY ARE HELPING ME GET MY LEGS AND WRIST BACK, BUT IT'S NOT ENOUGH.

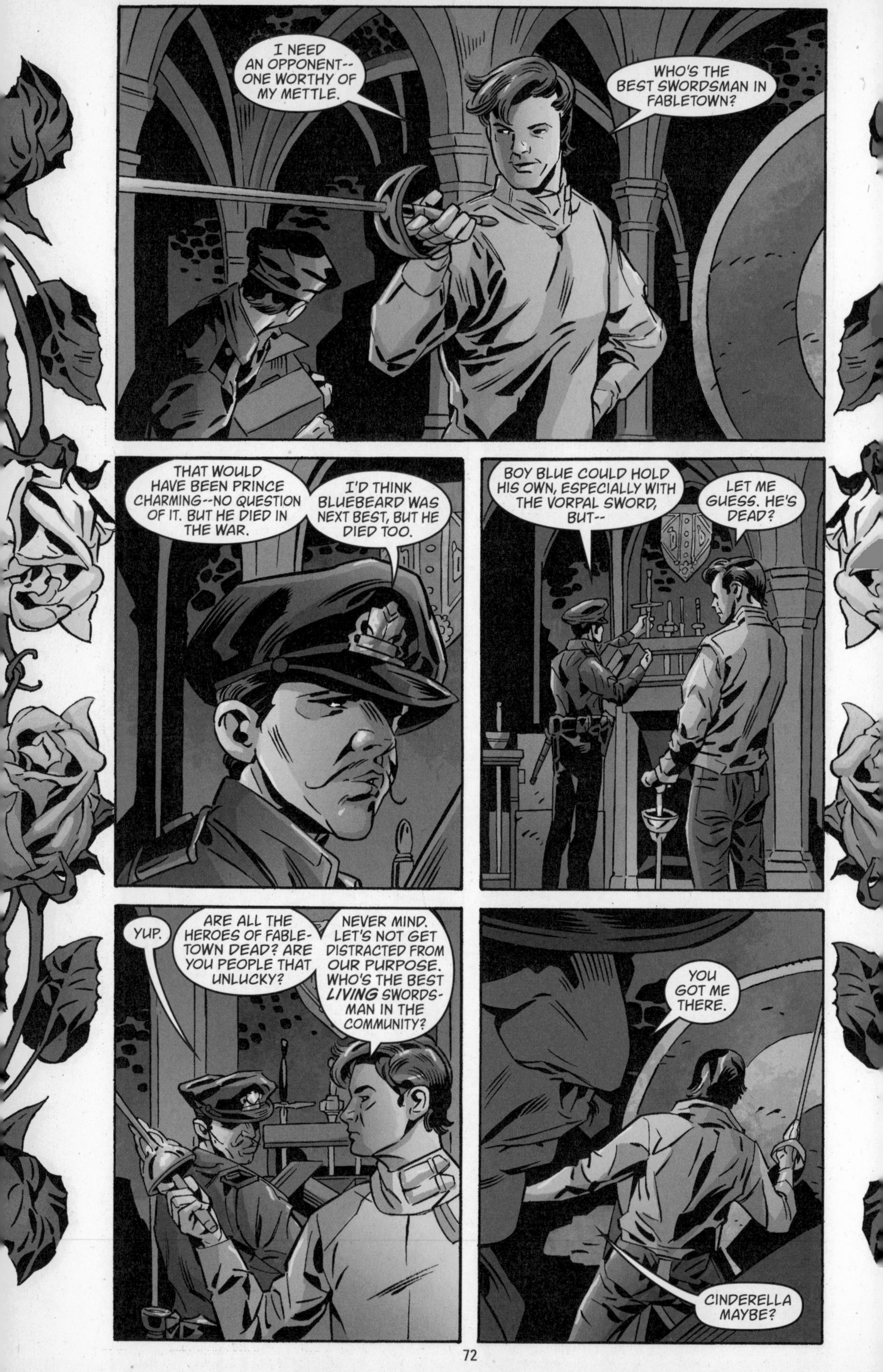
I NEED AN OPPONENT-- ONE WORTHY OF MY METTLE.
WHO'S THE BEST SWORDSMAN IN FABLETOWN?
THAT WOULD HAVE BEEN PRINCE CHARMING--NO QUESTION OF IT. BUT HE DIED IN THE WAR.
I'D THINK BLUEBEARD WAS NEXT BEST, BUT HE DIED TOO.
BOY BLUE COULD HOLD HIS OWN, ESPECIALLY WITH THE VORPAL SWORD, BUT--
LET ME GUESS. HE'S DEAD?
YUP.
ARE ALL THE HEROES OF FABLE-TOWN DEAD? ARE YOU PEOPLE THAT UNLUCKY?
NEVER MIND. LET'S NOT GET DISTRACTED FROM OUR PURPOSE. WHO'S THE BEST LIVING SWORDS-MAN IN THE COMMUNITY?
YOU GOT ME THERE.
CINDERELLA MAYBE?

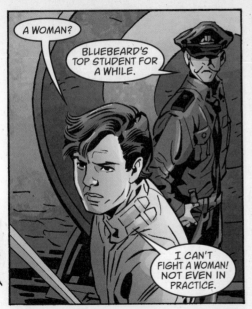

A WOMAN?

BLUEBEARD'S TOP STUDENT FOR A WHILE.

I CAN'T FIGHT A WOMAN! NOT EVEN IN PRACTICE.

WAIT. WHAT WAS I THINKING?

EDDIE DANTÈS USED TO RUN THE FENCING SCHOOL. THAT HAS TO MEAN HE'S PRETTY GOOD, WOULDN'T YOU THINK?

WANT ME TO FIND HIM?

WOULD YOU, PLEASE?

SURE. NO PROBLEM.

BUT MAYBE FIRST, YOU SHOULD EXPLAIN A THING OR TWO.

HOW IS IT YOU HAPPEN TO HAVE A SWORD THAT CAN MAGICALLY *CHANGE* FROM ONE TYPE OF SWORD TO ANOTHER, AT LEAST THREE TIMES WHILE I'VE BEEN WATCHING YOU?

I HAVE NO IDEA. I SIMPLY SELECTED ONE FROM THE RACKS TO PRACTICE. I ASSUMED IT WAS SOME SORT OF CLEVER MAGICAL TRAINING BLADE.

A TOOL TO GET A MAN USED TO FIGHTING WITH DIFFERENT WEAPONS, WITH VARYING WEIGHTS AND BALANCES AND SUCH.

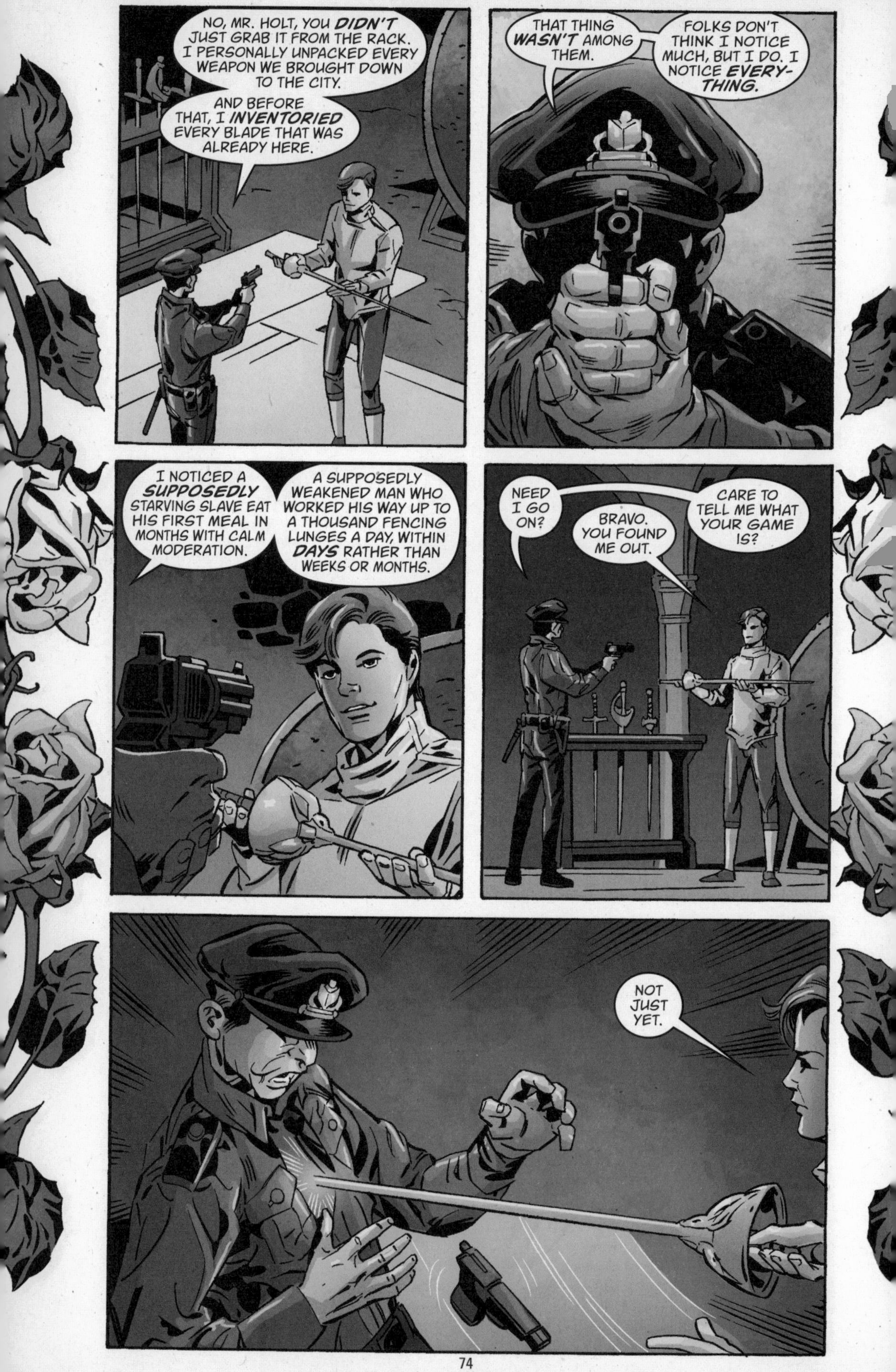
NO, MR. HOLT, YOU DIDN'T JUST GRAB IT FROM THE RACK. I PERSONALLY UNPACKED EVERY WEAPON WE BROUGHT DOWN TO THE CITY.
AND BEFORE THAT, I INVENTORIED EVERY BLADE THAT WAS ALREADY HERE.
THAT THING WASN'T AMONG THEM.
FOLKS DON'T THINK I NOTICE MUCH, BUT I DO. I NOTICE EVERYTHING.
I NOTICED A SUPPOSEDLY STARVING SLAVE EAT HIS FIRST MEAL IN MONTHS WITH CALM MODERATION.
A SUPPOSEDLY WEAKENED MAN WHO WORKED HIS WAY UP TO A THOUSAND FENCING LUNGES A DAY, WITHIN DAYS RATHER THAN WEEKS OR MONTHS.
NEED I GO ON?
BRAVO. YOU FOUND ME OUT.
CARE TO TELL ME WHAT YOUR GAME IS?
NOT JUST YET.

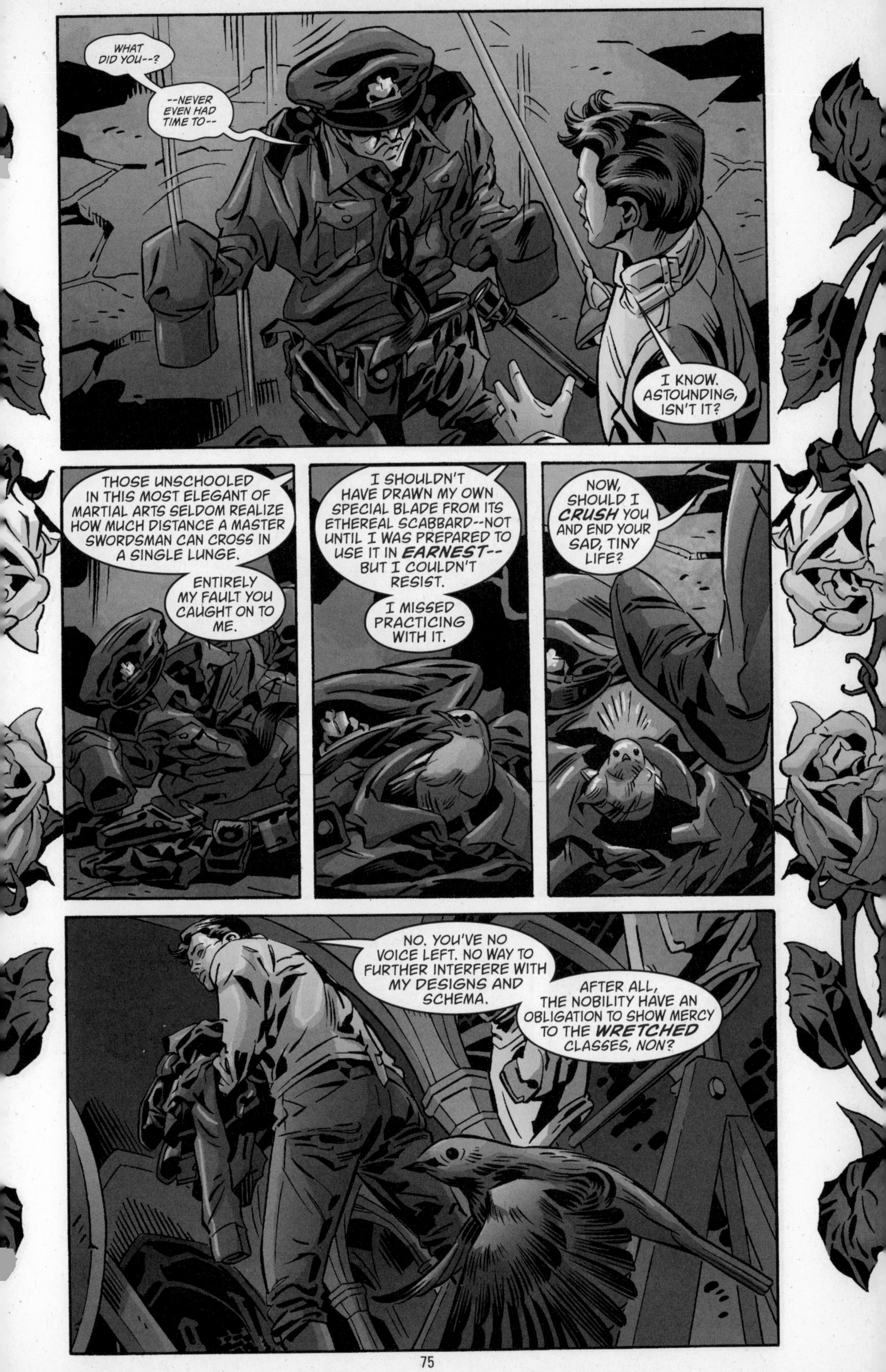
WHAT DID YOU--?
--NEVER EVEN HAD TIME TO--
I KNOW. ASTOUNDING, ISN'T IT?
THOSE UNSCHOOLED IN THIS MOST ELEGANT OF MARTIAL ARTS SELDOM REALIZE HOW MUCH DISTANCE A MASTER SWORDSMAN CAN CROSS IN A SINGLE LUNGE.
ENTIRELY MY FAULT YOU CAUGHT ON TO ME.
I SHOULDN'T HAVE DRAWN MY OWN SPECIAL BLADE FROM ITS ETHEREAL SCABBARD--NOT UNTIL I WAS PREPARED TO USE IT IN EARNEST--BUT I COULDN'T RESIST.
I MISSED PRACTICING WITH IT.
NOW, SHOULD I CRUSH YOU AND END YOUR SAD, TINY LIFE?
NO. YOU'VE NO VOICE LEFT. NO WAY TO FURTHER INTERFERE WITH MY DESIGNS AND SCHEMA.
AFTER ALL, THE NOBILITY HAVE AN OBLIGATION TO SHOW MERCY TO THE WRETCHED CLASSES, NON?

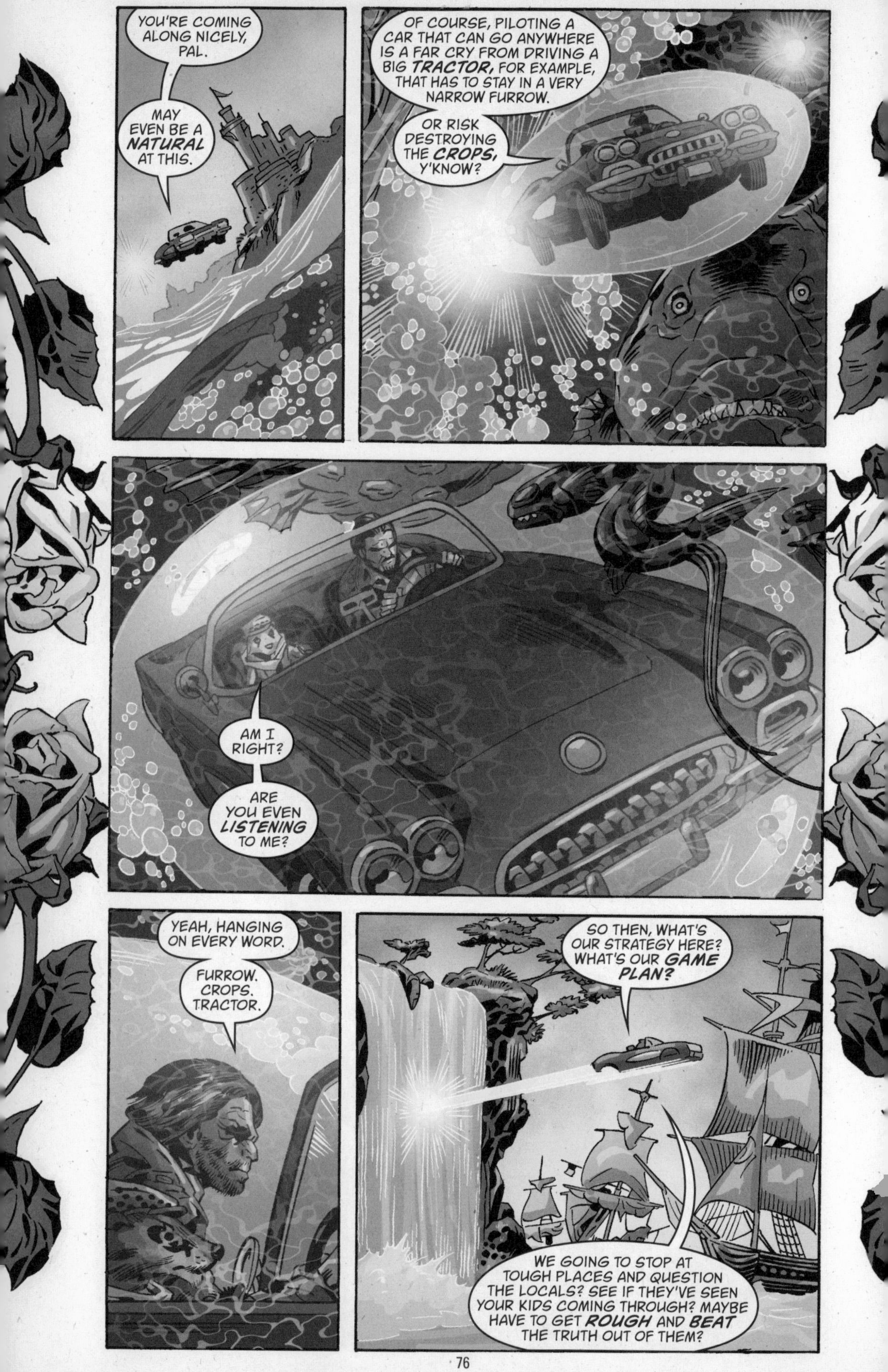
YOU'RE COMING ALONG NICELY, PAL.
MAY EVEN BE A NATURAL AT THIS.
OF COURSE, PILOTING A CAR THAT CAN GO ANYWHERE IS A FAR CRY FROM DRIVING A BIG TRACTOR, FOR EXAMPLE, THAT HAS TO STAY IN A VERY NARROW FURROW.
OR RISK DESTROYING THE CROPS, Y'KNOW?
AM I RIGHT?
ARE YOU EVEN LISTENING TO ME?
YEAH, HANGING ON EVERY WORD.
FURROW. CROPS. TRACTOR.
SO THEN, WHAT'S OUR STRATEGY HERE? WHAT'S OUR GAME PLAN?
WE GOING TO STOP AT TOUGH PLACES AND QUESTION THE LOCALS? SEE IF THEY'VE SEEN YOUR KIDS COMING THROUGH? MAYBE HAVE TO GET ROUGH AND BEAT THE TRUTH OUT OF THEM?

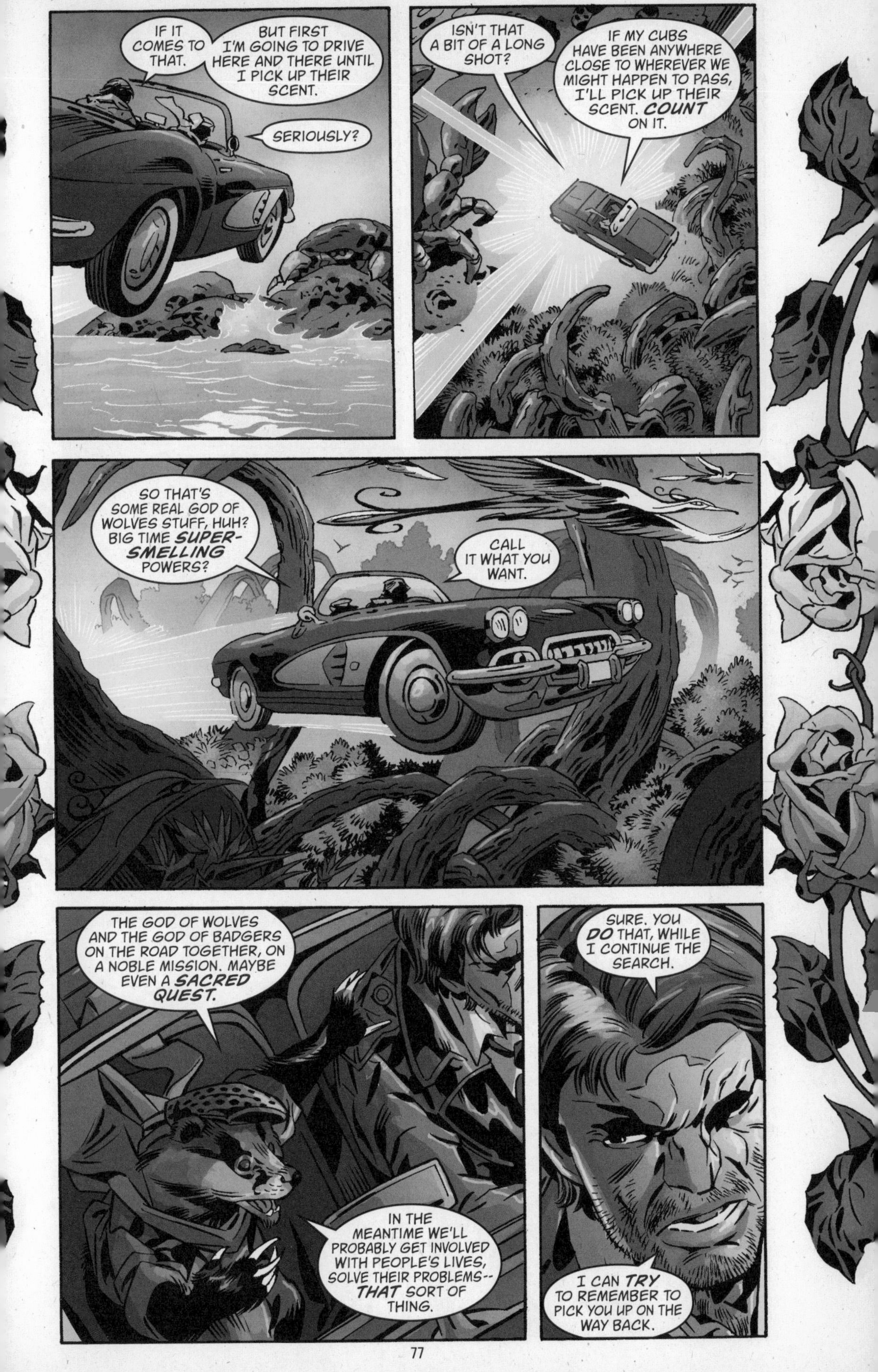

IF IT COMES TO THAT.
BUT FIRST I'M GOING TO DRIVE HERE AND THERE UNTIL I PICK UP THEIR SCENT.
SERIOUSLY?
ISN'T THAT A BIT OF A LONG SHOT?
IF MY CUBS HAVE BEEN ANYWHERE CLOSE TO WHEREVER WE MIGHT HAPPEN TO PASS, I'LL PICK UP THEIR SCENT. COUNT ON IT.
SO THAT'S SOME REAL GOD OF WOLVES STUFF, HUH? BIG TIME SUPER-SMELLING POWERS?
CALL IT WHAT YOU WANT.
THE GOD OF WOLVES AND THE GOD OF BADGERS ON THE ROAD TOGETHER, ON A NOBLE MISSION. MAYBE EVEN A SACRED QUEST.
IN THE MEANTIME WE'LL PROBABLY GET INVOLVED WITH PEOPLE'S LIVES, SOLVE THEIR PROBLEMS-- THAT SORT OF THING.
SURE. YOU DO THAT, WHILE I CONTINUE THE SEARCH.
I CAN TRY TO REMEMBER TO PICK YOU UP ON THE WAY BACK.

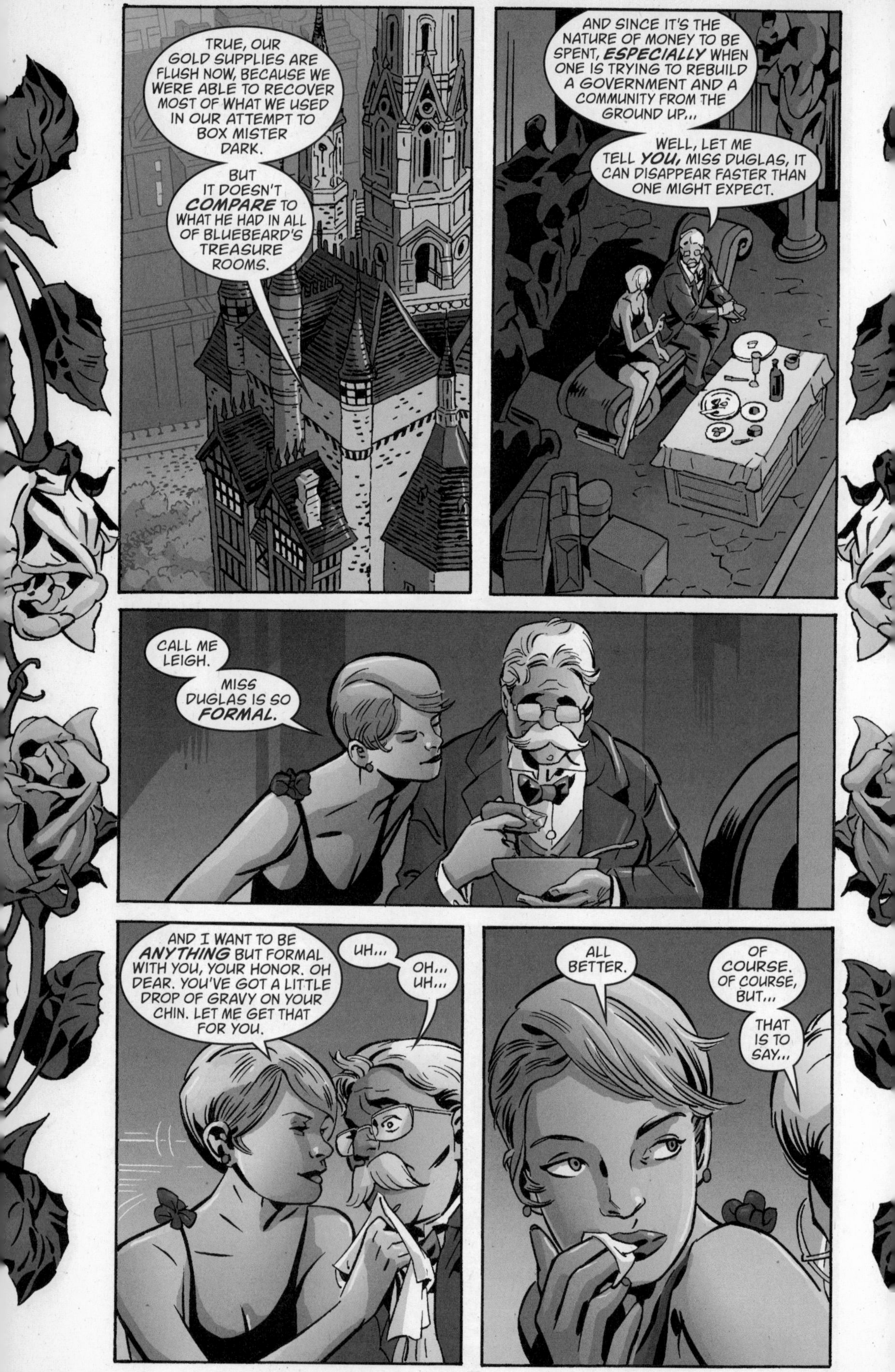

TRUE, OUR GOLD SUPPLIES ARE FLUSH NOW, BECAUSE WE WERE ABLE TO RECOVER MOST OF WHAT WE USED IN OUR ATTEMPT TO BOX MISTER DARK.
BUT IT DOESN'T COMPARE TO WHAT HE HAD IN ALL OF BLUEBEARD'S TREASURE ROOMS.
AND SINCE IT'S THE NATURE OF MONEY TO BE SPENT, ESPECIALLY WHEN ONE IS TRYING TO REBUILD A GOVERNMENT AND A COMMUNITY FROM THE GROUND UP...
WELL, LET ME TELL YOU, MISS DUGLAS, IT CAN DISAPPEAR FASTER THAN ONE MIGHT EXPECT.
CALL ME LEIGH.
MISS DUGLAS IS SO FORMAL.
AND I WANT TO BE ANYTHING BUT FORMAL WITH YOU, YOUR HONOR. OH DEAR. YOU'VE GOT A LITTLE DROP OF GRAVY ON YOUR CHIN. LET ME GET THAT FOR YOU.
UH...
OH... UH...
ALL BETTER.
OF COURSE. OF COURSE, BUT...
THAT IS TO SAY...

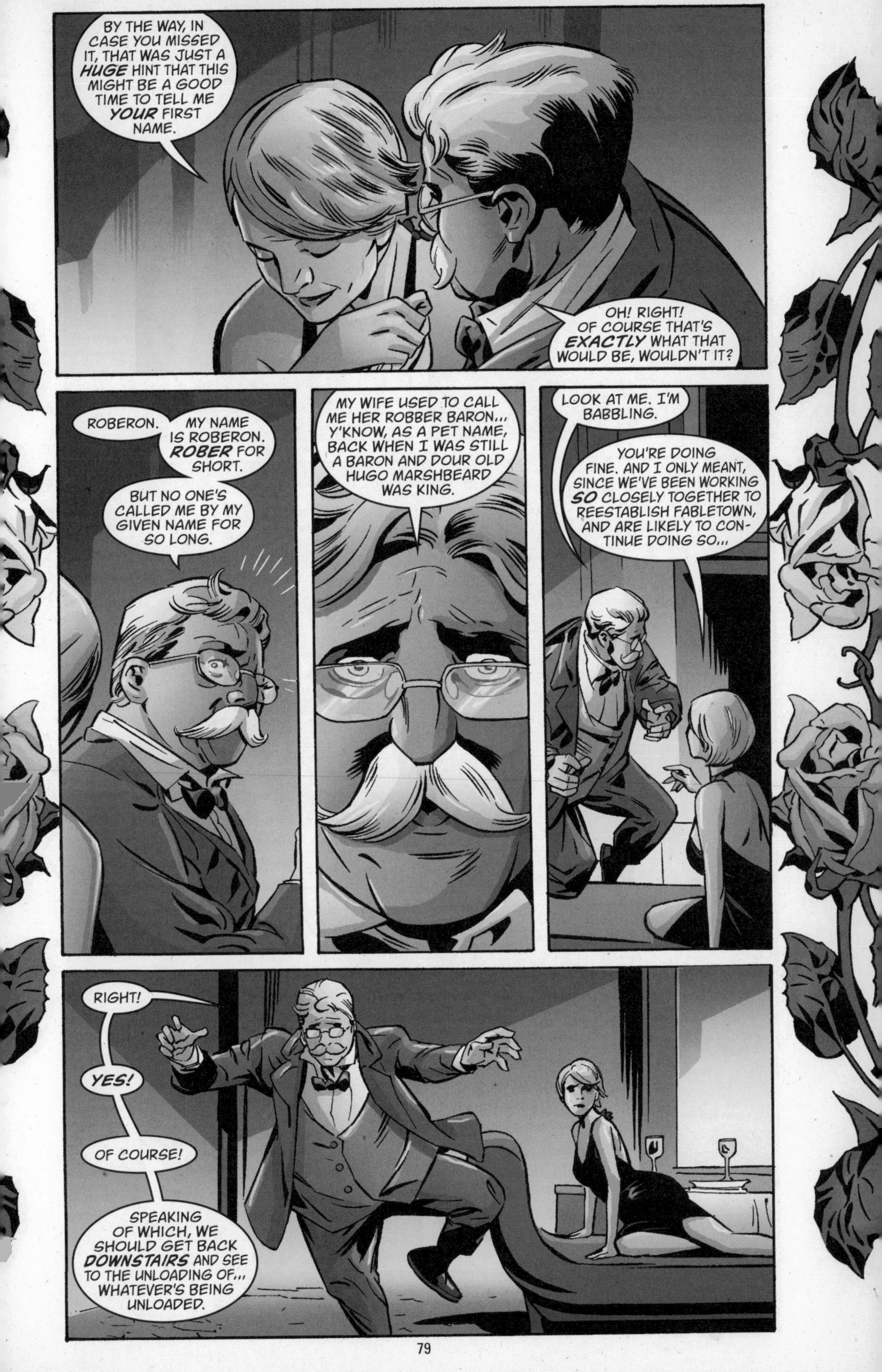
BY THE WAY, IN CASE YOU MISSED IT, THAT WAS JUST A HUGE HINT THAT THIS MIGHT BE A GOOD TIME TO TELL ME YOUR FIRST NAME.
OH! RIGHT! OF COURSE THAT'S EXACTLY WHAT THAT WOULD BE, WOULDN'T IT?
ROBERON.
MY NAME IS ROBERON. ROBER FOR SHORT.
BUT NO ONE'S CALLED ME BY MY GIVEN NAME FOR SO LONG.
MY WIFE USED TO CALL ME HER ROBBER BARON... Y'KNOW, AS A PET NAME, BACK WHEN I WAS STILL A BARON AND DOUR OLD HUGO MARSHBEARD WAS KING.
LOOK AT ME. I'M BABBLING.
YOU'RE DOING FINE. AND I ONLY MEANT, SINCE WE'VE BEEN WORKING SO CLOSELY TOGETHER TO REESTABLISH FABLETOWN, AND ARE LIKELY TO CONTINUE DOING SO...
RIGHT!
YES!
OF COURSE!
SPEAKING OF WHICH, WE SHOULD GET BACK DOWNSTAIRS AND SEE TO THE UNLOADING OF... WHATEVER'S BEING UNLOADED.

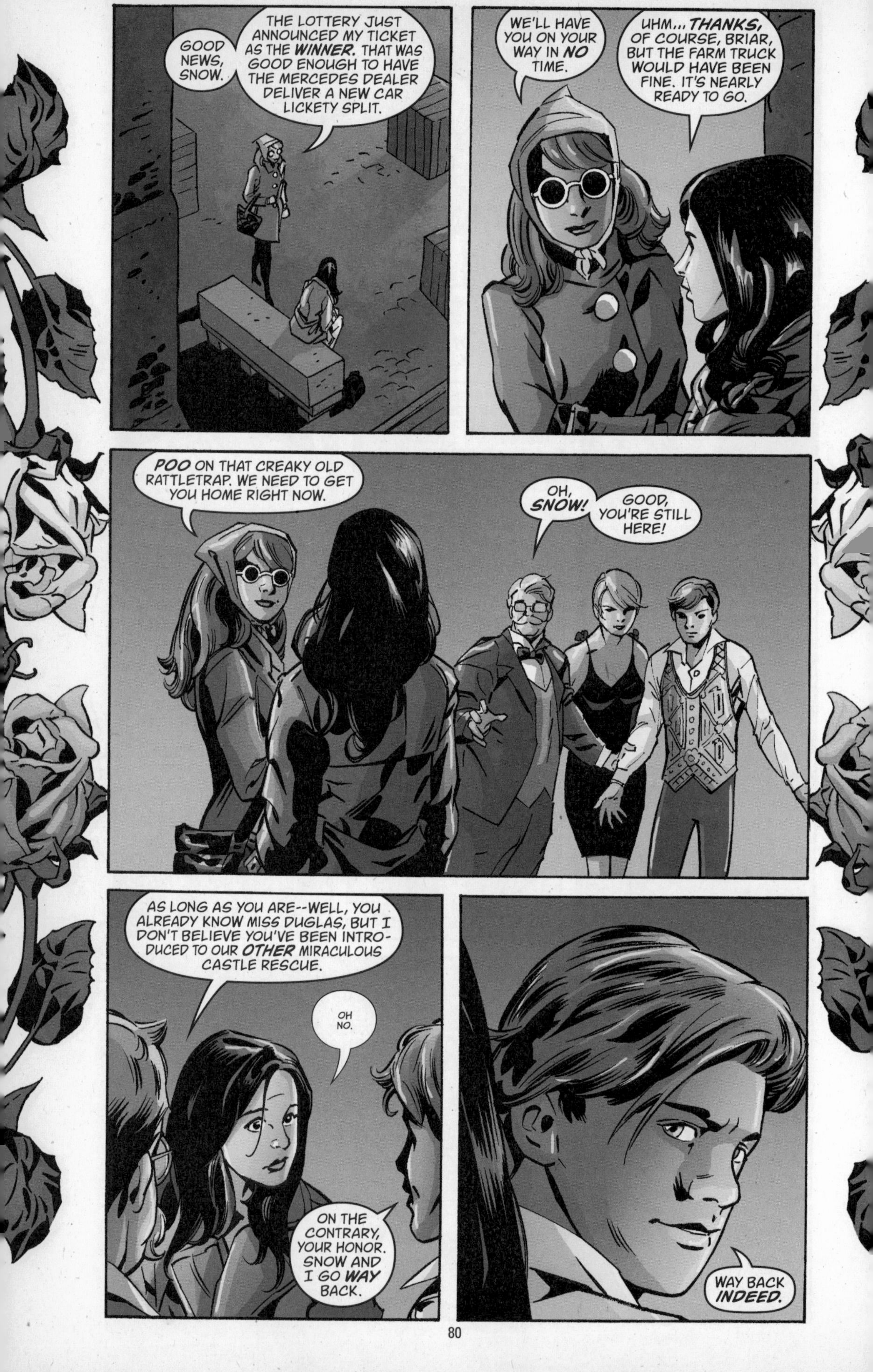
GOOD NEWS, SNOW.
THE LOTTERY JUST ANNOUNCED MY TICKET AS THE WINNER. THAT WAS GOOD ENOUGH TO HAVE THE MERCEDES DEALER DELIVER A NEW CAR LICKETY SPLIT.
WE'LL HAVE YOU ON YOUR WAY IN NO TIME.
UHM... THANKS, OF COURSE, BRIAR, BUT THE FARM TRUCK WOULD HAVE BEEN FINE. IT'S NEARLY READY TO GO.
POO ON THAT CREAKY OLD RATTLETRAP. WE NEED TO GET YOU HOME RIGHT NOW.
OH, SNOW!
GOOD, YOU'RE STILL HERE!
AS LONG AS YOU ARE--WELL, YOU ALREADY KNOW MISS DUGLAS, BUT I DON'T BELIEVE YOU'VE BEEN INTRO-DUCED TO OUR OTHER MIRACULOUS CASTLE RESCUE.
OH NO.
ON THE CONTRARY, YOUR HONOR. SNOW AND I GO WAY BACK.
WAY BACK INDEED.

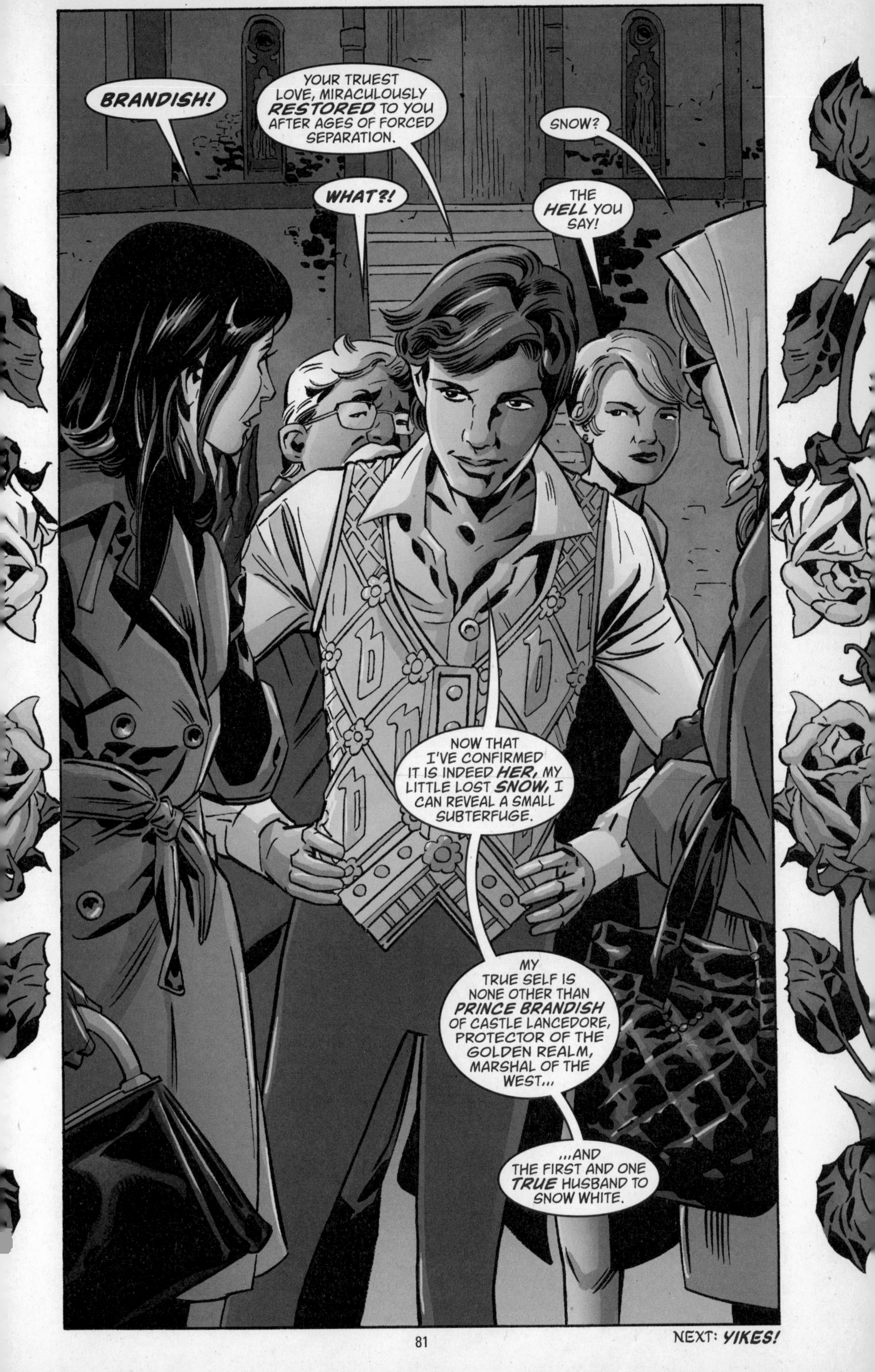
BRANDISH!
YOUR TRUEST LOVE, MIRACULOUSLY RESTORED TO YOU AFTER AGES OF FORCED SEPARATION.
SNOW?
WHAT?!
THE HELL YOU SAY!
NOW THAT I'VE CONFIRMED IT IS INDEED HER, MY LITTLE LOST SNOW, I CAN REVEAL A SMALL SUBTERFUGE.
MY TRUE SELF IS NONE OTHER THAN PRINCE BRANDISH OF CASTLE LANCEDORE, PROTECTOR OF THE GOLDEN REALM, MARSHAL OF THE WEST...
...AND THE FIRST AND ONE TRUE HUSBAND TO SNOW WHITE.

NEXT: ***YIKES!***

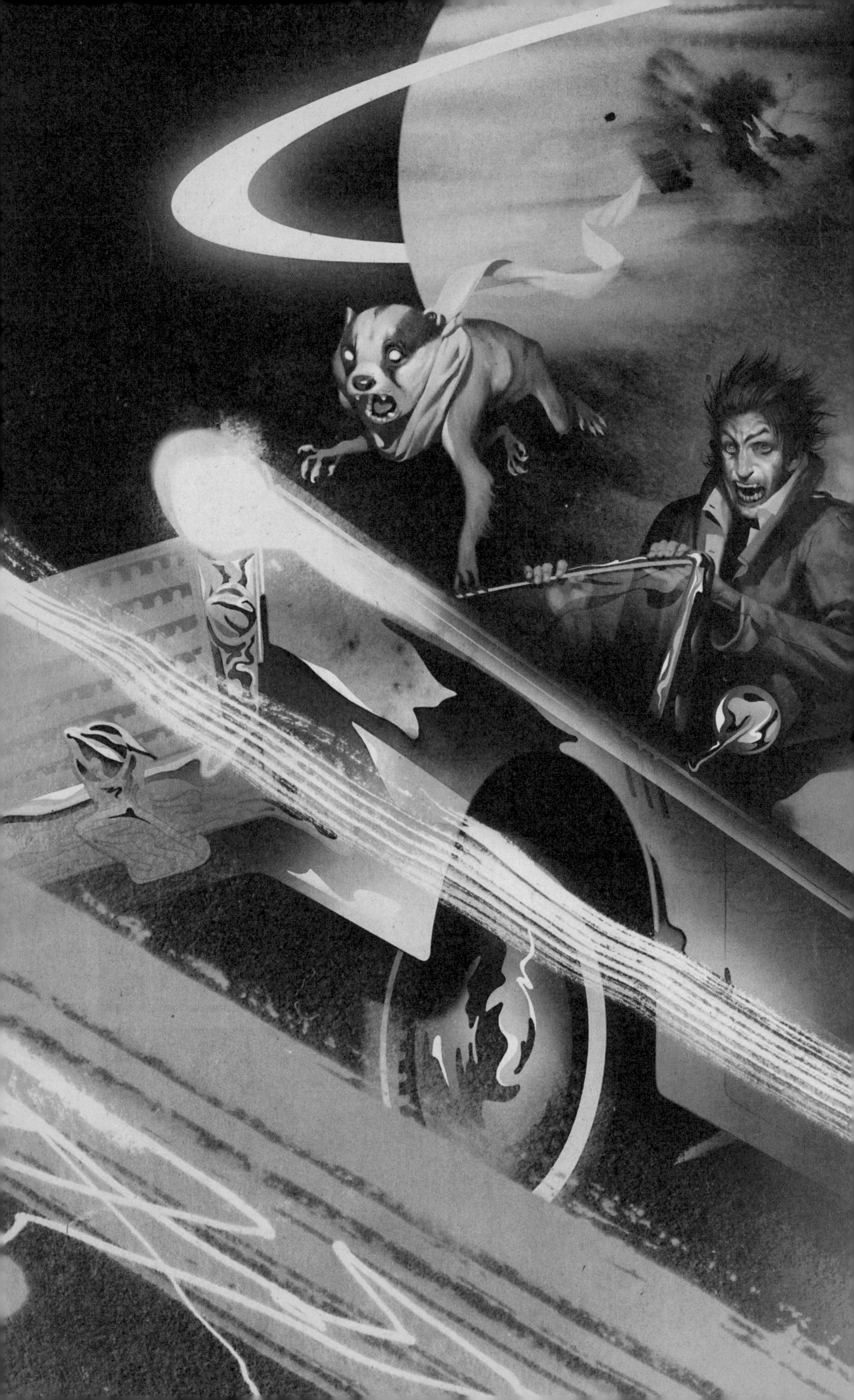

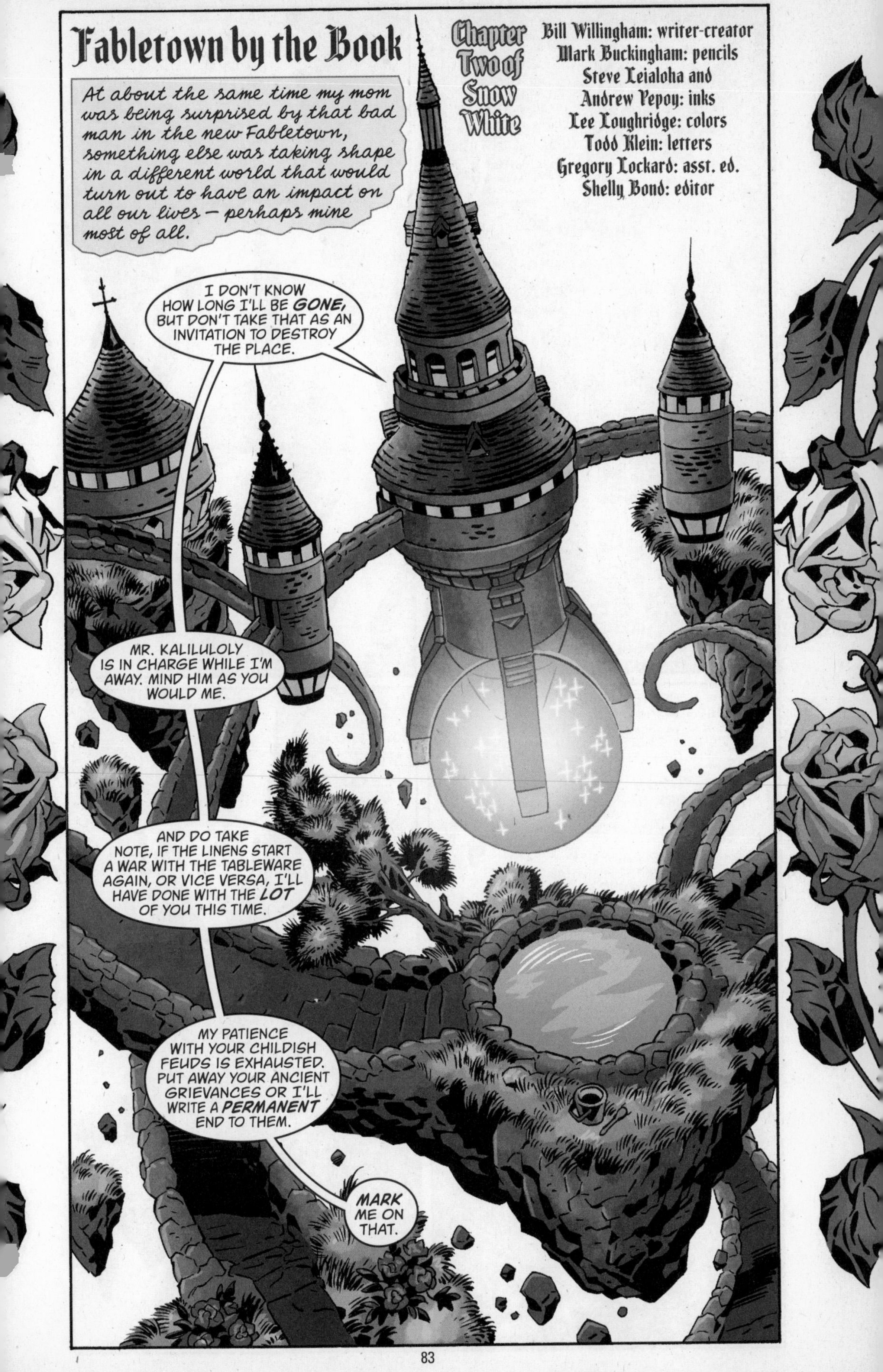

Fabletown by the Book
Chapter Two of Snow White
Bill Willingham: writer-creator
Mark Buckingham: pencils
Steve Leialoha and
Andrew Pepoy: inks
Lee Loughridge: colors
Todd Klein: letters
Gregory Lockard: asst. ed.
Shelly Bond: editor
At about the same time my mom was being surprised by that bad man in the new Fabletown, something else was taking shape in a different world that would turn out to have an impact on all our lives — perhaps mine most of all.
I DON'T KNOW HOW LONG I'LL BE GONE, BUT DON'T TAKE THAT AS AN INVITATION TO DESTROY THE PLACE.
MR. KALILULOLY IS IN CHARGE WHILE I'M AWAY. MIND HIM AS YOU WOULD ME.
AND DO TAKE NOTE, IF THE LINENS START A WAR WITH THE TABLEWARE AGAIN, OR VICE VERSA, I'LL HAVE DONE WITH THE LOT OF YOU THIS TIME.
MY PATIENCE WITH YOUR CHILDISH FEUDS IS EXHAUSTED. PUT AWAY YOUR ANCIENT GRIEVANCES OR I'LL WRITE A PERMANENT END TO THEM.
MARK ME ON THAT.

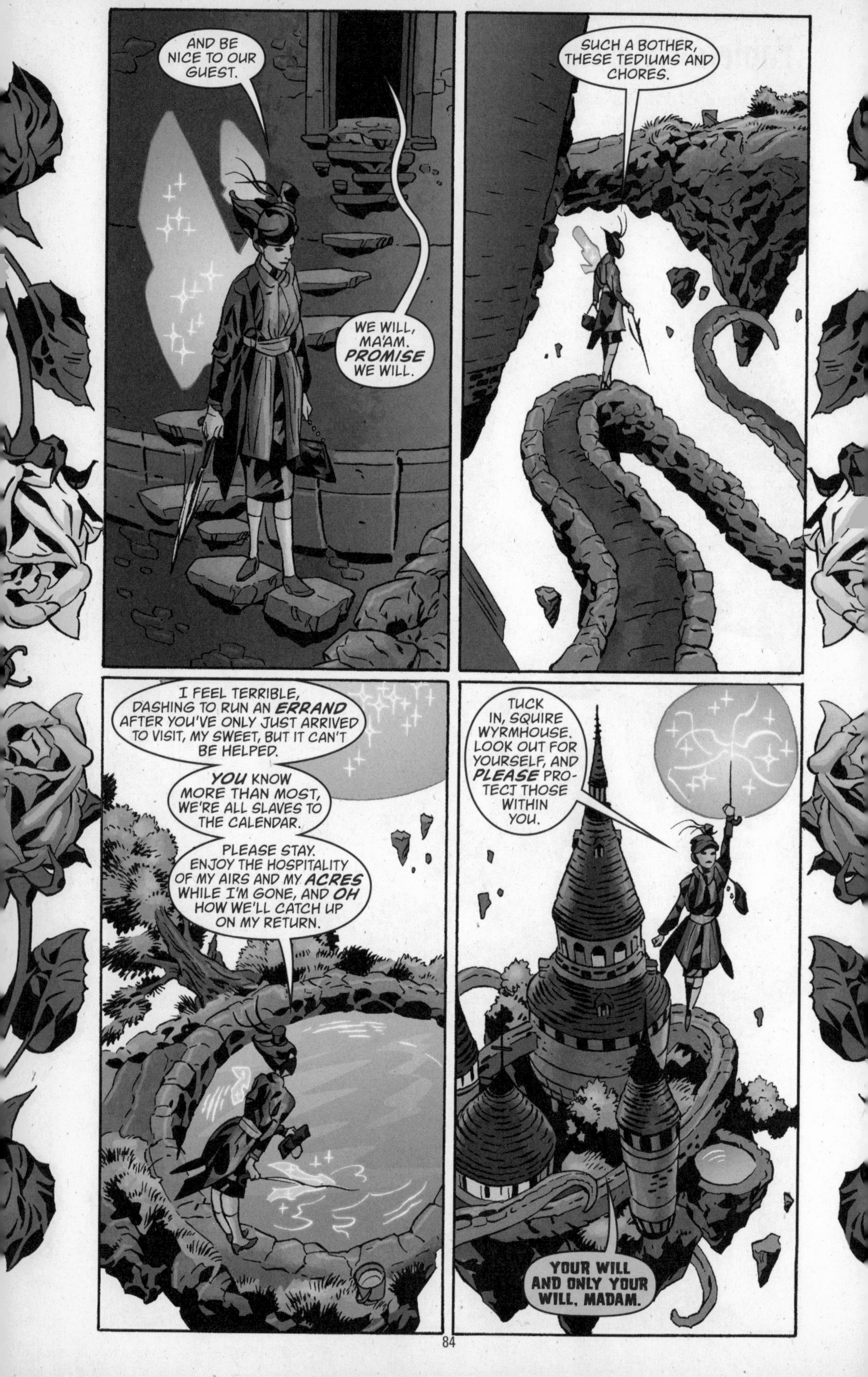
AND BE NICE TO OUR GUEST.
WE WILL, MA'AM. PROMISE WE WILL.
SUCH A BOTHER, THESE TEDIUMS AND CHORES.
I FEEL TERRIBLE, DASHING TO RUN AN ERRAND AFTER YOU'VE ONLY JUST ARRIVED TO VISIT, MY SWEET, BUT IT CAN'T BE HELPED.
YOU KNOW MORE THAN MOST, WE'RE ALL SLAVES TO THE CALENDAR.
PLEASE STAY. ENJOY THE HOSPITALITY OF MY AIRS AND MY ACRES WHILE I'M GONE, AND OH HOW WE'LL CATCH UP ON MY RETURN.
TUCK IN, SQUIRE WYRMHOUSE. LOOK OUT FOR YOURSELF, AND PLEASE PROTECT THOSE WITHIN YOU.
YOUR WILL AND ONLY YOUR WILL, MADAM.

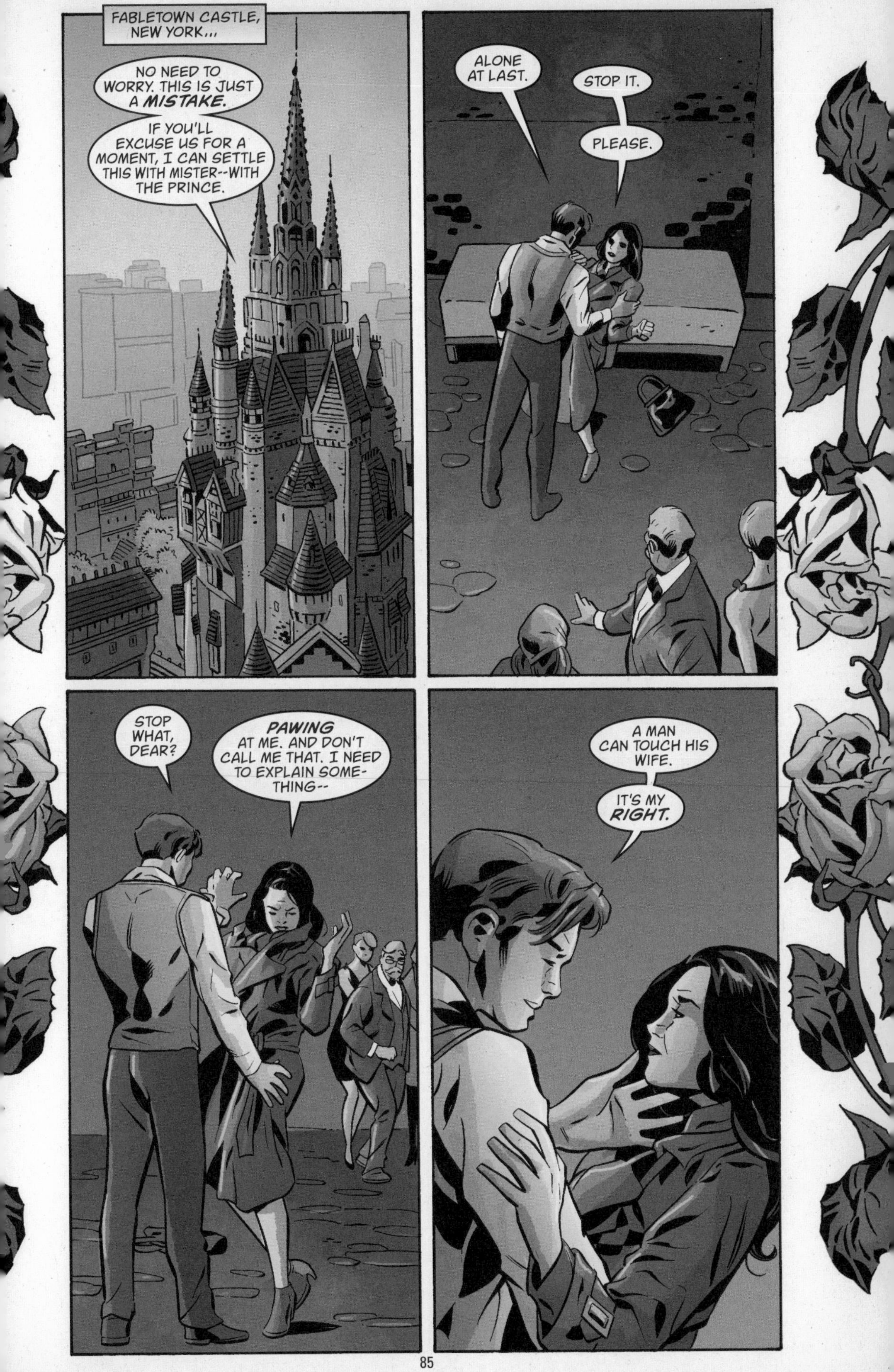
FABLETOWN CASTLE, NEW YORK...
NO NEED TO WORRY. THIS IS JUST A *MISTAKE.*
IF YOU'LL EXCUSE US FOR A MOMENT, I CAN SETTLE THIS WITH MISTER--WITH THE PRINCE.
ALONE AT LAST.
STOP IT.
PLEASE.
STOP WHAT, DEAR?
PAWING AT ME. AND DON'T CALL ME THAT. I NEED TO EXPLAIN SOME-THING--
A MAN CAN TOUCH HIS WIFE.
IT'S MY *RIGHT.*

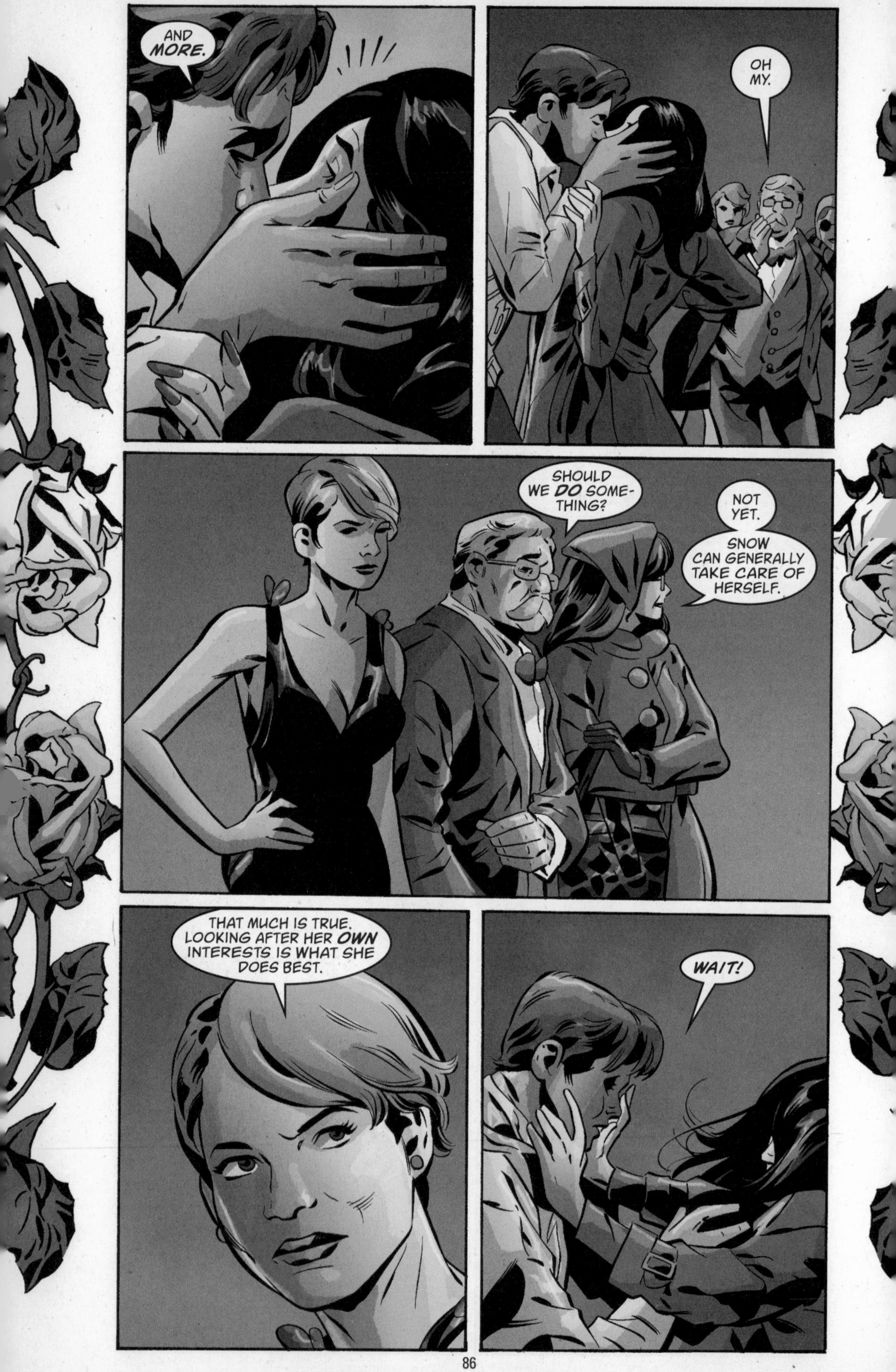
AND MORE.
OH MY.
SHOULD WE DO SOME-THING?
NOT YET.
SNOW CAN GENERALLY TAKE CARE OF HERSELF.
THAT MUCH IS TRUE. LOOKING AFTER HER OWN INTERESTS IS WHAT SHE DOES BEST.
WAIT!

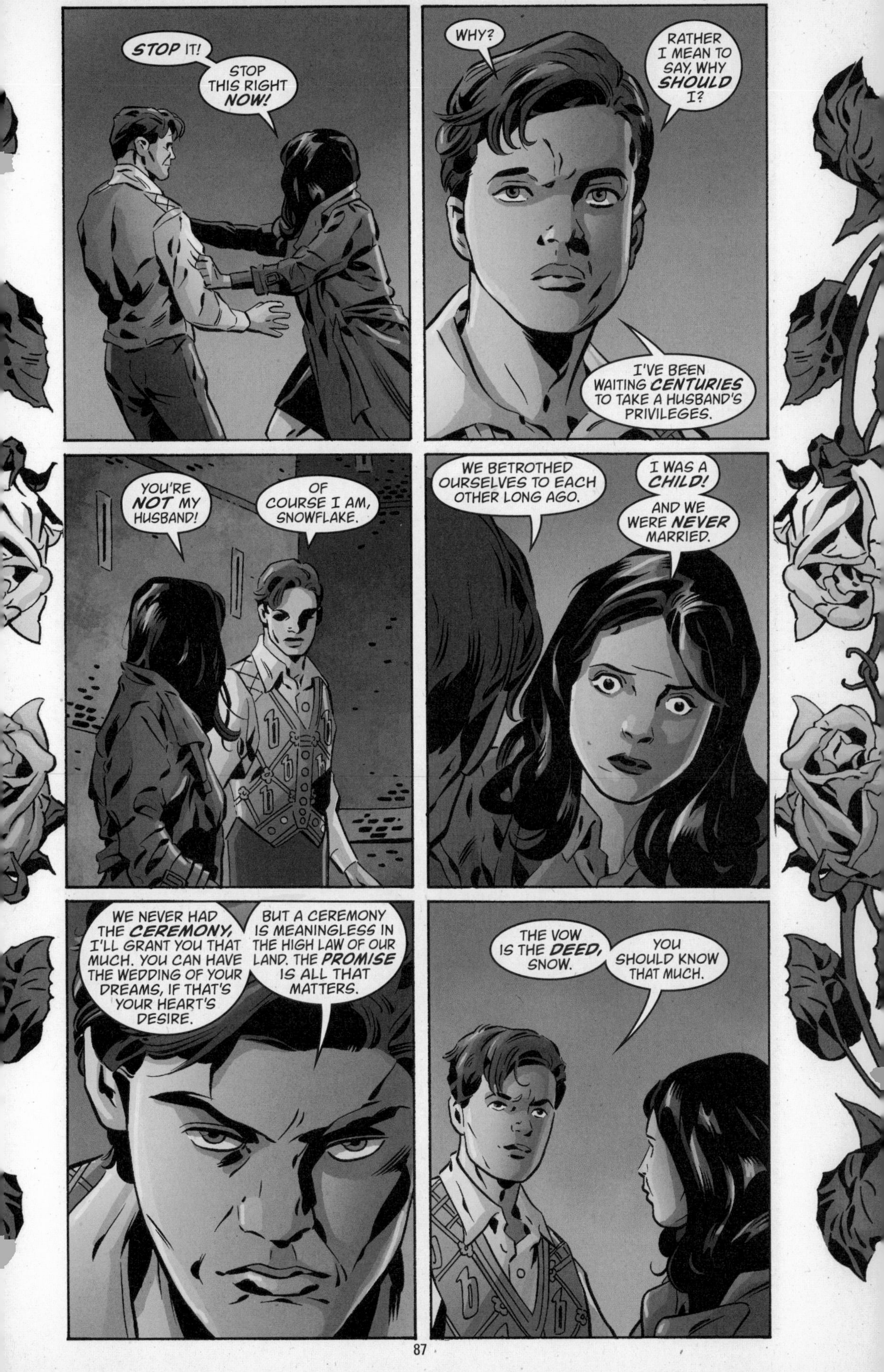
STOP IT!
STOP THIS RIGHT NOW!
WHY?
RATHER I MEAN TO SAY, WHY SHOULD I?
I'VE BEEN WAITING CENTURIES TO TAKE A HUSBAND'S PRIVILEGES.
YOU'RE NOT MY HUSBAND!
OF COURSE I AM, SNOWFLAKE.
WE BETROTHED OURSELVES TO EACH OTHER LONG AGO.
I WAS A CHILD!
AND WE WERE NEVER MARRIED.
WE NEVER HAD THE CEREMONY, I'LL GRANT YOU THAT MUCH. YOU CAN HAVE THE WEDDING OF YOUR DREAMS, IF THAT'S YOUR HEART'S DESIRE.
BUT A CEREMONY IS MEANINGLESS IN THE HIGH LAW OF OUR LAND. THE PROMISE IS ALL THAT MATTERS.
THE VOW IS THE DEED, SNOW.
YOU SHOULD KNOW THAT MUCH.

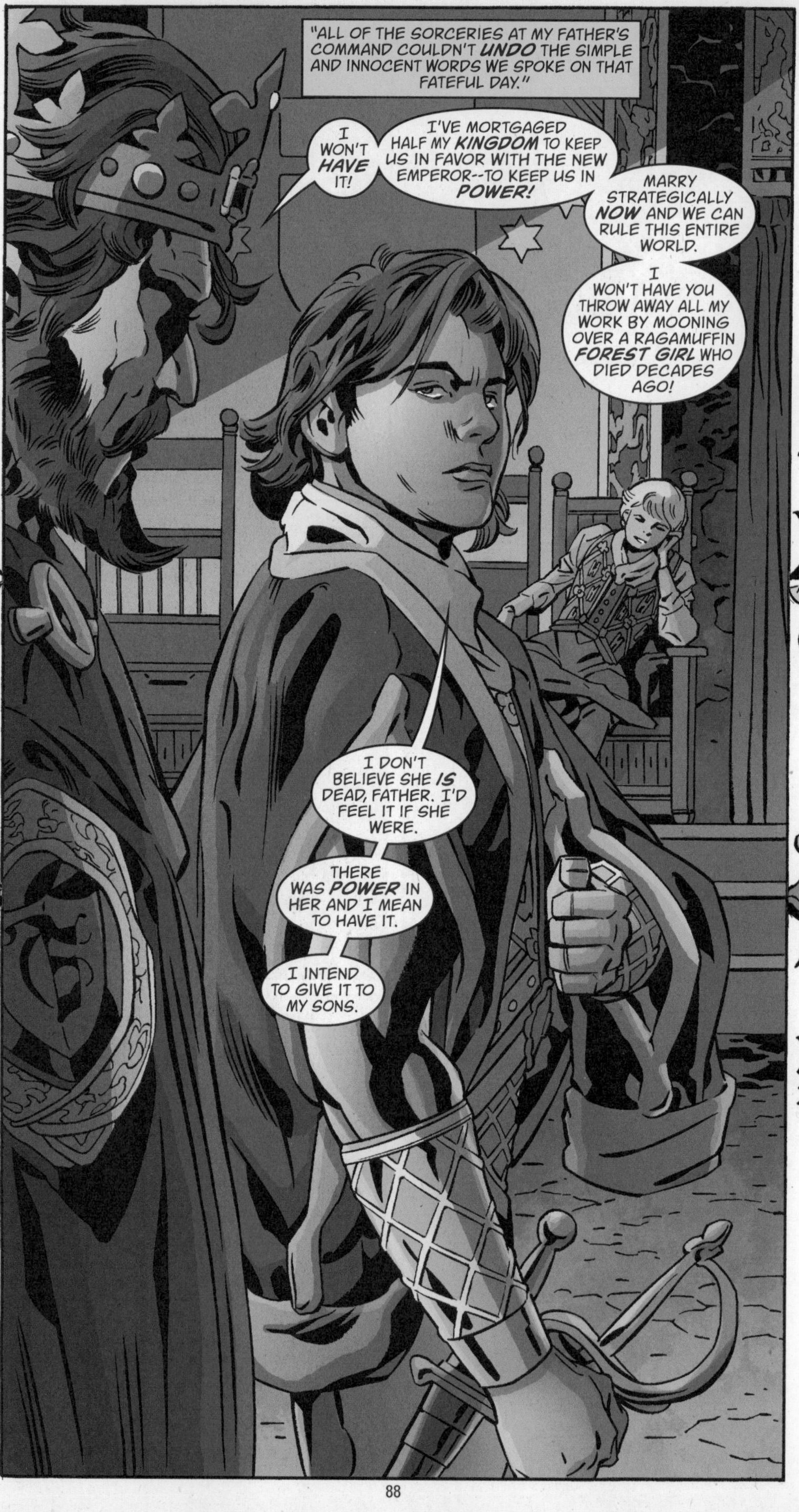
"ALL OF THE SORCERIES AT MY FATHER'S COMMAND COULDN'T UNDO THE SIMPLE AND INNOCENT WORDS WE SPOKE ON THAT FATEFUL DAY."
I WON'T HAVE IT!
I'VE MORTGAGED HALF MY KINGDOM TO KEEP US IN FAVOR WITH THE NEW EMPEROR--TO KEEP US IN POWER!
MARRY STRATEGICALLY NOW AND WE CAN RULE THIS ENTIRE WORLD.
I WON'T HAVE YOU THROW AWAY ALL MY WORK BY MOONING OVER A RAGAMUFFIN FOREST GIRL WHO DIED DECADES AGO!
I DON'T BELIEVE SHE IS DEAD, FATHER. I'D FEEL IT IF SHE WERE.
THERE WAS POWER IN HER AND I MEAN TO HAVE IT.
I INTEND TO GIVE IT TO MY SONS.

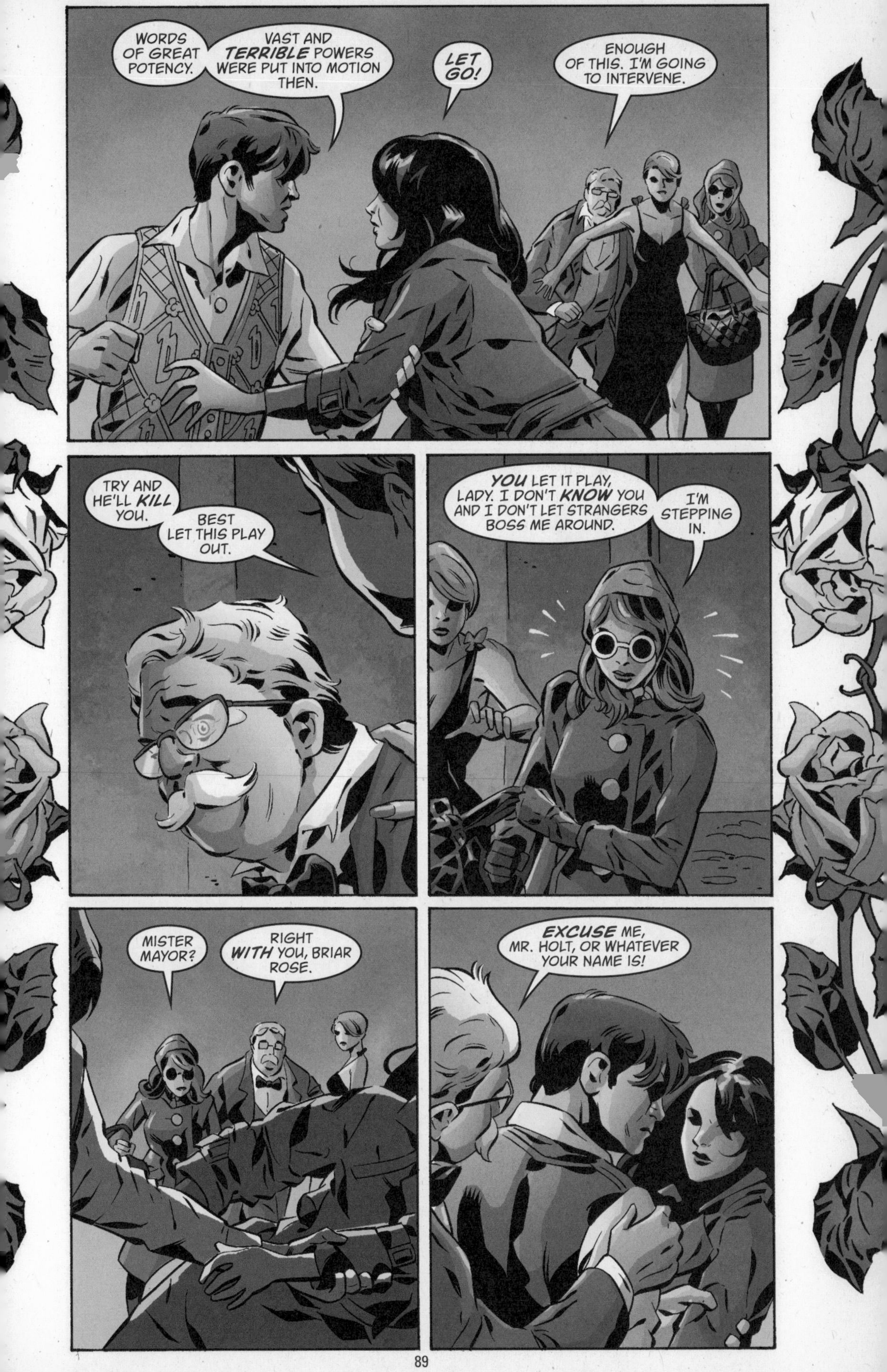
WORDS OF GREAT POTENCY.
VAST AND TERRIBLE POWERS WERE PUT INTO MOTION THEN.
LET GO!
ENOUGH OF THIS. I'M GOING TO INTERVENE.
TRY AND HE'LL KILL YOU.
BEST LET THIS PLAY OUT.
YOU LET IT PLAY, LADY. I DON'T KNOW YOU AND I DON'T LET STRANGERS BOSS ME AROUND.
I'M STEPPING IN.
MISTER MAYOR?
RIGHT WITH YOU, BRIAR ROSE.
EXCUSE ME, MR. HOLT, OR WHATEVER YOUR NAME IS!

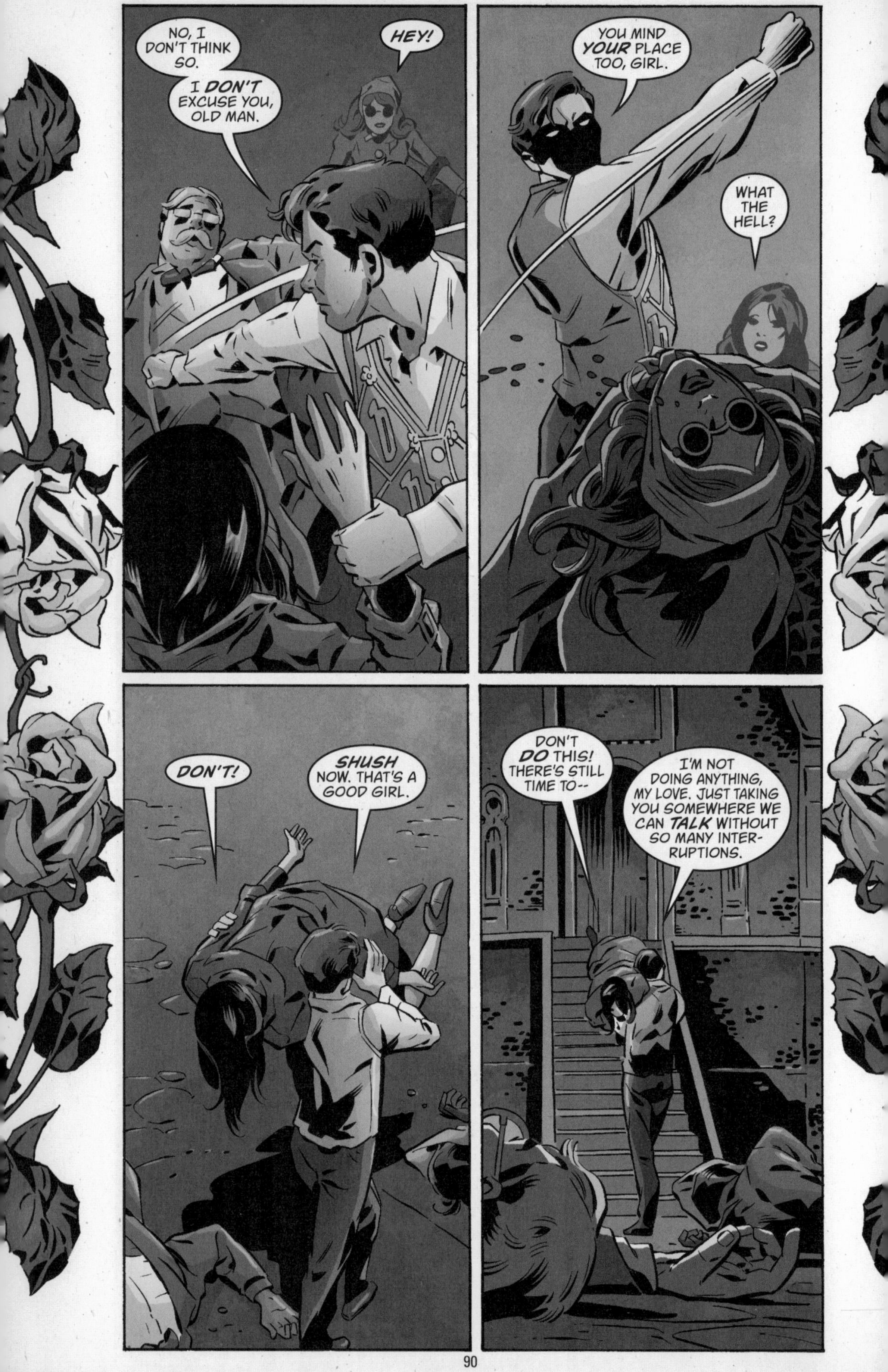
NO, I DON'T THINK SO.
I DON'T EXCUSE YOU, OLD MAN.
HEY!
YOU MIND YOUR PLACE TOO, GIRL.
WHAT THE HELL?
DON'T!
SHUSH NOW. THAT'S A GOOD GIRL.
DON'T DO THIS! THERE'S STILL TIME TO--
I'M NOT DOING ANYTHING, MY LOVE. JUST TAKING YOU SOMEWHERE WE CAN TALK WITHOUT SO MANY INTER-RUPTIONS.

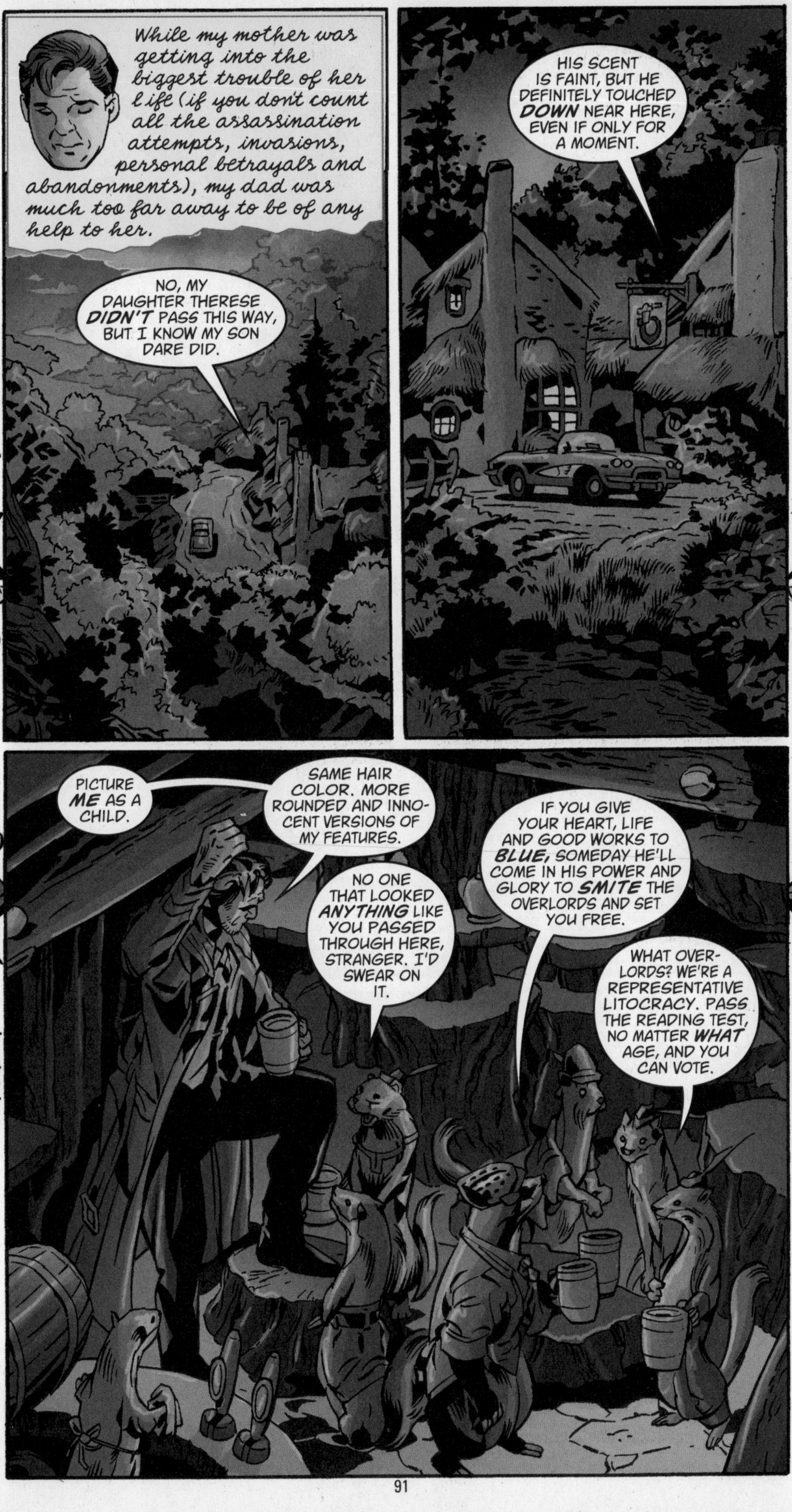
While my mother was getting into the biggest trouble of her life (if you don't count all the assassination attempts, invasions, personal betrayals and abandonments), my dad was much too far away to be of any help to her.
NO, MY DAUGHTER THERESE DIDN'T PASS THIS WAY, BUT I KNOW MY SON DARE DID.
HIS SCENT IS FAINT, BUT HE DEFINITELY TOUCHED DOWN NEAR HERE, EVEN IF ONLY FOR A MOMENT.
PICTURE ME AS A CHILD.
SAME HAIR COLOR. MORE ROUNDED AND INNOCENT VERSIONS OF MY FEATURES.
NO ONE THAT LOOKED ANYTHING LIKE YOU PASSED THROUGH HERE, STRANGER. I'D SWEAR ON IT.
IF YOU GIVE YOUR HEART, LIFE AND GOOD WORKS TO BLUE, SOMEDAY HE'LL COME IN HIS POWER AND GLORY TO SMITE THE OVERLORDS AND SET YOU FREE.
WHAT OVERLORDS? WE'RE A REPRESENTATIVE LITOCRACY. PASS THE READING TEST, NO MATTER WHAT AGE, AND YOU CAN VOTE.

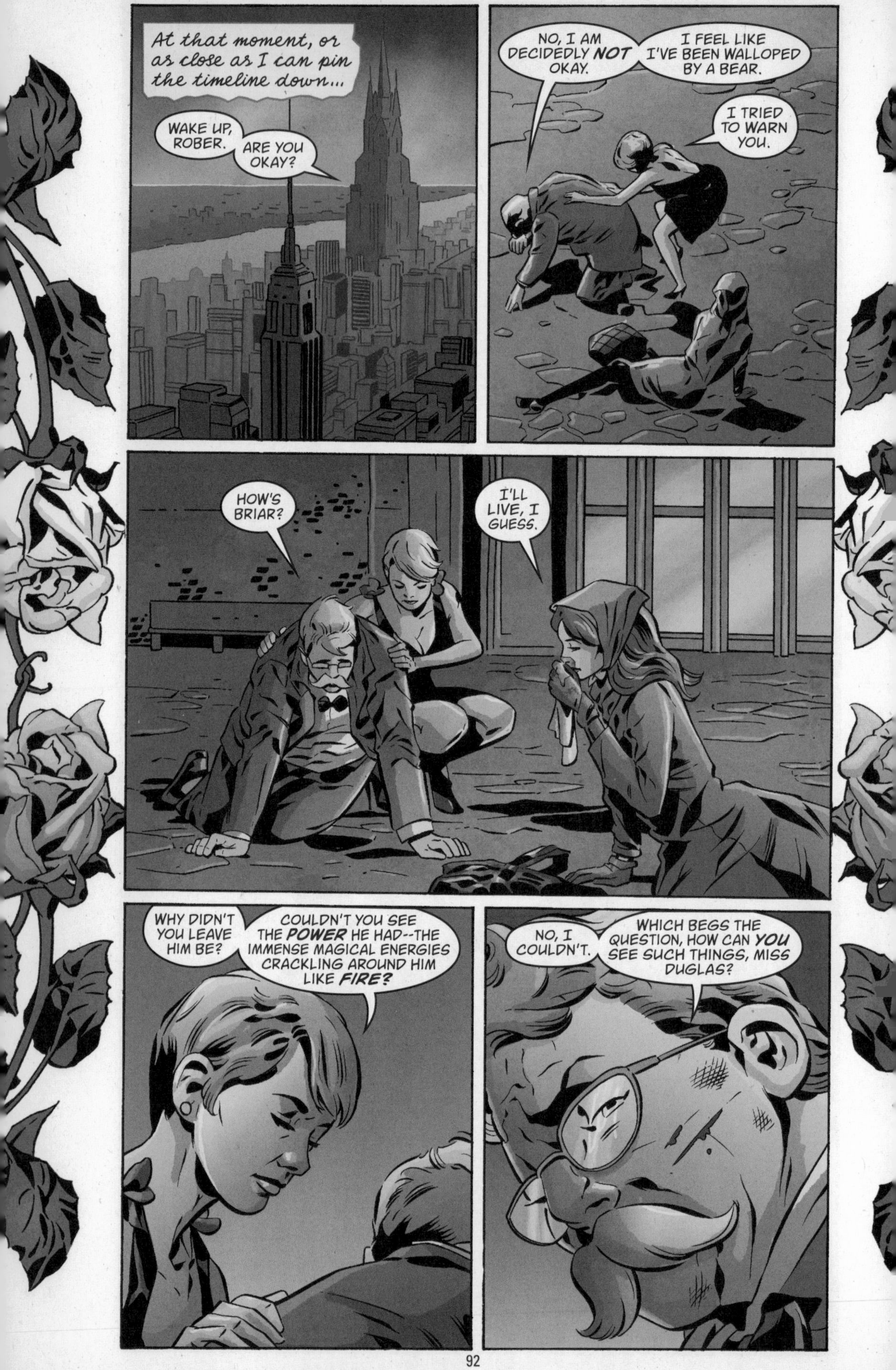

At that moment, or as close as I can pin the timeline down...
WAKE UP, ROBER.
ARE YOU OKAY?
NO, I AM DECIDEDLY NOT OKAY.
I FEEL LIKE I'VE BEEN WALLOPED BY A BEAR.
I TRIED TO WARN YOU.
HOW'S BRIAR?
I'LL LIVE, I GUESS.
WHY DIDN'T YOU LEAVE HIM BE?
COULDN'T YOU SEE THE POWER HE HAD--THE IMMENSE MAGICAL ENERGIES CRACKLING AROUND HIM LIKE FIRE?
NO, I COULDN'T.
WHICH BEGS THE QUESTION, HOW CAN YOU SEE SUCH THINGS, MISS DUGLAS?

THERE WE ARE, MY DOVE. SAFE AND SOUND, TUCKED IN BEHIND A STOUT DOOR.

GOOD LUCK ANYONE BREAKING *THIS* ONE DOWN BEFORE WE'VE HAD A CHANCE TO FINISH OUR TALK.

DO YOU LIKE MY SUITE OF ROOMS? LAVISH, ISN'T IT?

THE GOOD PEOPLE OF FABLETOWN WERE QUITE GENEROUS IN REWARDING MY SMALL PART IN KEEPING LEIGH DUGLAS *ALIVE* DURING HER ORDEALS.

BRANDISH, YOU HAVE TO *LISTEN* TO ME.

OF COURSE I WILL, DARLING. A HUSBAND AND WIFE *NEED* TO LISTEN TO EACH OTHER-- TO RELY CHIEFLY ON EACH OTHER.

WE'RE NOT MARRIED. WE *CAN'T* BE. I'M ALREADY MARRIED TO *BIGBY WOLF.*

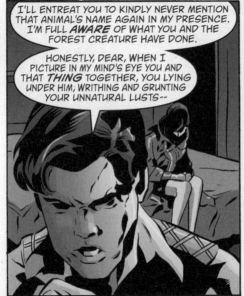

I'LL ENTREAT YOU TO KINDLY NEVER MENTION THAT ANIMAL'S NAME AGAIN IN MY PRESENCE. I'M FULL *AWARE* OF WHAT YOU AND THE FOREST CREATURE HAVE DONE.

HONESTLY, DEAR, WHEN I PICTURE IN MY MIND'S EYE YOU AND THAT *THING* TOGETHER, YOU LYING UNDER HIM; WRITHING AND GRUNTING YOUR UNNATURAL LUSTS--

WELL, IT'S ENOUGH TO TEMPT A GENTLEMAN TO ACT ALARMINGLY *UN-GENTLY* INDEED.

BUT I'M RESOLVED TO *FORGIVE* YOU YOUR WILD AND WICKED WAYS. WHAT EVILS YOU GOT UP TO, LACKING MY SUP-PORT AND GUIDANCE, ARE A THING OF THE PAST.

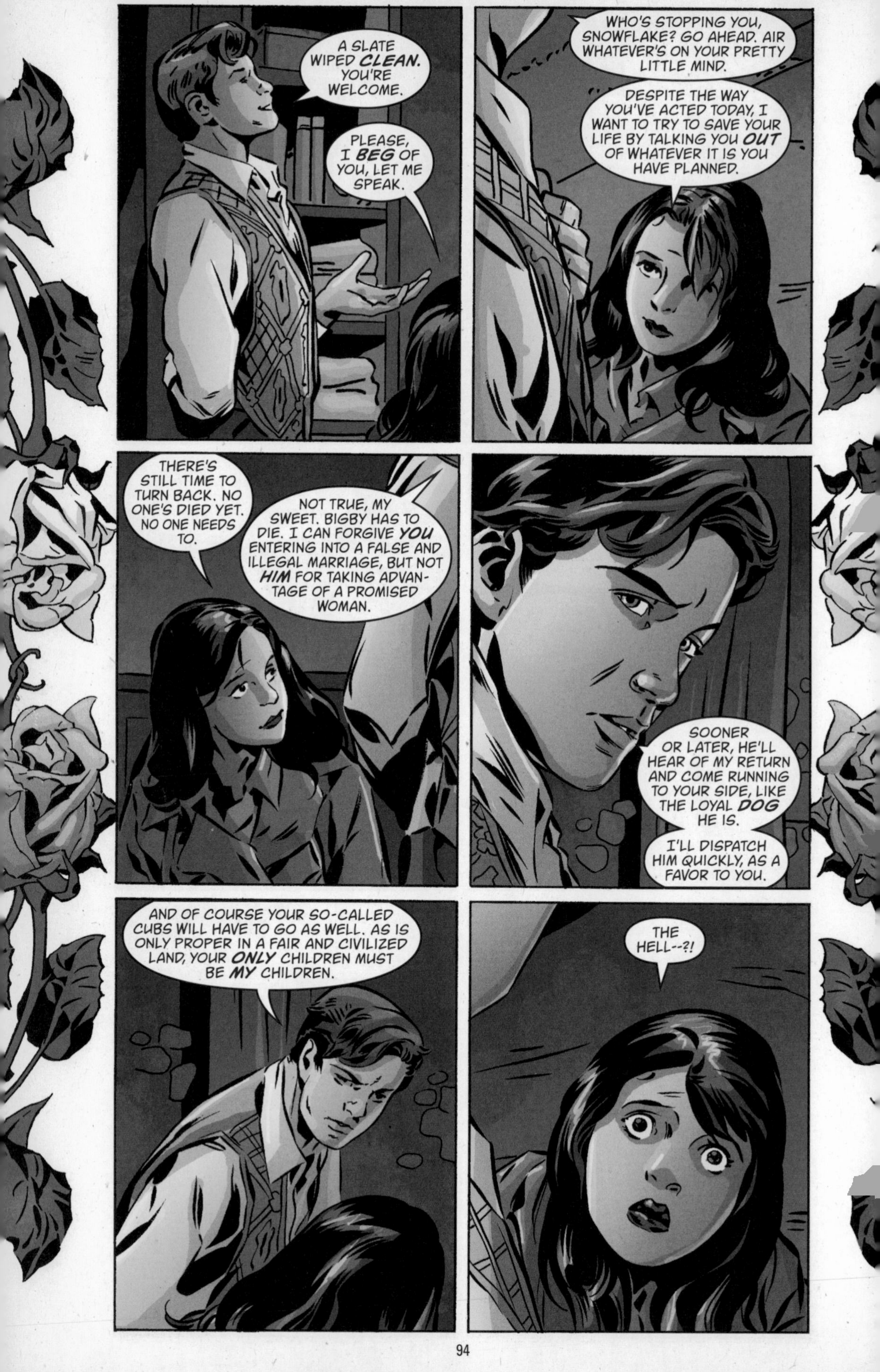
A SLATE WIPED CLEAN. YOU'RE WELCOME.
PLEASE, I BEG OF YOU, LET ME SPEAK.
WHO'S STOPPING YOU, SNOWFLAKE? GO AHEAD. AIR WHATEVER'S ON YOUR PRETTY LITTLE MIND.
DESPITE THE WAY YOU'VE ACTED TODAY, I WANT TO TRY TO SAVE YOUR LIFE BY TALKING YOU OUT OF WHATEVER IT IS YOU HAVE PLANNED.
THERE'S STILL TIME TO TURN BACK. NO ONE'S DIED YET. NO ONE NEEDS TO.
NOT TRUE, MY SWEET. BIGBY HAS TO DIE. I CAN FORGIVE YOU ENTERING INTO A FALSE AND ILLEGAL MARRIAGE, BUT NOT HIM FOR TAKING ADVANTAGE OF A PROMISED WOMAN.
SOONER OR LATER, HE'LL HEAR OF MY RETURN AND COME RUNNING TO YOUR SIDE, LIKE THE LOYAL DOG HE IS.
I'LL DISPATCH HIM QUICKLY, AS A FAVOR TO YOU.
AND OF COURSE YOUR SO-CALLED CUBS WILL HAVE TO GO AS WELL. AS IS ONLY PROPER IN A FAIR AND CIVILIZED LAND, YOUR ONLY CHILDREN MUST BE MY CHILDREN.
THE HELL--?!

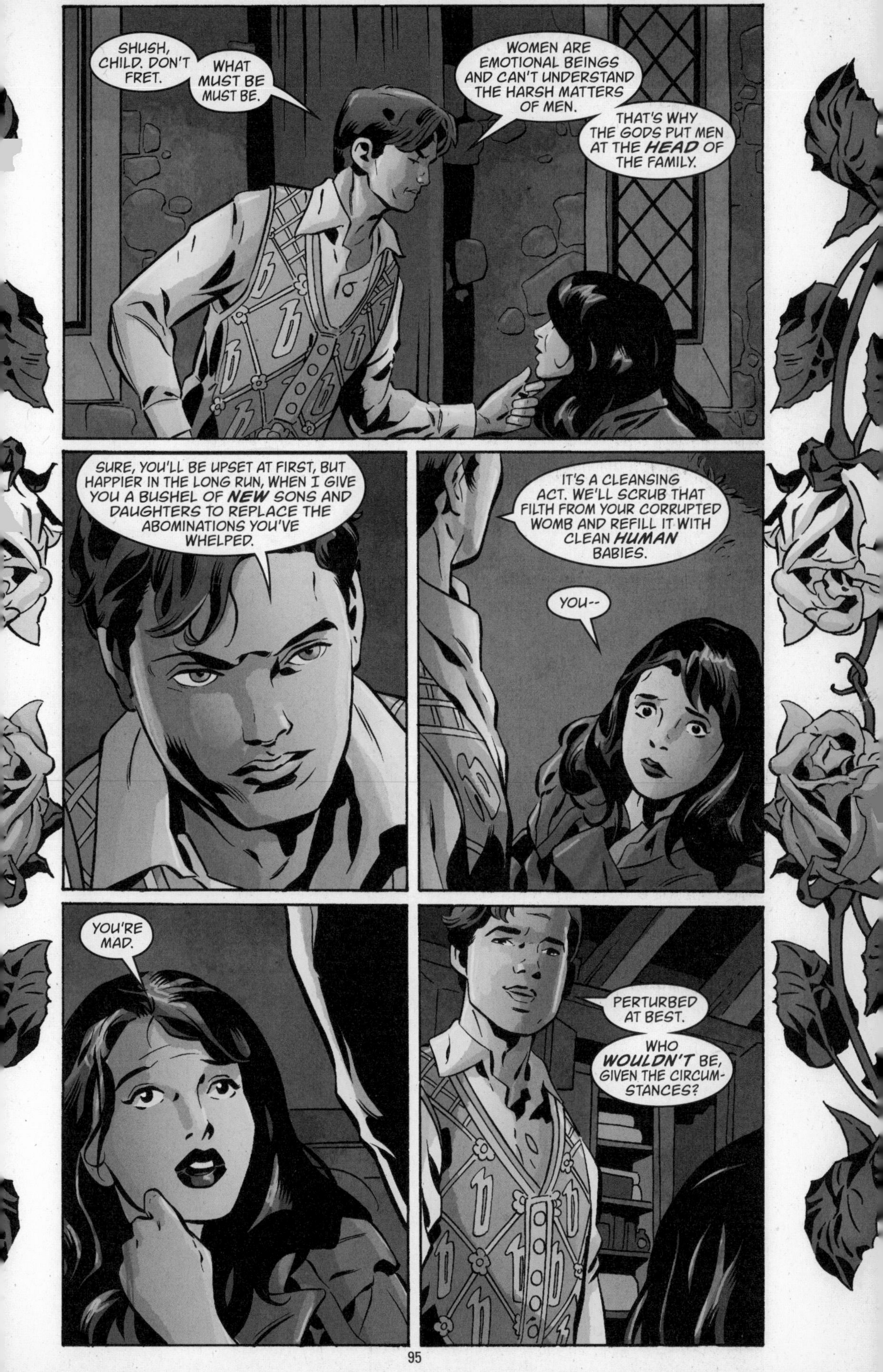
SHUSH, CHILD. DON'T FRET.
WHAT MUST BE MUST BE.
WOMEN ARE EMOTIONAL BEINGS AND CAN'T UNDERSTAND THE HARSH MATTERS OF MEN.
THAT'S WHY THE GODS PUT MEN AT THE HEAD OF THE FAMILY.
SURE, YOU'LL BE UPSET AT FIRST, BUT HAPPIER IN THE LONG RUN, WHEN I GIVE YOU A BUSHEL OF NEW SONS AND DAUGHTERS TO REPLACE THE ABOMINATIONS YOU'VE WHELPED.
IT'S A CLEANSING ACT. WE'LL SCRUB THAT FILTH FROM YOUR CORRUPTED WOMB AND REFILL IT WITH CLEAN HUMAN BABIES.
YOU--
YOU'RE MAD.
PERTURBED AT BEST.
WHO WOULDN'T BE, GIVEN THE CIRCUMSTANCES?

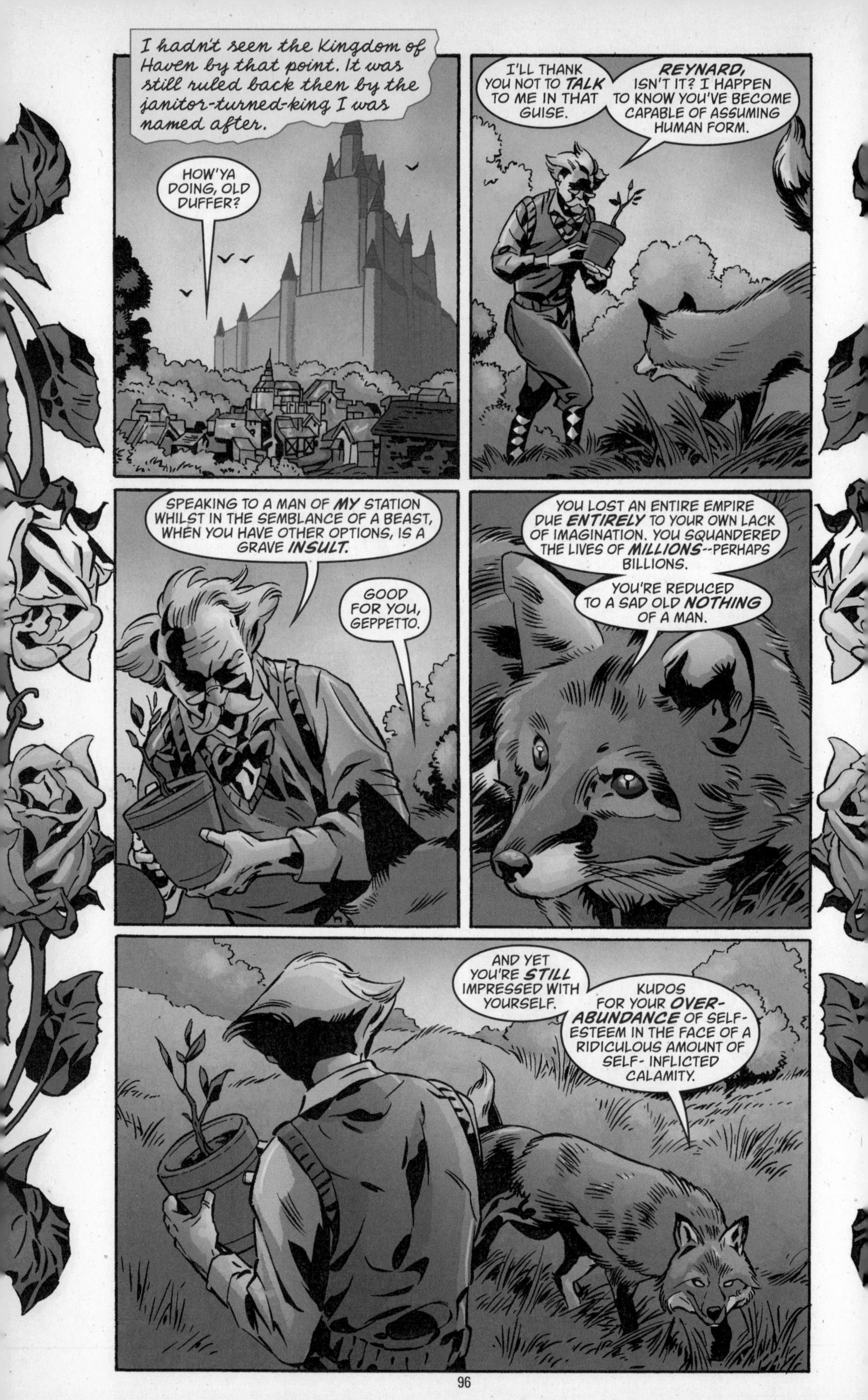
I hadn't seen the Kingdom of Haven by that point. It was still ruled back then by the janitor-turned-king I was named after.
HOW'YA DOING, OLD DUFFER?
I'LL THANK YOU NOT TO TALK TO ME IN THAT GUISE.
REYNARD, ISN'T IT? I HAPPEN TO KNOW YOU'VE BECOME CAPABLE OF ASSUMING HUMAN FORM.
SPEAKING TO A MAN OF MY STATION WHILST IN THE SEMBLANCE OF A BEAST, WHEN YOU HAVE OTHER OPTIONS, IS A GRAVE INSULT.
GOOD FOR YOU, GEPPETTO.
YOU LOST AN ENTIRE EMPIRE DUE ENTIRELY TO YOUR OWN LACK OF IMAGINATION. YOU SQUANDERED THE LIVES OF MILLIONS--PERHAPS BILLIONS.
YOU'RE REDUCED TO A SAD OLD NOTHING OF A MAN.
AND YET YOU'RE STILL IMPRESSED WITH YOURSELF.
KUDOS FOR YOUR OVER-ABUNDANCE OF SELF-ESTEEM IN THE FACE OF A RIDICULOUS AMOUNT OF SELF- INFLICTED CALAMITY.

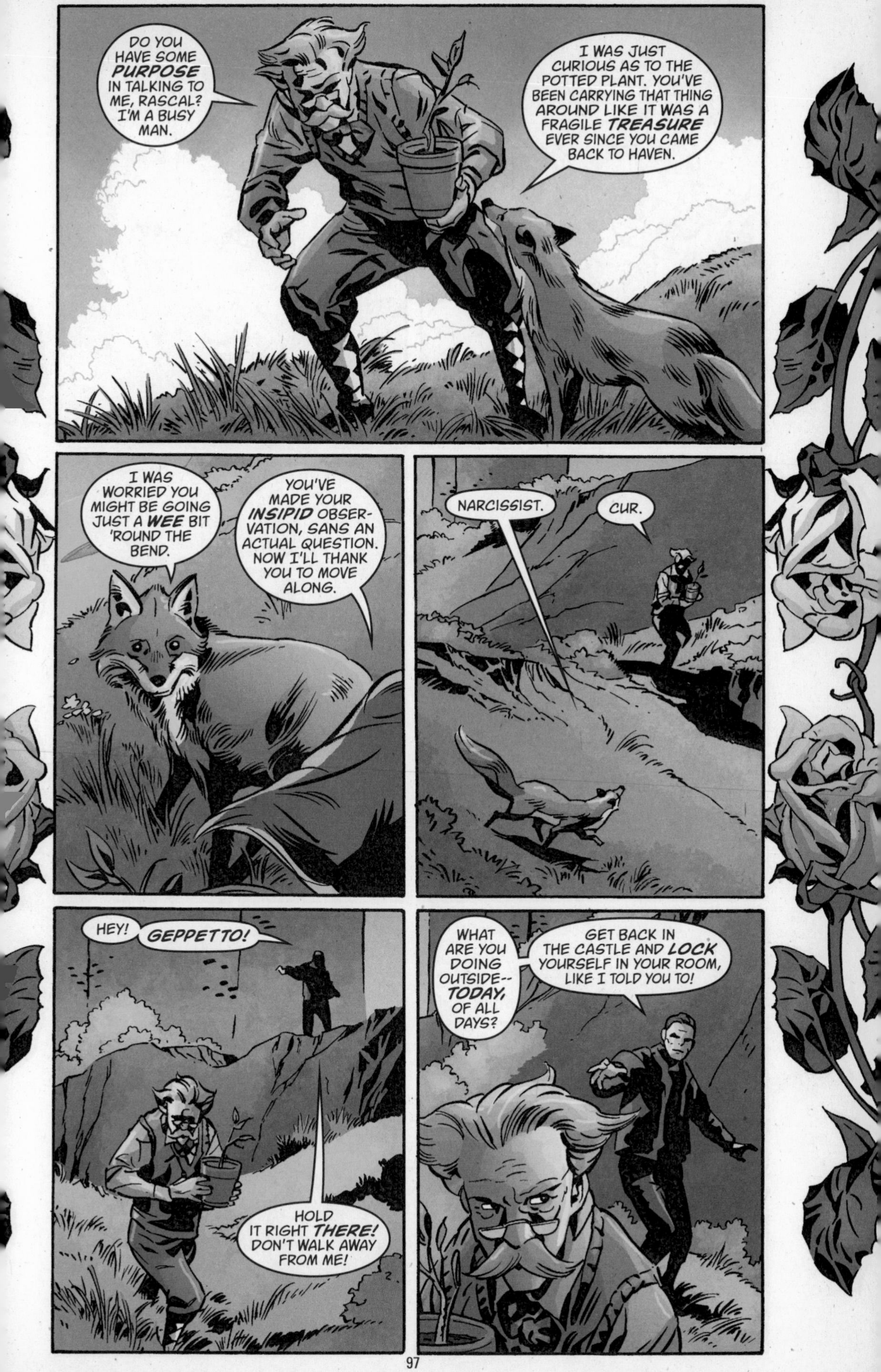

DO YOU HAVE SOME PURPOSE IN TALKING TO ME, RASCAL? I'M A BUSY MAN.
I WAS JUST CURIOUS AS TO THE POTTED PLANT. YOU'VE BEEN CARRYING THAT THING AROUND LIKE IT WAS A FRAGILE TREASURE EVER SINCE YOU CAME BACK TO HAVEN.
I WAS WORRIED YOU MIGHT BE GOING JUST A WEE BIT 'ROUND THE BEND.
YOU'VE MADE YOUR INSIPID OBSERVATION, SANS AN ACTUAL QUESTION. NOW I'LL THANK YOU TO MOVE ALONG.
NARCISSIST.
CUR.
HEY!
GEPPETTO!
HOLD IT RIGHT THERE! DON'T WALK AWAY FROM ME!
WHAT ARE YOU DOING OUTSIDE-- TODAY, OF ALL DAYS?
GET BACK IN THE CASTLE AND LOCK YOURSELF IN YOUR ROOM, LIKE I TOLD YOU TO!

THIS **PLANT** NEEDS SOME FRESH AIR AND WATER. I TOOK IT OUT FOR BOTH. AND SINCE **WHEN** DO I TAKE ORDERS FROM YOU, BEAST?

SINCE I WENT **WAY** OUT ON A LIMB TO SAVE YOUR BONY ASS FROM THE BLUE FAIRY, WHO MIGHT ARRIVE ANY SECOND. SHE CAN'T SEE YOU HERE OR WE'RE **BOTH** COOKED.

ALSO SINCE I'M SHERIFF OF THE WHOLE DAMNED **KINGDOM** NOW.

YOU?

ME. OFFICIALLY APPOINTED BY **HIS HIGHNESS**, AMBROSE THE FIRST, LAST WEEK.

IS THAT FLY-EATING MORON **MORE** DAFT THAN EVEN I SUSPECTED?

HEY, WATCH IT, PAL. YOU JUST SPOKE **TREASON.**

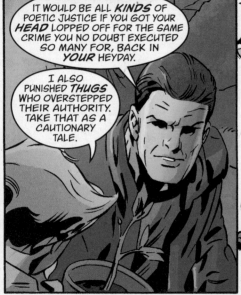

IT WOULD BE ALL **KINDS** OF POETIC JUSTICE IF YOU GOT YOUR **HEAD** LOPPED OFF FOR THE SAME CRIME YOU NO DOUBT EXECUTED SO MANY FOR, BACK IN **YOUR** HEYDAY.

I ALSO PUNISHED **THUGS** WHO OVERSTEPPED THEIR AUTHORITY. TAKE THAT AS A CAUTIONARY TALE.

NO, **YOU** TAKE IT. TAKE YOURSELF AND YOUR VANITY **AND** YOUR LITTLE PET PLANT BACK INTO THE CASTLE, RIGHT **NOW.**

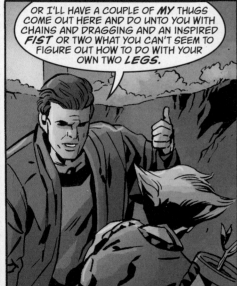

OR I'LL HAVE A COUPLE OF **MY** THUGS COME OUT HERE AND DO UNTO YOU WITH CHAINS AND DRAGGING AND AN INSPIRED **FIST** OR TWO WHAT YOU CAN'T SEEM TO FIGURE OUT HOW TO DO WITH YOUR OWN TWO **LEGS.**

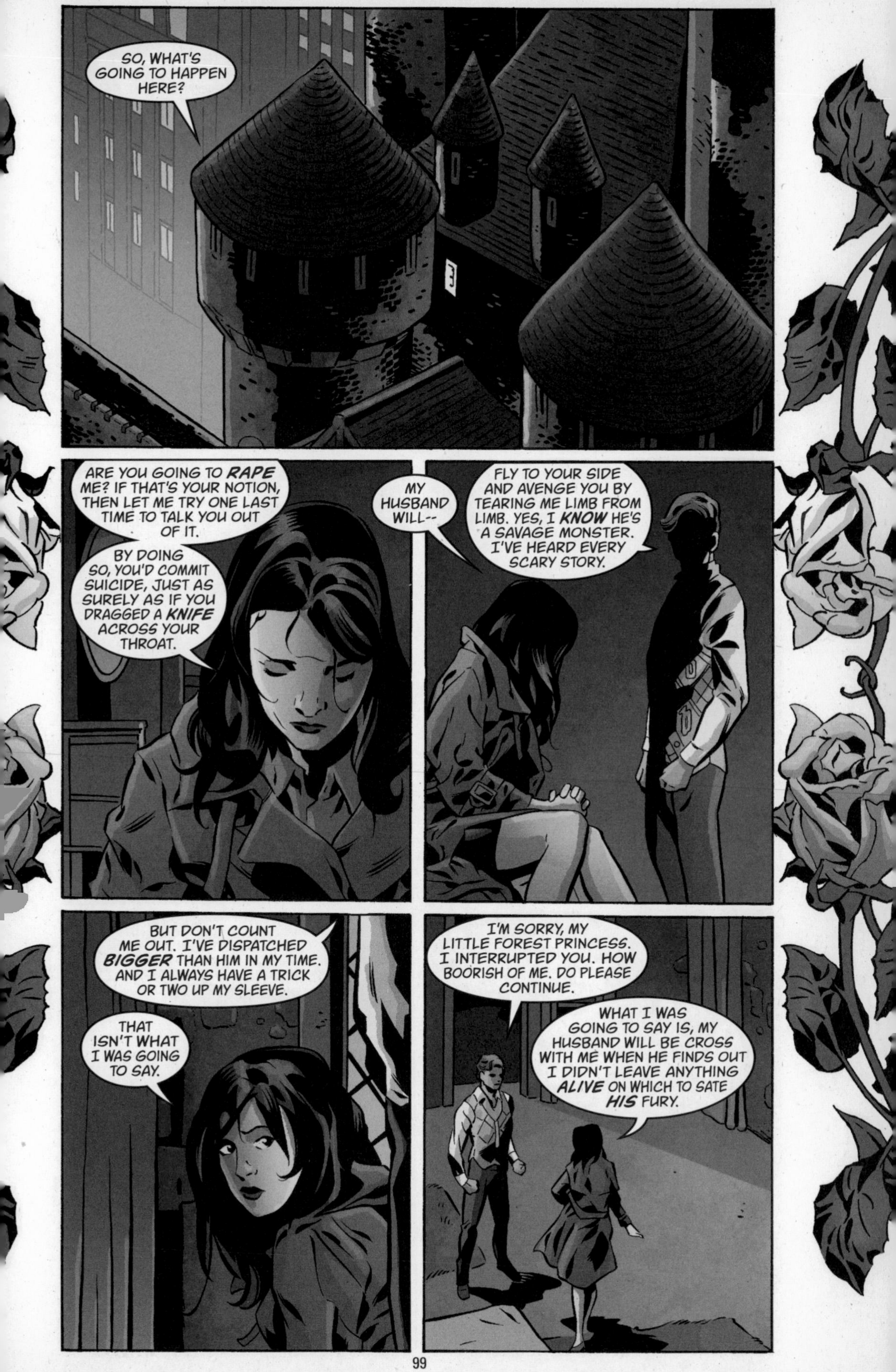
SO, WHAT'S GOING TO HAPPEN HERE?
ARE YOU GOING TO *RAPE* ME? IF THAT'S YOUR NOTION, THEN LET ME TRY ONE LAST TIME TO TALK YOU OUT OF IT.
BY DOING SO, YOU'D COMMIT SUICIDE, JUST AS SURELY AS IF YOU DRAGGED A *KNIFE* ACROSS YOUR THROAT.
MY HUSBAND WILL--
FLY TO YOUR SIDE AND AVENGE YOU BY TEARING ME LIMB FROM LIMB. YES, I *KNOW* HE'S A SAVAGE MONSTER. I'VE HEARD EVERY SCARY STORY.
BUT DON'T COUNT ME OUT. I'VE DISPATCHED *BIGGER* THAN HIM IN MY TIME. AND I ALWAYS HAVE A TRICK OR TWO UP MY SLEEVE.
THAT ISN'T WHAT I WAS GOING TO SAY.
I'M SORRY, MY LITTLE FOREST PRINCESS. I INTERRUPTED YOU. HOW BOORISH OF ME. DO PLEASE CONTINUE.
WHAT I WAS GOING TO SAY IS, MY HUSBAND WILL BE CROSS WITH ME WHEN HE FINDS OUT I DIDN'T LEAVE ANYTHING *ALIVE* ON WHICH TO SATE *HIS* FURY.

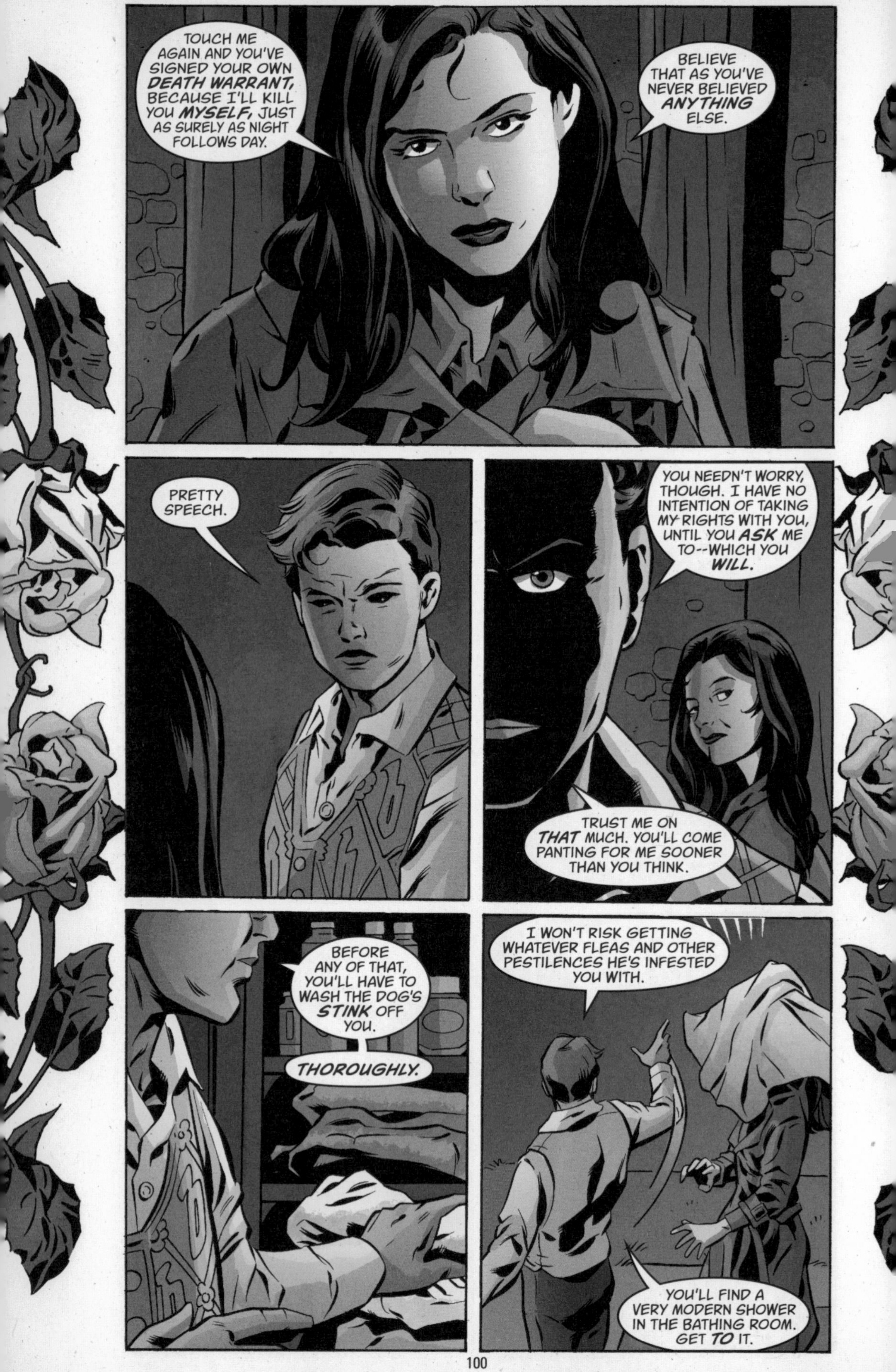
TOUCH ME AGAIN AND YOU'VE SIGNED YOUR OWN DEATH WARRANT, BECAUSE I'LL KILL YOU MYSELF, JUST AS SURELY AS NIGHT FOLLOWS DAY.
BELIEVE THAT AS YOU'VE NEVER BELIEVED ANYTHING ELSE.
PRETTY SPEECH.
YOU NEEDN'T WORRY, THOUGH. I HAVE NO INTENTION OF TAKING MY RIGHTS WITH YOU, UNTIL YOU ASK ME TO--WHICH YOU WILL.
TRUST ME ON THAT MUCH. YOU'LL COME PANTING FOR ME SOONER THAN YOU THINK.
BEFORE ANY OF THAT, YOU'LL HAVE TO WASH THE DOG'S STINK OFF YOU.
THOROUGHLY.
I WON'T RISK GETTING WHATEVER FLEAS AND OTHER PESTILENCES HE'S INFESTED YOU WITH.
YOU'LL FIND A VERY MODERN SHOWER IN THE BATHING ROOM. GET TO IT.

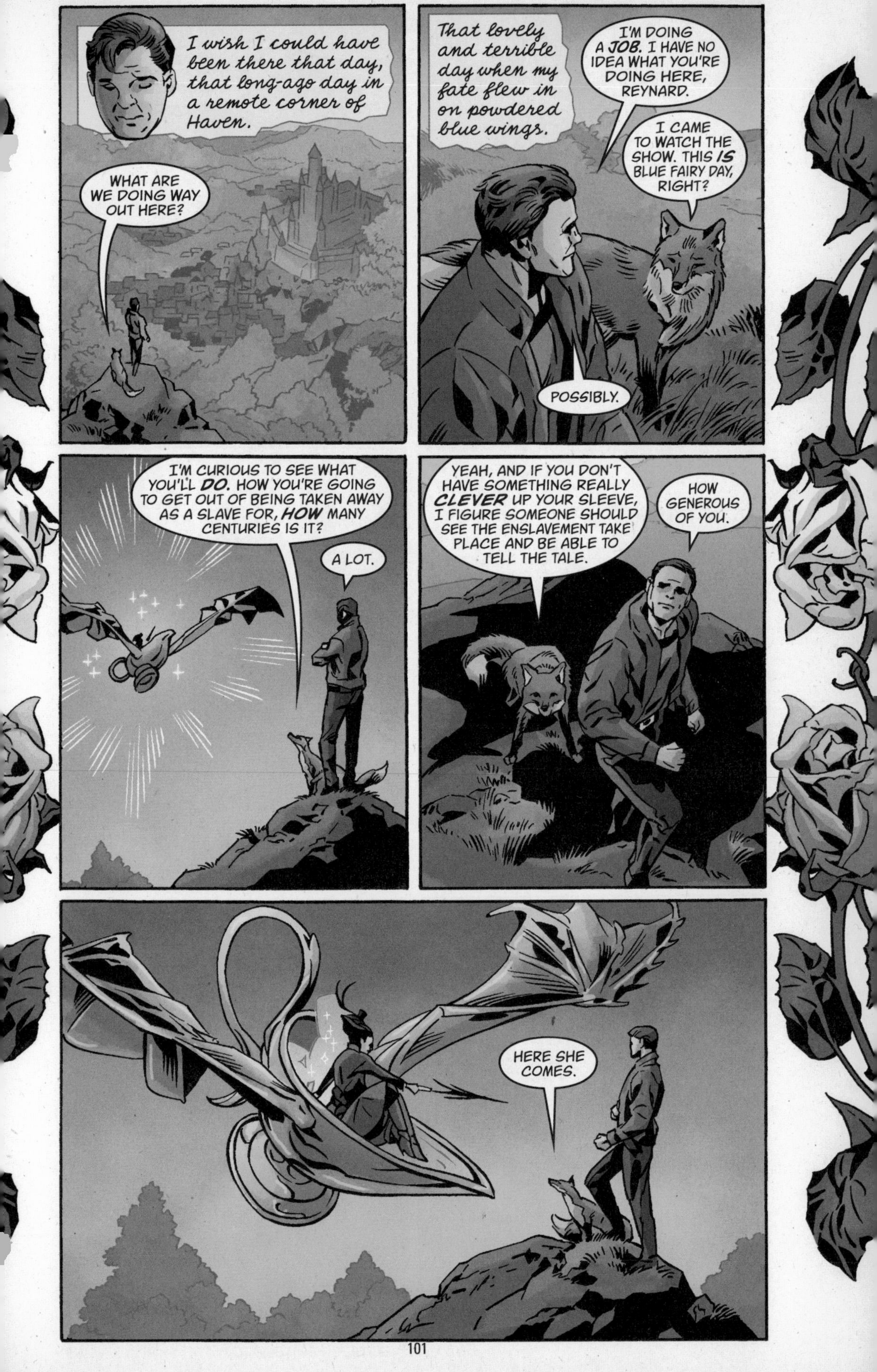

I wish I could have been there that day, that long-ago day in a remote corner of Haven.
WHAT ARE WE DOING WAY OUT HERE?
That lovely and terrible day when my fate flew in on powdered blue wings.
I'M DOING A JOB. I HAVE NO IDEA WHAT YOU'RE DOING HERE, REYNARD.
I CAME TO WATCH THE SHOW. THIS IS BLUE FAIRY DAY, RIGHT?
POSSIBLY.
I'M CURIOUS TO SEE WHAT YOU'LL DO. HOW YOU'RE GOING TO GET OUT OF BEING TAKEN AWAY AS A SLAVE FOR, HOW MANY CENTURIES IS IT?
A LOT.
YEAH, AND IF YOU DON'T HAVE SOMETHING REALLY CLEVER UP YOUR SLEEVE, I FIGURE SOMEONE SHOULD SEE THE ENSLAVEMENT TAKE PLACE AND BE ABLE TO TELL THE TALE.
HOW GENEROUS OF YOU.
HERE SHE COMES.

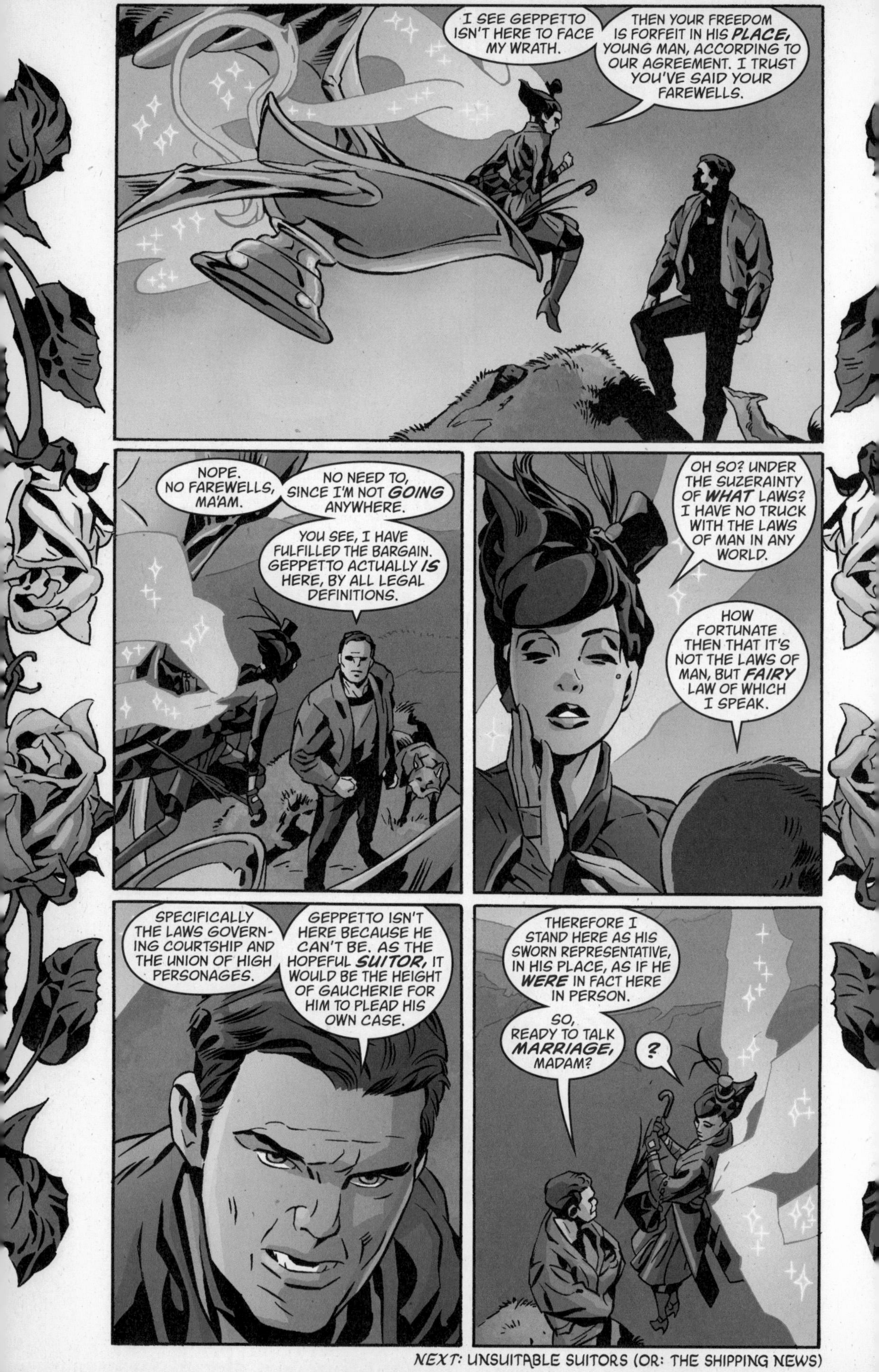
I SEE GEPPETTO ISN'T HERE TO FACE MY WRATH.
THEN YOUR FREEDOM IS FORFEIT IN HIS PLACE, YOUNG MAN, ACCORDING TO OUR AGREEMENT. I TRUST YOU'VE SAID YOUR FAREWELLS.
NOPE. NO FAREWELLS, MA'AM.
NO NEED TO, SINCE I'M NOT GOING ANYWHERE.
YOU SEE, I HAVE FULFILLED THE BARGAIN. GEPPETTO ACTUALLY IS HERE, BY ALL LEGAL DEFINITIONS.
OH SO? UNDER THE SUZERAINTY OF WHAT LAWS? I HAVE NO TRUCK WITH THE LAWS OF MAN IN ANY WORLD.
HOW FORTUNATE THEN THAT IT'S NOT THE LAWS OF MAN, BUT FAIRY LAW OF WHICH I SPEAK.
SPECIFICALLY THE LAWS GOVERN-ING COURTSHIP AND THE UNION OF HIGH PERSONAGES.
GEPPETTO ISN'T HERE BECAUSE HE CAN'T BE. AS THE HOPEFUL SUITOR, IT WOULD BE THE HEIGHT OF GAUCHERIE FOR HIM TO PLEAD HIS OWN CASE.
THEREFORE I STAND HERE AS HIS SWORN REPRESENTATIVE, IN HIS PLACE, AS IF HE WERE IN FACT HERE IN PERSON.
SO, READY TO TALK MARRIAGE, MADAM?
?

NEXT: UNSUITABLE SUITORS (OR: THE SHIPPING NEWS)

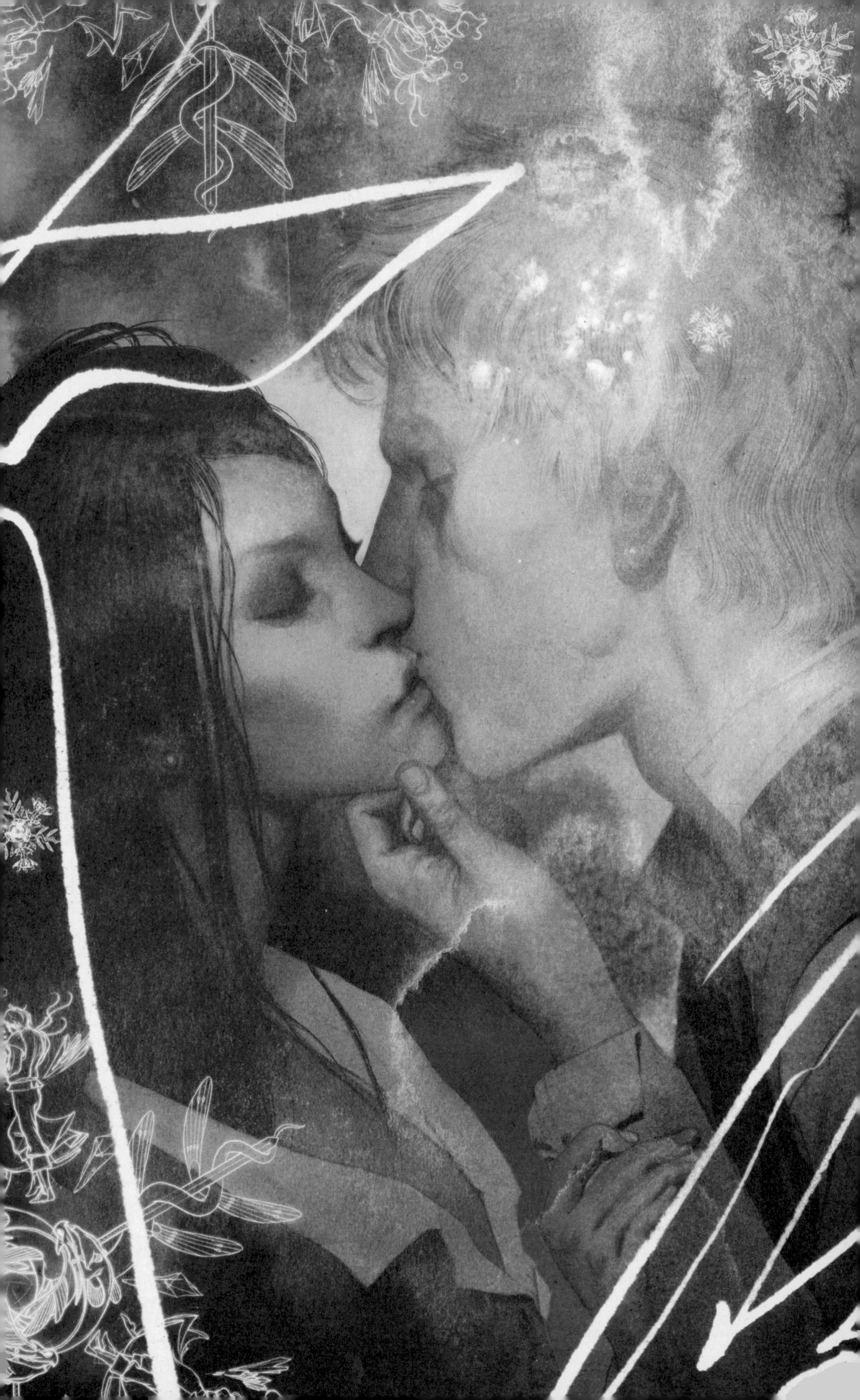

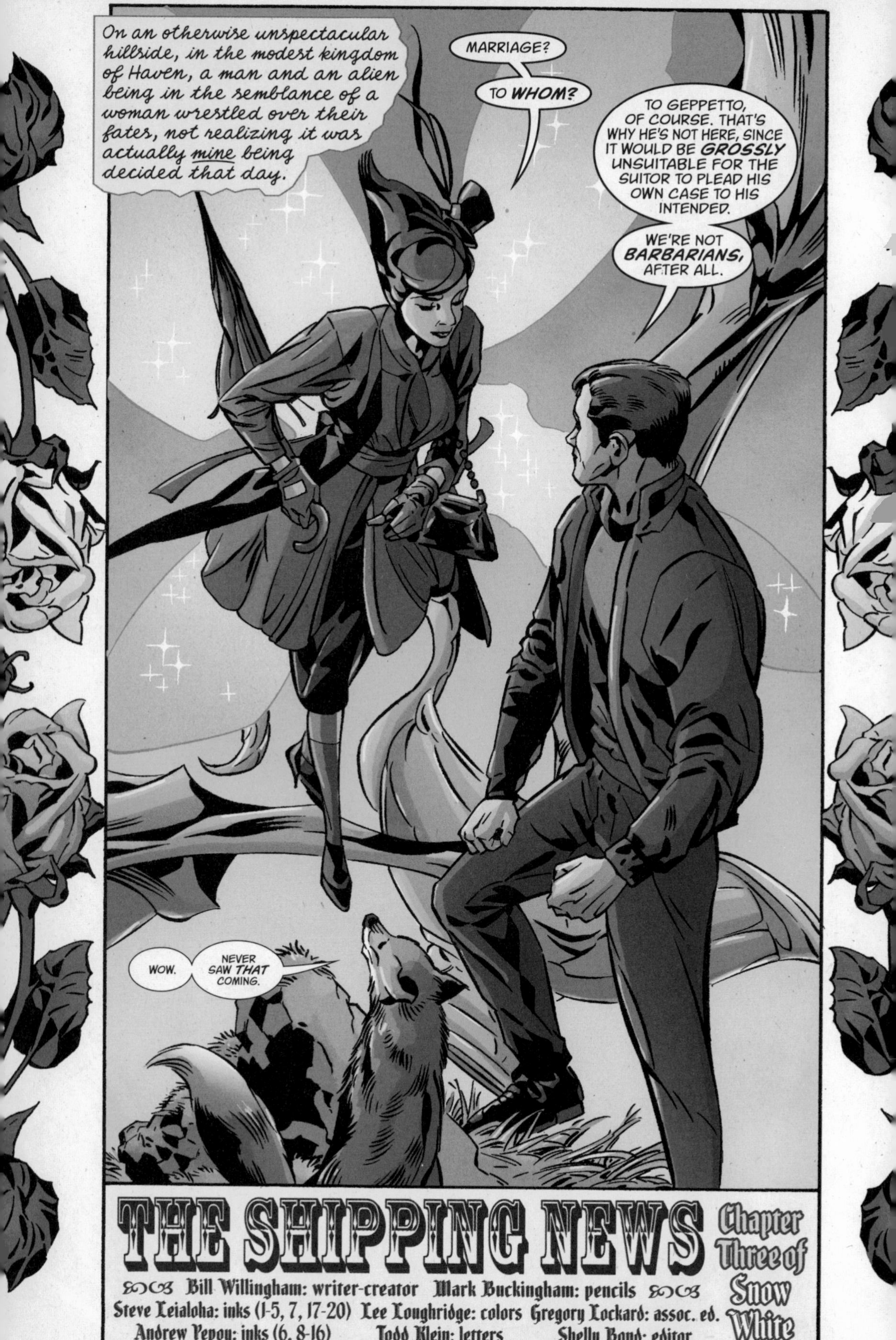
On an otherwise unspectacular hillside, in the modest kingdom of Haven, a man and an alien being in the semblance of a woman wrestled over their fates, not realizing it was actually mine being decided that day.
MARRIAGE?
TO WHOM?
TO GEPPETTO, OF COURSE. THAT'S WHY HE'S NOT HERE, SINCE IT WOULD BE GROSSLY UNSUITABLE FOR THE SUITOR TO PLEAD HIS OWN CASE TO HIS INTENDED.
WE'RE NOT BARBARIANS, AFTER ALL.
WOW.
NEVER SAW THAT COMING.
THE SHIPPING NEWS
Chapter Three of Snow White
Bill Willingham: writer-creator
Mark Buckingham: pencils
Steve Leialoha: inks (1-5, 7, 17-20)
Lee Loughridge: colors
Gregory Lockard: assoc. ed.
Andrew Pepoy: inks (6, 8-16)
Todd Klein: letters
Shelly Bond: editor

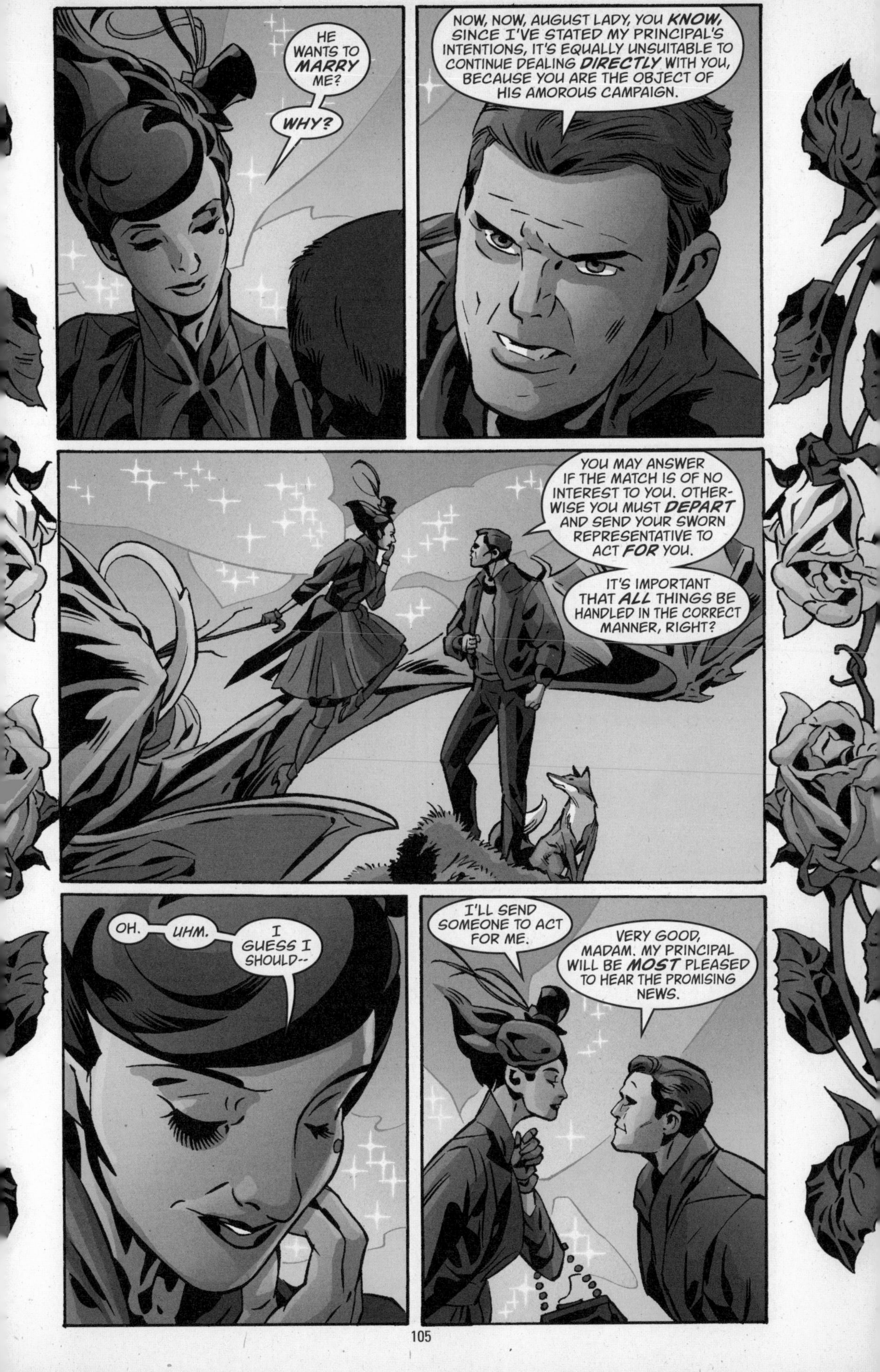
HE WANTS TO MARRY ME?
WHY?
NOW, NOW, AUGUST LADY, YOU KNOW, SINCE I'VE STATED MY PRINCIPAL'S INTENTIONS, IT'S EQUALLY UNSUITABLE TO CONTINUE DEALING DIRECTLY WITH YOU, BECAUSE YOU ARE THE OBJECT OF HIS AMOROUS CAMPAIGN.
YOU MAY ANSWER IF THE MATCH IS OF NO INTEREST TO YOU. OTHER-WISE YOU MUST DEPART AND SEND YOUR SWORN REPRESENTATIVE TO ACT FOR YOU.
IT'S IMPORTANT THAT ALL THINGS BE HANDLED IN THE CORRECT MANNER, RIGHT?
OH.
UHM.
I GUESS I SHOULD--
I'LL SEND SOMEONE TO ACT FOR ME.
VERY GOOD, MADAM. MY PRINCIPAL WILL BE MOST PLEASED TO HEAR THE PROMISING NEWS.

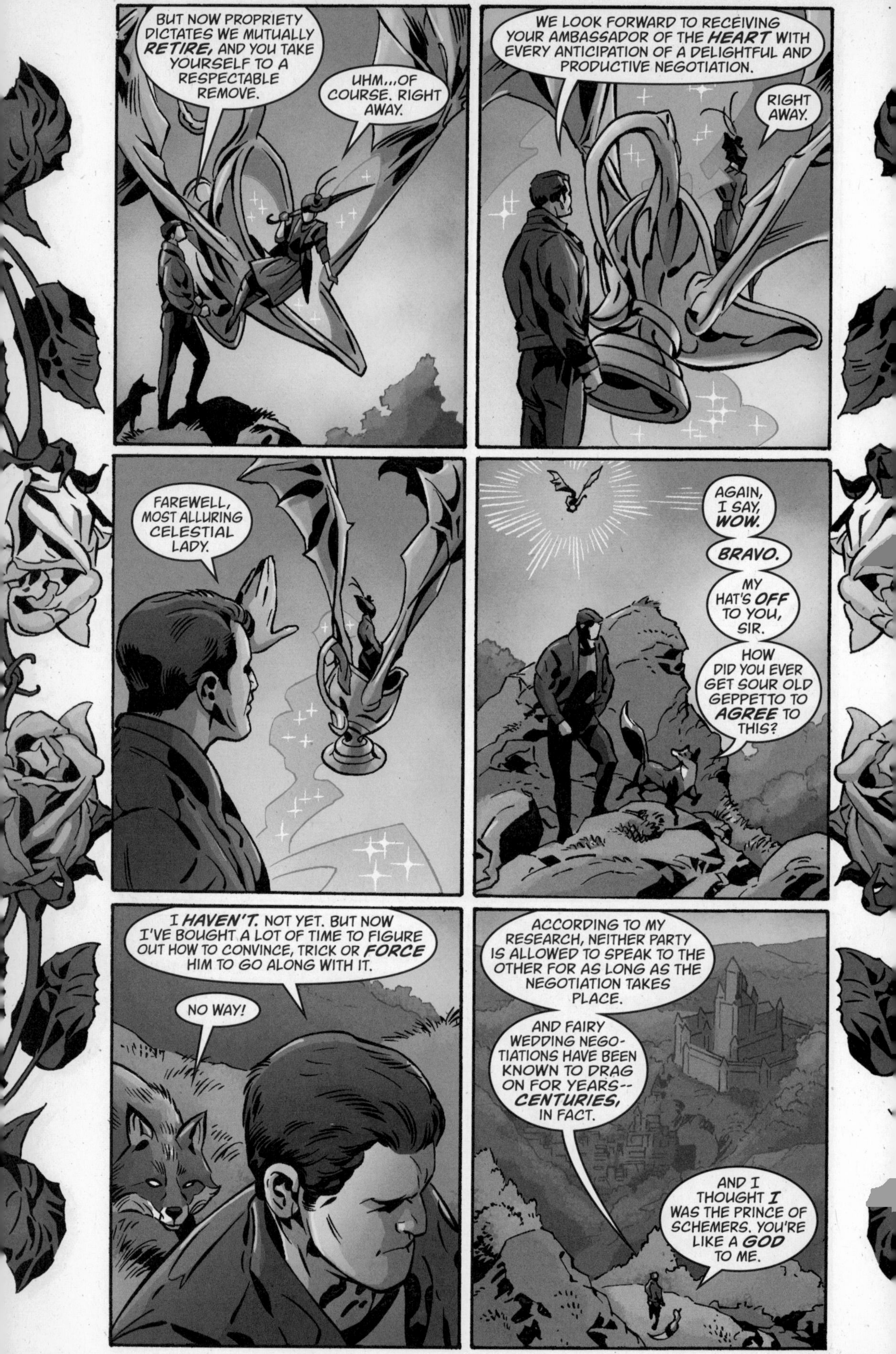
BUT NOW PROPRIETY DICTATES WE MUTUALLY RETIRE, AND YOU TAKE YOURSELF TO A RESPECTABLE REMOVE.
UHM...OF COURSE. RIGHT AWAY.
WE LOOK FORWARD TO RECEIVING YOUR AMBASSADOR OF THE HEART WITH EVERY ANTICIPATION OF A DELIGHTFUL AND PRODUCTIVE NEGOTIATION.
RIGHT AWAY.
FAREWELL, MOST ALLURING CELESTIAL LADY.
AGAIN, I SAY, WOW.
BRAVO.
MY HAT'S OFF TO YOU, SIR.
HOW DID YOU EVER GET SOUR OLD GEPPETTO TO AGREE TO THIS?
I HAVEN'T. NOT YET. BUT NOW I'VE BOUGHT A LOT OF TIME TO FIGURE OUT HOW TO CONVINCE, TRICK OR FORCE HIM TO GO ALONG WITH IT.
NO WAY!
ACCORDING TO MY RESEARCH, NEITHER PARTY IS ALLOWED TO SPEAK TO THE OTHER FOR AS LONG AS THE NEGOTIATION TAKES PLACE.
AND FAIRY WEDDING NEGO-TIATIONS HAVE BEEN KNOWN TO DRAG ON FOR YEARS--CENTURIES, IN FACT.
AND I THOUGHT I WAS THE PRINCE OF SCHEMERS. YOU'RE LIKE A GOD TO ME.

MEANWHILE...

SHOULD WE BREAK IT DOWN?

HOW?

THIS DOOR'S SOLID *OAK*. WE'D NEED A BATTERING RAM.

OR A SHAPED CHARGE.

OR BIGBY. OR BEAST. WHERE ARE OUR BIG GUNS WHEN WE *NEED* THEM?

GRIMBLE IS BIG ENOUGH TO TAKE THIS DOOR DOWN, WHEN HE'S BEING ALL TROLLISH, AND HE MAY EVEN HAVE EXPLOSIVES. WHERE'S *HE*?

I HAVE NO IDEA. COME TO THINK OF IT, I HAVEN'T SEEN HIM SINCE THIS MORNING.

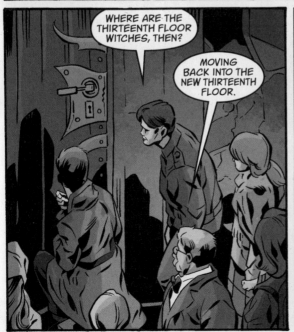

WHERE ARE THE THIRTEENTH FLOOR WITCHES, THEN?

MOVING BACK INTO THE NEW THIRTEENTH FLOOR.

WELL, ONE OF THEM COULD-- I DON'T KNOW--TURN THE DOOR INTO *BUTTERFLIES* OR SOMETHING.

SURE, BECAUSE THEY ALWAYS JUST HAPPEN TO HAVE A "TURN THE DOOR INTO BUTTERFLIES" SPELL ALL CONJURED UP AND READY TO *FIRE*.

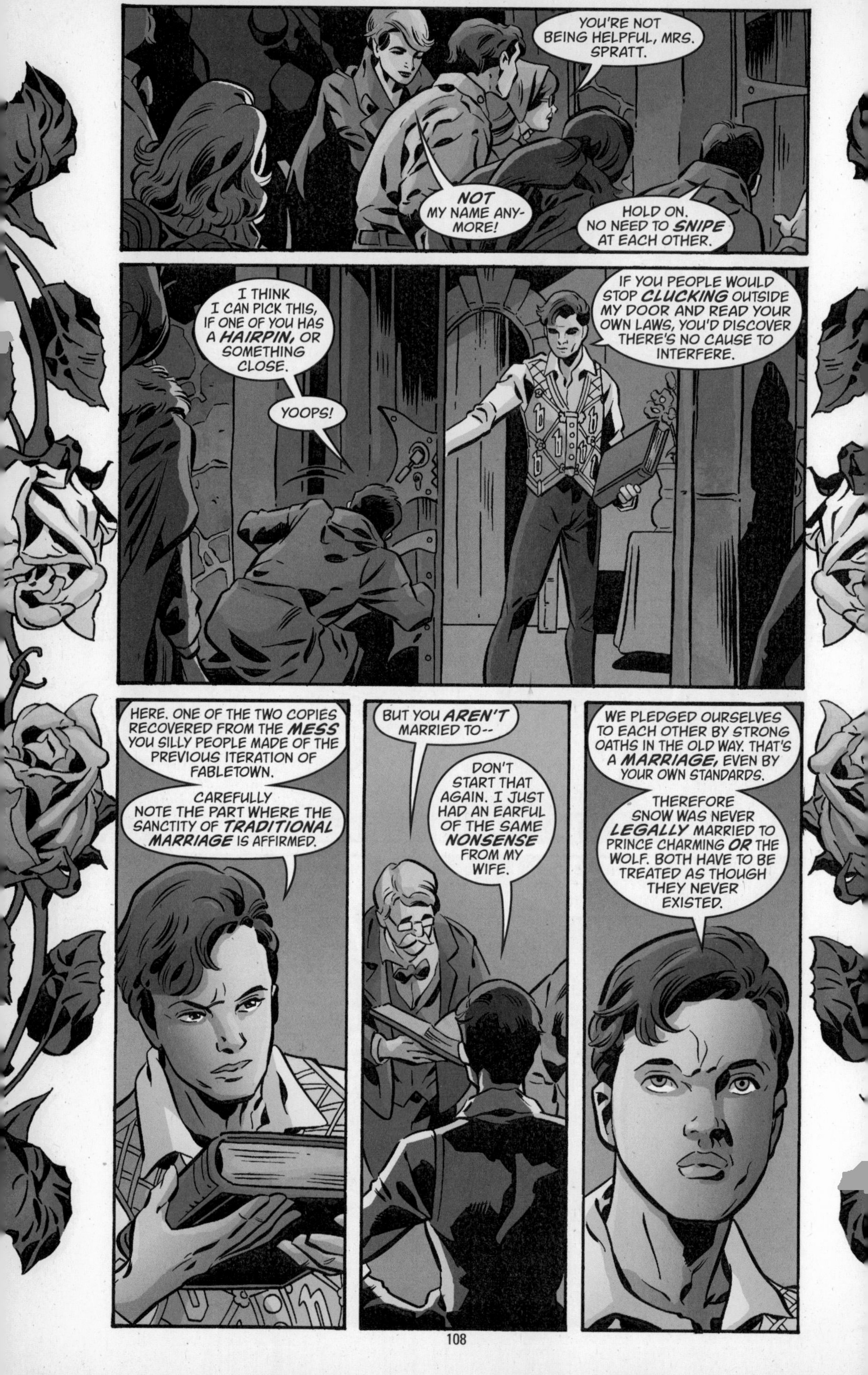
YOU'RE NOT BEING HELPFUL, MRS. SPRATT.
NOT MY NAME ANY-MORE!
HOLD ON. NO NEED TO SNIPE AT EACH OTHER.
I THINK I CAN PICK THIS, IF ONE OF YOU HAS A HAIRPIN, OR SOMETHING CLOSE.
YOOPS!
IF YOU PEOPLE WOULD STOP CLUCKING OUTSIDE MY DOOR AND READ YOUR OWN LAWS, YOU'D DISCOVER THERE'S NO CAUSE TO INTERFERE.
HERE. ONE OF THE TWO COPIES RECOVERED FROM THE MESS YOU SILLY PEOPLE MADE OF THE PREVIOUS ITERATION OF FABLETOWN.
CAREFULLY NOTE THE PART WHERE THE SANCTITY OF TRADITIONAL MARRIAGE IS AFFIRMED.
BUT YOU AREN'T MARRIED TO--
DON'T START THAT AGAIN. I JUST HAD AN EARFUL OF THE SAME NONSENSE FROM MY WIFE.
WE PLEDGED OURSELVES TO EACH OTHER BY STRONG OATHS IN THE OLD WAY. THAT'S A MARRIAGE, EVEN BY YOUR OWN STANDARDS.
THEREFORE SNOW WAS NEVER LEGALLY MARRIED TO PRINCE CHARMING OR THE WOLF. BOTH HAVE TO BE TREATED AS THOUGH THEY NEVER EXISTED.

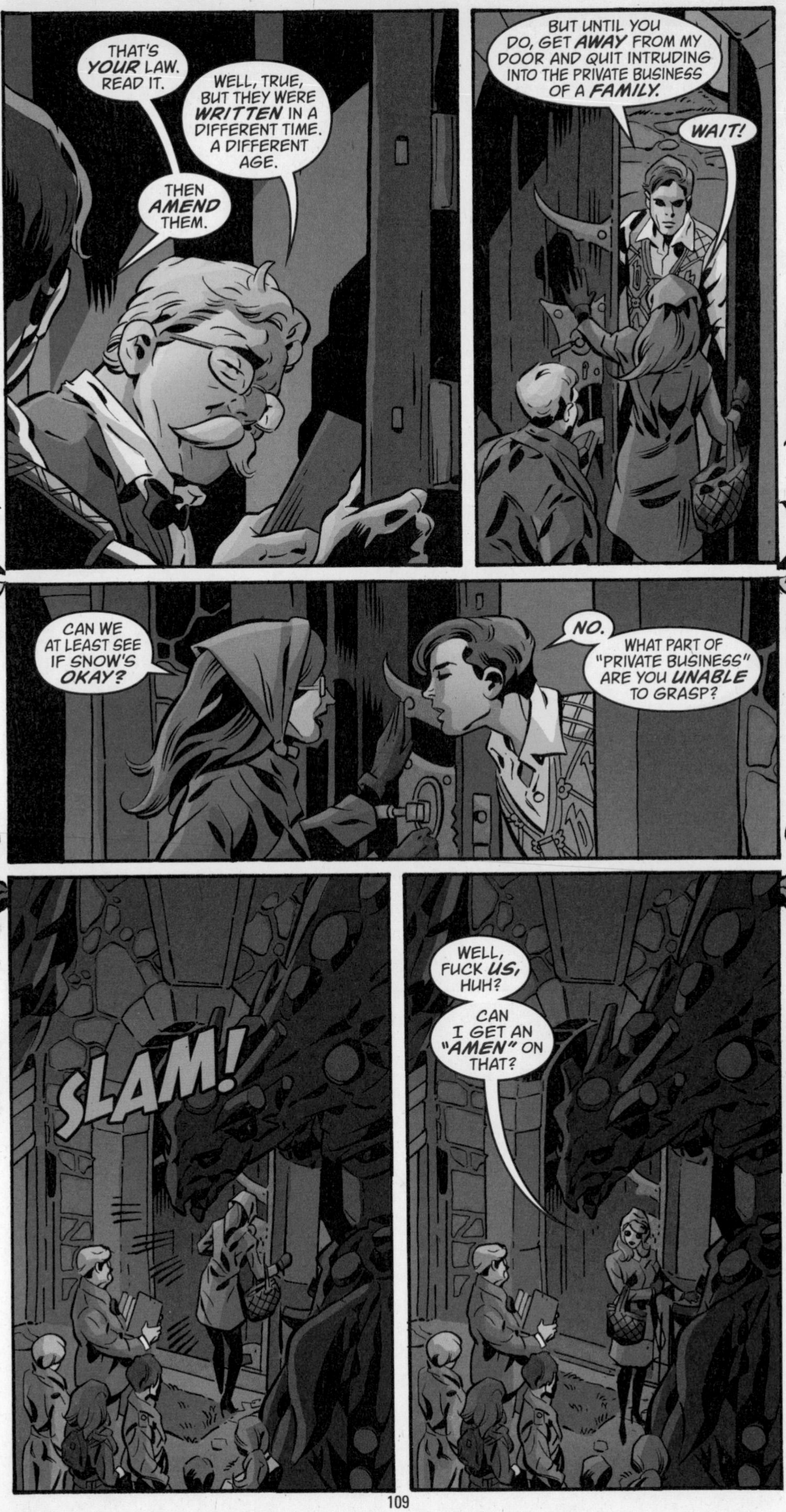
THAT'S YOUR LAW. READ IT.
WELL, TRUE, BUT THEY WERE WRITTEN IN A DIFFERENT TIME. A DIFFERENT AGE.
THEN AMEND THEM.
BUT UNTIL YOU DO, GET AWAY FROM MY DOOR AND QUIT INTRUDING INTO THE PRIVATE BUSINESS OF A FAMILY.
WAIT!
CAN WE AT LEAST SEE IF SNOW'S OKAY?
NO.
WHAT PART OF "PRIVATE BUSINESS" ARE YOU UNABLE TO GRASP?
SLAM!
WELL, FUCK US, HUH?
CAN I GET AN "AMEN" ON THAT?

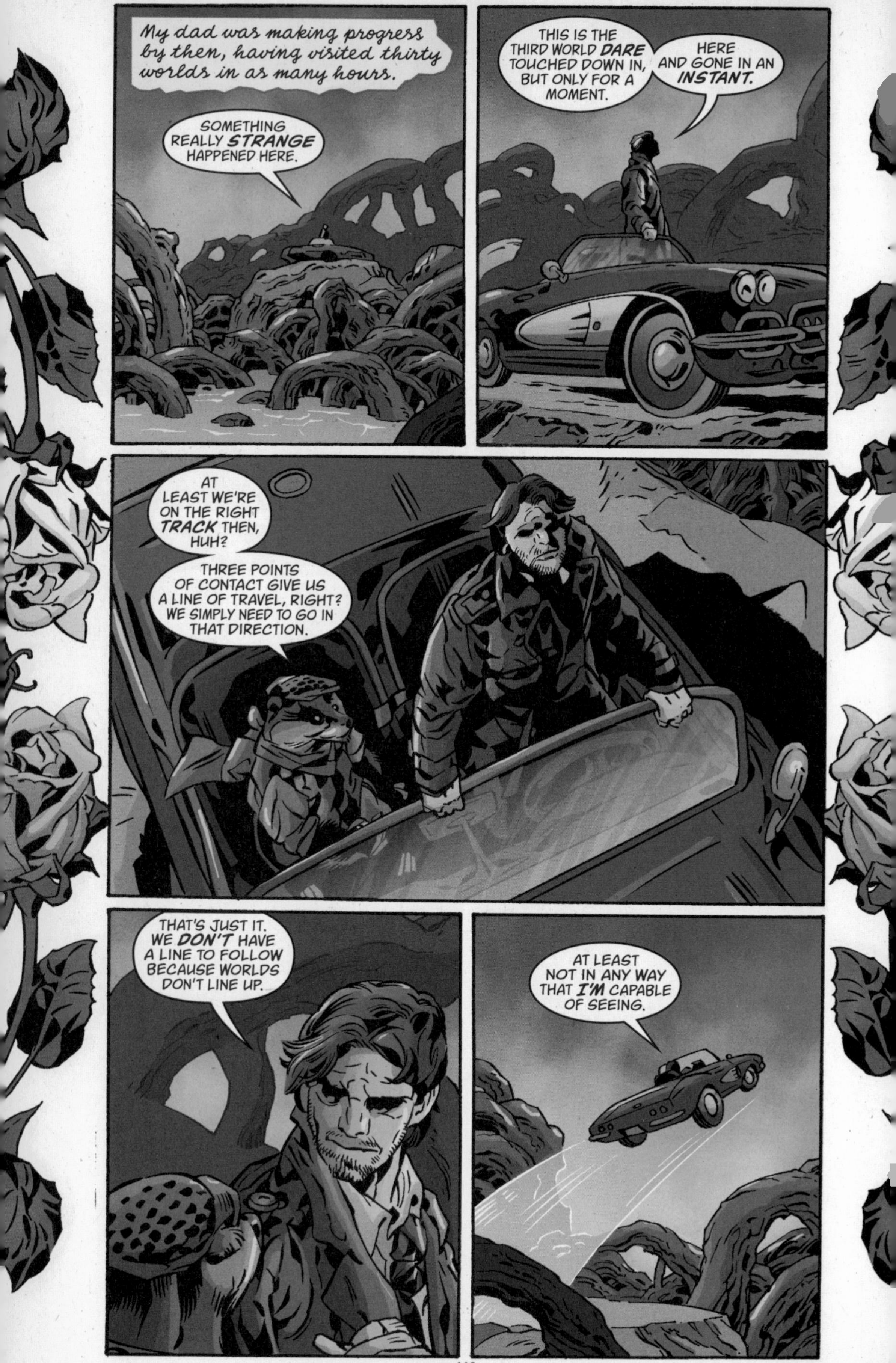
My dad was making progress by then, having visited thirty worlds in as many hours.
SOMETHING REALLY STRANGE HAPPENED HERE.
THIS IS THE THIRD WORLD DARE TOUCHED DOWN IN, BUT ONLY FOR A MOMENT.
HERE AND GONE IN AN INSTANT.
AT LEAST WE'RE ON THE RIGHT TRACK THEN, HUH?
THREE POINTS OF CONTACT GIVE US A LINE OF TRAVEL, RIGHT? WE SIMPLY NEED TO GO IN THAT DIRECTION.
THAT'S JUST IT. WE DON'T HAVE A LINE TO FOLLOW BECAUSE WORLDS DON'T LINE UP.
AT LEAST NOT IN ANY WAY THAT I'M CAPABLE OF SEEING.

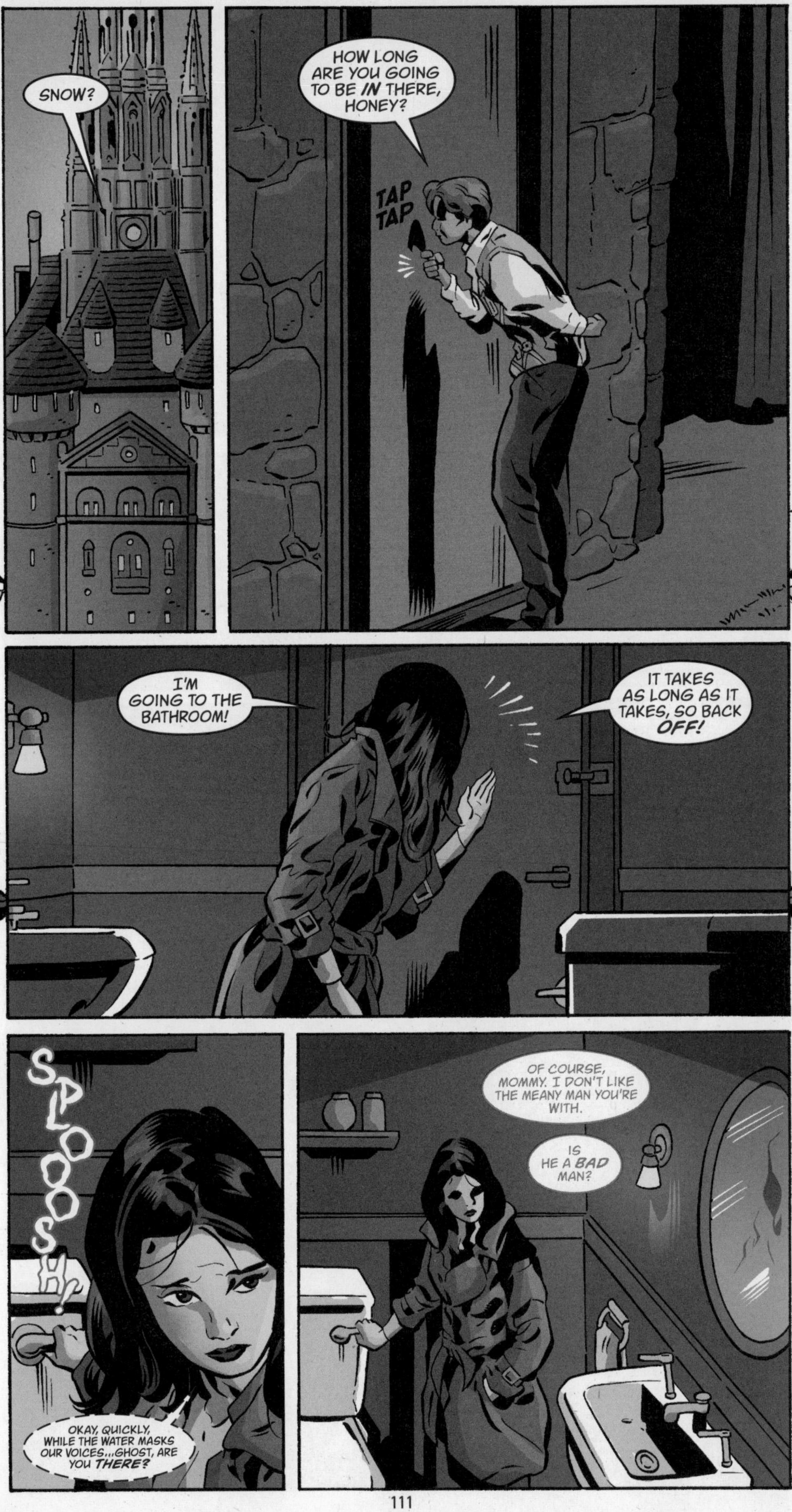
SNOW?
HOW LONG ARE YOU GOING TO BE IN THERE, HONEY?
TAP TAP
I'M GOING TO THE BATHROOM!
IT TAKES AS LONG AS IT TAKES, SO BACK OFF!
SPLOOOSH!
OKAY, QUICKLY, WHILE THE WATER MASKS OUR VOICES... GHOST, ARE YOU THERE?
OF COURSE, MOMMY. I DON'T LIKE THE MEANY MAN YOU'RE WITH.
IS HE A BAD MAN?

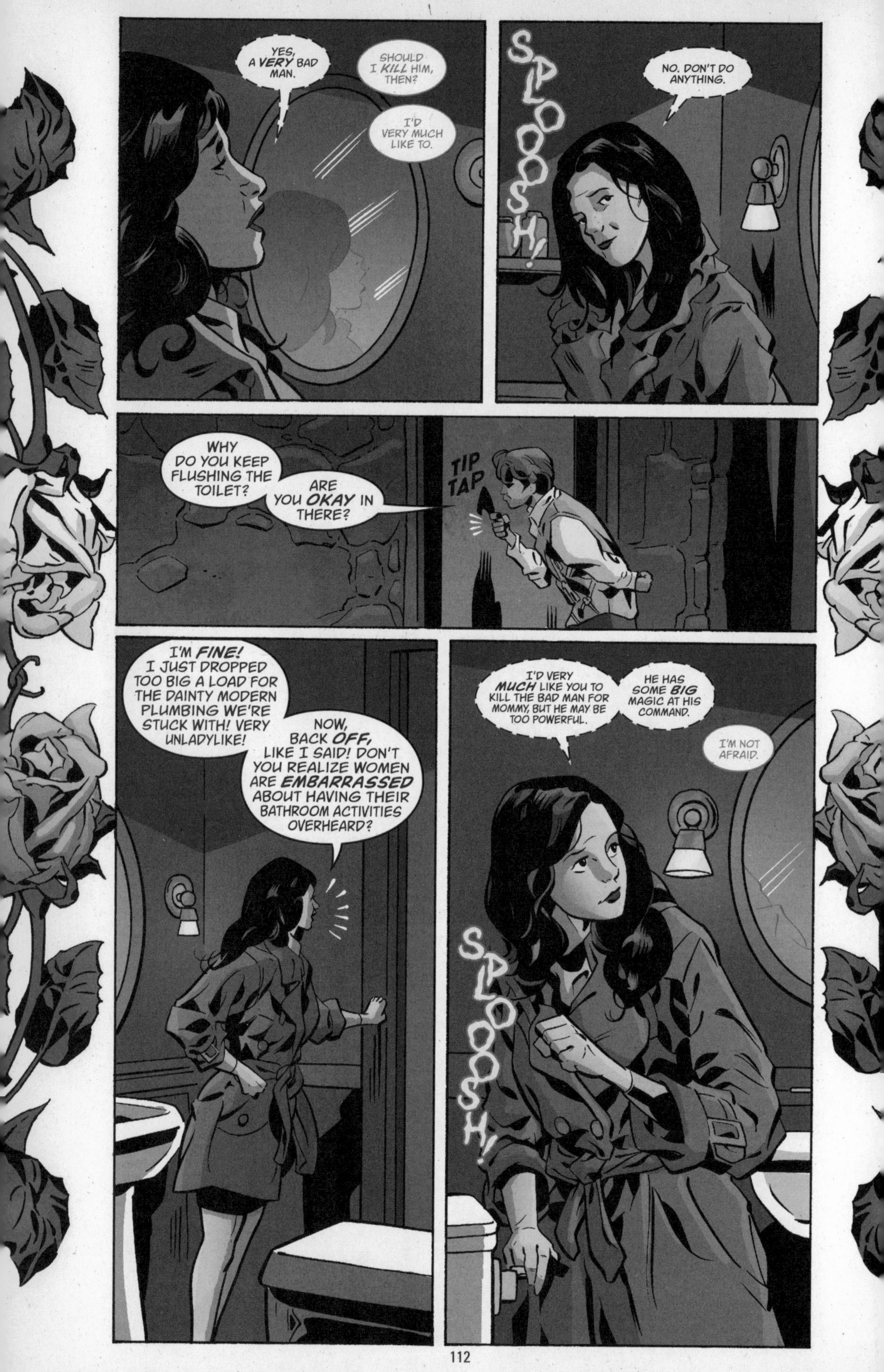
YES, A VERY BAD MAN.
SHOULD I KILL HIM, THEN?
I'D VERY MUCH LIKE TO.
SPLOOOSH!
NO. DON'T DO ANYTHING.
WHY DO YOU KEEP FLUSHING THE TOILET?
ARE YOU OKAY IN THERE?
TIP TAP
I'M FINE! I JUST DROPPED TOO BIG A LOAD FOR THE DAINTY MODERN PLUMBING WE'RE STUCK WITH! VERY UNLADYLIKE!
NOW, BACK OFF, LIKE I SAID! DON'T YOU REALIZE WOMEN ARE EMBARRASSED ABOUT HAVING THEIR BATHROOM ACTIVITIES OVERHEARD?
I'D VERY MUCH LIKE YOU TO KILL THE BAD MAN FOR MOMMY, BUT HE MAY BE TOO POWERFUL.
HE HAS SOME BIG MAGIC AT HIS COMMAND.
I'M NOT AFRAID.
SPLOOOSH!

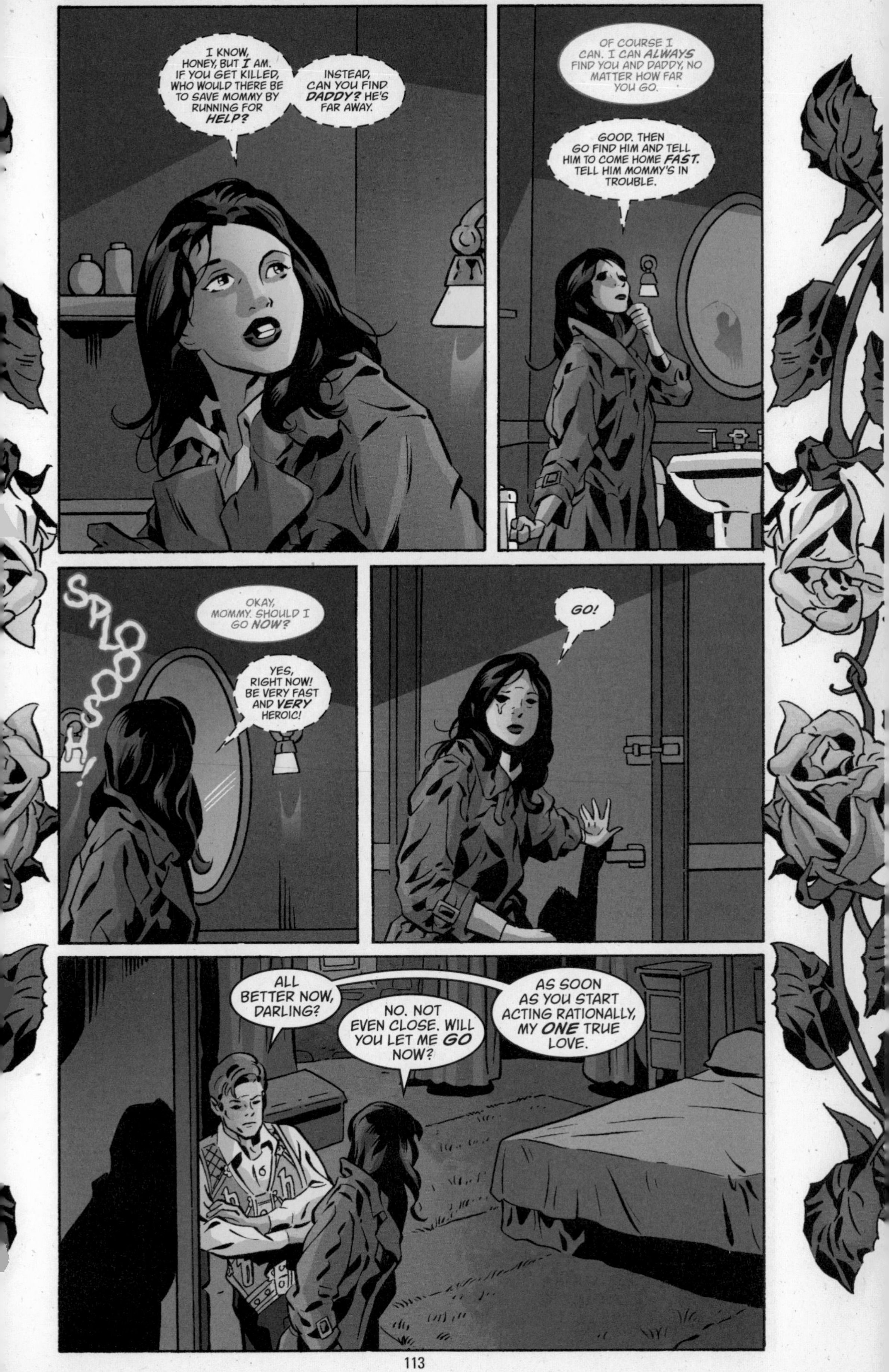
I KNOW, HONEY, BUT I AM. IF YOU GET KILLED, WHO WOULD THERE BE TO SAVE MOMMY BY RUNNING FOR HELP?
INSTEAD, CAN YOU FIND DADDY? HE'S FAR AWAY.
OF COURSE I CAN. I CAN ALWAYS FIND YOU AND DADDY, NO MATTER HOW FAR YOU GO.
GOOD. THEN GO FIND HIM AND TELL HIM TO COME HOME FAST. TELL HIM MOMMY'S IN TROUBLE.
SPLOOOSH!
OKAY, MOMMY. SHOULD I GO NOW?
YES, RIGHT NOW! BE VERY FAST AND VERY HEROIC!
GO!
ALL BETTER NOW, DARLING?
NO. NOT EVEN CLOSE. WILL YOU LET ME GO NOW?
AS SOON AS YOU START ACTING RATIONALLY, MY ONE TRUE LOVE.

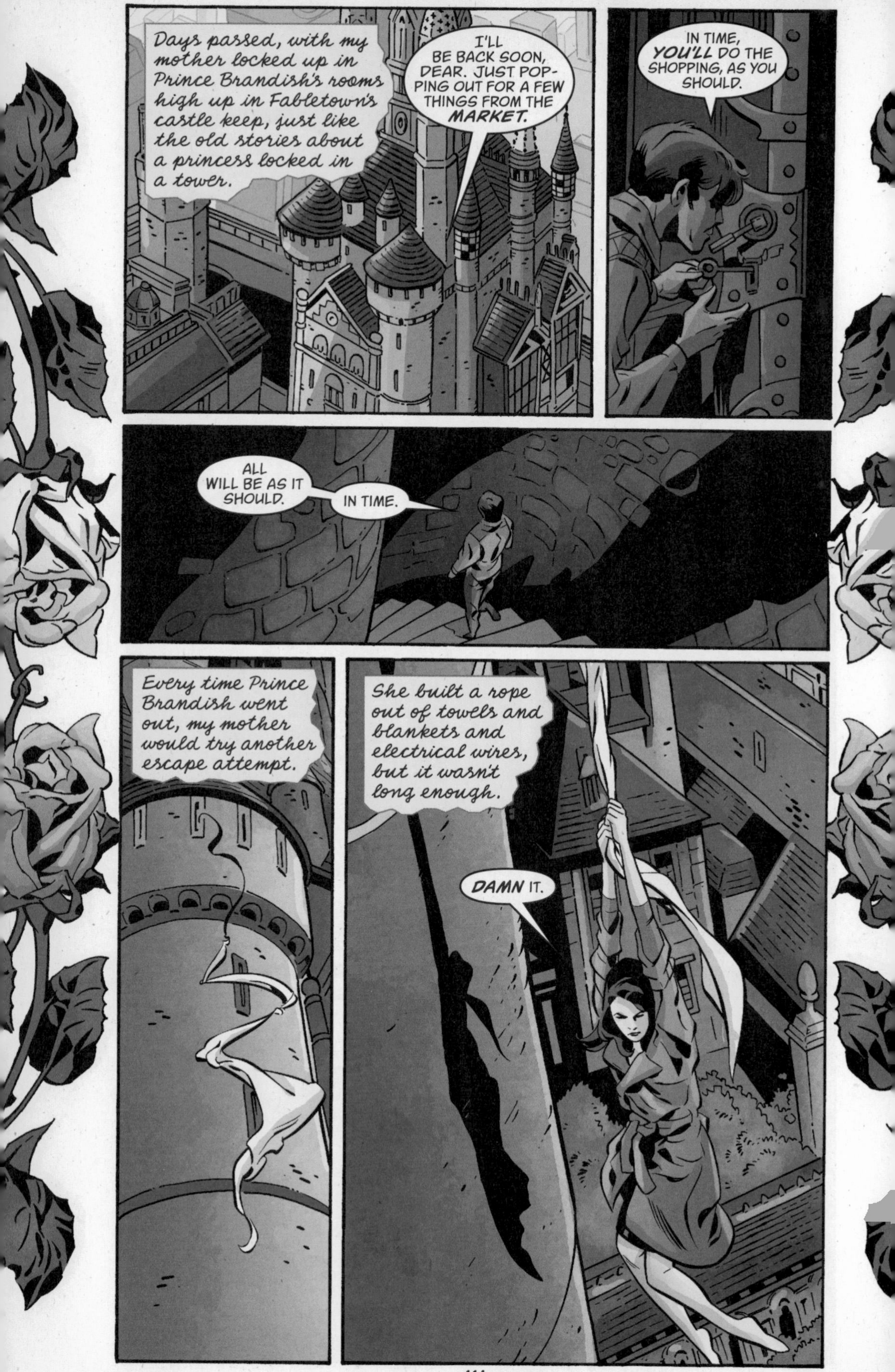
Days passed, with my mother locked up in Prince Brandish's rooms high up in Fabletown's castle keep, just like the old stories about a princess locked in a tower.
I'LL BE BACK SOON, DEAR. JUST POPPING OUT FOR A FEW THINGS FROM THE MARKET.
IN TIME, YOU'LL DO THE SHOPPING, AS YOU SHOULD.
ALL WILL BE AS IT SHOULD.
IN TIME.
Every time Prince Brandish went out, my mother would try another escape attempt.
She built a rope out of towels and blankets and electrical wires, but it wasn't long enough.
DAMN IT.

She tried to talk others into helping her.

DON'T BE SO TIMID. JUST DANGLE A PISTOL FROM A STRING DOWN TO MY *WINDOW* FROM ABOVE, AND I'LL DO THE REST.

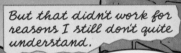

But that didn't work for reasons I still don't quite understand.

I'M SORRY, SNOW, BUT WE CAN'T INTERFERE. NOT *YET*.

THE GOOD NEWS IS WE'RE MAKING PROGRESS ON AMENDING VARIOUS APPLICABLE LAWS, BUT IT'S A SLOW PROCESS AT THE *BEST* OF TIMES.

CHANGING THE LAWS OF AGES CAN BE TOUGH SLED-DING.

THE BAD NEWS IS WE'RE STUCK ON WHETHER OR NOT WE CAN FAIRLY MAKE THE NEW LAWS RETRO-ACTIVE, SO AS TO BE ABLE TO HELP YOU WITH YOUR *SPECIFIC* DILEMMA.

FOR CRAP'S SAKE, YOUR HONOR, JUST HELP ME ESCAPE AND *KILL* THE MAN, AND YOU CAN TRY ME UNDER *ANY* SET OF LAWS YOU LIKE.

IT DOESN'T HELP TO GIVE IN TO DESPAIR, SNOW. WE'LL THINK OF *SOMETHING*. WE SPOKE TO ROSE AT THE FARM. YOU'LL BE PLEASED TO KNOW YOUR CHILDREN ARE FINE.

WELL--YOU KNOW--THE ONES WHO AREN'T CURRENTLY *MISSING*.

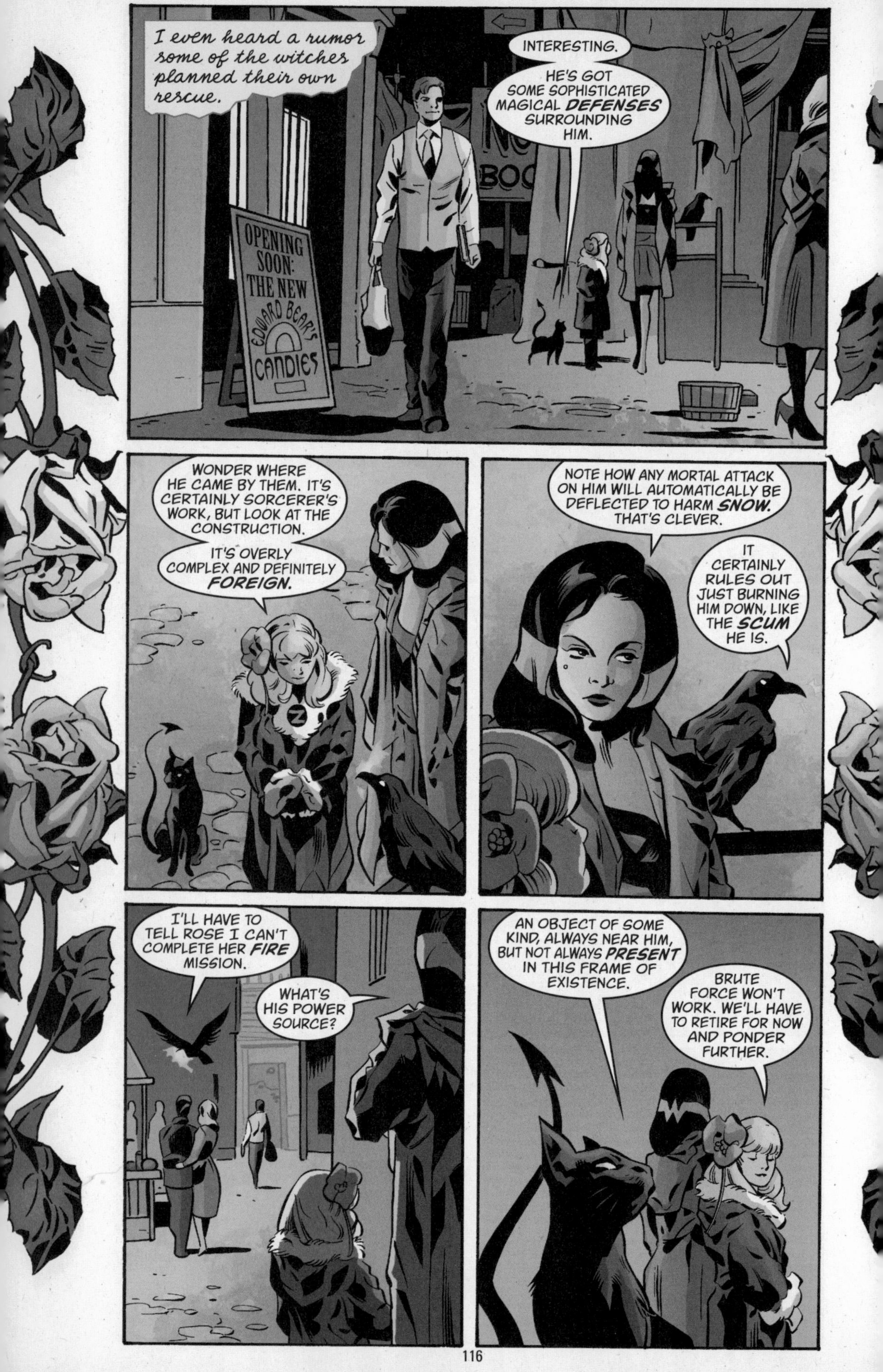
I even heard a rumor some of the witches planned their own rescue.
INTERESTING.
HE'S GOT SOME SOPHISTICATED MAGICAL DEFENSES SURROUNDING HIM.
OPENING SOON: THE NEW EDWARD BEAR'S CANDIES
WONDER WHERE HE CAME BY THEM. IT'S CERTAINLY SORCERER'S WORK, BUT LOOK AT THE CONSTRUCTION.
IT'S OVERLY COMPLEX AND DEFINITELY FOREIGN.
NOTE HOW ANY MORTAL ATTACK ON HIM WILL AUTOMATICALLY BE DEFLECTED TO HARM SNOW. THAT'S CLEVER.
IT CERTAINLY RULES OUT JUST BURNING HIM DOWN, LIKE THE SCUM HE IS.
I'LL HAVE TO TELL ROSE I CAN'T COMPLETE HER FIRE MISSION.
WHAT'S HIS POWER SOURCE?
AN OBJECT OF SOME KIND, ALWAYS NEAR HIM, BUT NOT ALWAYS PRESENT IN THIS FRAME OF EXISTENCE.
BRUTE FORCE WON'T WORK. WE'LL HAVE TO RETIRE FOR NOW AND PONDER FURTHER.

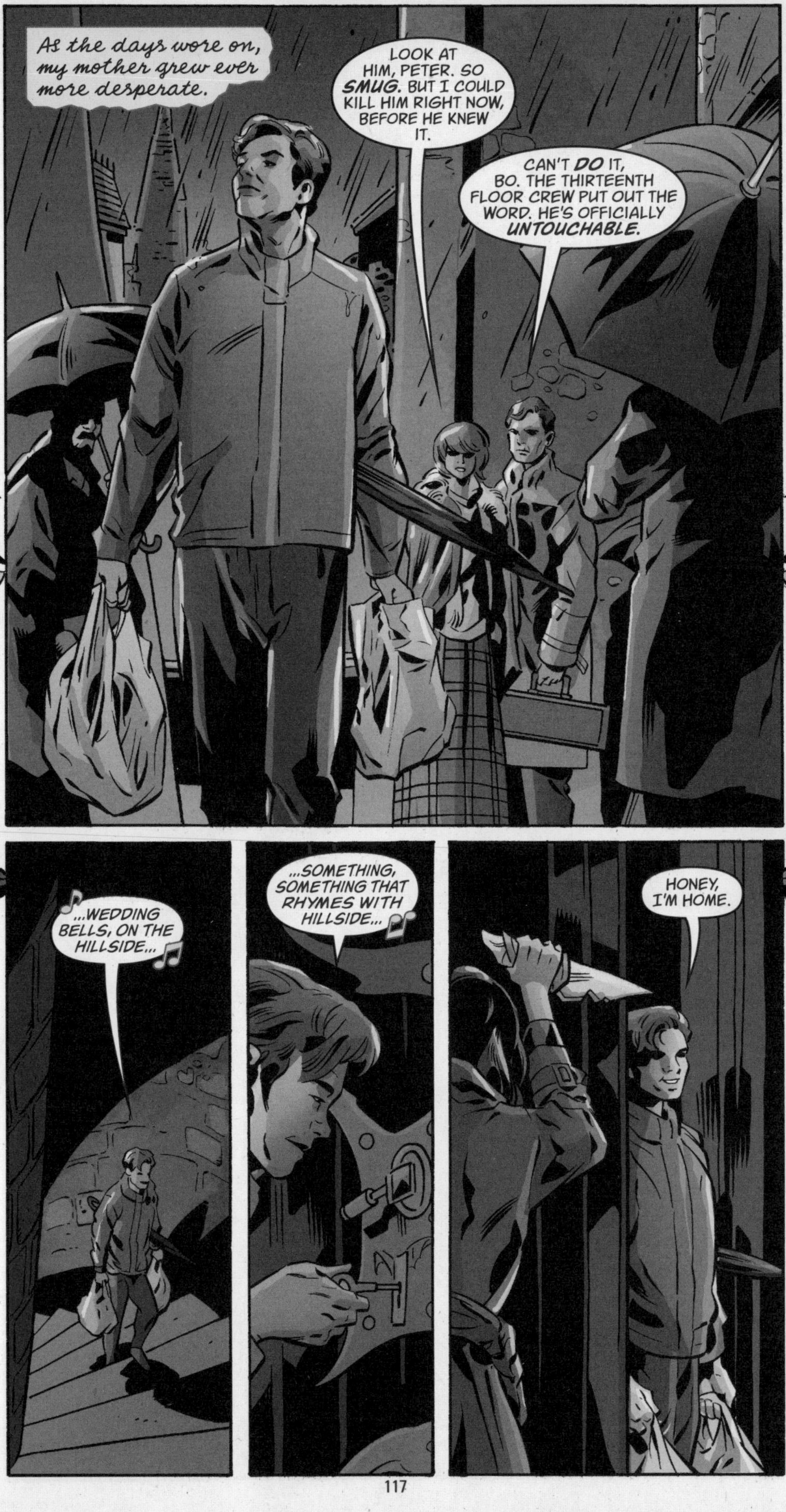
As the days wore on, my mother grew ever more desperate.
LOOK AT HIM, PETER. SO SMUG. BUT I COULD KILL HIM RIGHT NOW, BEFORE HE KNEW IT.
CAN'T DO IT, BO. THE THIRTEENTH FLOOR CREW PUT OUT THE WORD. HE'S OFFICIALLY UNTOUCHABLE.
...WEDDING BELLS, ON THE HILLSIDE...
...SOMETHING, SOMETHING THAT RHYMES WITH HILLSIDE...
HONEY, I'M HOME.

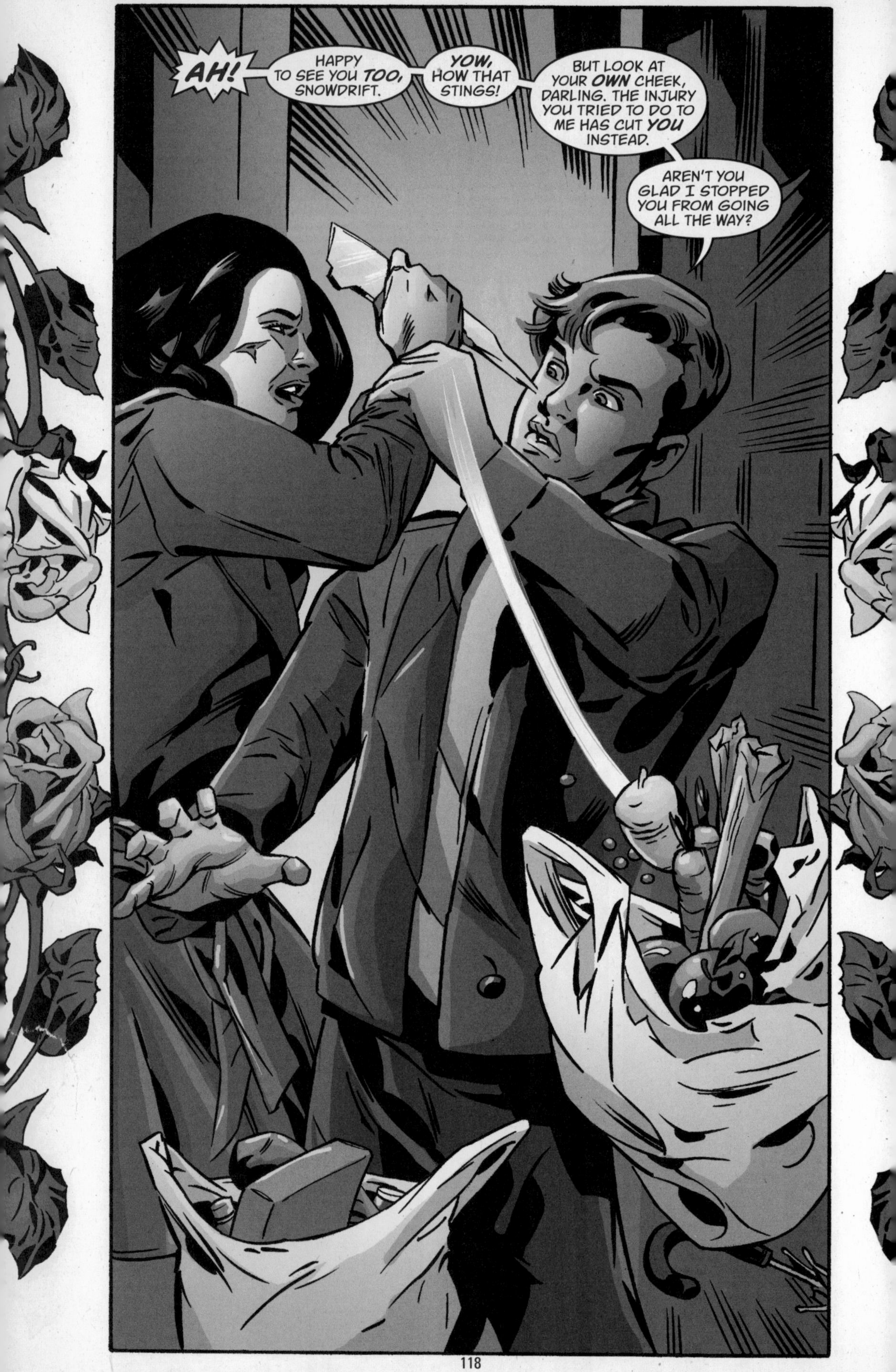
AH!
HAPPY TO SEE YOU TOO, SNOWDRIFT.
YOW, HOW THAT STINGS!
BUT LOOK AT YOUR OWN CHEEK, DARLING. THE INJURY YOU TRIED TO DO TO ME HAS CUT YOU INSTEAD.
AREN'T YOU GLAD I STOPPED YOU FROM GOING ALL THE WAY?

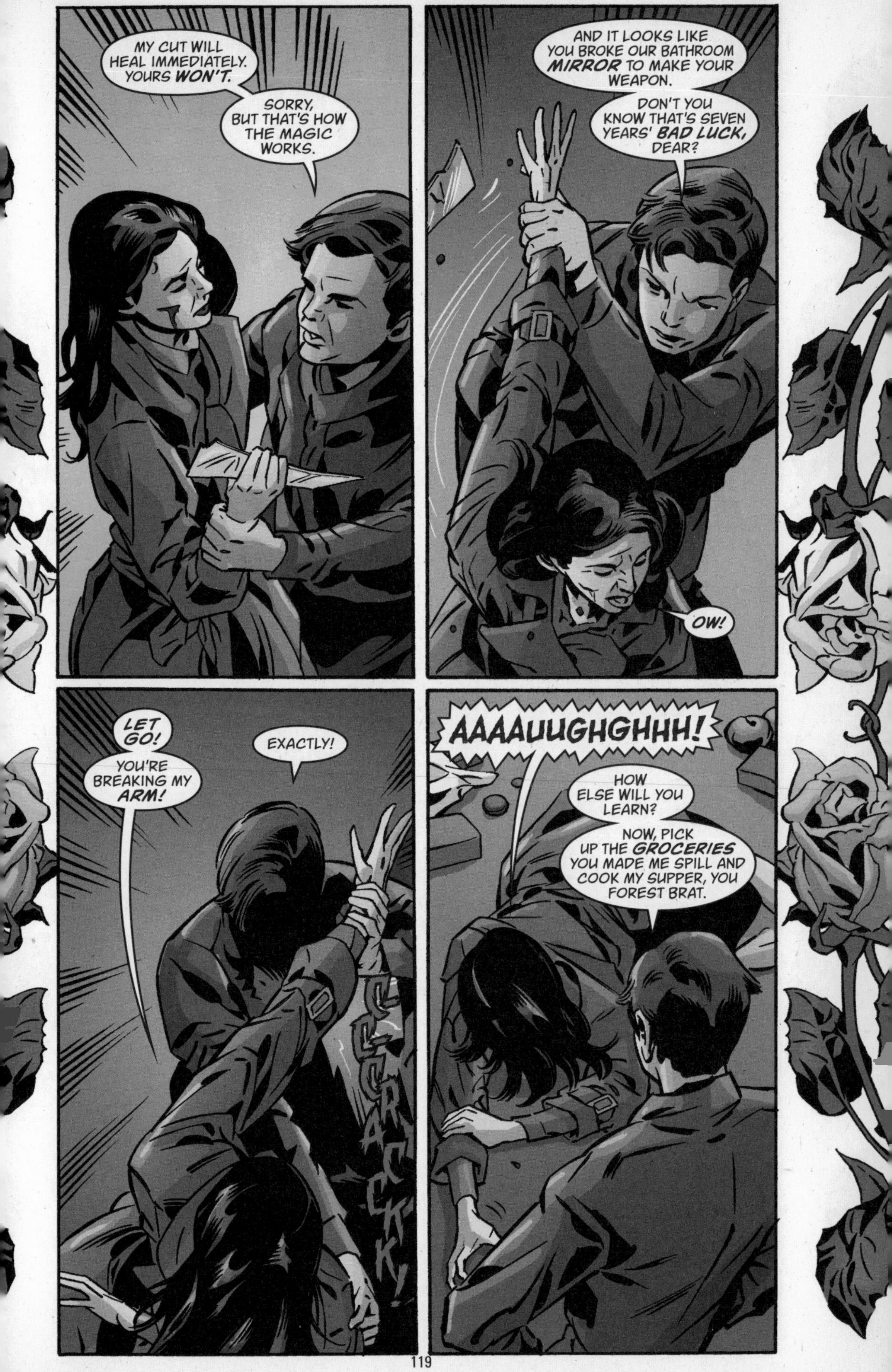
MY CUT WILL HEAL IMMEDIATELY. YOURS WON'T.
SORRY, BUT THAT'S HOW THE MAGIC WORKS.
AND IT LOOKS LIKE YOU BROKE OUR BATHROOM MIRROR TO MAKE YOUR WEAPON.
DON'T YOU KNOW THAT'S SEVEN YEARS' BAD LUCK, DEAR?
OW!
LET GO!
YOU'RE BREAKING MY ARM!
EXACTLY!
CCCRACK!
AAAAUUGHGHHH!
HOW ELSE WILL YOU LEARN?
NOW, PICK UP THE GROCERIES YOU MADE ME SPILL AND COOK MY SUPPER, YOU FOREST BRAT.

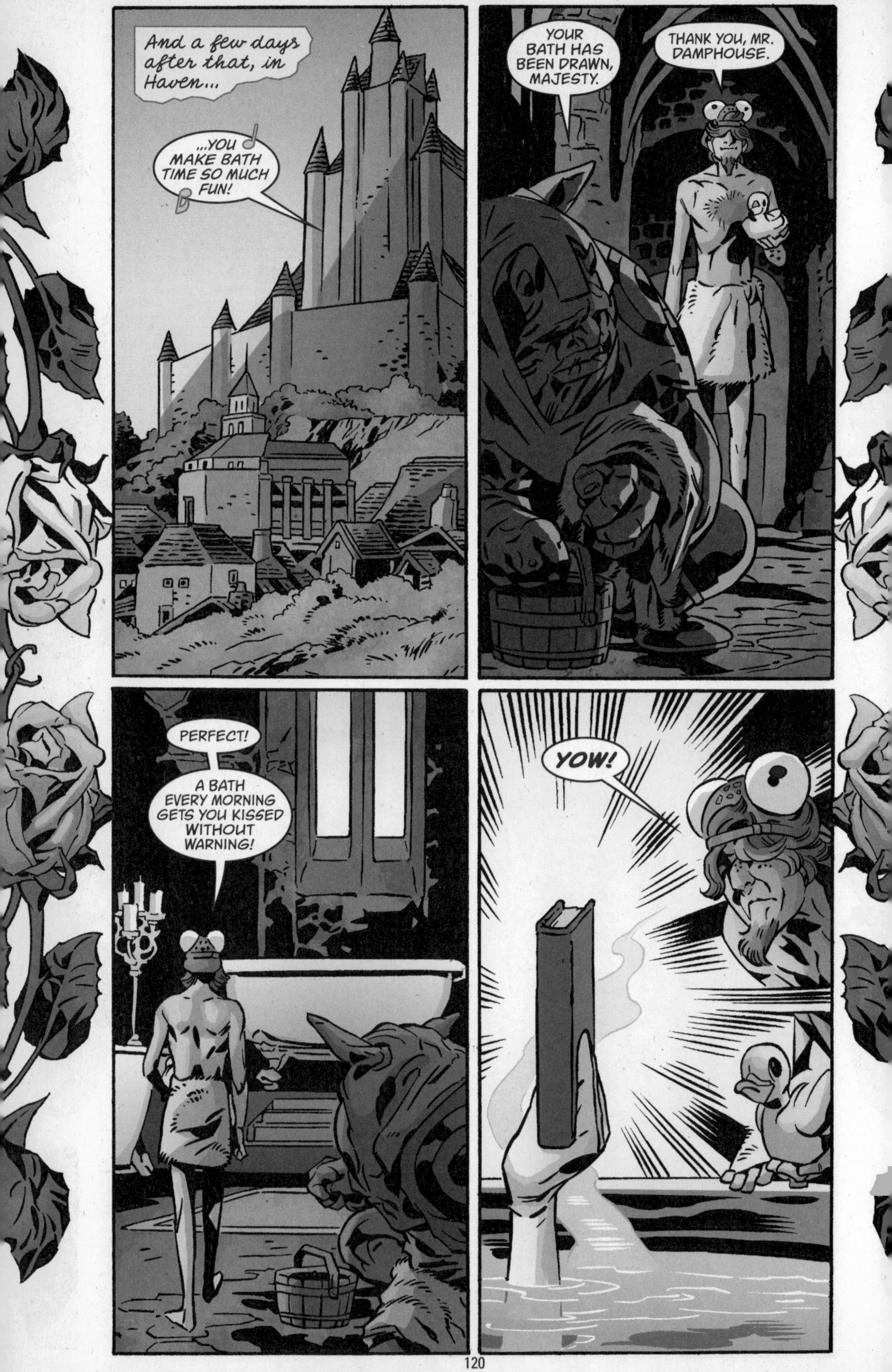
And a few days after that, in Haven...
...YOU MAKE BATH TIME SO MUCH FUN!
YOUR BATH HAS BEEN DRAWN, MAJESTY.
THANK YOU, MR. DAMPHOUSE.
PERFECT!
A BATH EVERY MORNING GETS YOU KISSED WITHOUT WARNING!
YOW!

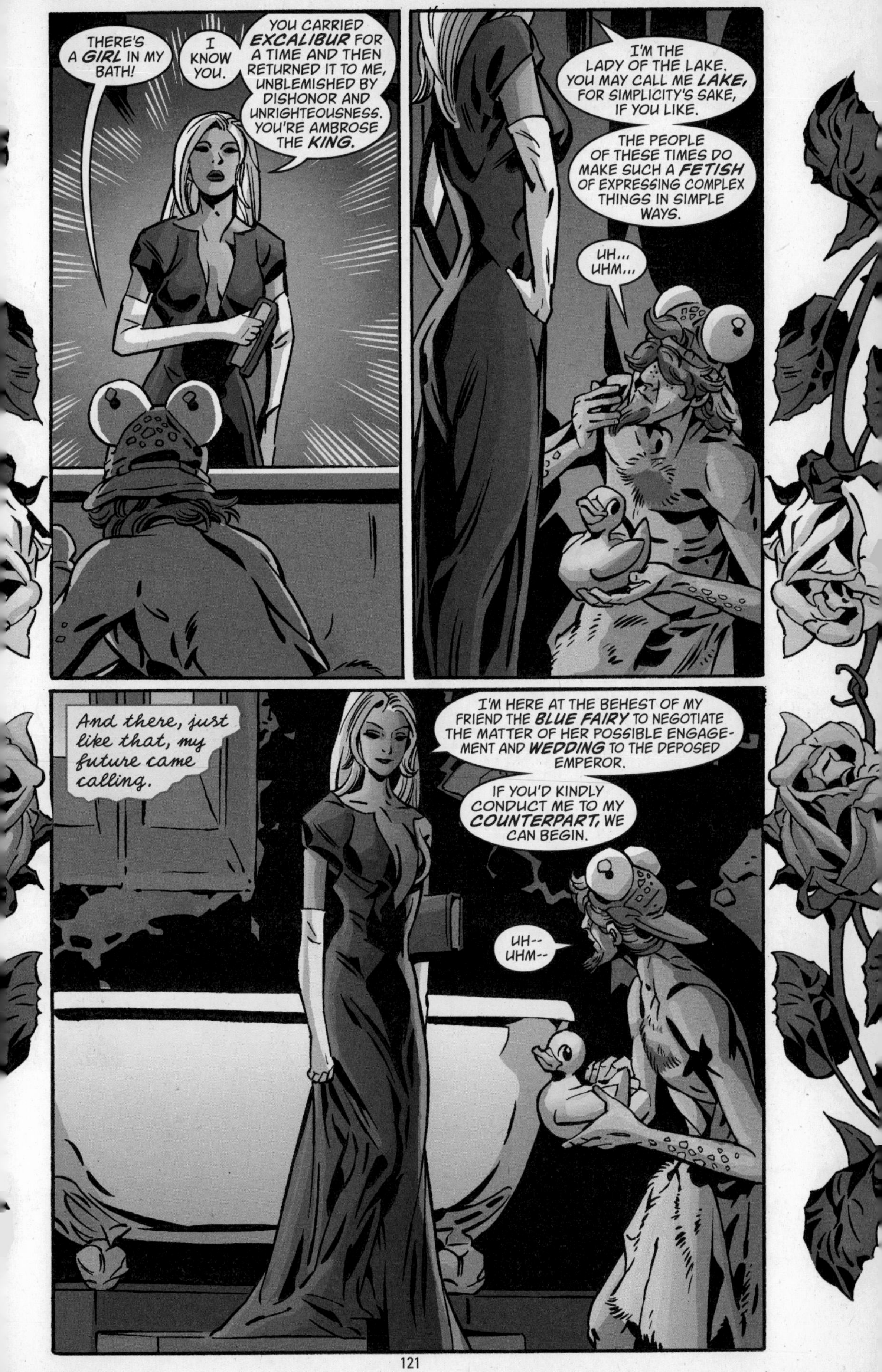
THERE'S A GIRL IN MY BATH!
I KNOW YOU.
YOU CARRIED EXCALIBUR FOR A TIME AND THEN RETURNED IT TO ME, UNBLEMISHED BY DISHONOR AND UNRIGHTEOUSNESS. YOU'RE AMBROSE THE KING.
I'M THE LADY OF THE LAKE. YOU MAY CALL ME LAKE, FOR SIMPLICITY'S SAKE, IF YOU LIKE.
THE PEOPLE OF THESE TIMES DO MAKE SUCH A FETISH OF EXPRESSING COMPLEX THINGS IN SIMPLE WAYS.
UH... UHM...
And there, just like that, my future came calling.
I'M HERE AT THE BEHEST OF MY FRIEND THE BLUE FAIRY TO NEGOTIATE THE MATTER OF HER POSSIBLE ENGAGEMENT AND WEDDING TO THE DEPOSED EMPEROR.
IF YOU'D KINDLY CONDUCT ME TO MY COUNTERPART, WE CAN BEGIN.
UH-- UHM--

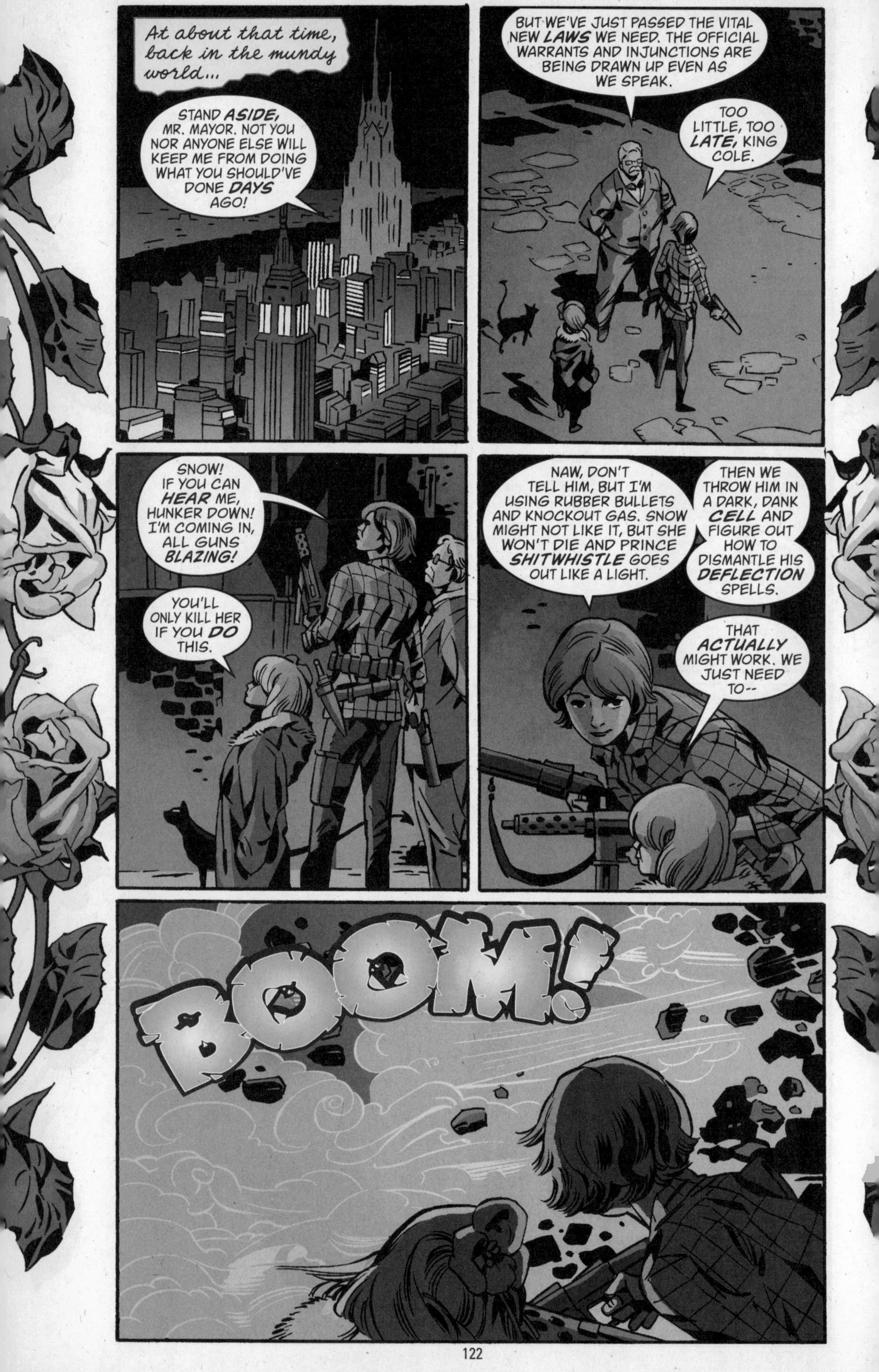
At about that time, back in the mundy world...
STAND ASIDE, MR. MAYOR. NOT YOU NOR ANYONE ELSE WILL KEEP ME FROM DOING WHAT YOU SHOULD'VE DONE DAYS AGO!
BUT WE'VE JUST PASSED THE VITAL NEW LAWS WE NEED. THE OFFICIAL WARRANTS AND INJUNCTIONS ARE BEING DRAWN UP EVEN AS WE SPEAK.
TOO LITTLE, TOO LATE, KING COLE.
SNOW! IF YOU CAN HEAR ME, HUNKER DOWN! I'M COMING IN, ALL GUNS BLAZING!
YOU'LL ONLY KILL HER IF YOU DO THIS.
NAW, DON'T TELL HIM, BUT I'M USING RUBBER BULLETS AND KNOCKOUT GAS. SNOW MIGHT NOT LIKE IT, BUT SHE WON'T DIE AND PRINCE SHITWHISTLE GOES OUT LIKE A LIGHT.
THEN WE THROW HIM IN A DARK, DANK CELL AND FIGURE OUT HOW TO DISMANTLE HIS DEFLECTION SPELLS.
THAT ACTUALLY MIGHT WORK. WE JUST NEED TO--
BOOM!

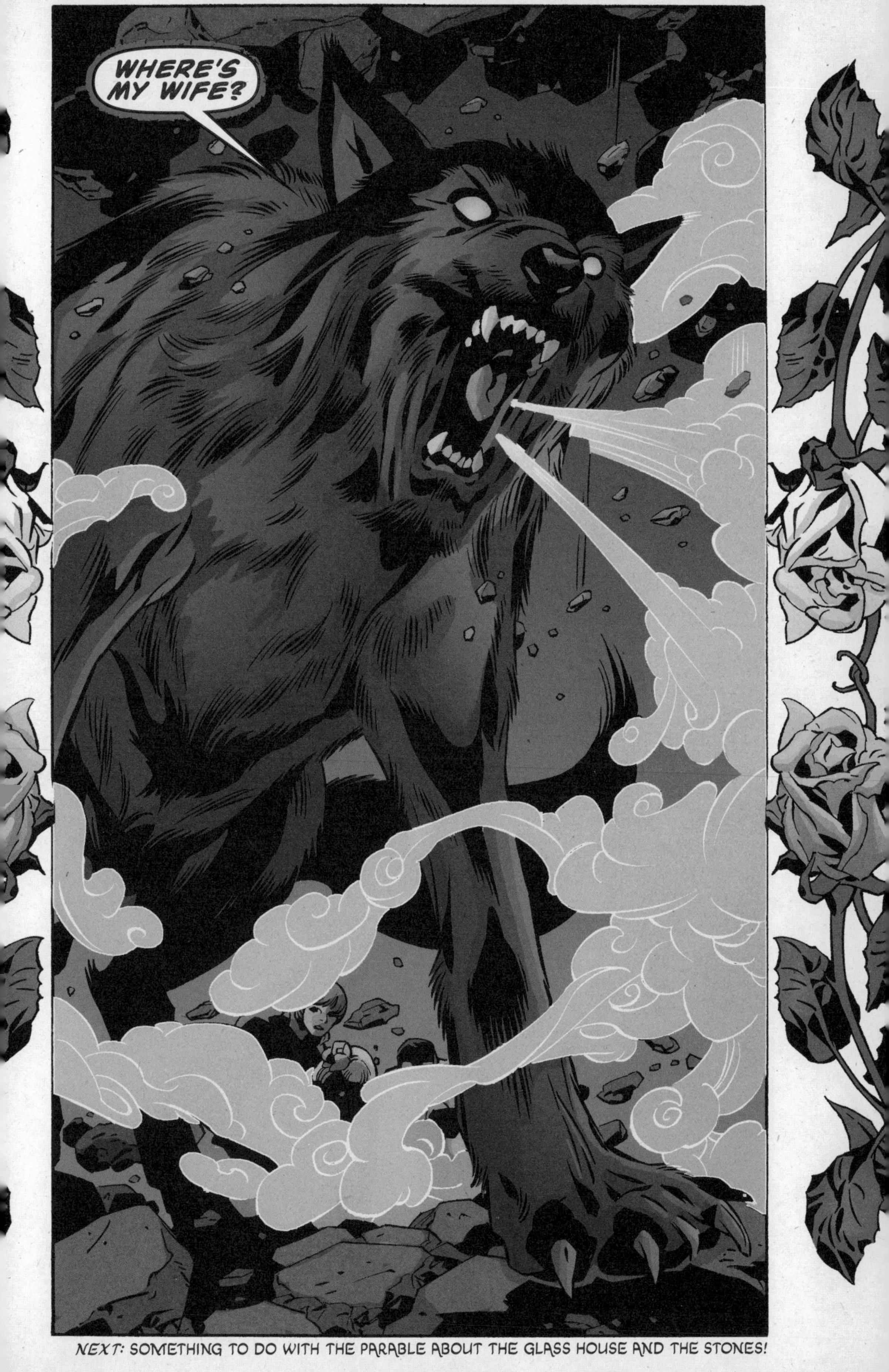
WHERE'S MY WIFE?

NEXT: SOMETHING TO DO WITH THE PARABLE ABOUT THE GLASS HOUSE AND THE STONES!

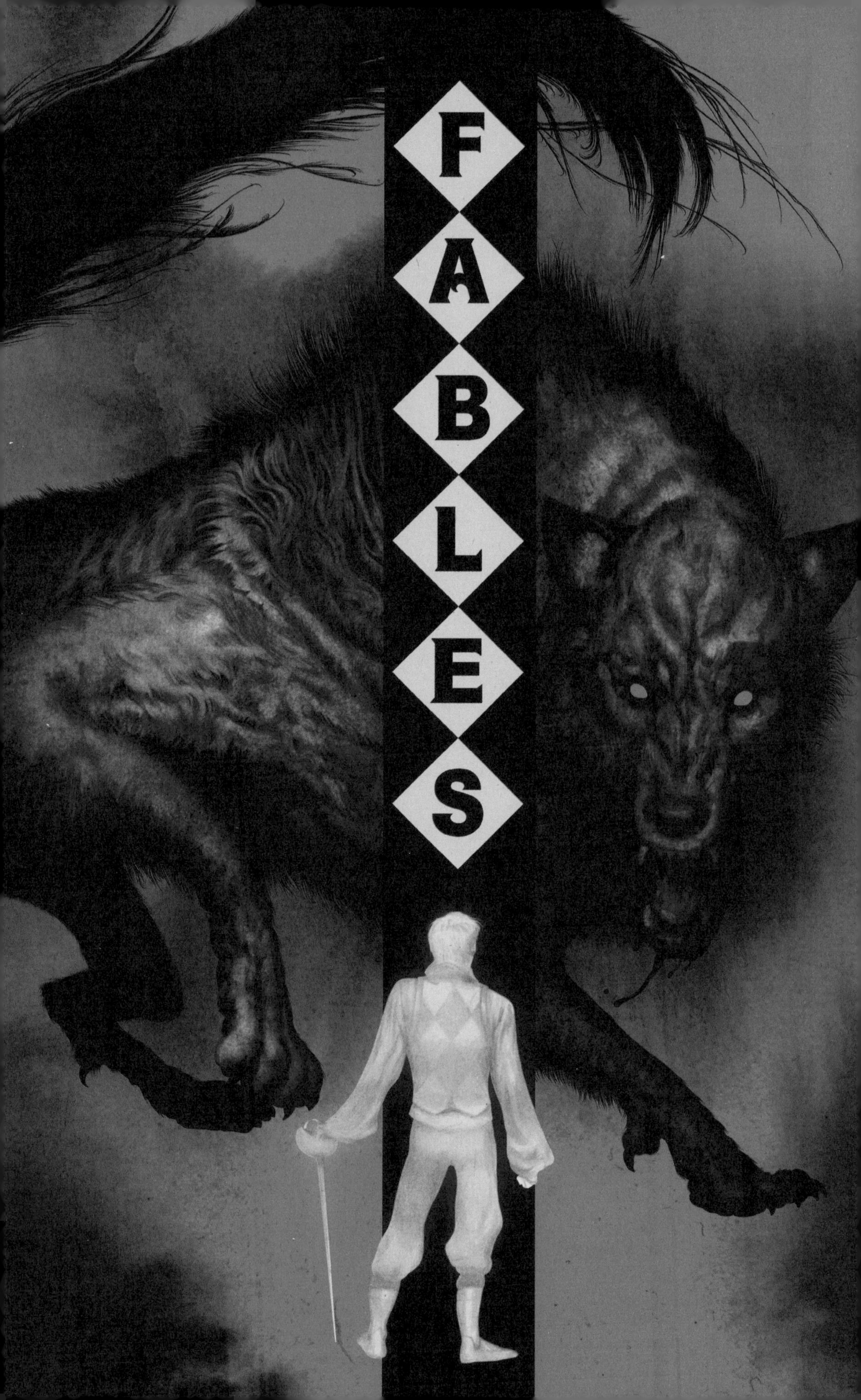
FABLES

MEANWHILE, IN THE BIGGEST COURTYARD OF FABLETOWN RESTORED...

AT LAST!

THE ANIMAL *BRIDEGROOM* IS HOME!

YOU MADE GOOD TIME, TOO.

YOUR SECRET AND INVISIBLE SON IS QUITE POWERFUL IN HIS *OWN* RIGHT, ABLE TO CROSS ENTIRE UNIVERSES IN A VERITABLE "BLINK."

HOW DOES THAT *WORK*?

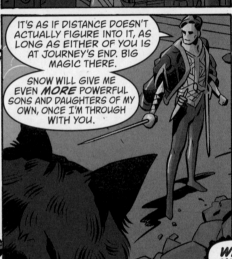

IT'S AS IF DISTANCE DOESN'T ACTUALLY FIGURE INTO IT, AS LONG AS EITHER OF YOU IS AT JOURNEY'S END. BIG MAGIC THERE.

SNOW WILL GIVE ME EVEN *MORE* POWERFUL SONS AND DAUGHTERS OF MY OWN, ONCE I'M THROUGH WITH YOU.

WHERE'S MY WIFE?

Through a Glass Darkly
Chapter Four of Snow White

Bill Willingham: writer-creator ❄ Mark Buckingham: pencils
❄ Steve Leialoha: inks (2-3, 6-7, 10-11, 14-15, 18-19) ❄
❄ Andrew Pepoy: inks (1, 4-5, 8-9, 12-13, 16-17, 20) ❄
Lee Loughridge: colors ❄ ❄ Gregory Lockard: assoc. ed.
❄ Todd Klein: letters ❄ ❄ ❄ Shelly Bond: editor ❄

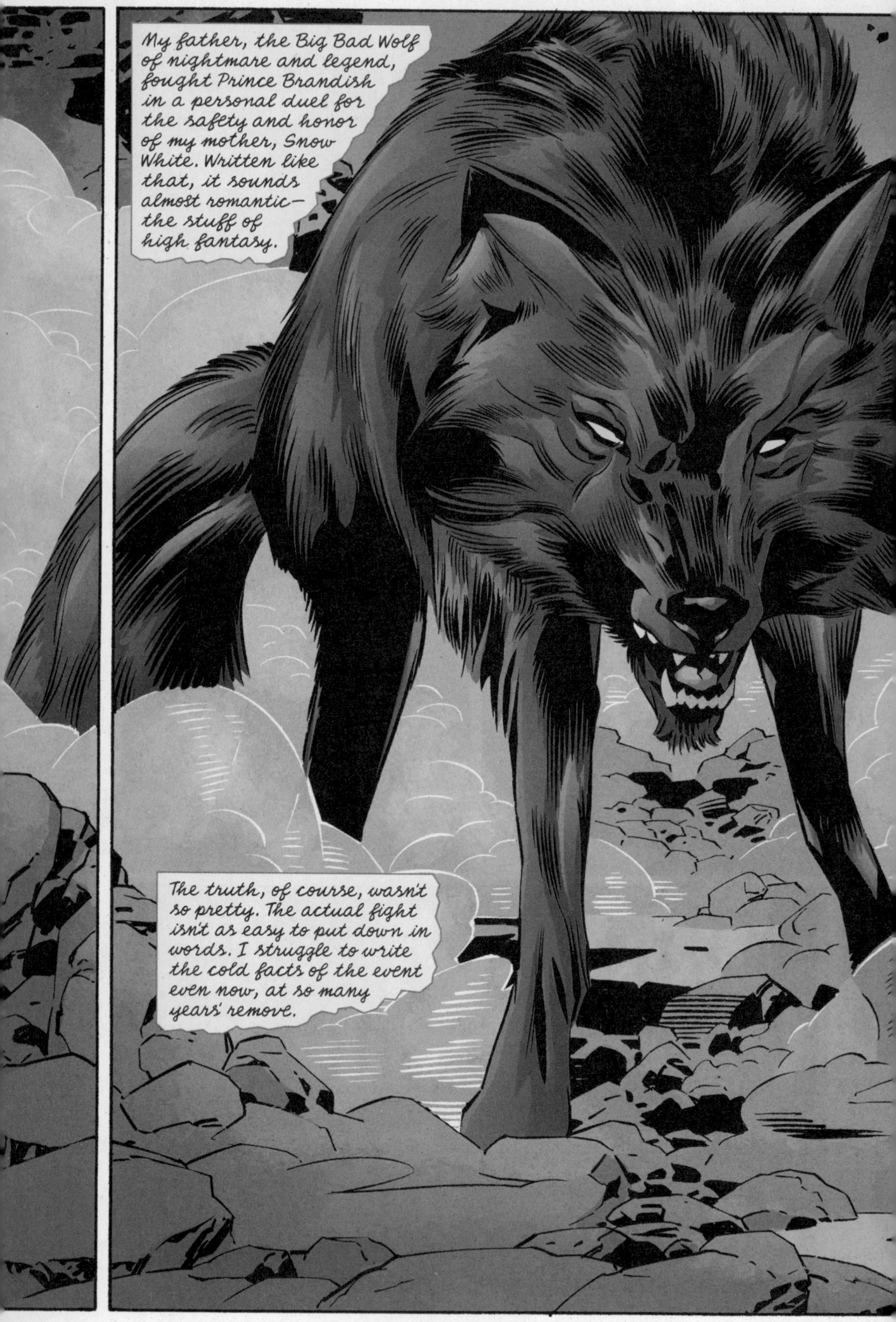
My father, the Big Bad Wolf of nightmare and legend, fought Prince Brandish in a personal duel for the safety and honor of my mother, Snow White. Written like that, it sounds almost romantic—the stuff of high fantasy.
The truth, of course, wasn't so pretty. The actual fight isn't as easy to put down in words. I struggle to write the cold facts of the event even now, at so many years' remove.

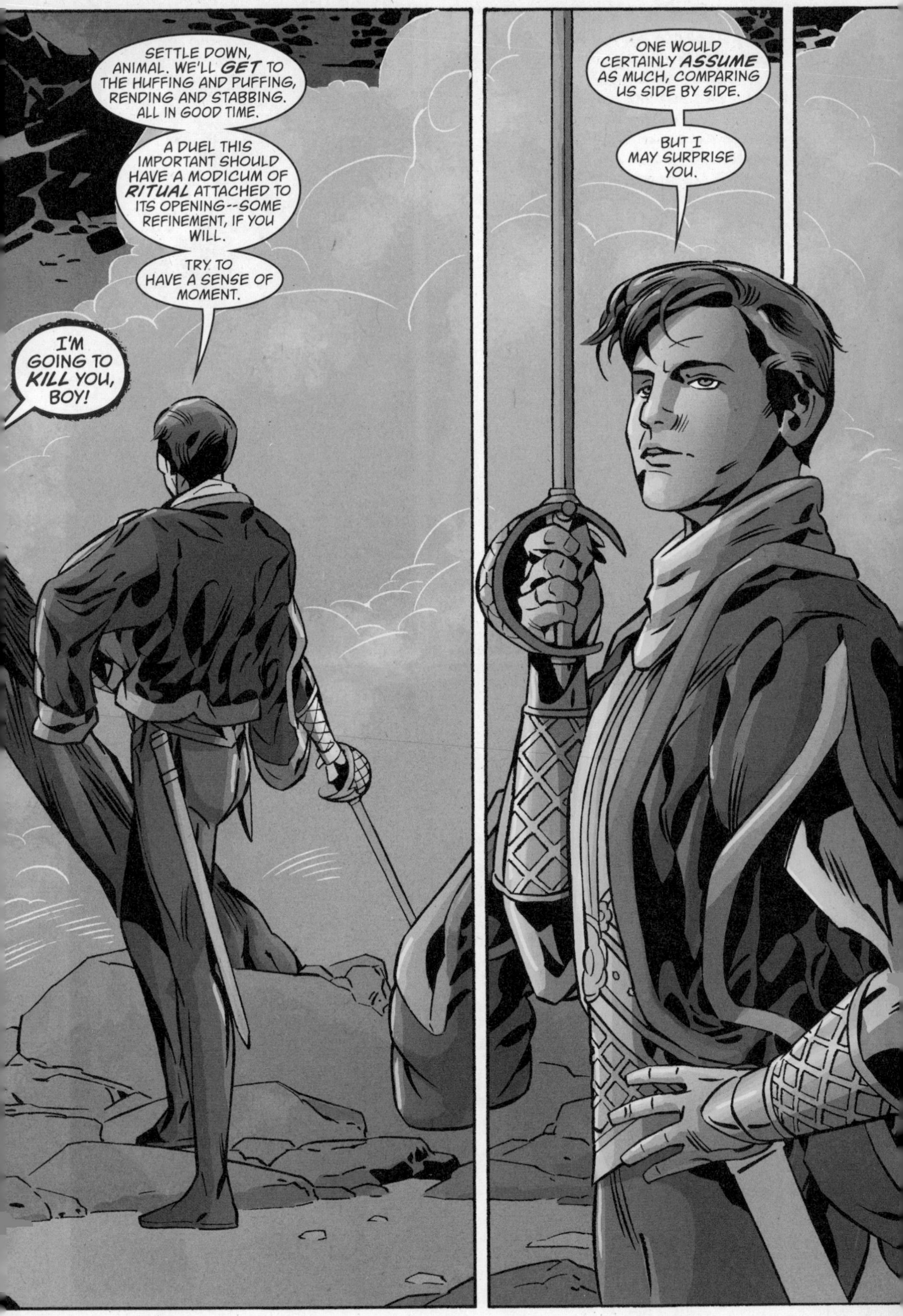
SETTLE DOWN, ANIMAL. WE'LL GET TO THE HUFFING AND PUFFING, RENDING AND STABBING. ALL IN GOOD TIME.
A DUEL THIS IMPORTANT SHOULD HAVE A MODICUM OF RITUAL ATTACHED TO ITS OPENING--SOME REFINEMENT, IF YOU WILL.
TRY TO HAVE A SENSE OF MOMENT.
I'M GOING TO KILL YOU, BOY!
ONE WOULD CERTAINLY ASSUME AS MUCH, COMPARING US SIDE BY SIDE.
BUT I MAY SURPRISE YOU.

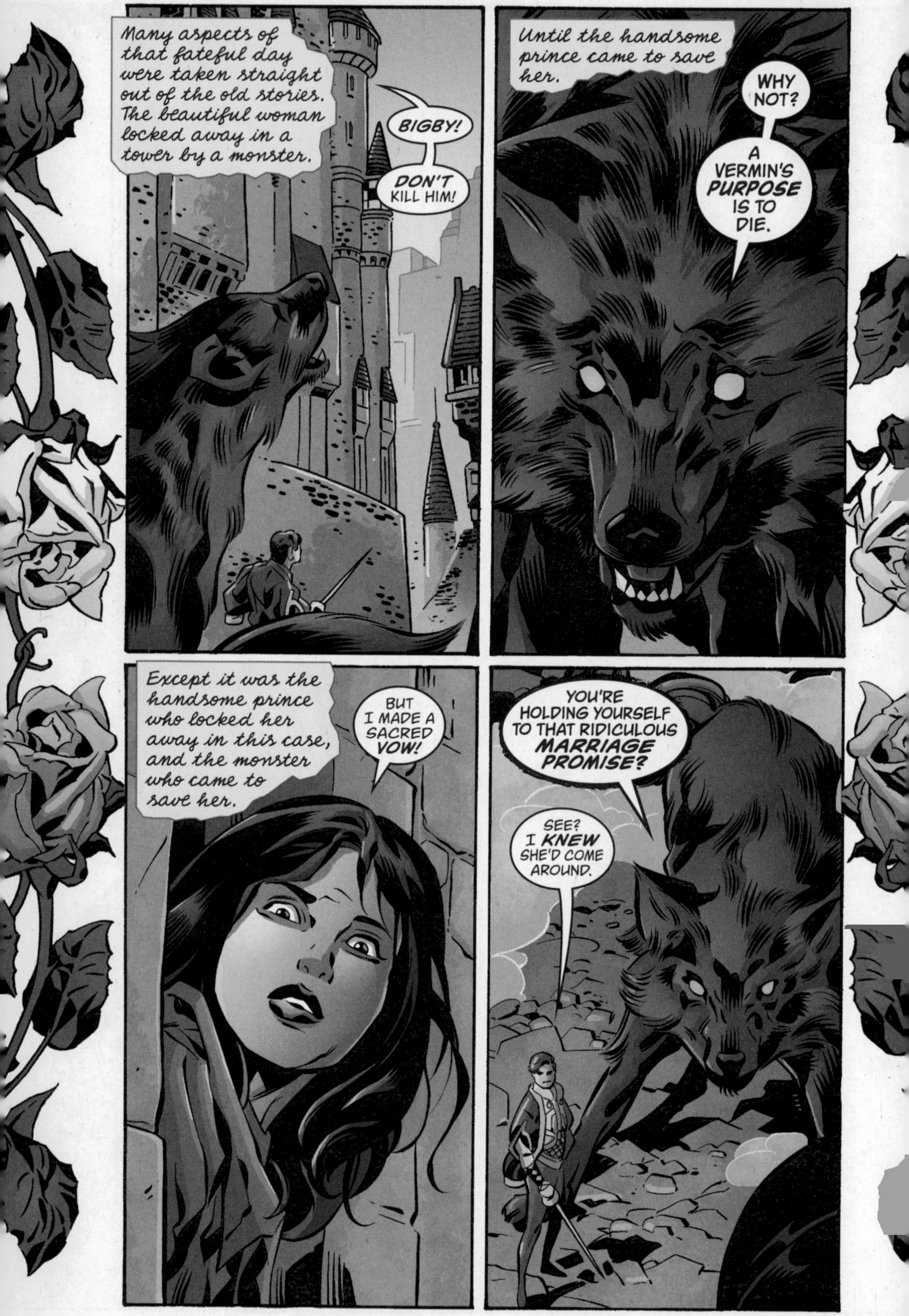
Many aspects of that fateful day were taken straight out of the old stories. The beautiful woman locked away in a tower by a monster.
BIGBY!
DON'T KILL HIM!
Until the handsome prince came to save her.
WHY NOT?
A VERMIN'S PURPOSE IS TO DIE.
Except it was the handsome prince who locked her away in this case, and the monster who came to save her.
BUT I MADE A SACRED VOW!
YOU'RE HOLDING YOURSELF TO THAT RIDICULOUS MARRIAGE PROMISE?
SEE? I KNEW SHE'D COME AROUND.

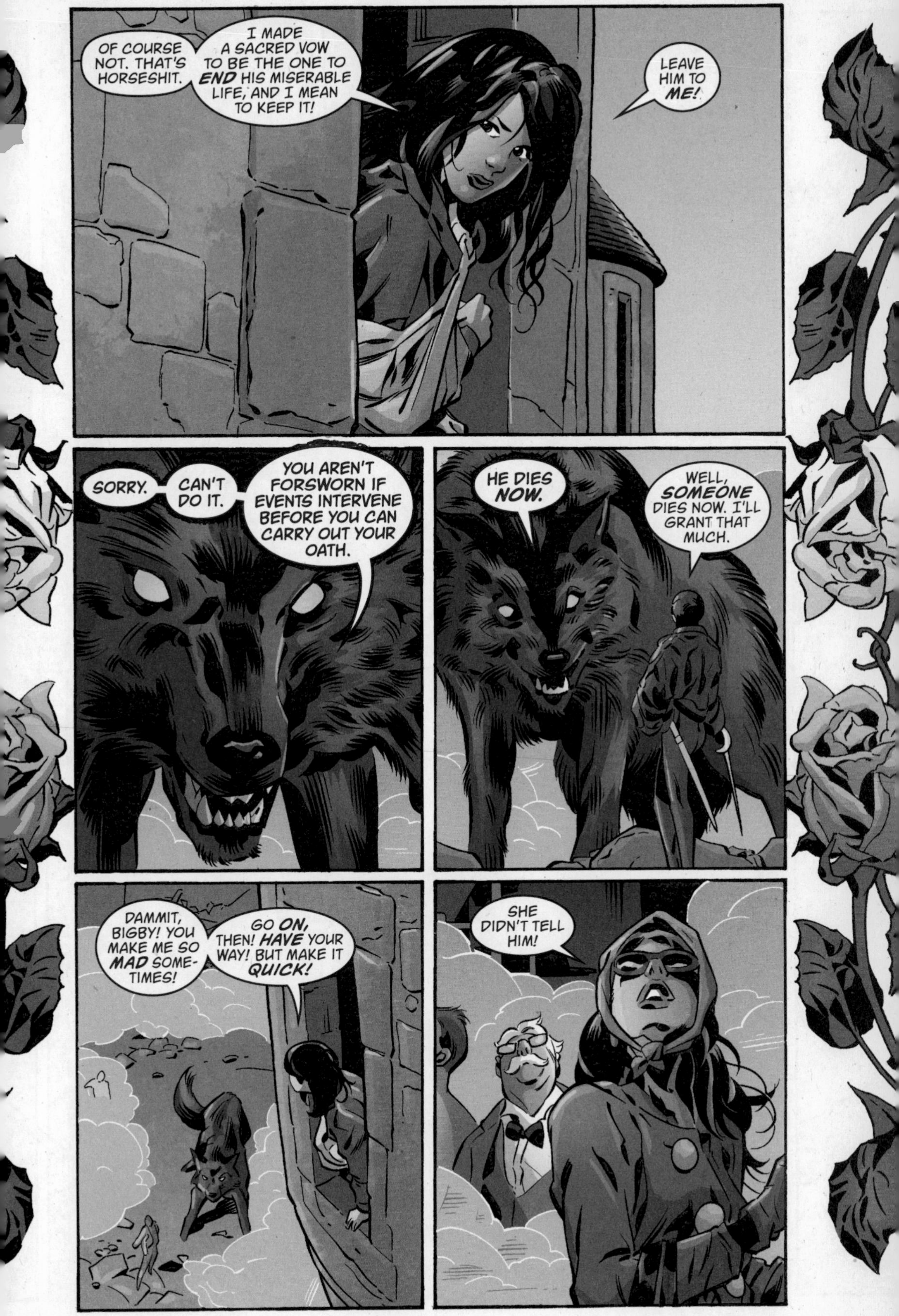
OF COURSE NOT. THAT'S HORSESHIT.
I MADE A SACRED VOW TO BE THE ONE TO END HIS MISERABLE LIFE, AND I MEAN TO KEEP IT!
LEAVE HIM TO ME!
SORRY.
CAN'T DO IT.
YOU AREN'T FORSWORN IF EVENTS INTERVENE BEFORE YOU CAN CARRY OUT YOUR OATH.
HE DIES NOW.
WELL, SOMEONE DIES NOW. I'LL GRANT THAT MUCH.
DAMMIT, BIGBY! YOU MAKE ME SO MAD SOMETIMES!
GO ON, THEN! HAVE YOUR WAY! BUT MAKE IT QUICK!
SHE DIDN'T TELL HIM!

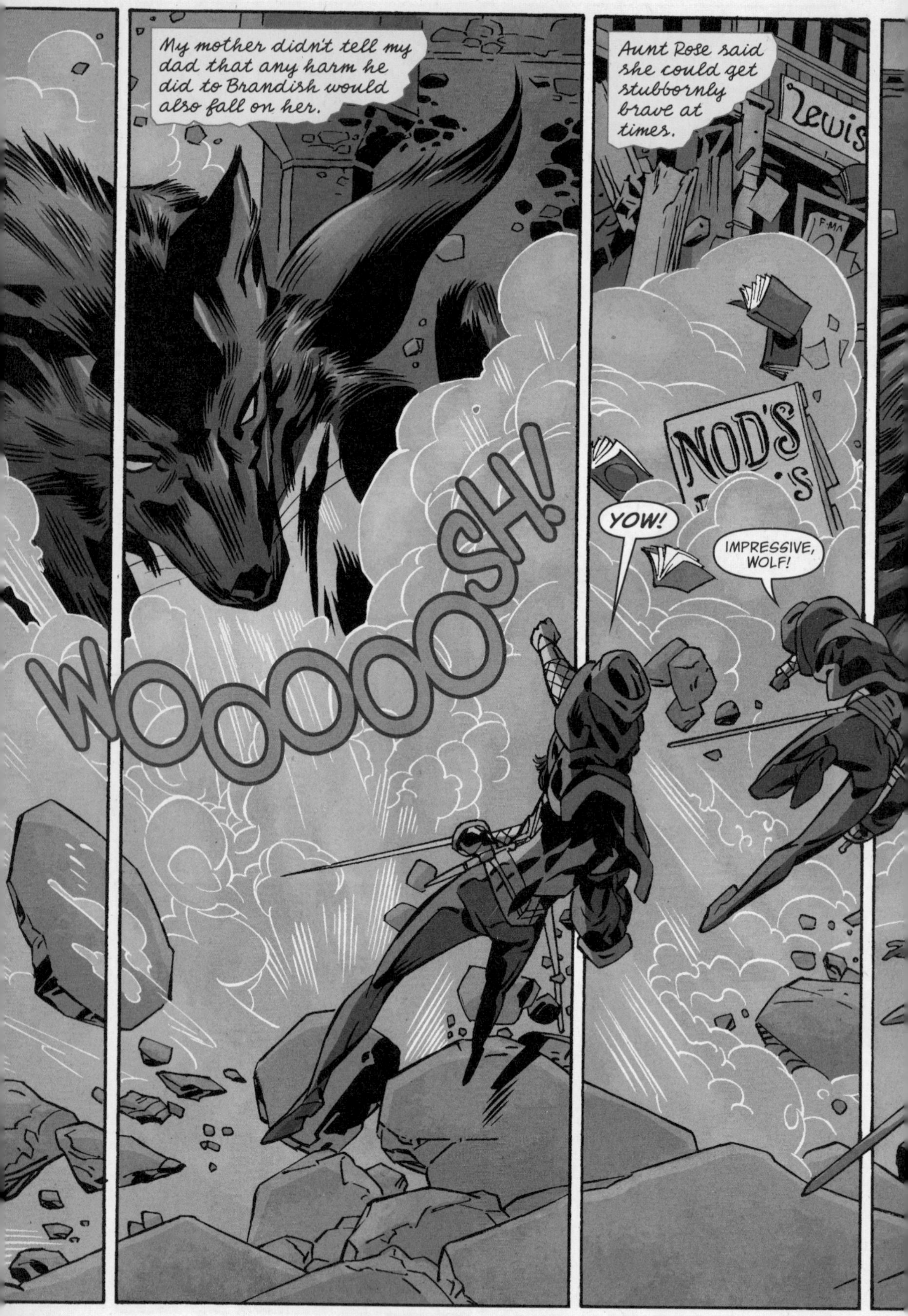
My mother didn't tell my dad that any harm he did to Brandish would also fall on her.
WOOOOOOSH!
Aunt Rose said she could get stubbornly brave at times.
Lewis
NOD'S
YOW!
IMPRESSIVE, WOLF!

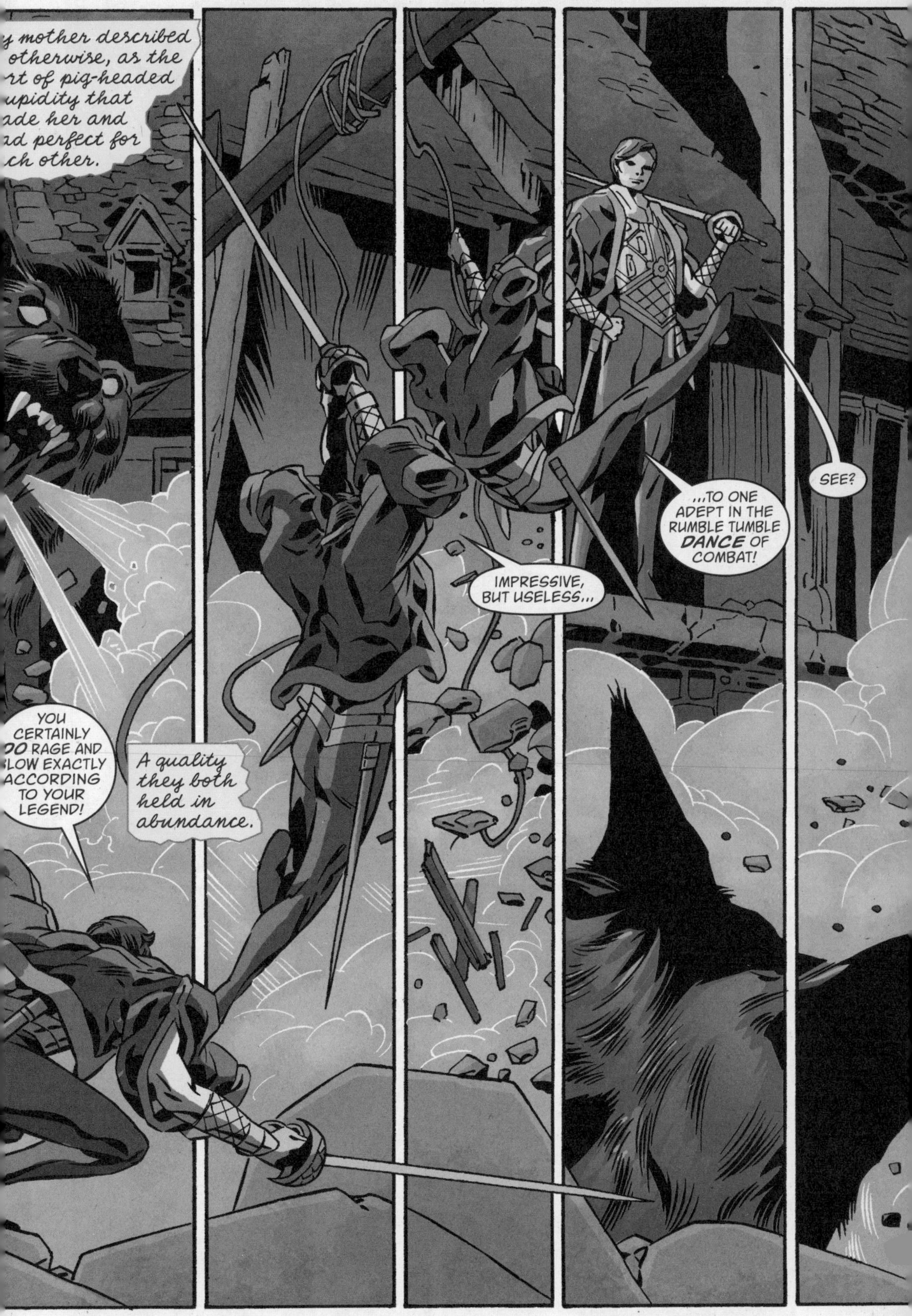

y mother described
otherwise, as the
rt of pig-headed
upidity that
ade her and
ad perfect for
ch other.
YOU CERTAINLY DO RAGE AND BLOW EXACTLY ACCORDING TO YOUR LEGEND!
A quality they both held in abundance.
IMPRESSIVE, BUT USELESS...
...TO ONE ADEPT IN THE RUMBLE TUMBLE DANCE OF COMBAT!
SEE?

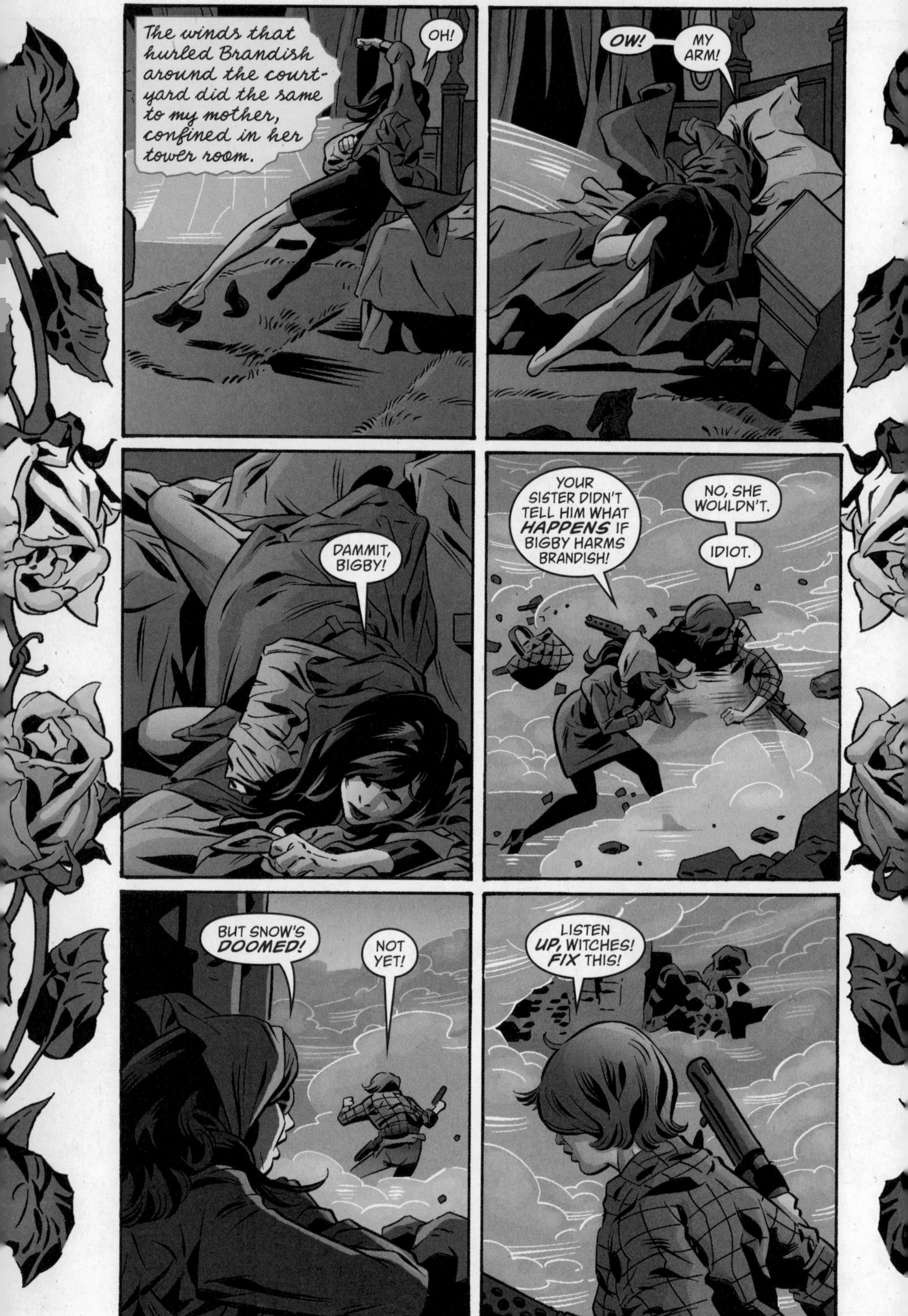
The winds that hurled Brandish around the courtyard did the same to my mother, confined in her tower room.
OH!
OW!
MY ARM!
DAMMIT, BIGBY!
YOUR SISTER DIDN'T TELL HIM WHAT HAPPENS IF BIGBY HARMS BRANDISH!
NO, SHE WOULDN'T.
IDIOT.
BUT SNOW'S DOOMED!
NOT YET!
LISTEN UP, WITCHES! FIX THIS!

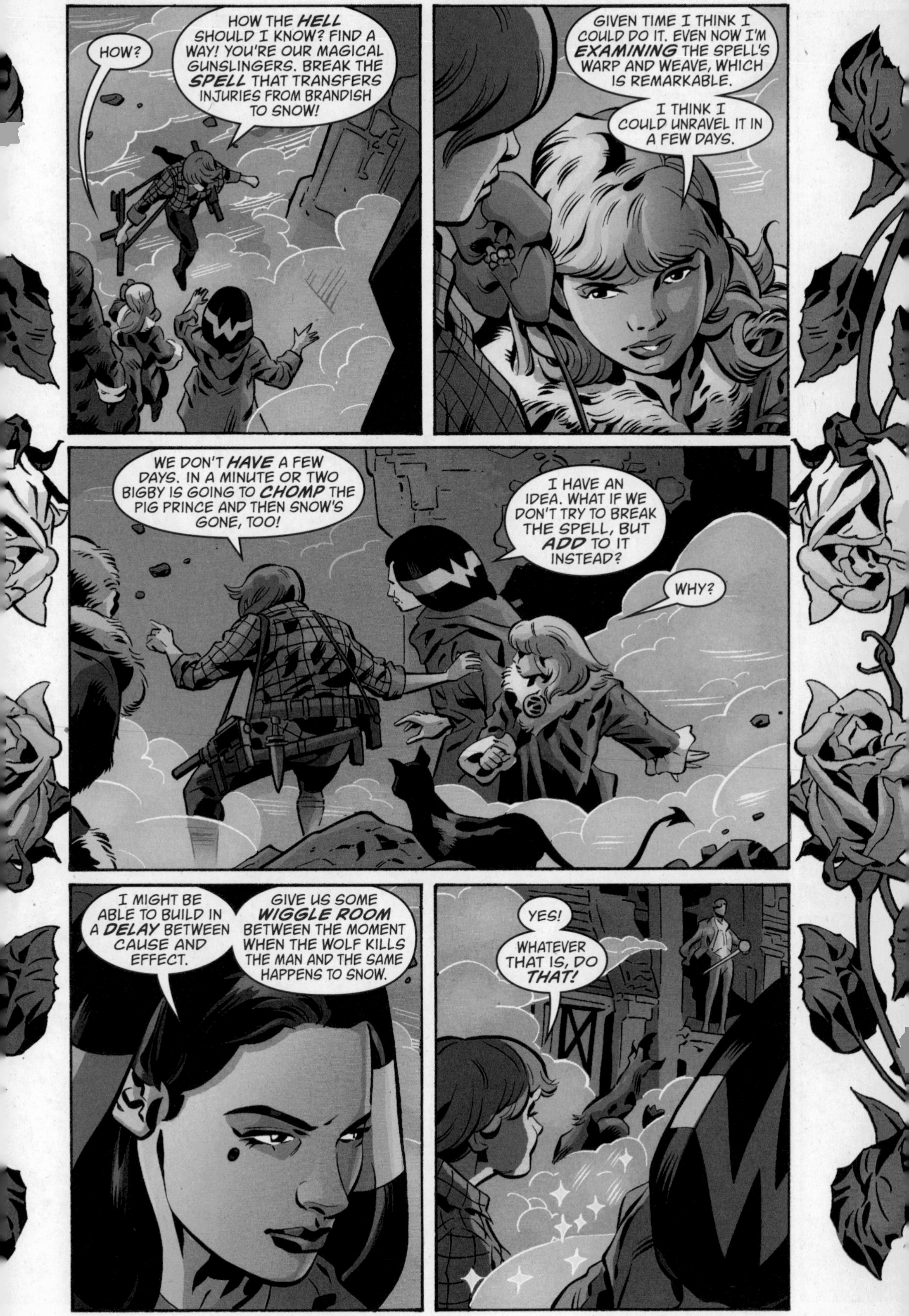
HOW?
HOW THE HELL SHOULD I KNOW? FIND A WAY! YOU'RE OUR MAGICAL GUNSLINGERS. BREAK THE SPELL THAT TRANSFERS INJURIES FROM BRANDISH TO SNOW!
GIVEN TIME I THINK I COULD DO IT. EVEN NOW I'M EXAMINING THE SPELL'S WARP AND WEAVE, WHICH IS REMARKABLE.
I THINK I COULD UNRAVEL IT IN A FEW DAYS.
WE DON'T HAVE A FEW DAYS. IN A MINUTE OR TWO BIGBY IS GOING TO CHOMP THE PIG PRINCE AND THEN SNOW'S GONE, TOO!
I HAVE AN IDEA. WHAT IF WE DON'T TRY TO BREAK THE SPELL, BUT ADD TO IT INSTEAD?
WHY?
I MIGHT BE ABLE TO BUILD IN A DELAY BETWEEN CAUSE AND EFFECT.
GIVE US SOME WIGGLE ROOM BETWEEN THE MOMENT WHEN THE WOLF KILLS THE MAN AND THE SAME HAPPENS TO SNOW.
YES!
WHATEVER THAT IS, DO THAT!

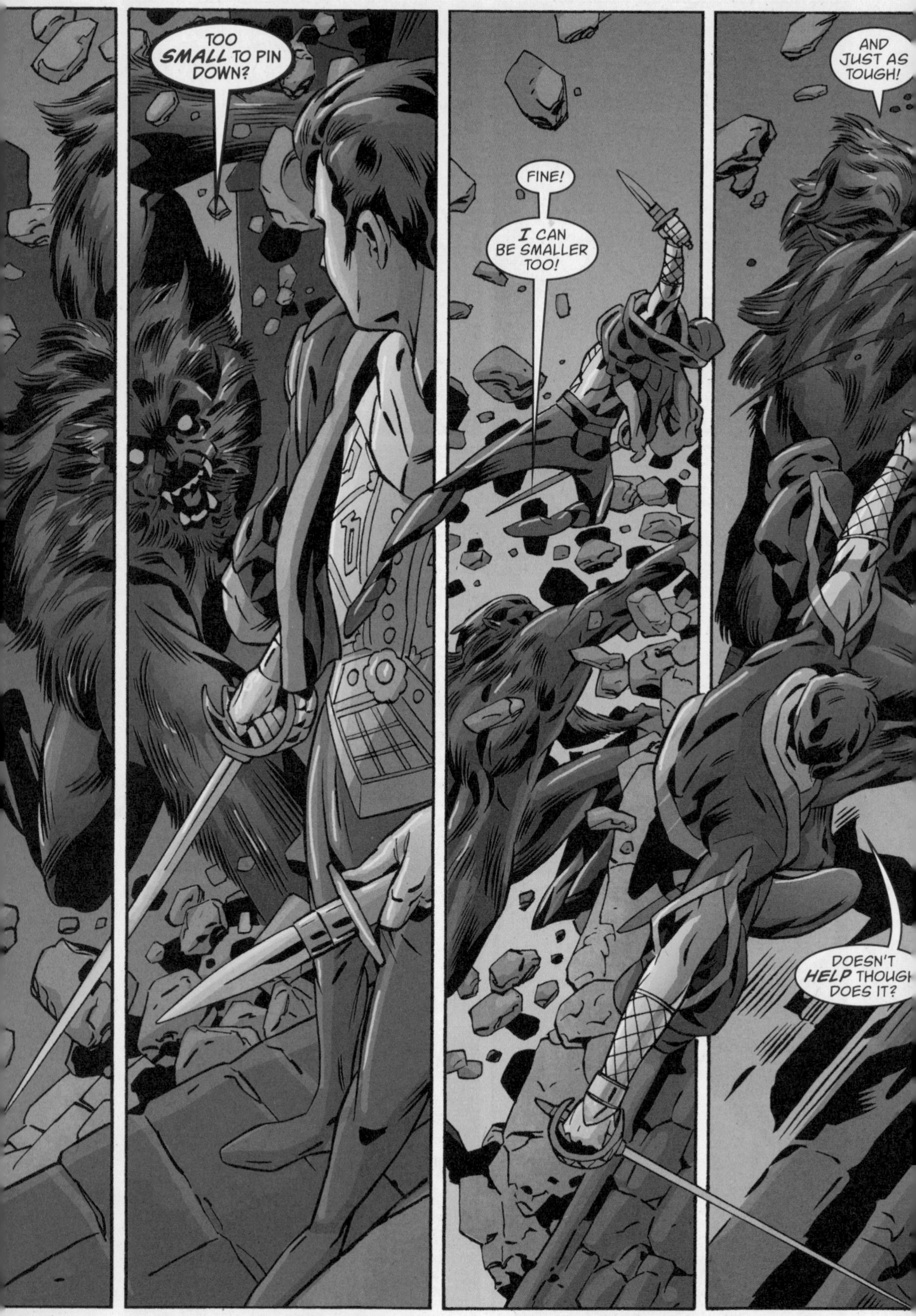
TOO SMALL TO PIN DOWN?
FINE!
I CAN BE SMALLER TOO!
AND JUST AS TOUGH!
DOESN'T HELP THOUGH DOES IT?

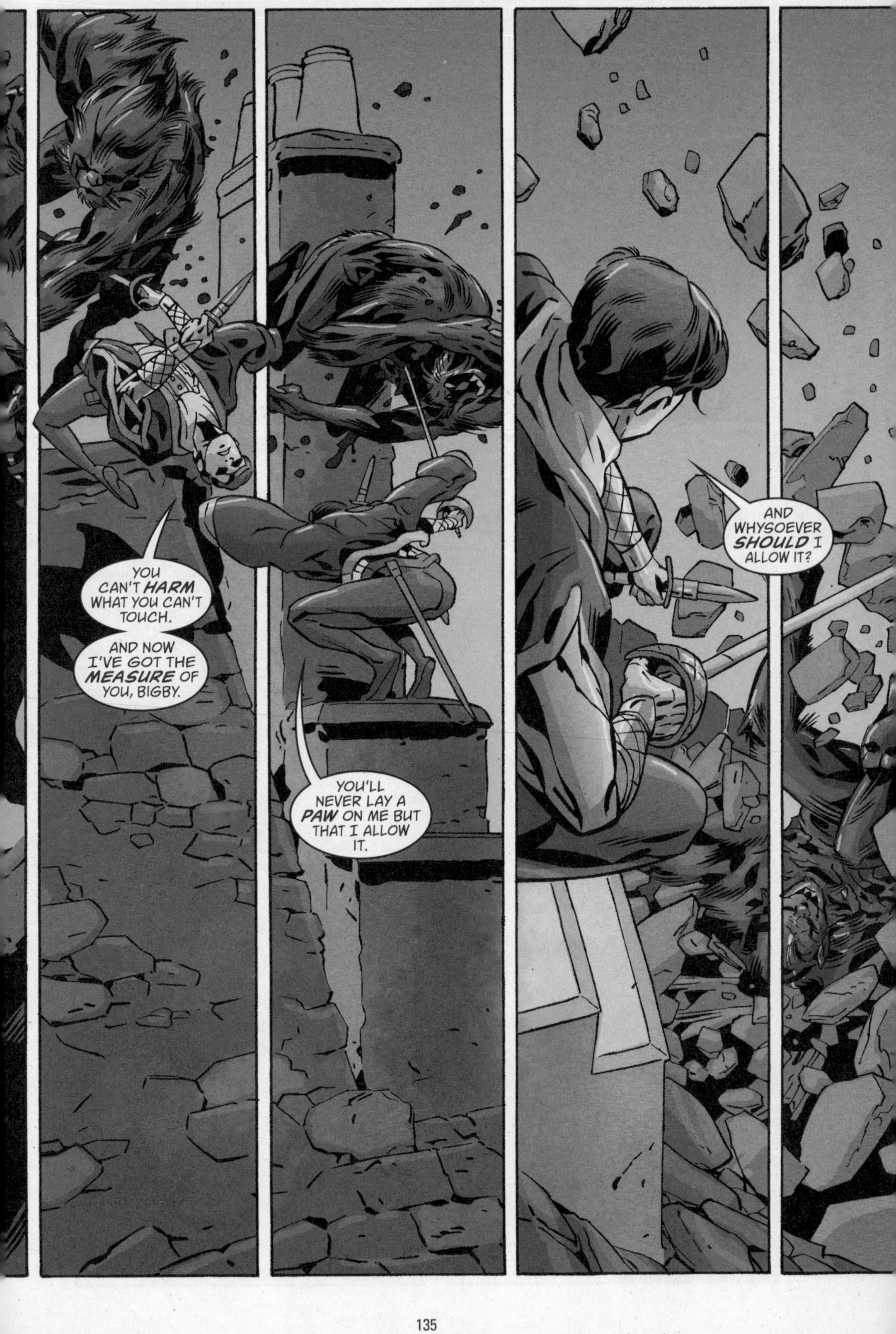
YOU CAN'T HARM WHAT YOU CAN'T TOUCH.
AND NOW I'VE GOT THE MEASURE OF YOU, BIGBY.
YOU'LL NEVER LAY A PAW ON ME BUT THAT I ALLOW IT.
AND WHYSOEVER SHOULD I ALLOW IT?

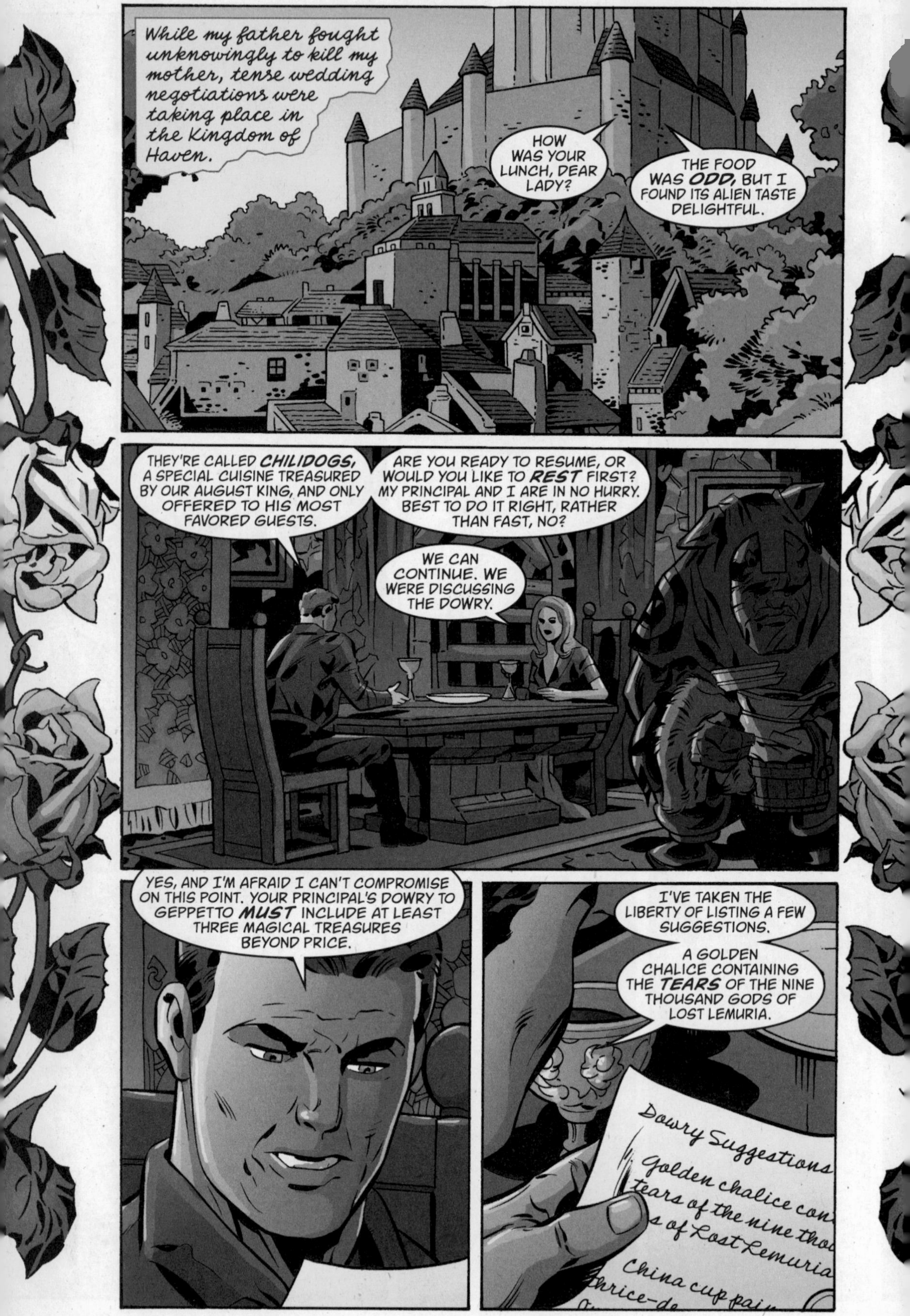
While my father fought unknowingly to kill my mother, tense wedding negotiations were taking place in the Kingdom of Haven.
HOW WAS YOUR LUNCH, DEAR LADY?
THE FOOD WAS ODD, BUT I FOUND ITS ALIEN TASTE DELIGHTFUL.
THEY'RE CALLED CHILIDOGS, A SPECIAL CUISINE TREASURED BY OUR AUGUST KING, AND ONLY OFFERED TO HIS MOST FAVORED GUESTS.
ARE YOU READY TO RESUME, OR WOULD YOU LIKE TO REST FIRST? MY PRINCIPAL AND I ARE IN NO HURRY. BEST TO DO IT RIGHT, RATHER THAN FAST, NO?
WE CAN CONTINUE. WE WERE DISCUSSING THE DOWRY.
YES, AND I'M AFRAID I CAN'T COMPROMISE ON THIS POINT. YOUR PRINCIPAL'S DOWRY TO GEPPETTO MUST INCLUDE AT LEAST THREE MAGICAL TREASURES BEYOND PRICE.
I'VE TAKEN THE LIBERTY OF LISTING A FEW SUGGESTIONS.
A GOLDEN CHALICE CONTAINING THE TEARS OF THE NINE THOUSAND GODS OF LOST LEMURIA.
Dowry Suggestions
Golden chalice con
tears of the nine thou
s of Lost Lemuria
China cup pai
thrice-de

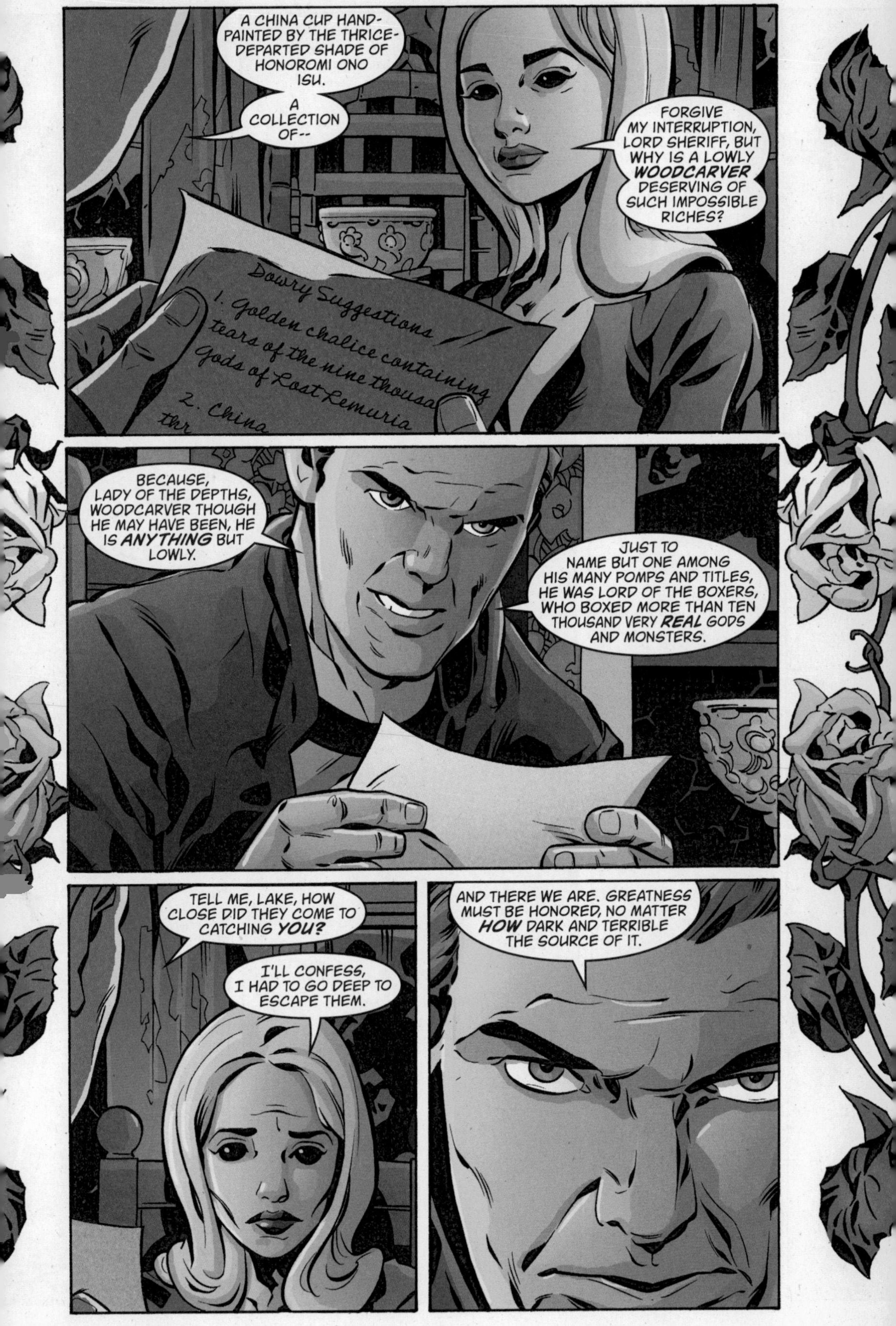
A CHINA CUP HAND-PAINTED BY THE THRICE-DEPARTED SHADE OF HONOROMI ONO ISU.
A COLLECTION OF--
FORGIVE MY INTERRUPTION, LORD SHERIFF, BUT WHY IS A LOWLY **WOODCARVER** DESERVING OF SUCH IMPOSSIBLE RICHES?
Dowry Suggestions
1. Golden chalice containing
tears of the nine thousa
Gods of Lost Lemuria
2. China
thr
BECAUSE, LADY OF THE DEPTHS, WOODCARVER THOUGH HE MAY HAVE BEEN, HE IS ***ANYTHING*** BUT LOWLY.
JUST TO NAME BUT ONE AMONG HIS MANY POMPS AND TITLES, HE WAS LORD OF THE BOXERS, WHO BOXED MORE THAN TEN THOUSAND VERY ***REAL*** GODS AND MONSTERS.
TELL ME, LAKE, HOW CLOSE DID THEY COME TO CATCHING ***YOU?***
I'LL CONFESS, I HAD TO GO DEEP TO ESCAPE THEM.
AND THERE WE ARE. GREATNESS MUST BE HONORED, NO MATTER ***HOW*** DARK AND TERRIBLE THE SOURCE OF IT.

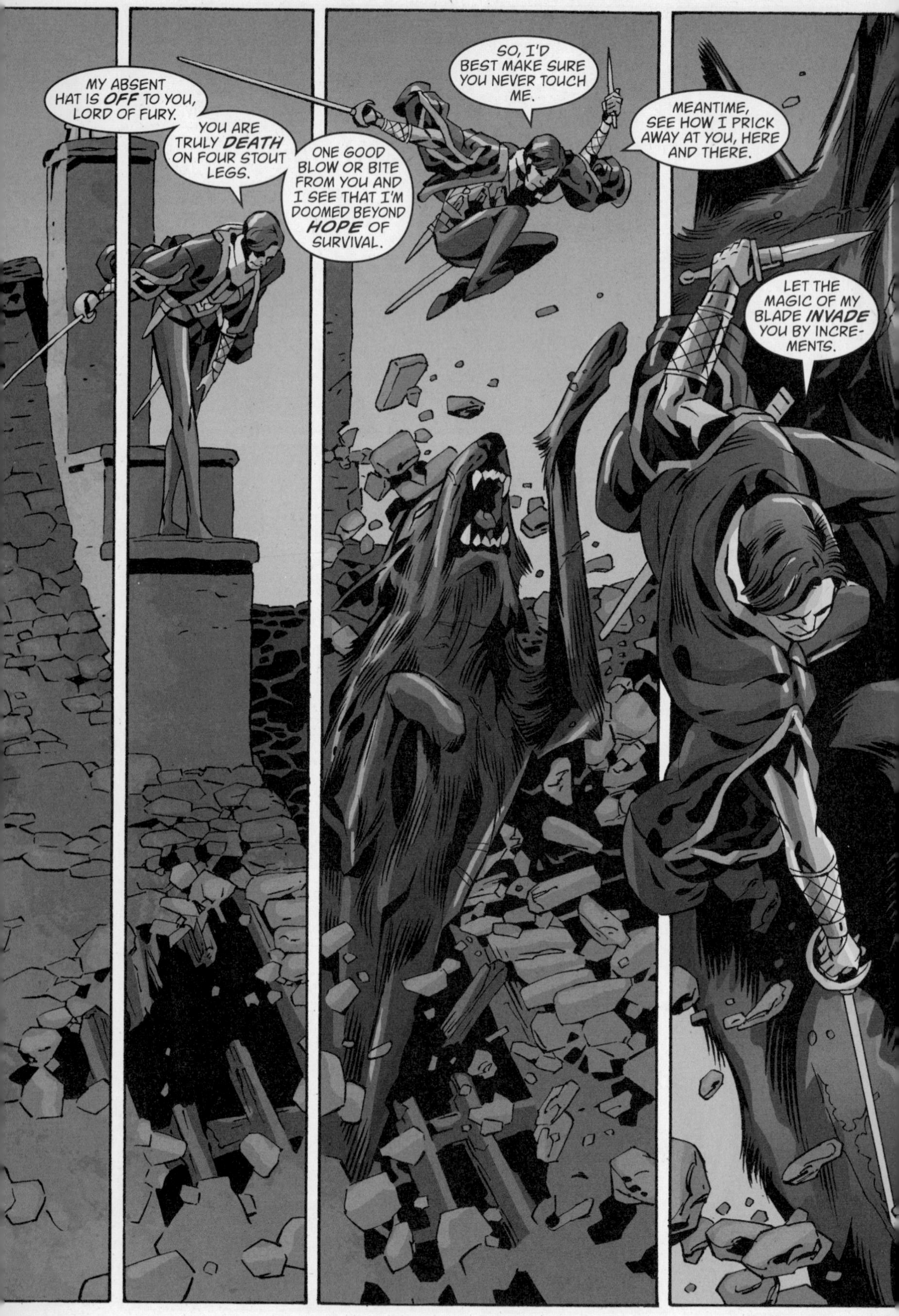
MY ABSENT HAT IS OFF TO YOU, LORD OF FURY.
YOU ARE TRULY DEATH ON FOUR STOUT LEGS.
ONE GOOD BLOW OR BITE FROM YOU AND I SEE THAT I'M DOOMED BEYOND HOPE OF SURVIVAL.
SO, I'D BEST MAKE SURE YOU NEVER TOUCH ME.
MEANTIME, SEE HOW I PRICK AWAY AT YOU, HERE AND THERE.
LET THE MAGIC OF MY BLADE INVADE YOU BY INCREMENTS.

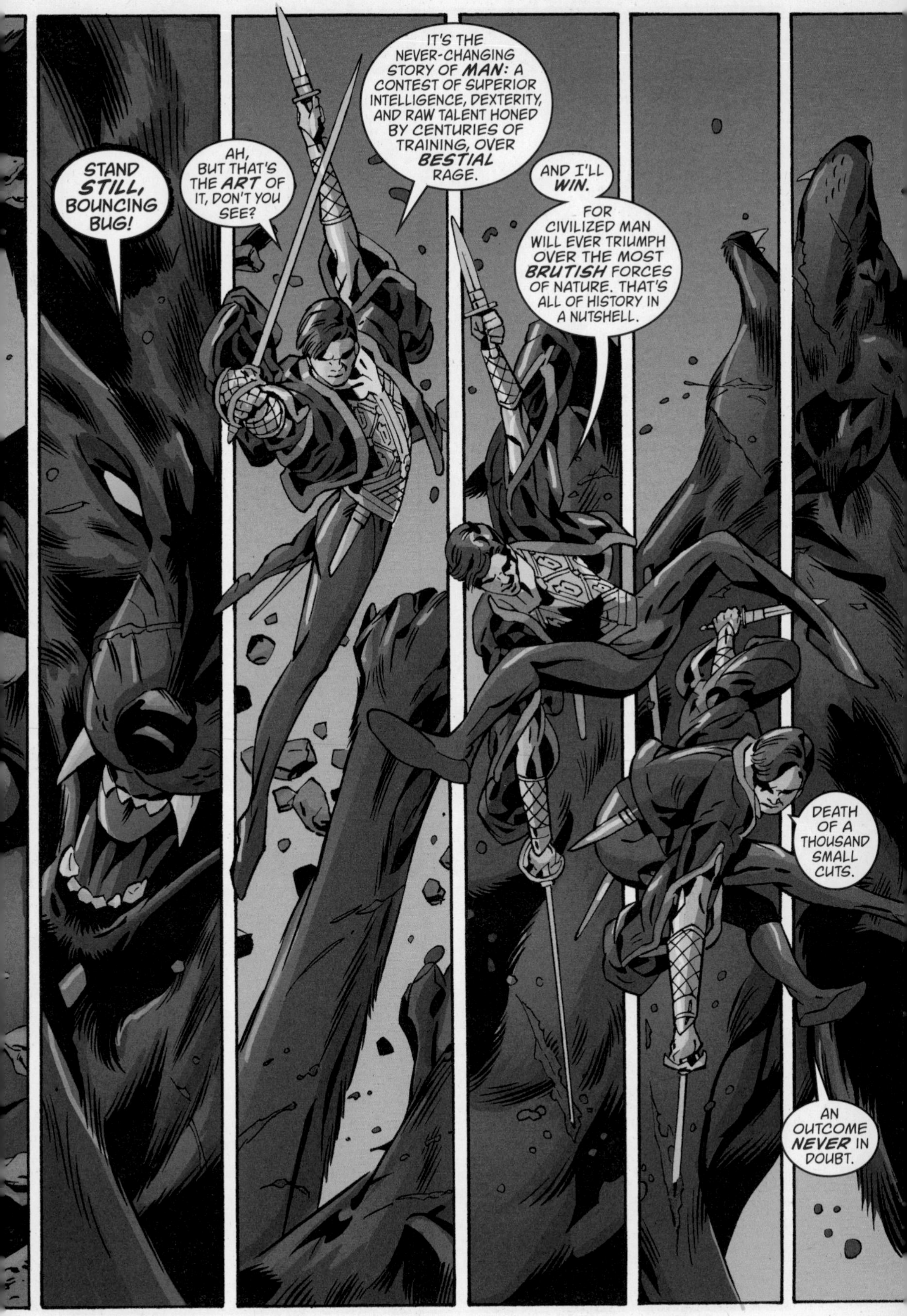
STAND STILL, BOUNCING BUG!
AH, BUT THAT'S THE ART OF IT, DON'T YOU SEE?
IT'S THE NEVER-CHANGING STORY OF MAN: A CONTEST OF SUPERIOR INTELLIGENCE, DEXTERITY, AND RAW TALENT HONED BY CENTURIES OF TRAINING, OVER BESTIAL RAGE.
AND I'LL WIN.
FOR CIVILIZED MAN WILL EVER TRIUMPH OVER THE MOST BRUTISH FORCES OF NATURE. THAT'S ALL OF HISTORY IN A NUTSHELL.
DEATH OF A THOUSAND SMALL CUTS.
AN OUTCOME NEVER IN DOUBT.

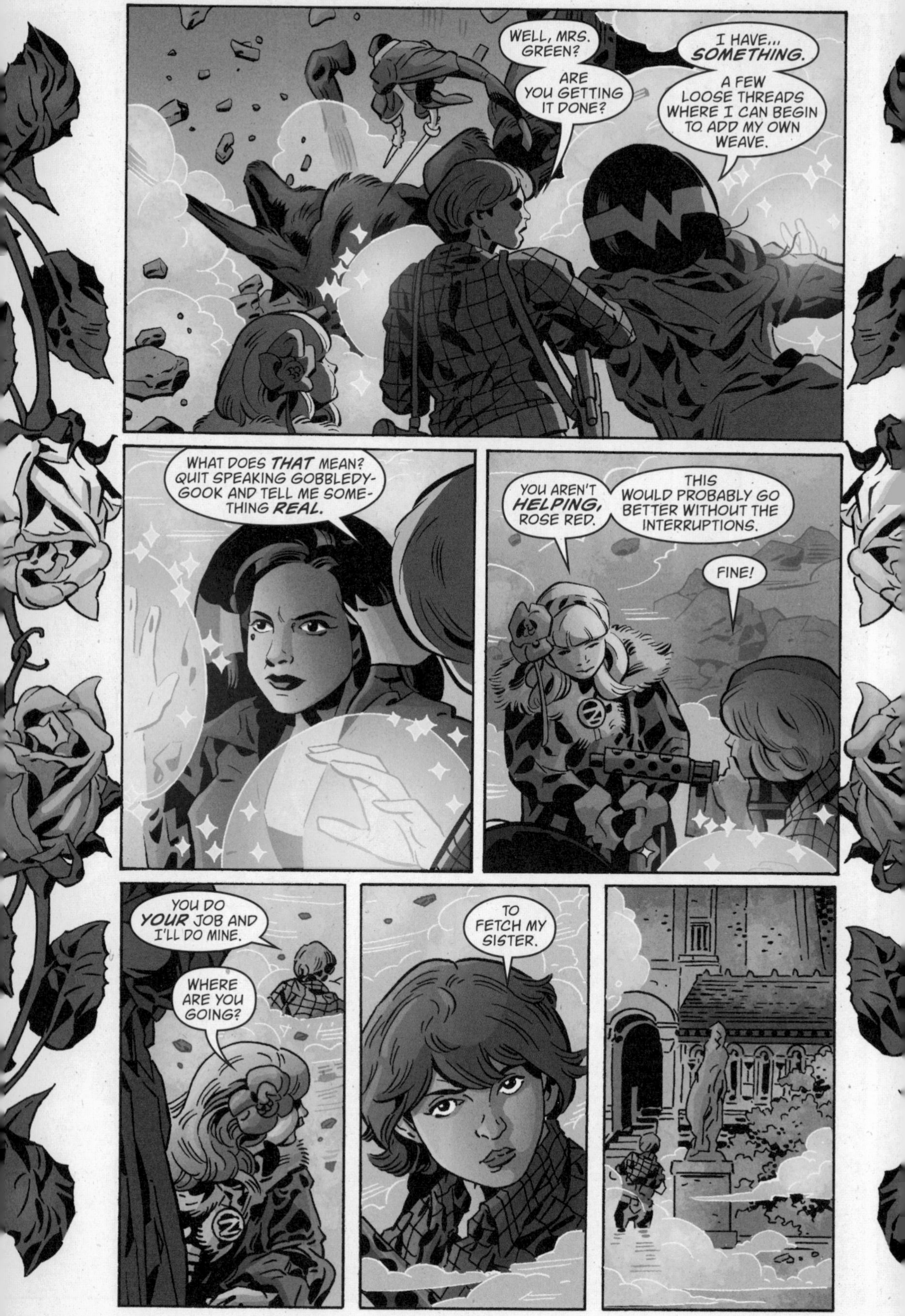
WELL, MRS. GREEN?
ARE YOU GETTING IT DONE?
I HAVE... SOMETHING.
A FEW LOOSE THREADS WHERE I CAN BEGIN TO ADD MY OWN WEAVE.
WHAT DOES THAT MEAN? QUIT SPEAKING GOBBLEDY-GOOK AND TELL ME SOME-THING REAL.
YOU AREN'T HELPING, ROSE RED.
THIS WOULD PROBABLY GO BETTER WITHOUT THE INTERRUPTIONS.
FINE!
YOU DO YOUR JOB AND I'LL DO MINE.
WHERE ARE YOU GOING?
TO FETCH MY SISTER.

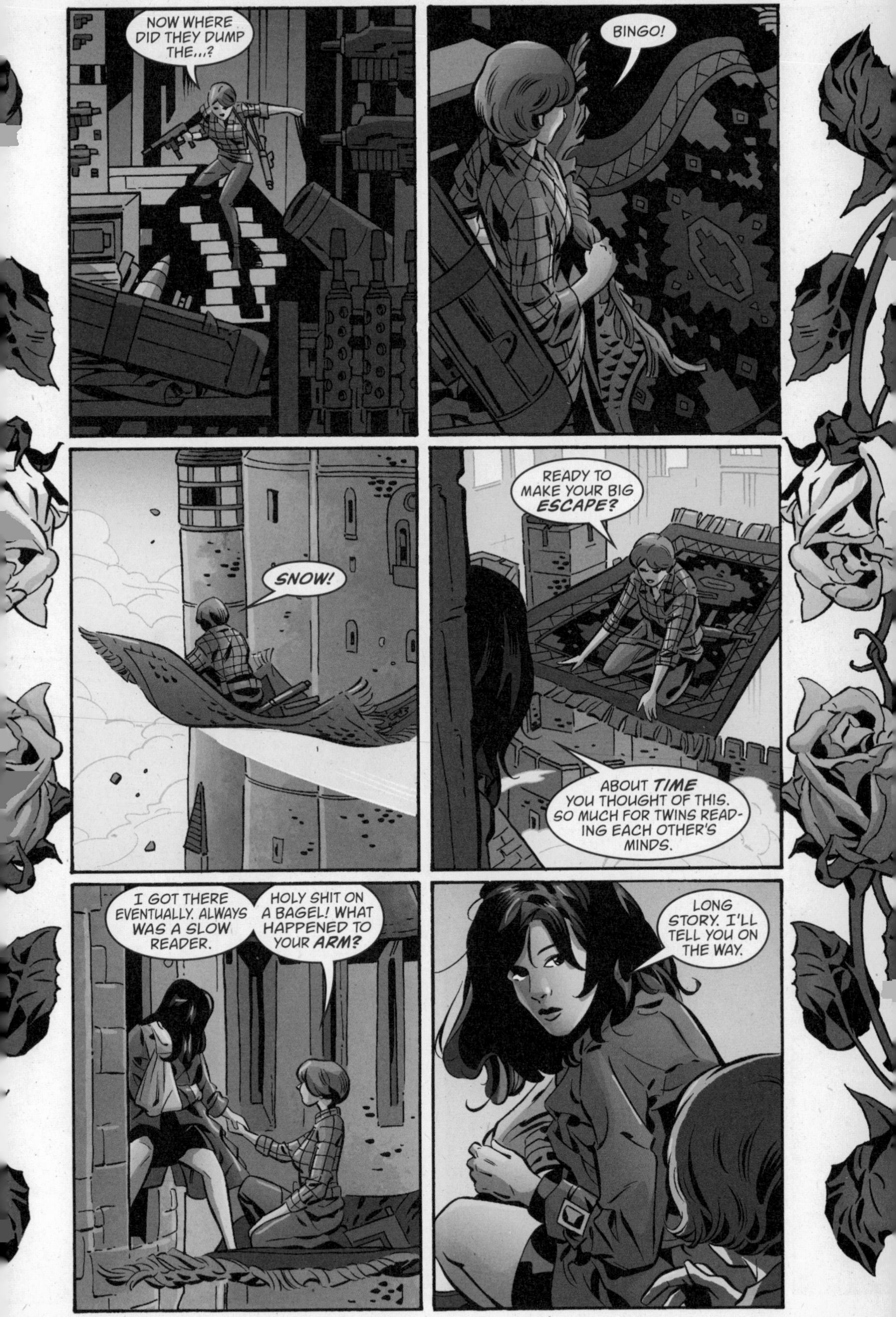

NOW WHERE DID THEY DUMP THE...?
BINGO!
SNOW!
READY TO MAKE YOUR BIG ESCAPE?
ABOUT TIME YOU THOUGHT OF THIS. SO MUCH FOR TWINS READ-ING EACH OTHER'S MINDS.
I GOT THERE EVENTUALLY. ALWAYS WAS A SLOW READER.
HOLY SHIT ON A BAGEL! WHAT HAPPENED TO YOUR ARM?
LONG STORY. I'LL TELL YOU ON THE WAY.

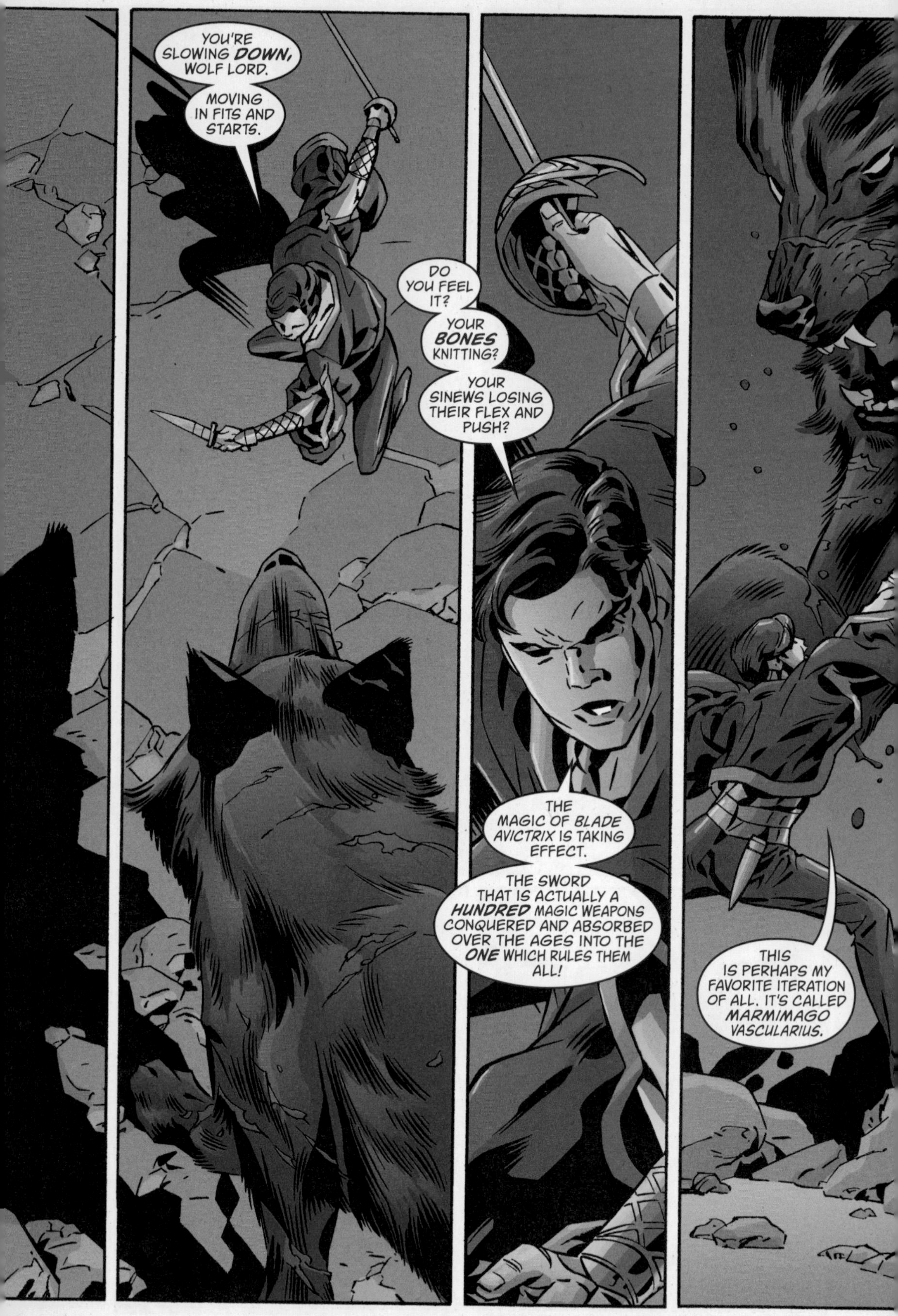
YOU'RE SLOWING DOWN, WOLF LORD.
MOVING IN FITS AND STARTS.
DO YOU FEEL IT?
YOUR BONES KNITTING?
YOUR SINEWS LOSING THEIR FLEX AND PUSH?
THE MAGIC OF BLADE AVICTRIX IS TAKING EFFECT.
THE SWORD THAT IS ACTUALLY A HUNDRED MAGIC WEAPONS CONQUERED AND ABSORBED OVER THE AGES INTO THE ONE WHICH RULES THEM ALL!
THIS IS PERHAPS MY FAVORITE ITERATION OF ALL. IT'S CALLED MARMIMAGO VASCULARIUS.

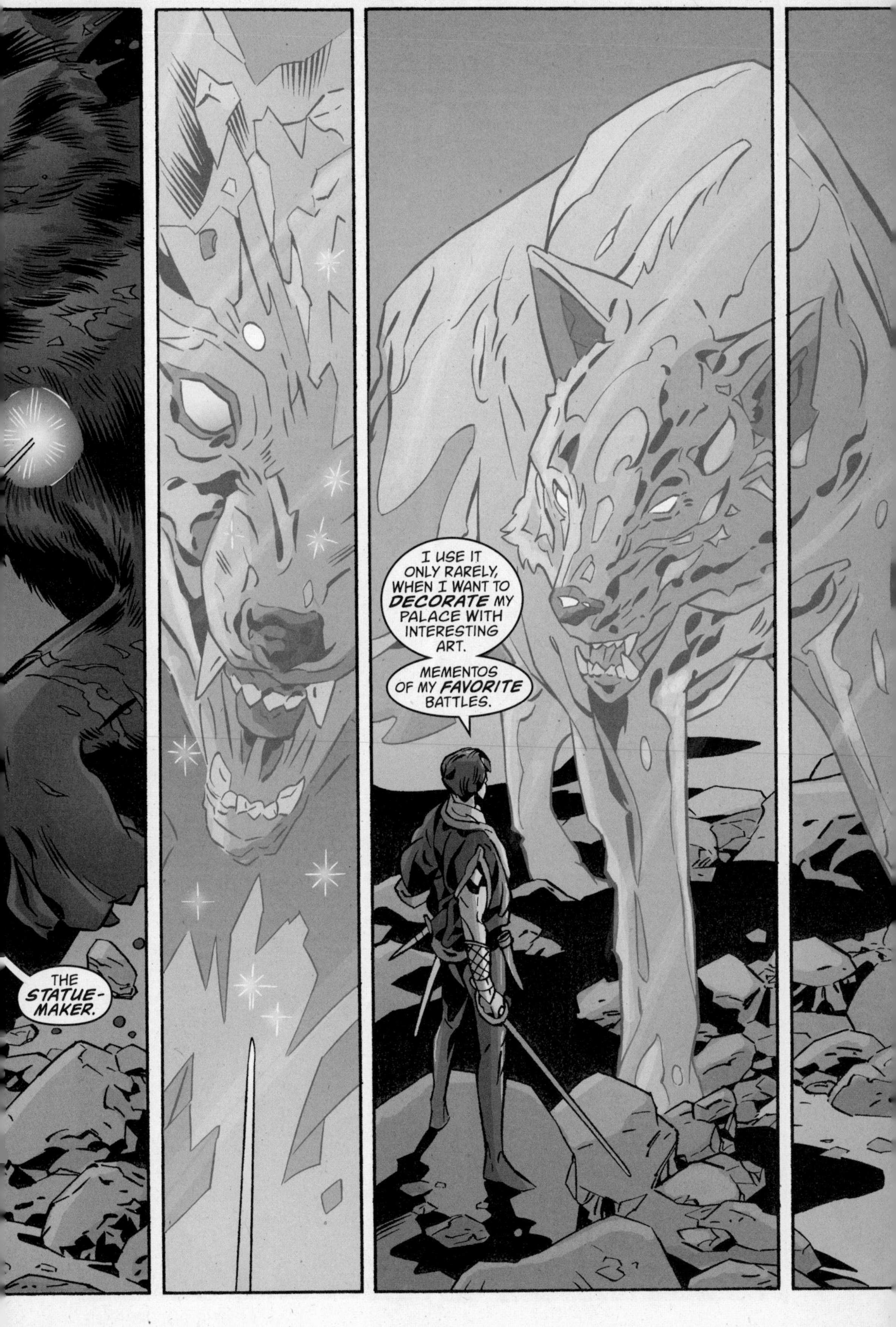
THE STATUE-MAKER.
I USE IT ONLY RARELY, WHEN I WANT TO DECORATE MY PALACE WITH INTERESTING ART.
MEMENTOS OF MY FAVORITE BATTLES.

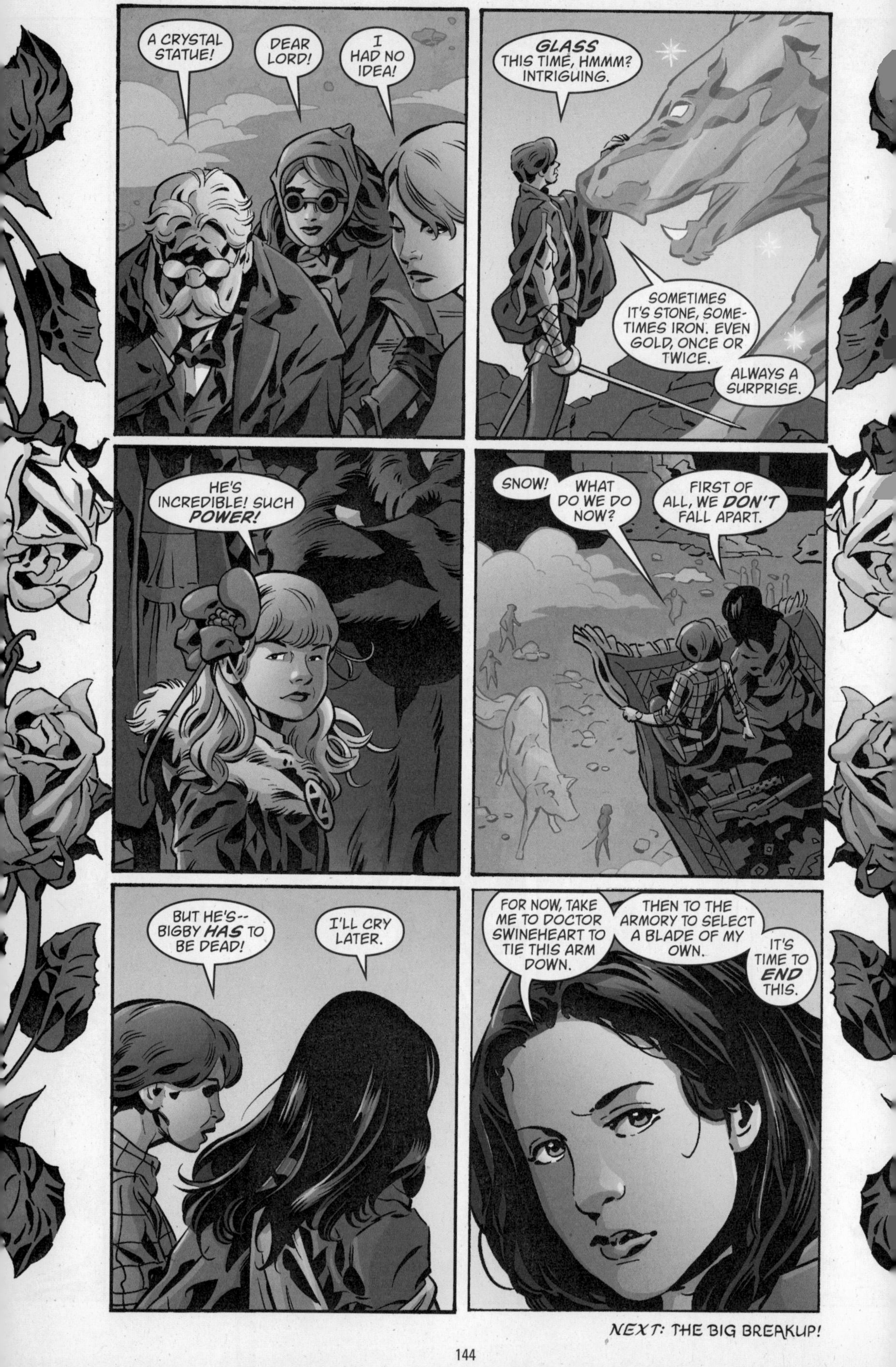
A CRYSTAL STATUE!
DEAR LORD!
I HAD NO IDEA!
GLASS THIS TIME, HMMM? INTRIGUING.
SOMETIMES IT'S STONE, SOMETIMES IRON. EVEN GOLD, ONCE OR TWICE.
ALWAYS A SURPRISE.
HE'S INCREDIBLE! SUCH POWER!
SNOW!
WHAT DO WE DO NOW?
FIRST OF ALL, WE DON'T FALL APART.
BUT HE'S-- BIGBY HAS TO BE DEAD!
I'LL CRY LATER.
FOR NOW, TAKE ME TO DOCTOR SWINEHEART TO TIE THIS ARM DOWN.
THEN TO THE ARMORY TO SELECT A BLADE OF MY OWN.
IT'S TIME TO END THIS.

NEXT: THE BIG BREAKUP!

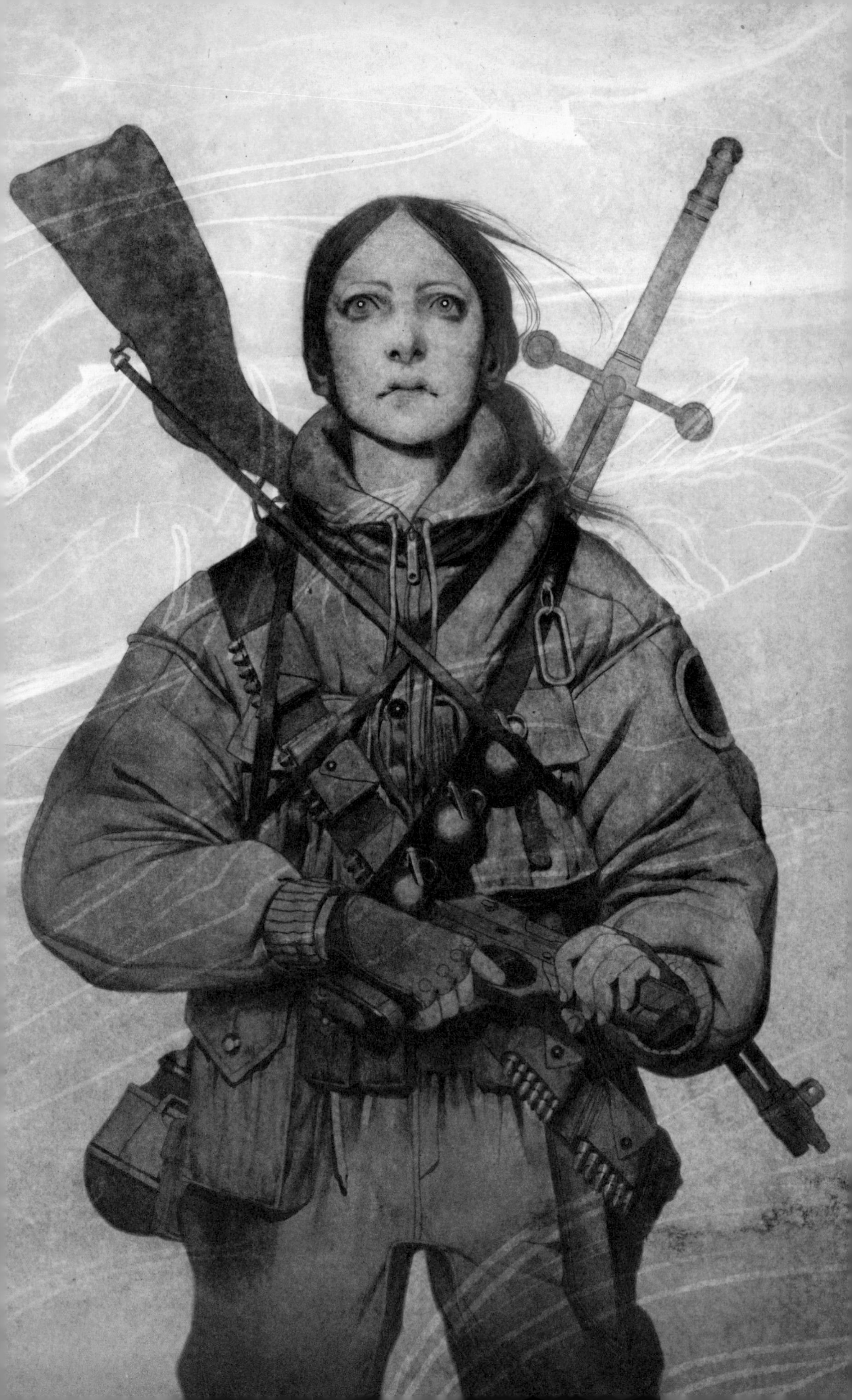

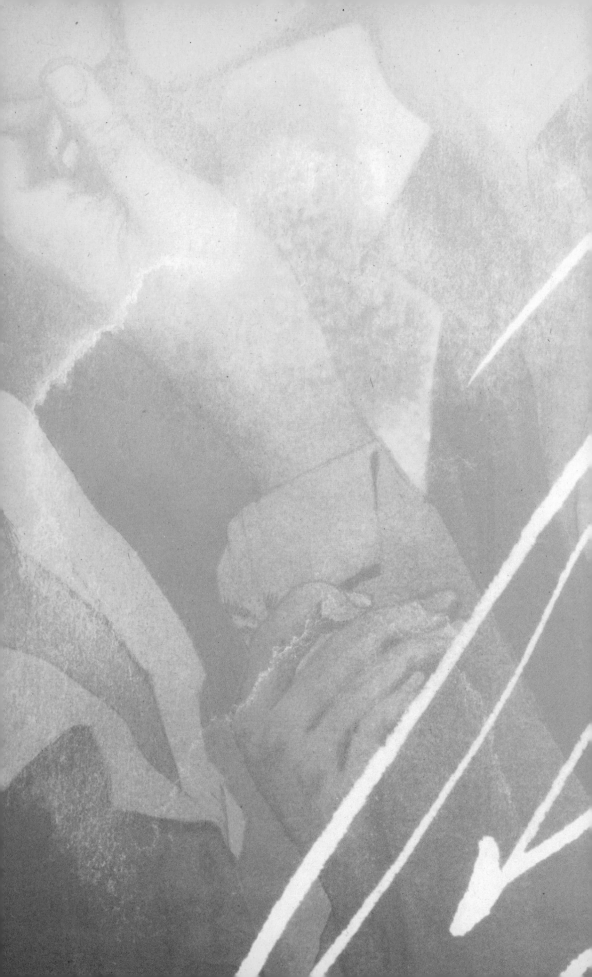

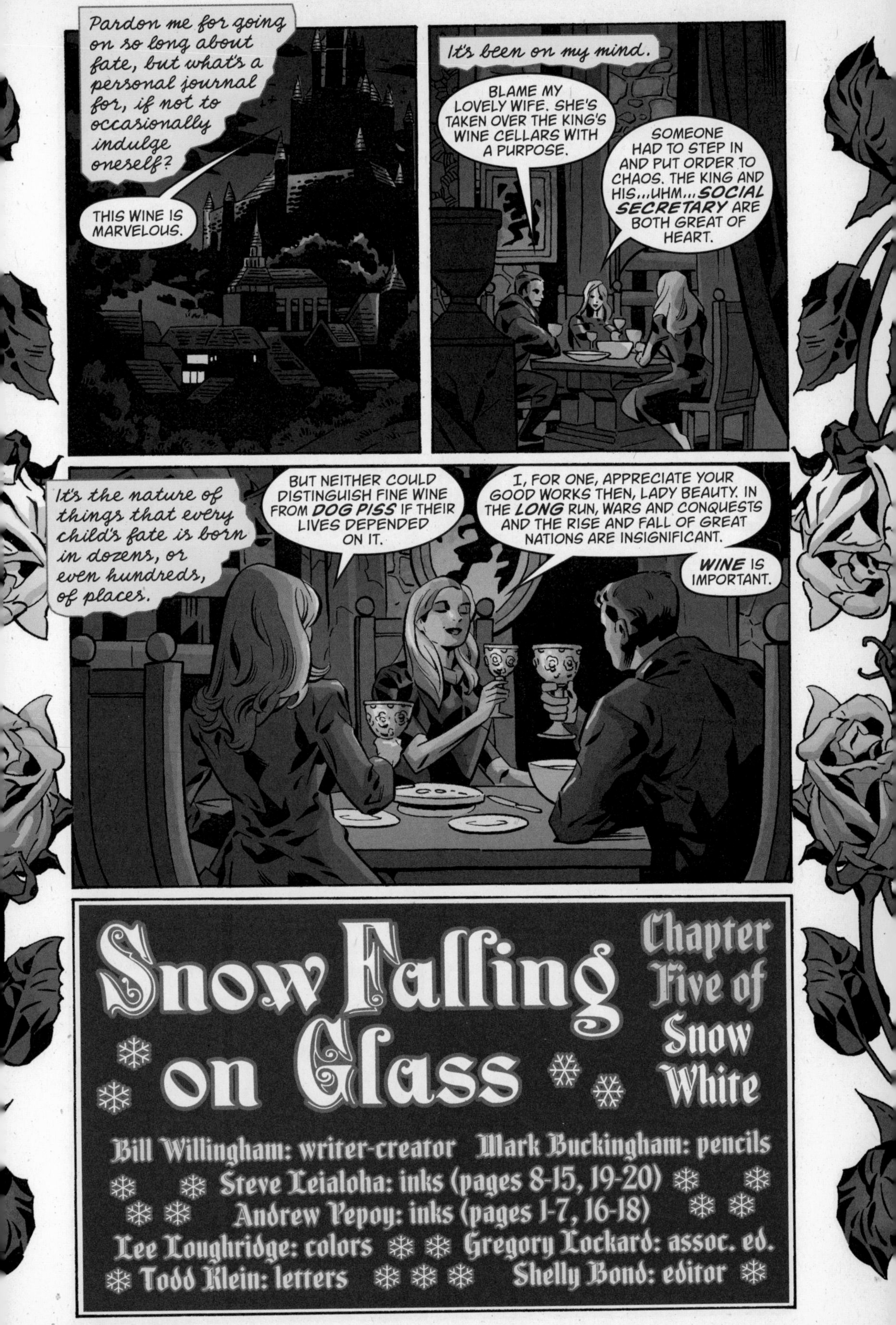
Pardon me for going on so long about fate, but what's a personal journal for, if not to occasionally indulge oneself?
THIS WINE IS MARVELOUS.
It's been on my mind.
BLAME MY LOVELY WIFE. SHE'S TAKEN OVER THE KING'S WINE CELLARS WITH A PURPOSE.
SOMEONE HAD TO STEP IN AND PUT ORDER TO CHAOS. THE KING AND HIS...UHM...SOCIAL SECRETARY ARE BOTH GREAT OF HEART.
It's the nature of things that every child's fate is born in dozens, or even hundreds, of places.
BUT NEITHER COULD DISTINGUISH FINE WINE FROM DOG PISS IF THEIR LIVES DEPENDED ON IT.
I, FOR ONE, APPRECIATE YOUR GOOD WORKS THEN, LADY BEAUTY. IN THE LONG RUN, WARS AND CONQUESTS AND THE RISE AND FALL OF GREAT NATIONS ARE INSIGNIFICANT.
WINE IS IMPORTANT.
Snow Falling on Glass
Chapter Five of Snow White
Bill Willingham: writer-creator
Mark Buckingham: pencils
Steve Leialoha: inks (pages 8-15, 19-20)
Andrew Pepoy: inks (pages 1-7, 16-18)
Lee Loughridge: colors
Gregory Lockard: assoc. ed.
Todd Klein: letters
Shelly Bond: editor

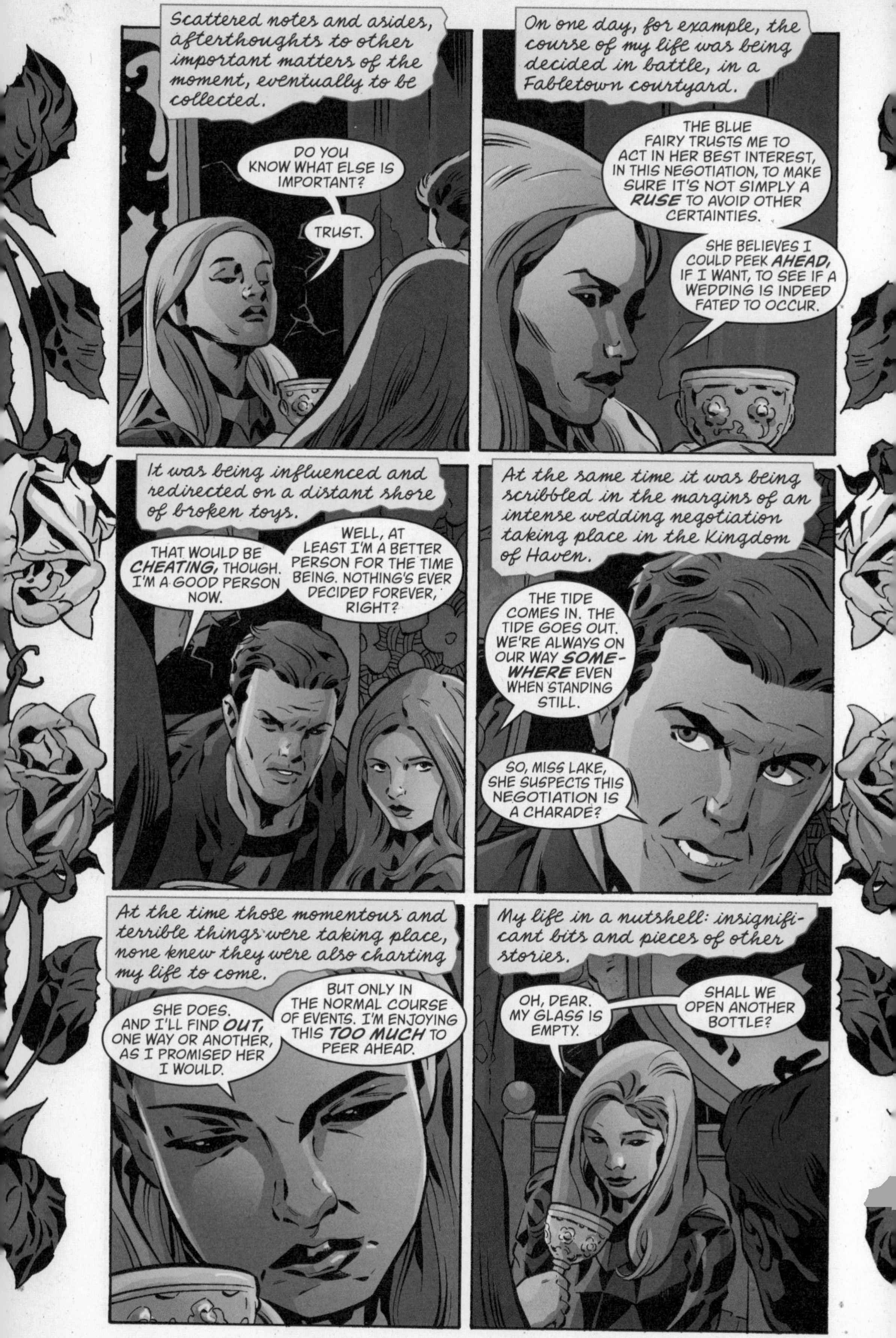
Scattered notes and asides, afterthoughts to other important matters of the moment, eventually to be collected.
DO YOU KNOW WHAT ELSE IS IMPORTANT?
TRUST.
On one day, for example, the course of my life was being decided in battle, in a Fabletown courtyard.
THE BLUE FAIRY TRUSTS ME TO ACT IN HER BEST INTEREST, IN THIS NEGOTIATION, TO MAKE SURE IT'S NOT SIMPLY A RUSE TO AVOID OTHER CERTAINTIES.
SHE BELIEVES I COULD PEEK AHEAD, IF I WANT, TO SEE IF A WEDDING IS INDEED FATED TO OCCUR.
It was being influenced and redirected on a distant shore of broken toys.
THAT WOULD BE CHEATING, THOUGH. I'M A GOOD PERSON NOW.
WELL, AT LEAST I'M A BETTER PERSON FOR THE TIME BEING. NOTHING'S EVER DECIDED FOREVER, RIGHT?
At the same time it was being scribbled in the margins of an intense wedding negotiation taking place in the Kingdom of Haven.
THE TIDE COMES IN. THE TIDE GOES OUT. WE'RE ALWAYS ON OUR WAY SOME-WHERE EVEN WHEN STANDING STILL.
SO, MISS LAKE, SHE SUSPECTS THIS NEGOTIATION IS A CHARADE?
At the time those momentous and terrible things were taking place, none knew they were also charting my life to come.
SHE DOES. AND I'LL FIND OUT, ONE WAY OR ANOTHER, AS I PROMISED HER I WOULD.
BUT ONLY IN THE NORMAL COURSE OF EVENTS. I'M ENJOYING THIS TOO MUCH TO PEER AHEAD.
My life in a nutshell: insignificant bits and pieces of other stories.
OH, DEAR. MY GLASS IS EMPTY.
SHALL WE OPEN ANOTHER BOTTLE?

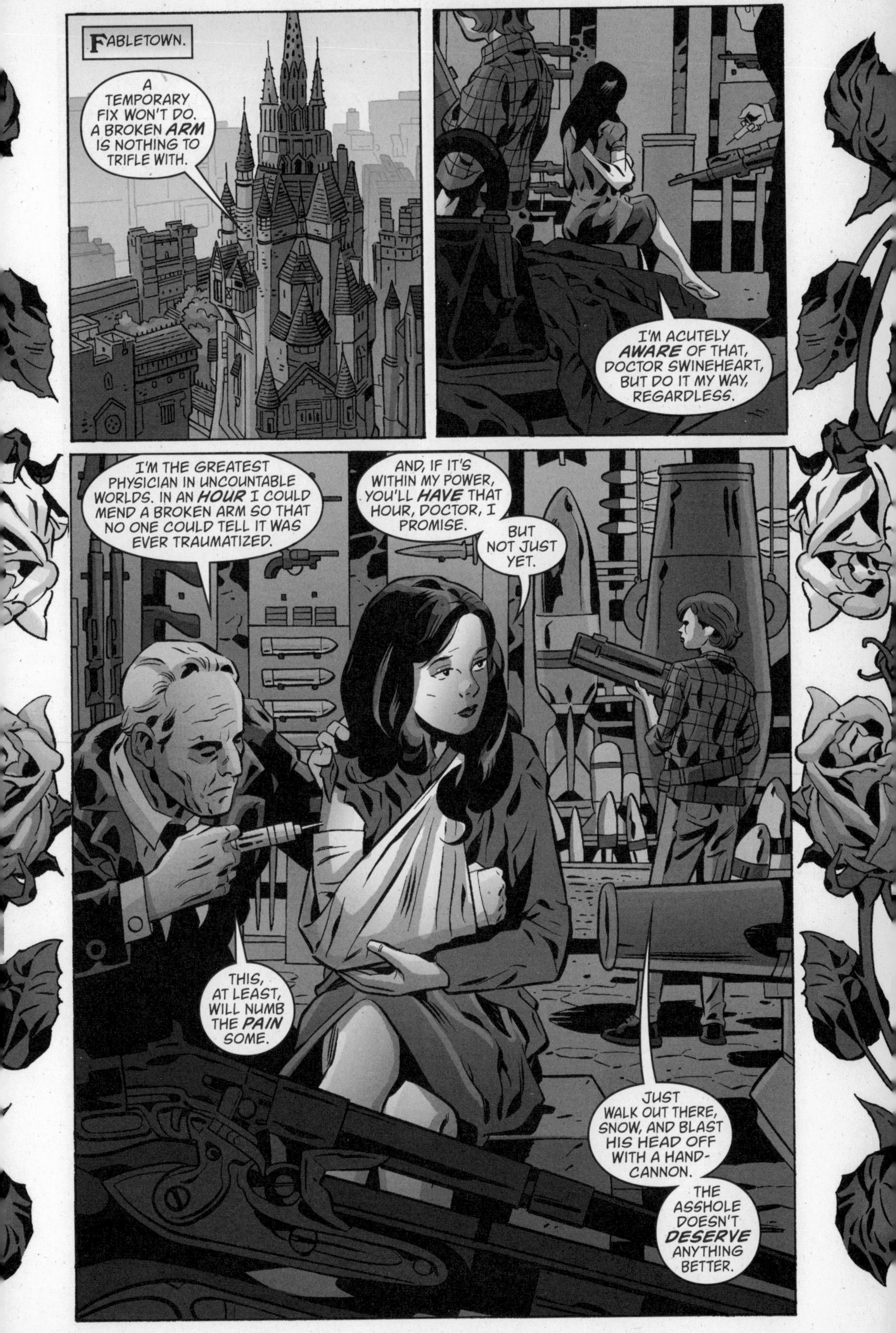
FABLETOWN.
A TEMPORARY FIX WON'T DO. A BROKEN ARM IS NOTHING TO TRIFLE WITH.
I'M ACUTELY AWARE OF THAT, DOCTOR SWINEHEART, BUT DO IT MY WAY, REGARDLESS.
I'M THE GREATEST PHYSICIAN IN UNCOUNTABLE WORLDS. IN AN HOUR I COULD MEND A BROKEN ARM SO THAT NO ONE COULD TELL IT WAS EVER TRAUMATIZED.
AND, IF IT'S WITHIN MY POWER, YOU'LL HAVE THAT HOUR, DOCTOR, I PROMISE.
BUT NOT JUST YET.
THIS, AT LEAST, WILL NUMB THE PAIN SOME.
JUST WALK OUT THERE, SNOW, AND BLAST HIS HEAD OFF WITH A HAND-CANNON.
THE ASSHOLE DOESN'T DESERVE ANYTHING BETTER.

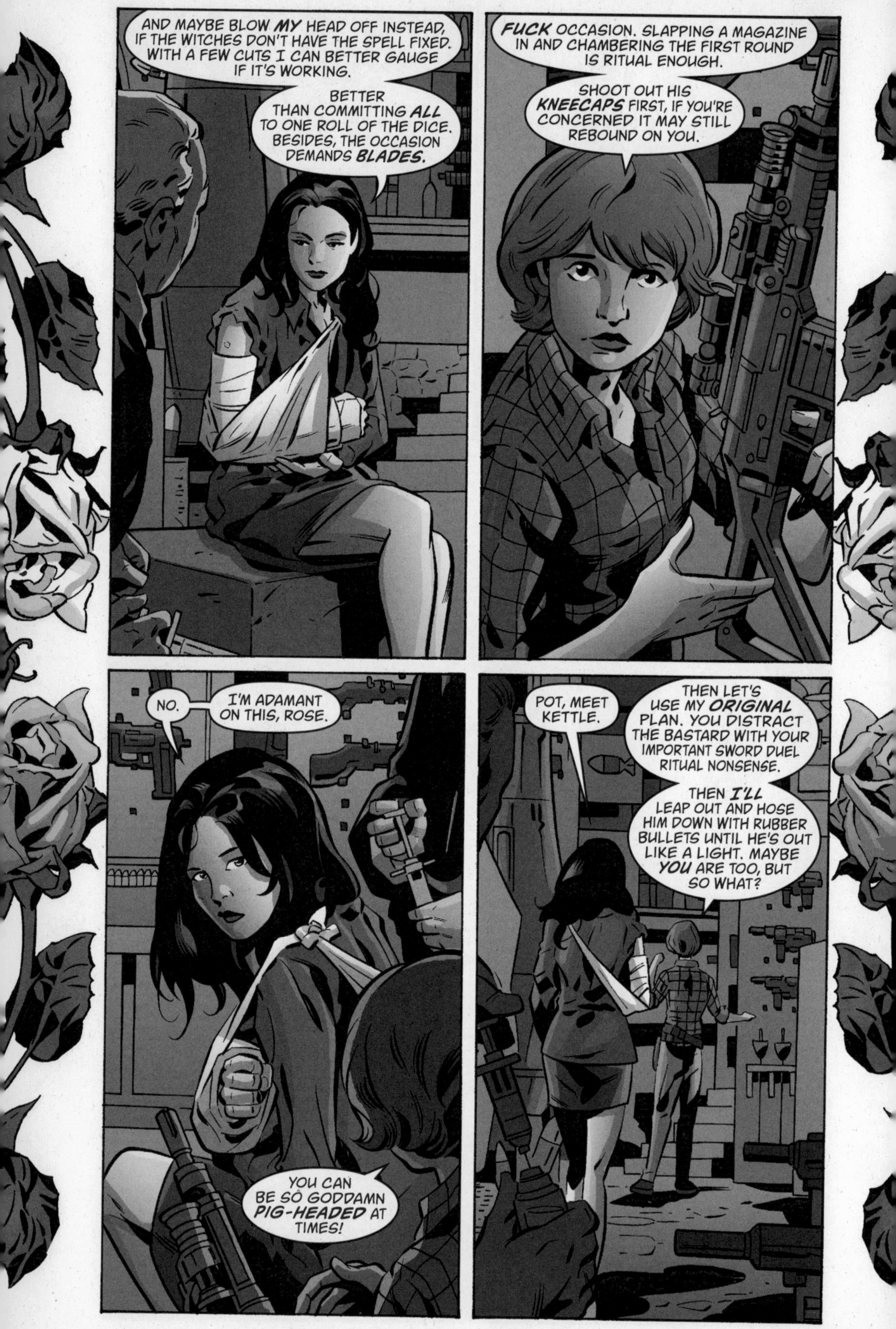
AND MAYBE BLOW MY HEAD OFF INSTEAD, IF THE WITCHES DON'T HAVE THE SPELL FIXED. WITH A FEW CUTS I CAN BETTER GAUGE IF IT'S WORKING.
BETTER THAN COMMITTING ALL TO ONE ROLL OF THE DICE. BESIDES, THE OCCASION DEMANDS BLADES.
FUCK OCCASION. SLAPPING A MAGAZINE IN AND CHAMBERING THE FIRST ROUND IS RITUAL ENOUGH.
SHOOT OUT HIS KNEECAPS FIRST, IF YOU'RE CONCERNED IT MAY STILL REBOUND ON YOU.
NO.
I'M ADAMANT ON THIS, ROSE.
YOU CAN BE SO GODDAMN PIG-HEADED AT TIMES!
POT, MEET KETTLE.
THEN LET'S USE MY ORIGINAL PLAN. YOU DISTRACT THE BASTARD WITH YOUR IMPORTANT SWORD DUEL RITUAL NONSENSE.
THEN I'LL LEAP OUT AND HOSE HIM DOWN WITH RUBBER BULLETS UNTIL HE'S OUT LIKE A LIGHT. MAYBE YOU ARE TOO, BUT SO WHAT?

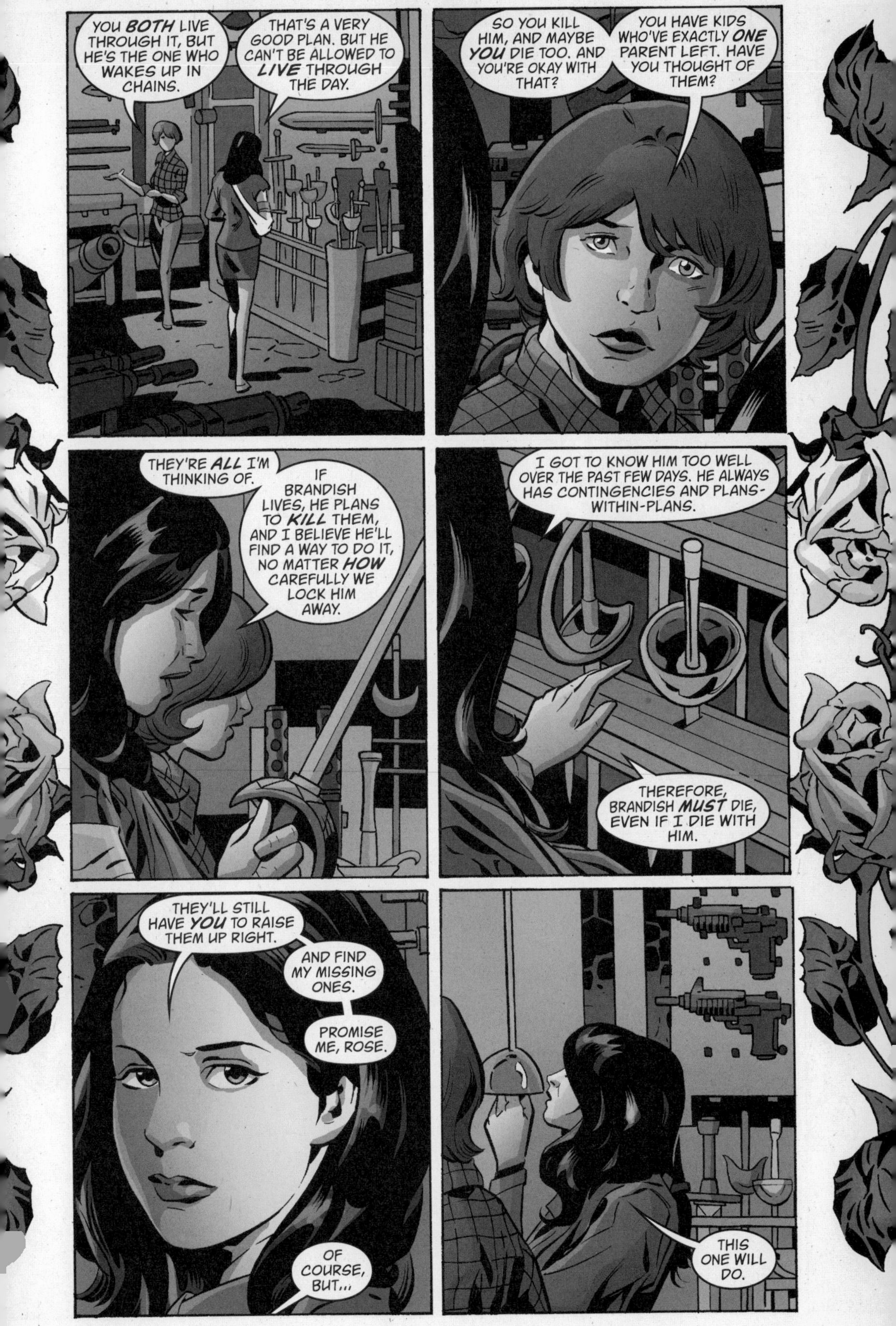
YOU BOTH LIVE THROUGH IT, BUT HE'S THE ONE WHO WAKES UP IN CHAINS.
THAT'S A VERY GOOD PLAN. BUT HE CAN'T BE ALLOWED TO LIVE THROUGH THE DAY.
SO YOU KILL HIM, AND MAYBE YOU DIE TOO. AND YOU'RE OKAY WITH THAT?
YOU HAVE KIDS WHO'VE EXACTLY ONE PARENT LEFT. HAVE YOU THOUGHT OF THEM?
THEY'RE ALL I'M THINKING OF.
IF BRANDISH LIVES, HE PLANS TO KILL THEM, AND I BELIEVE HE'LL FIND A WAY TO DO IT, NO MATTER HOW CAREFULLY WE LOCK HIM AWAY.
I GOT TO KNOW HIM TOO WELL OVER THE PAST FEW DAYS. HE ALWAYS HAS CONTINGENCIES AND PLANS-WITHIN-PLANS.
THEREFORE, BRANDISH MUST DIE, EVEN IF I DIE WITH HIM.
THEY'LL STILL HAVE YOU TO RAISE THEM UP RIGHT.
AND FIND MY MISSING ONES.
PROMISE ME, ROSE.
OF COURSE, BUT...
THIS ONE WILL DO.

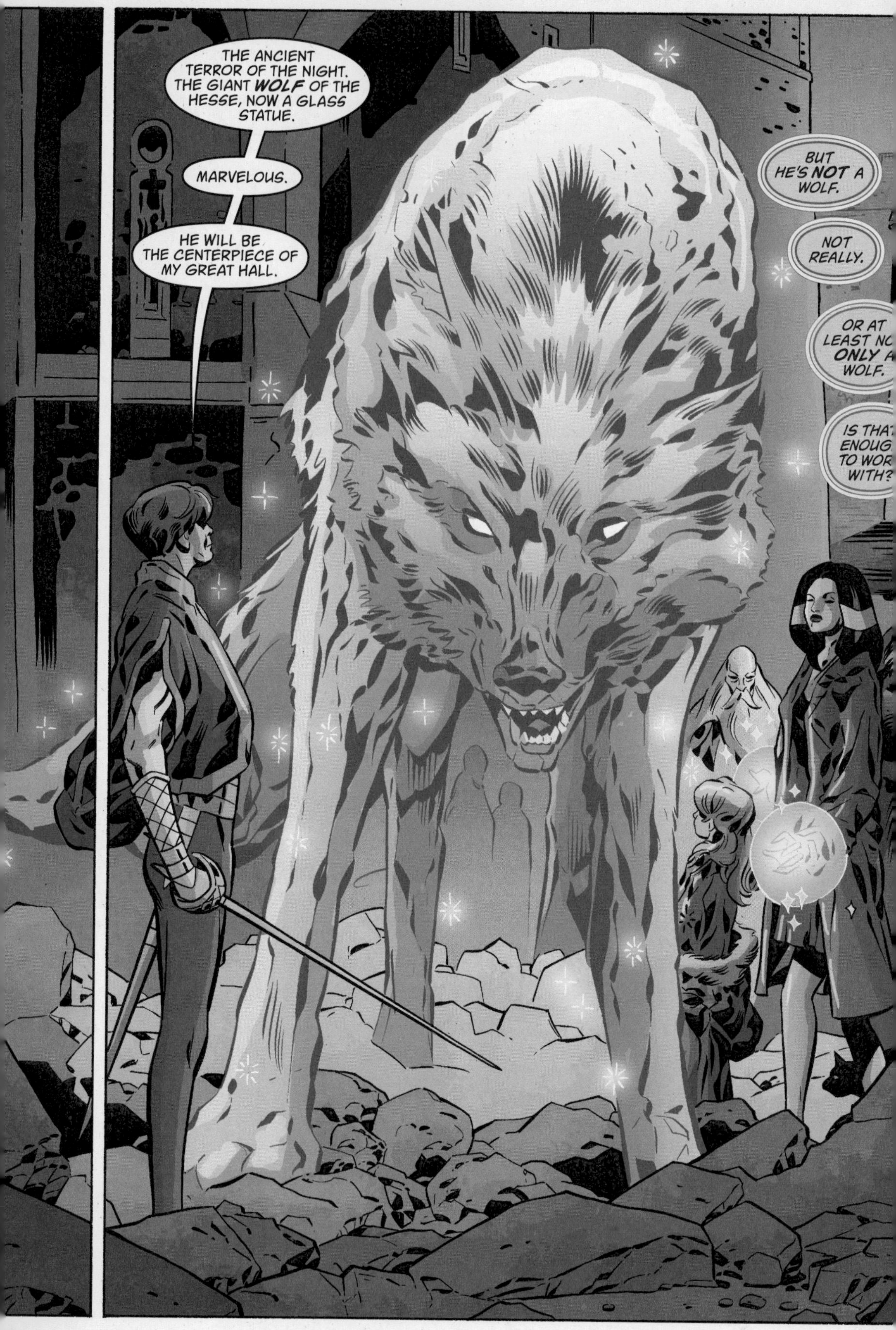
THE ANCIENT TERROR OF THE NIGHT. THE GIANT WOLF OF THE HESSE, NOW A GLASS STATUE.
MARVELOUS.
HE WILL BE THE CENTERPIECE OF MY GREAT HALL.
BUT HE'S NOT A WOLF.
NOT REALLY.
OR AT LEAST NO ONLY A WOLF.
IS THAT ENOUG TO WOR WITH?

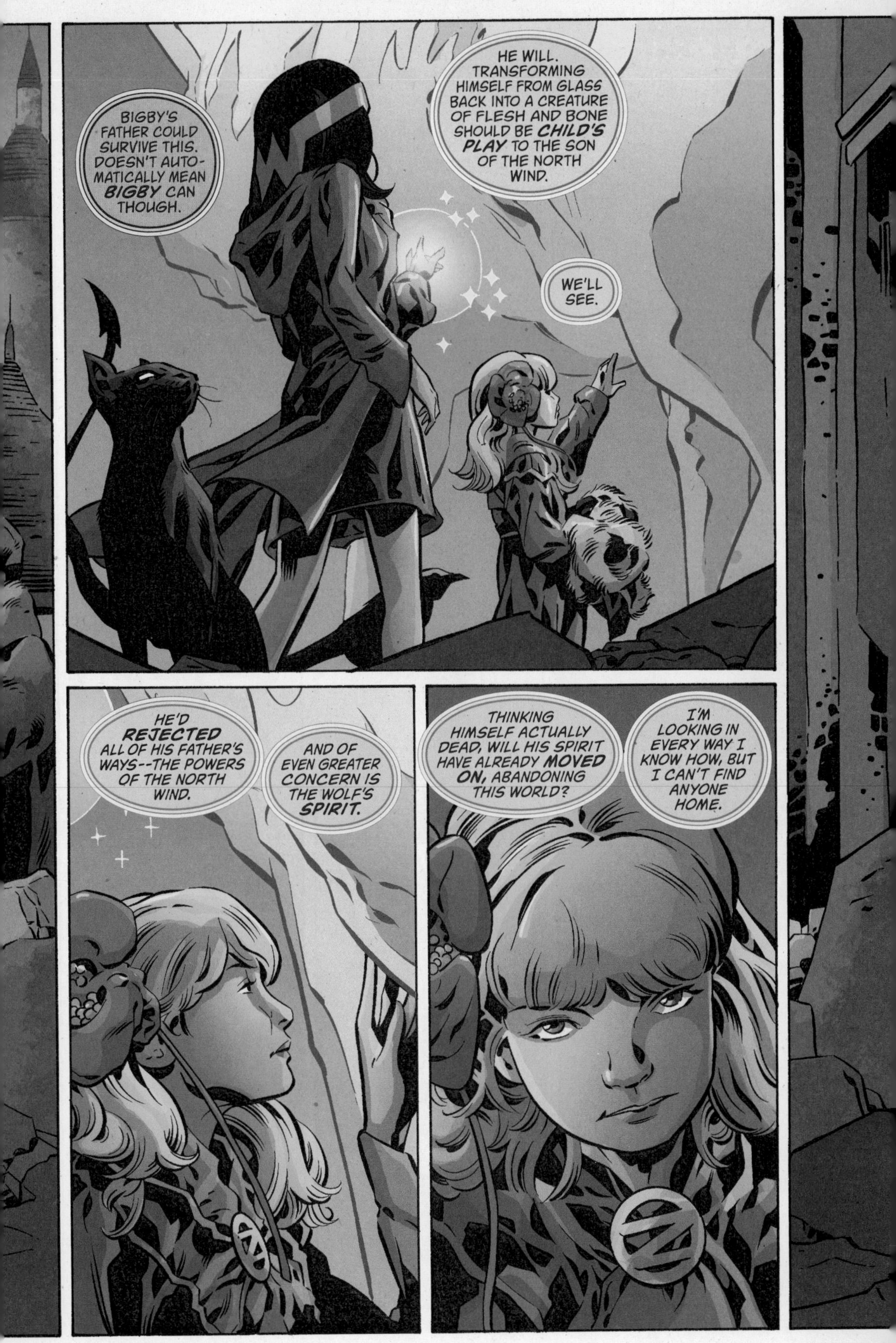
BIGBY'S FATHER COULD SURVIVE THIS. DOESN'T AUTOMATICALLY MEAN BIGBY CAN THOUGH.
HE WILL. TRANSFORMING HIMSELF FROM GLASS BACK INTO A CREATURE OF FLESH AND BONE SHOULD BE CHILD'S PLAY TO THE SON OF THE NORTH WIND.
WE'LL SEE.
HE'D REJECTED ALL OF HIS FATHER'S WAYS--THE POWERS OF THE NORTH WIND.
AND OF EVEN GREATER CONCERN IS THE WOLF'S SPIRIT.
THINKING HIMSELF ACTUALLY DEAD, WILL HIS SPIRIT HAVE ALREADY MOVED ON, ABANDONING THIS WORLD?
I'M LOOKING IN EVERY WAY I KNOW HOW, BUT I CAN'T FIND ANYONE HOME.

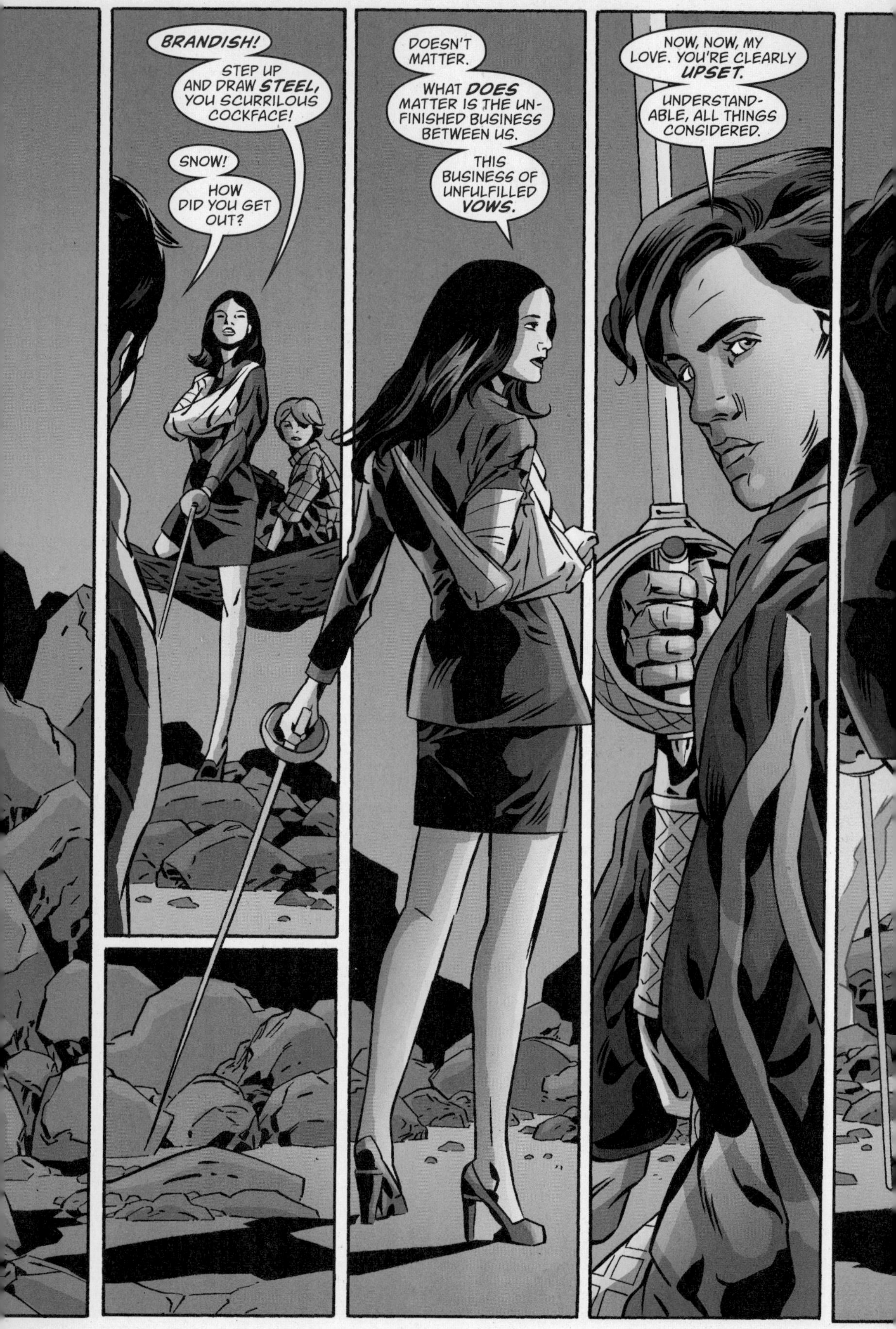
BRANDISH!
STEP UP AND DRAW STEEL, YOU SCURRILOUS COCKFACE!
SNOW!
HOW DID YOU GET OUT?
DOESN'T MATTER.
WHAT DOES MATTER IS THE UN-FINISHED BUSINESS BETWEEN US.
THIS BUSINESS OF UNFULFILLED VOWS.
NOW, NOW, MY LOVE. YOU'RE CLEARLY UPSET.
UNDERSTAND-ABLE, ALL THINGS CONSIDERED.

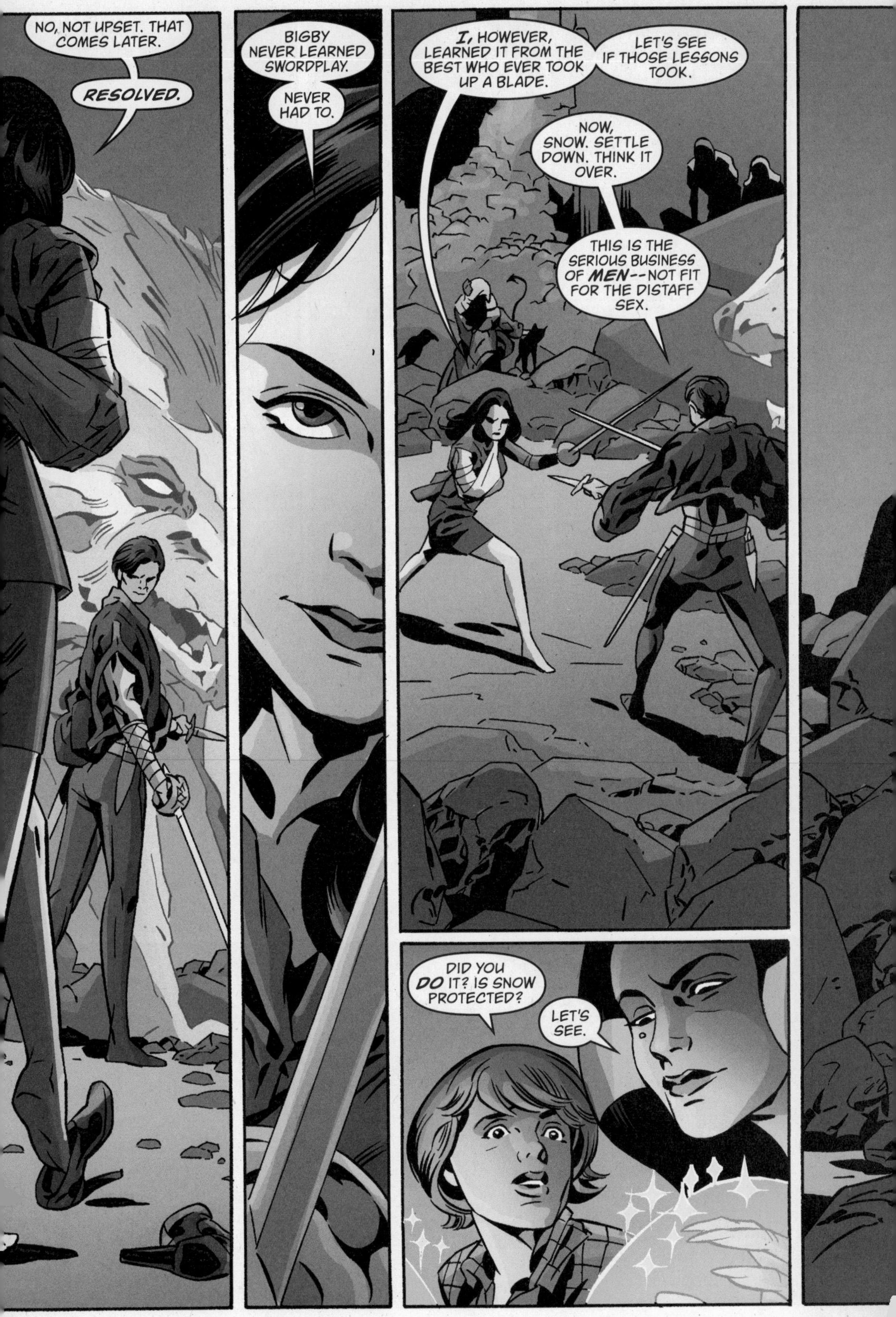
NO, NOT UPSET. THAT COMES LATER.
RESOLVED.
BIGBY NEVER LEARNED SWORDPLAY.
NEVER HAD TO.
I, HOWEVER, LEARNED IT FROM THE BEST WHO EVER TOOK UP A BLADE.
LET'S SEE IF THOSE LESSONS TOOK.
NOW, SNOW. SETTLE DOWN. THINK IT OVER.
THIS IS THE SERIOUS BUSINESS OF MEN--NOT FIT FOR THE DISTAFF SEX.
DID YOU DO IT? IS SNOW PROTECTED?
LET'S SEE.

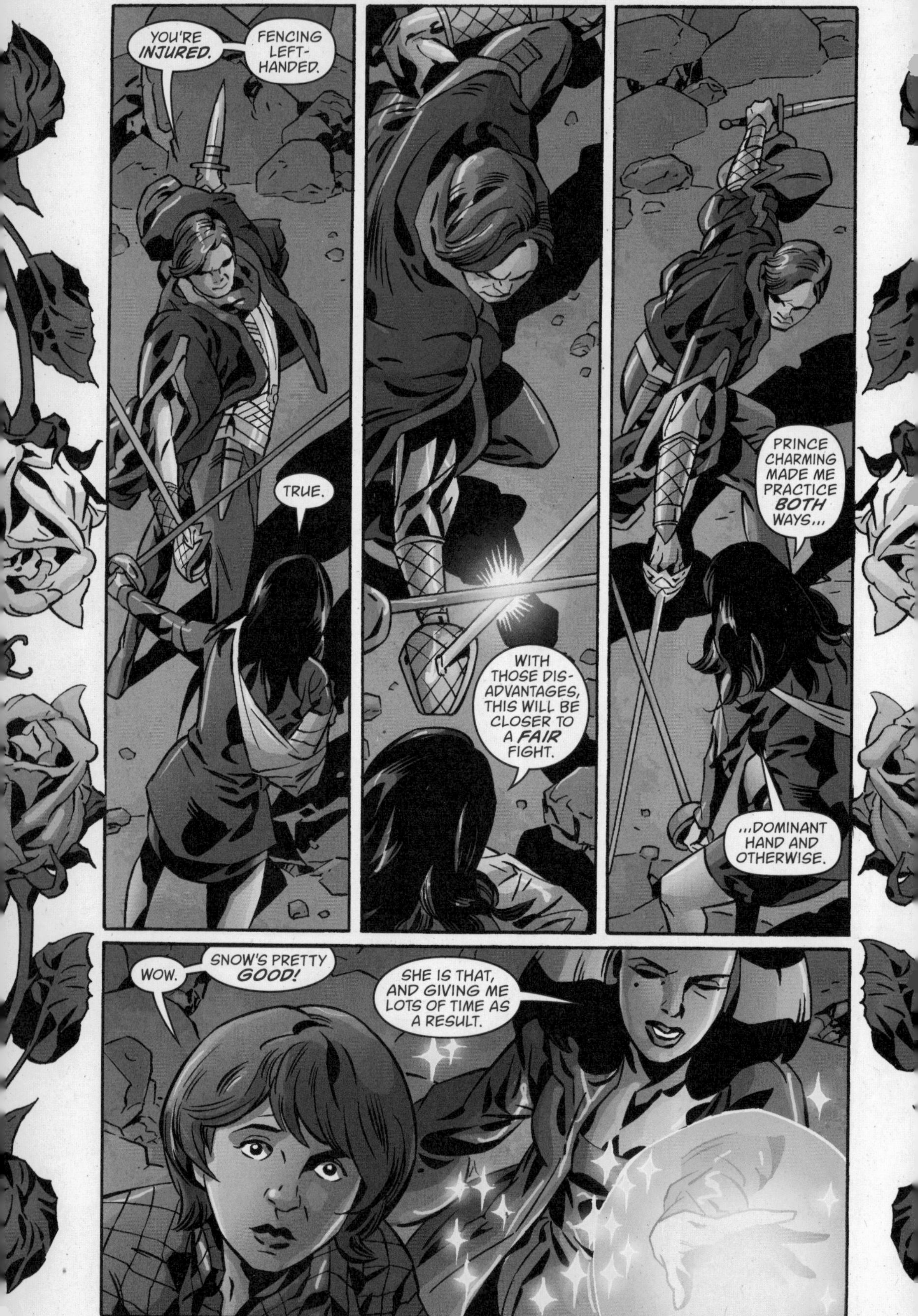
YOU'RE INJURED.
FENCING LEFT-HANDED.
TRUE.
WITH THOSE DIS-ADVANTAGES, THIS WILL BE CLOSER TO A FAIR FIGHT.
PRINCE CHARMING MADE ME PRACTICE BOTH WAYS...
...DOMINANT HAND AND OTHERWISE.
WOW.
SNOW'S PRETTY GOOD!
SHE IS THAT, AND GIVING ME LOTS OF TIME AS A RESULT.

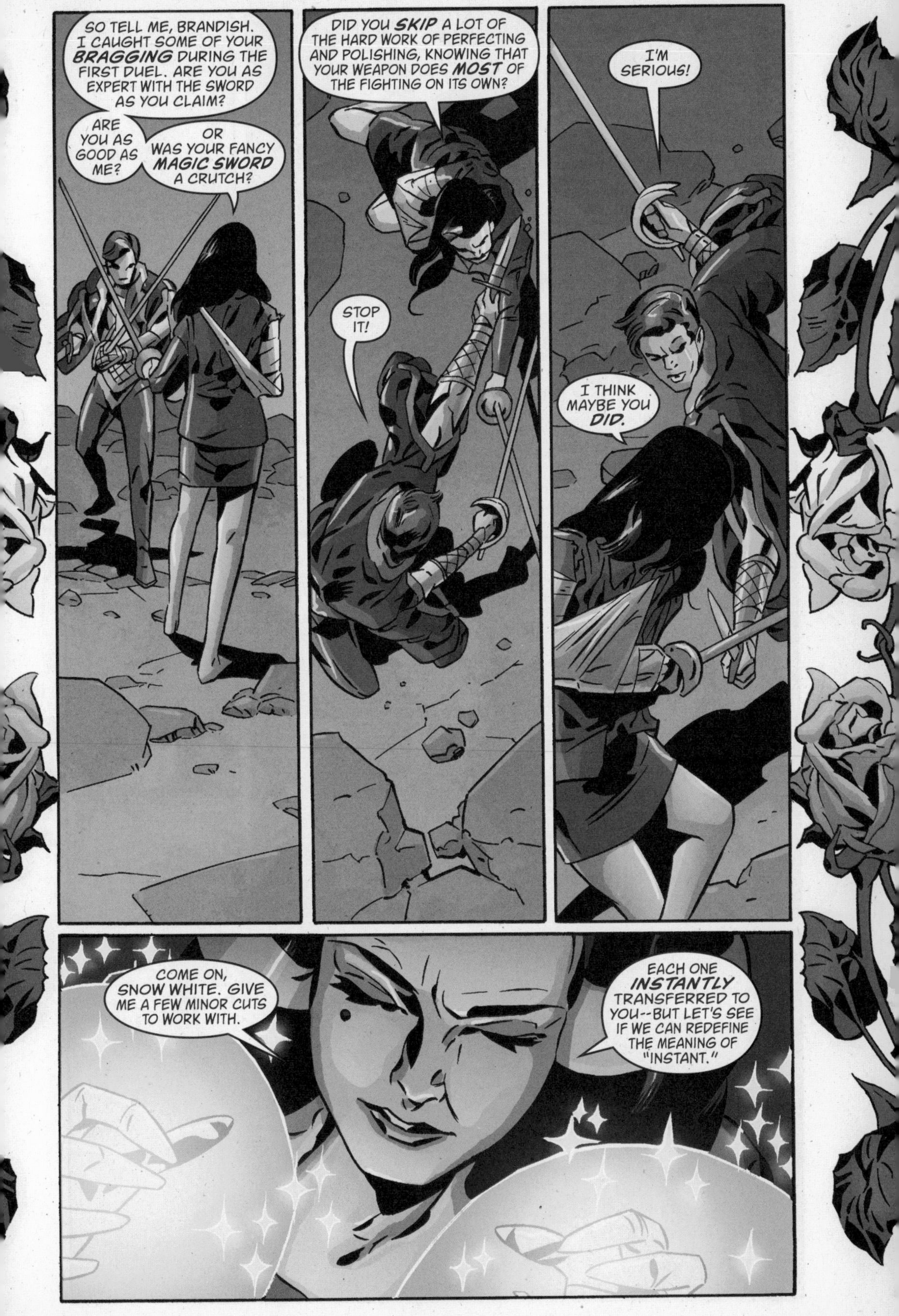

SO TELL ME, BRANDISH. I CAUGHT SOME OF YOUR BRAGGING DURING THE FIRST DUEL. ARE YOU AS EXPERT WITH THE SWORD AS YOU CLAIM?
ARE YOU AS GOOD AS ME?
OR WAS YOUR FANCY MAGIC SWORD A CRUTCH?
DID YOU SKIP A LOT OF THE HARD WORK OF PERFECTING AND POLISHING, KNOWING THAT YOUR WEAPON DOES MOST OF THE FIGHTING ON ITS OWN?
STOP IT!
I'M SERIOUS!
I THINK MAYBE YOU DID.
COME ON, SNOW WHITE. GIVE ME A FEW MINOR CUTS TO WORK WITH.
EACH ONE INSTANTLY TRANSFERRED TO YOU--BUT LET'S SEE IF WE CAN REDEFINE THE MEANING OF "INSTANT."

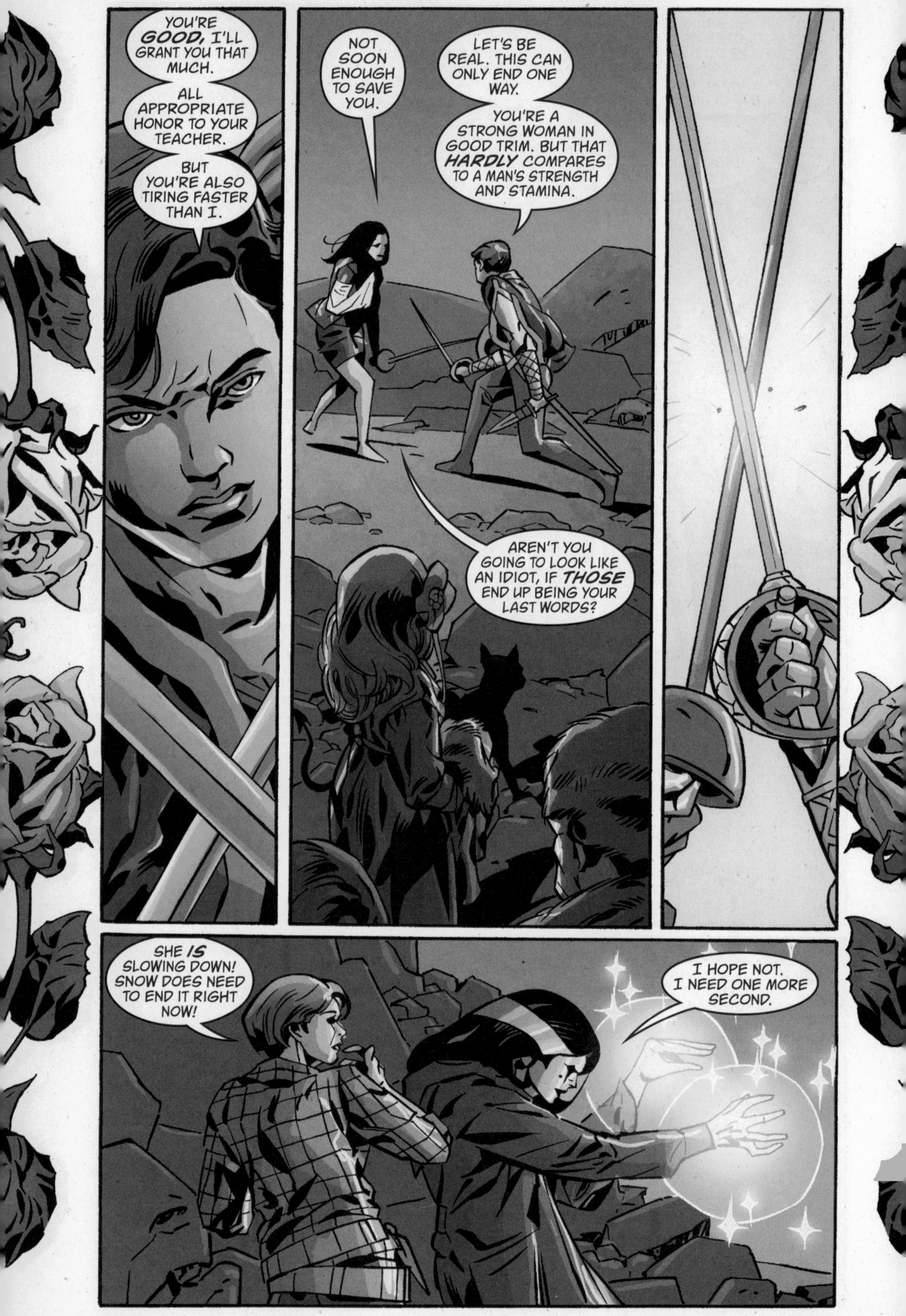
YOU'RE GOOD, I'LL GRANT YOU THAT MUCH.
ALL APPROPRIATE HONOR TO YOUR TEACHER.
BUT YOU'RE ALSO TIRING FASTER THAN I.
NOT SOON ENOUGH TO SAVE YOU.
LET'S BE REAL. THIS CAN ONLY END ONE WAY.
YOU'RE A STRONG WOMAN IN GOOD TRIM. BUT THAT HARDLY COMPARES TO A MAN'S STRENGTH AND STAMINA.
AREN'T YOU GOING TO LOOK LIKE AN IDIOT, IF THOSE END UP BEING YOUR LAST WORDS?
SHE IS SLOWING DOWN! SNOW DOES NEED TO END IT RIGHT NOW!
I HOPE NOT. I NEED ONE MORE SECOND.

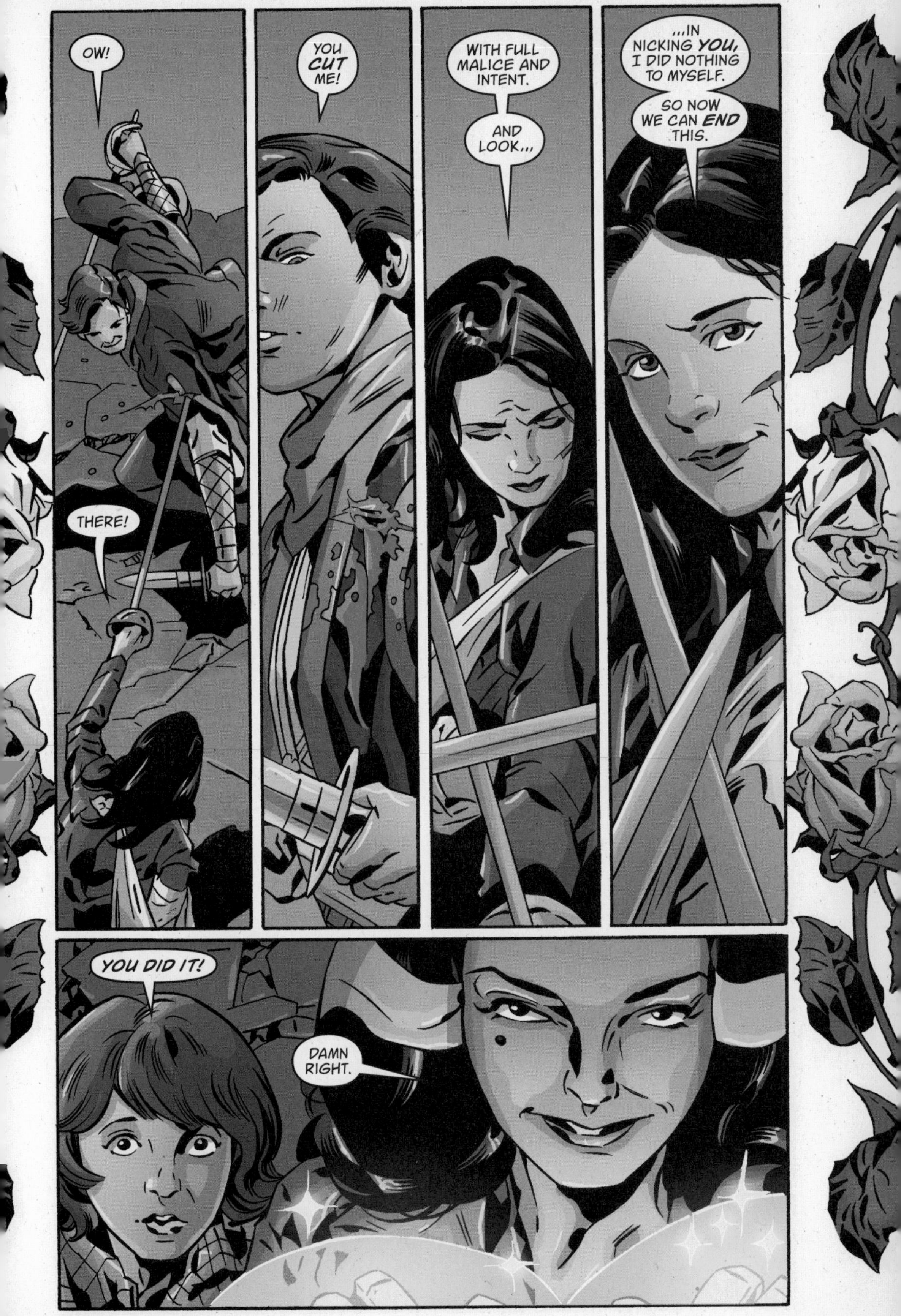
OW!
THERE!
YOU CUT ME!
WITH FULL MALICE AND INTENT.
AND LOOK...
...IN NICKING YOU, I DID NOTHING TO MYSELF.
SO NOW WE CAN END THIS.
YOU DID IT!
DAMN RIGHT.

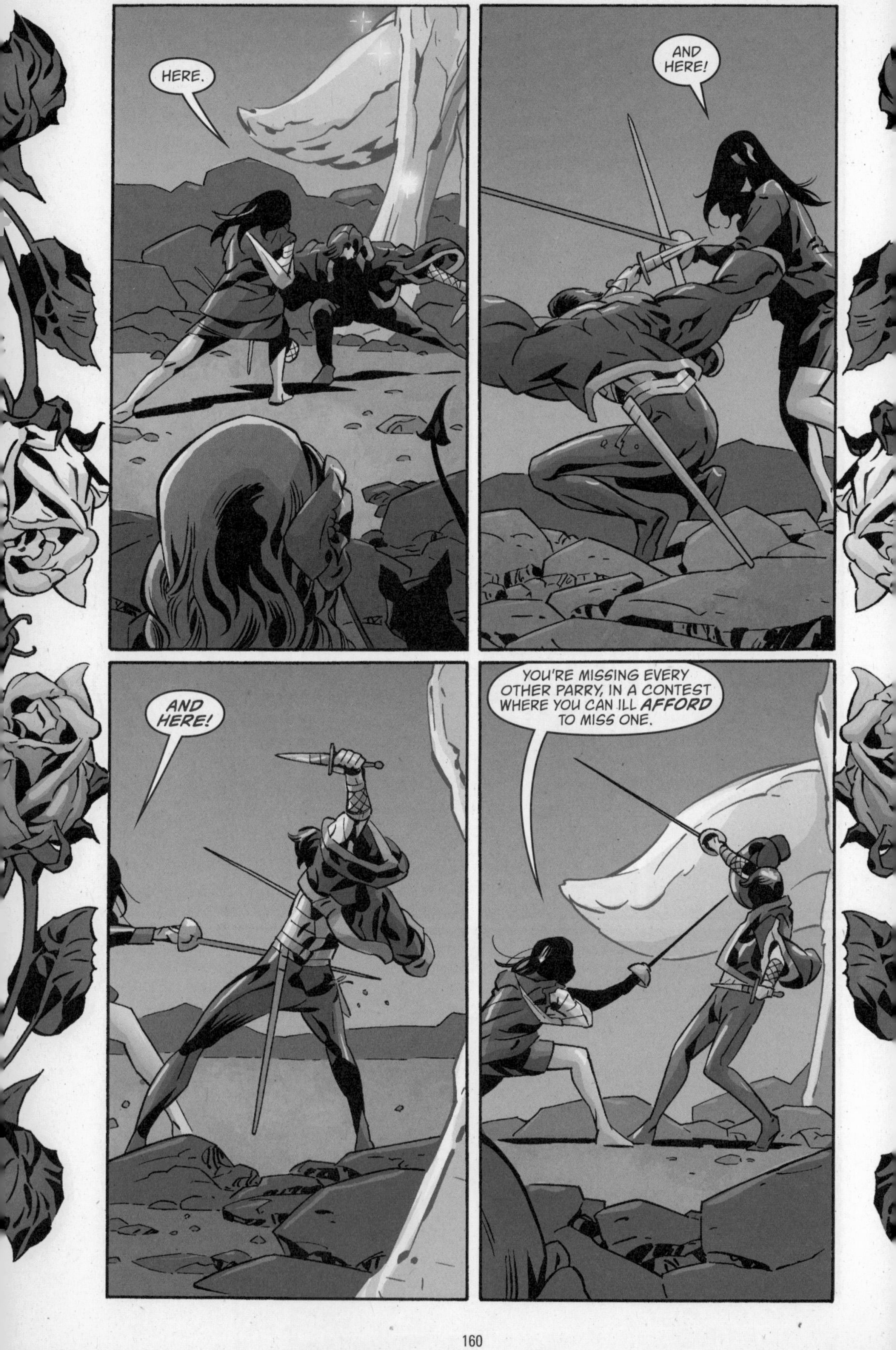
HERE.
AND HERE!
AND HERE!
YOU'RE MISSING EVERY OTHER PARRY, IN A CONTEST WHERE YOU CAN ILL AFFORD TO MISS ONE.

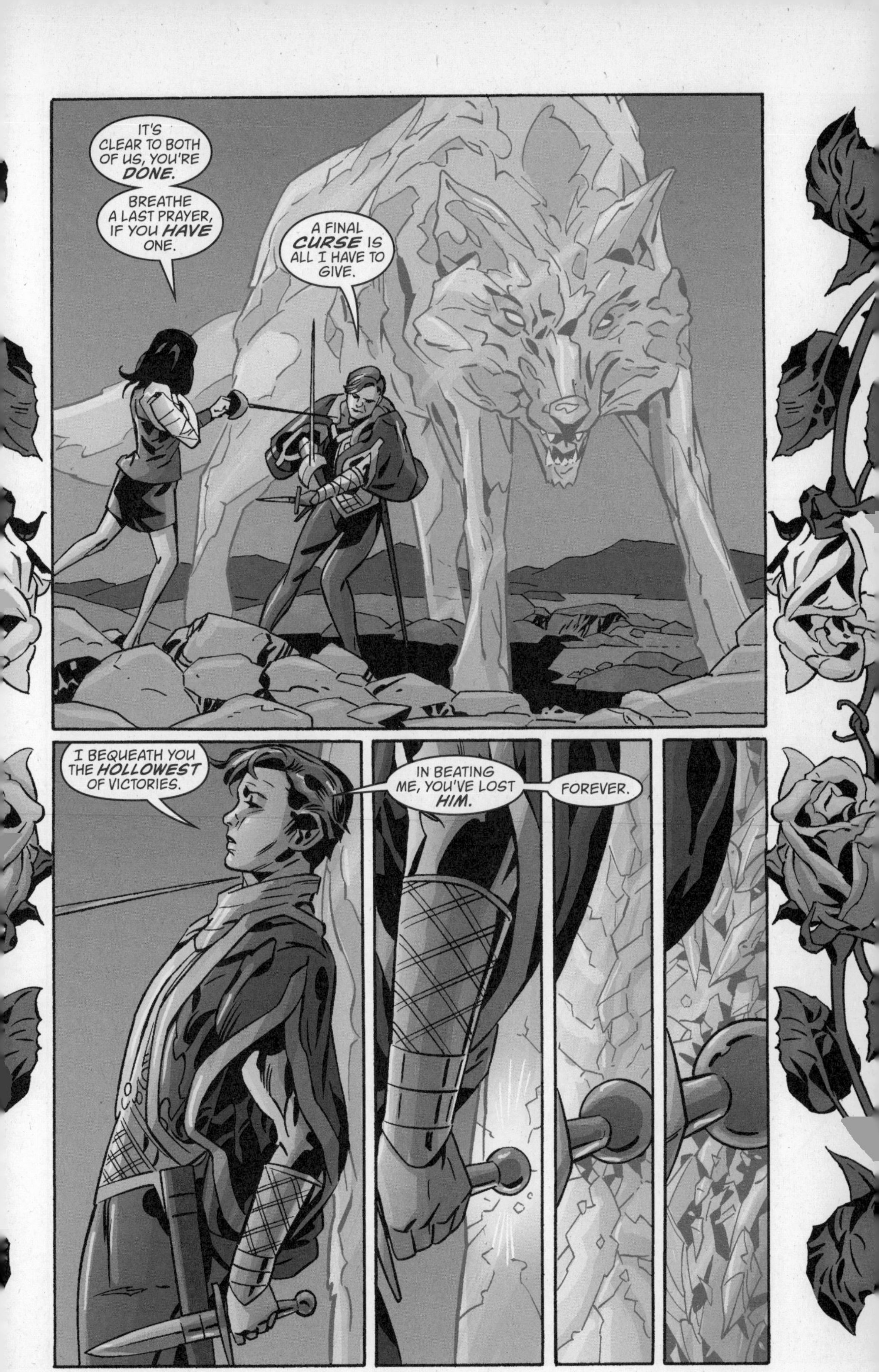
IT'S CLEAR TO BOTH OF US, YOU'RE DONE.
BREATHE A LAST PRAYER, IF YOU HAVE ONE.
A FINAL CURSE IS ALL I HAVE TO GIVE.
I BEQUEATH YOU THE HOLLOWEST OF VICTORIES.
IN BEATING ME, YOU'VE LOST HIM.
FOREVER.

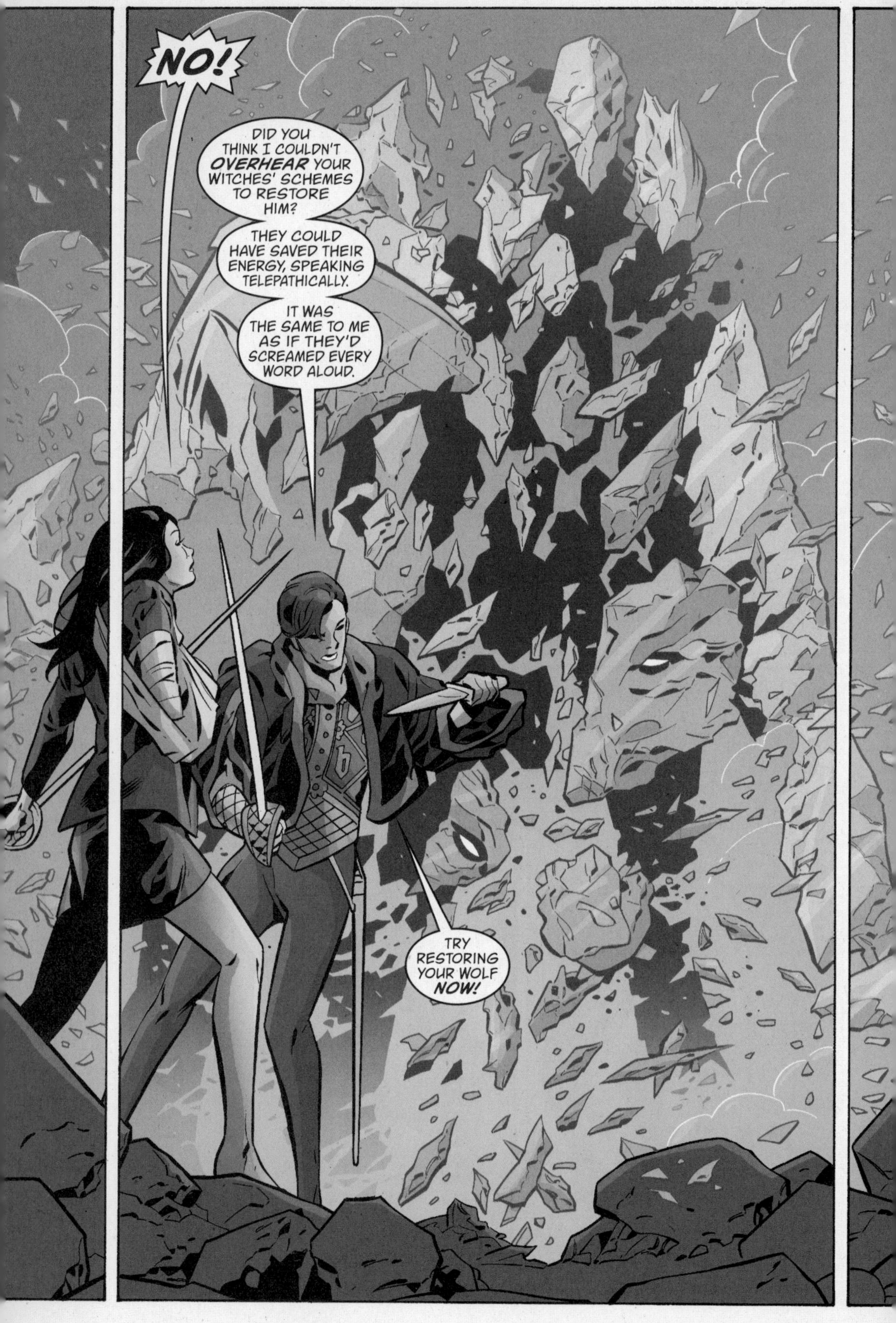

NO!
DID YOU THINK I COULDN'T OVERHEAR YOUR WITCHES' SCHEMES TO RESTORE HIM?
THEY COULD HAVE SAVED THEIR ENERGY, SPEAKING TELEPATHICALLY.
IT WAS THE SAME TO ME AS IF THEY'D SCREAMED EVERY WORD ALOUD.
TRY RESTORING YOUR WOLF NOW!

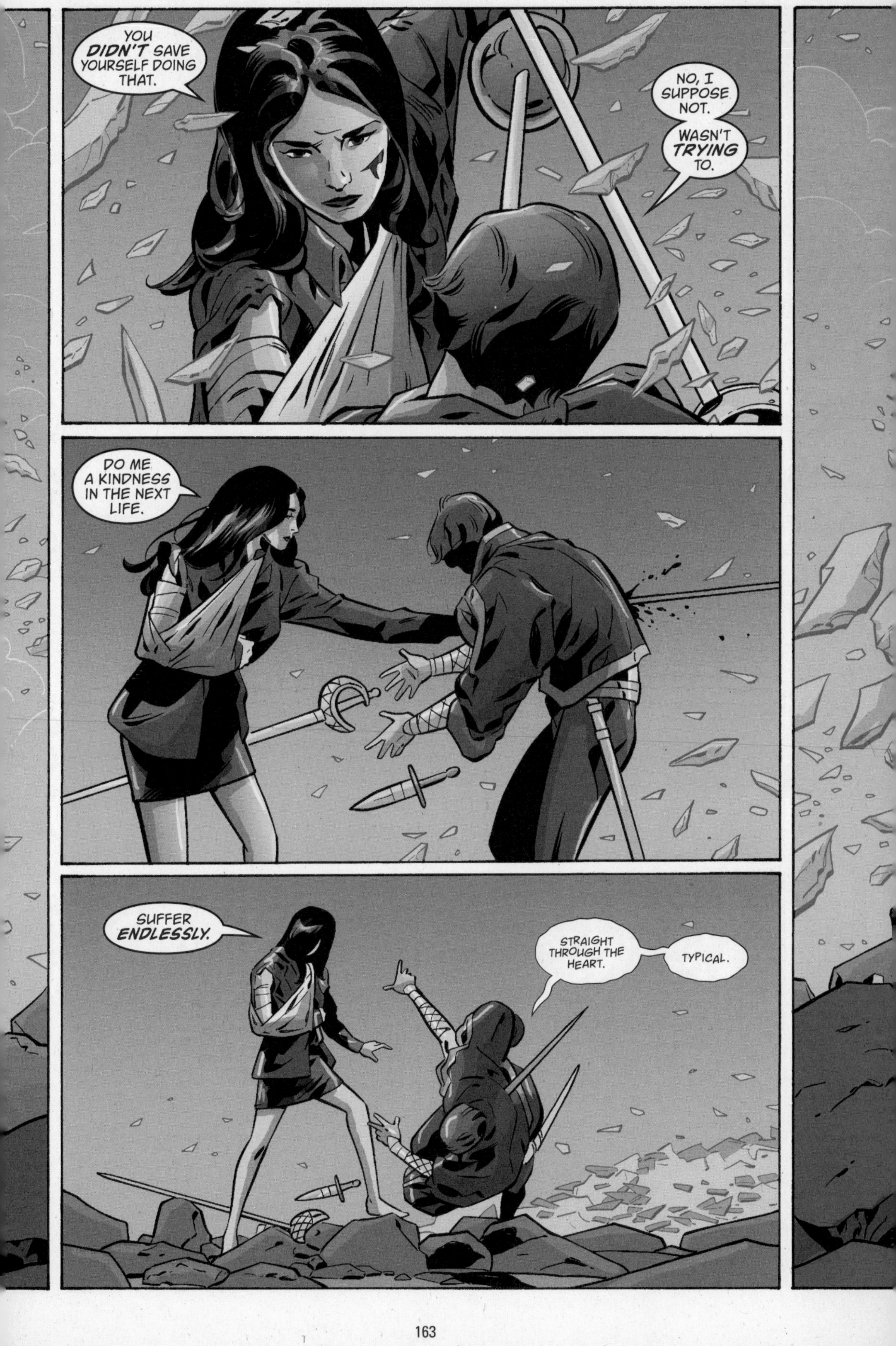
YOU DIDN'T SAVE YOURSELF DOING THAT.
NO, I SUPPOSE NOT.
WASN'T TRYING TO.
DO ME A KINDNESS IN THE NEXT LIFE.
SUFFER ENDLESSLY.
STRAIGHT THROUGH THE HEART.
TYPICAL.

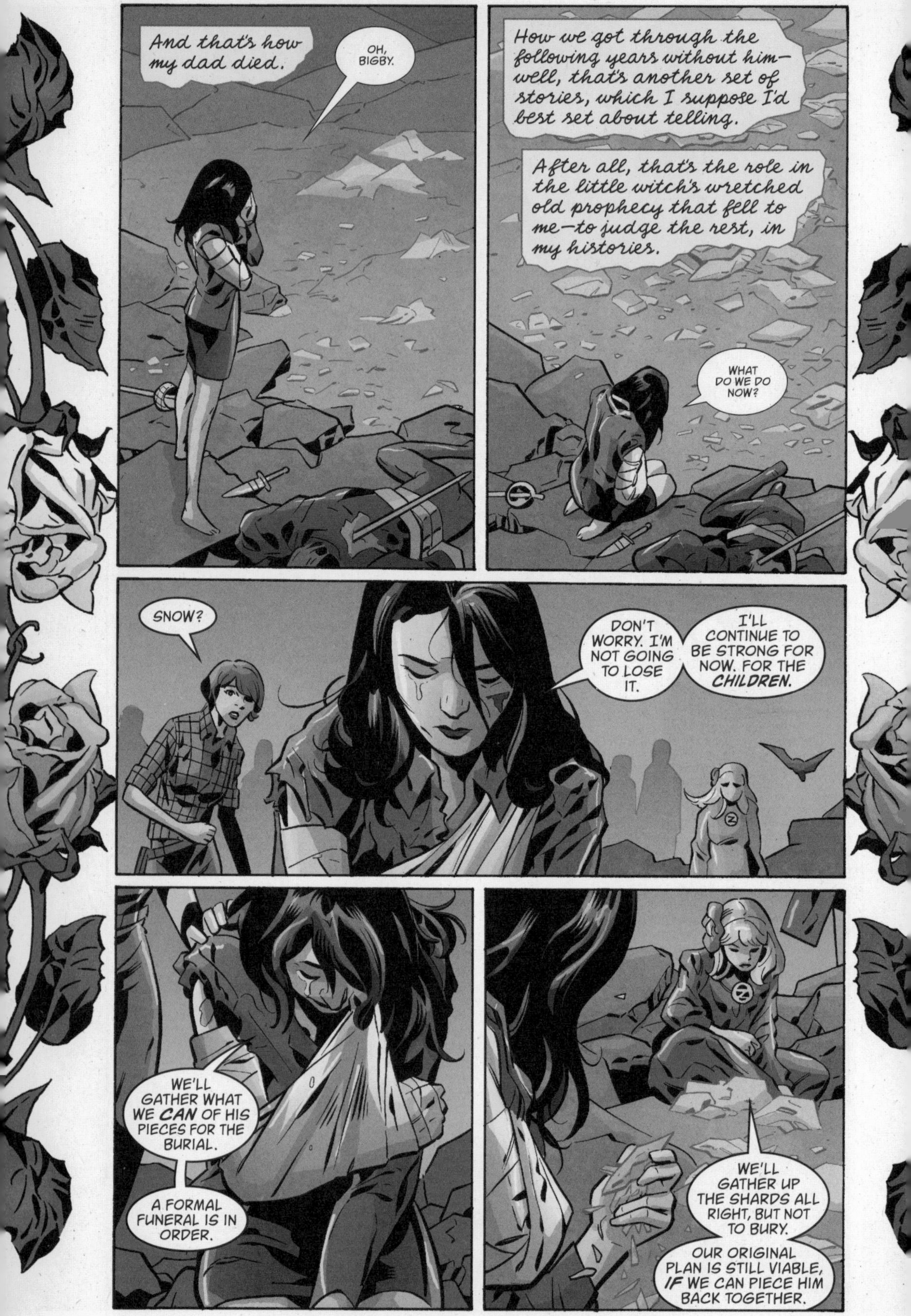

And that's how my dad died.
OH, BIGBY.
How we got through the following years without him—well, that's another set of stories, which I suppose I'd best set about telling.
After all, that's the role in the little witch's wretched old prophecy that fell to me—to judge the rest, in my histories.
WHAT DO WE DO NOW?
SNOW?
DON'T WORRY. I'M NOT GOING TO LOSE IT.
I'LL CONTINUE TO BE STRONG FOR NOW. FOR THE CHILDREN.
WE'LL GATHER WHAT WE CAN OF HIS PIECES FOR THE BURIAL.
A FORMAL FUNERAL IS IN ORDER.
WE'LL GATHER UP THE SHARDS ALL RIGHT, BUT NOT TO BURY.
OUR ORIGINAL PLAN IS STILL VIABLE, IF WE CAN PIECE HIM BACK TOGETHER.

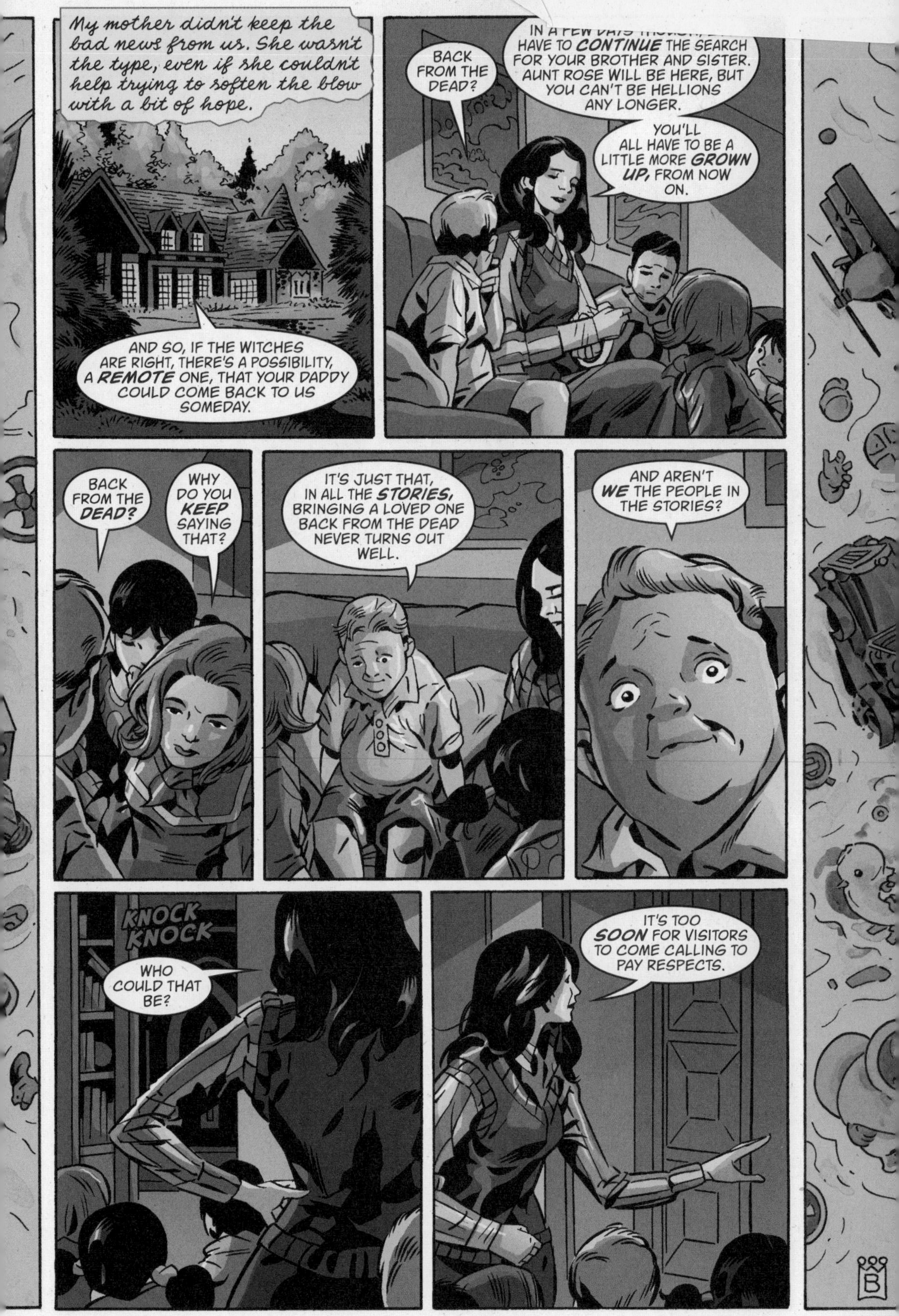
My mother didn't keep the bad news from us. She wasn't the type, even if she couldn't help trying to soften the blow with a bit of hope.
AND SO, IF THE WITCHES ARE RIGHT, THERE'S A POSSIBILITY, A REMOTE ONE, THAT YOUR DADDY COULD COME BACK TO US SOMEDAY.
BACK FROM THE DEAD?
IN A FEW DAYS
HAVE TO CONTINUE THE SEARCH FOR YOUR BROTHER AND SISTER. AUNT ROSE WILL BE HERE, BUT YOU CAN'T BE HELLIONS ANY LONGER.
YOU'LL ALL HAVE TO BE A LITTLE MORE GROWN UP, FROM NOW ON.
BACK FROM THE DEAD?
WHY DO YOU KEEP SAYING THAT?
IT'S JUST THAT, IN ALL THE STORIES, BRINGING A LOVED ONE BACK FROM THE DEAD NEVER TURNS OUT WELL.
AND AREN'T WE THE PEOPLE IN THE STORIES?
KNOCK KNOCK
WHO COULD THAT BE?
IT'S TOO SOON FOR VISITORS TO COME CALLING TO PAY RESPECTS.

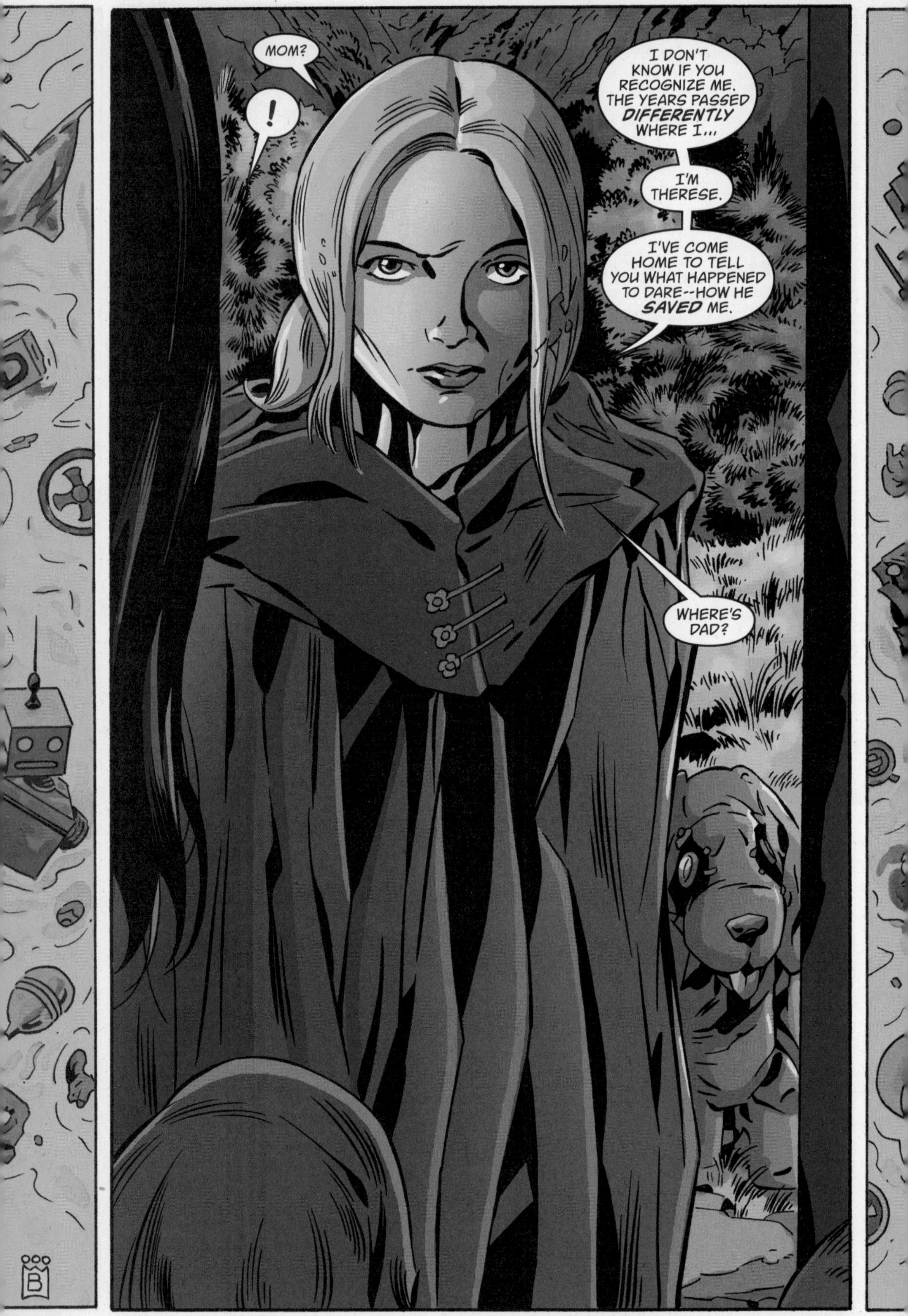
MOM?
!
I DON'T KNOW IF YOU RECOGNIZE ME. THE YEARS PASSED DIFFERENTLY WHERE I...
I'M THERESE.
I'VE COME HOME TO TELL YOU WHAT HAPPENED TO DARE--HOW HE SAVED ME.
WHERE'S DAD?

NEXT: A SMALL MATTER OF MONSTERS LURKING IN SHADOWS.

"Fables is an excellent series in the tradition of Sandman, one that rewards careful attention and loyalty."
—PUBLISHERS WEEKLY

"[A] wonderfully twisted concept..." "features fairy tale characters banished to the noirish world of present-day New York." —
WASHINGTON POST

"Great fun." —BOOKLIST

BILL WILLINGHAM
FABLES VOL. 1: LEGENDS IN EXILE

THE #1 NEW YORK TIMES BEST-SELLING SERIES

FABLES

Legends in Exile

"A top-notch fantasy comic that is on a par with SANDMAN."
— *Variety*

DIRECTOR

BULLFINCH STREET

Bill Willingham

Lan Medina

Steve Leialoha

Craig Hamilton

VERTIGO

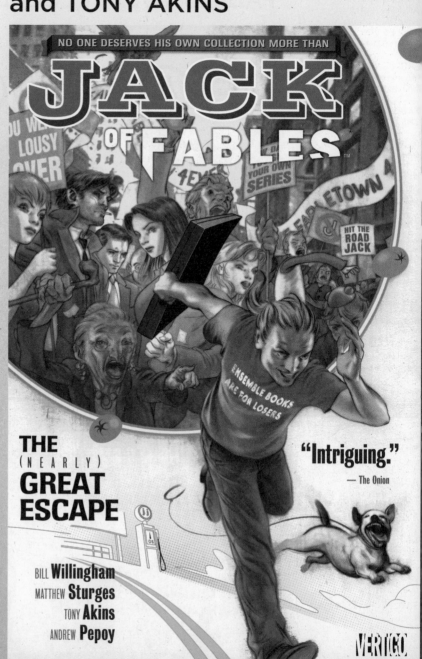